snapshots

an introduction
to tourism

third canadian edition

Norma Polovitz Nickerson
University of Montana

Paula Kerr
Algonquin College

PEARSON

Prentice
Hall

Toronto

National Library of Canada Cataloguing in Publication Data

Nickerson, Norma Polovitz
    Snapshots: an introduction to tourism / Norma Polovitz
Nickerson, Paula Kerr. — 3rd Canadian ed.

Includes bibliographical references and index.
ISBN 0-13-120126-3

1. Tourist trade. 2. Tourist trade — Canada. I. Kerr, Paula, 1944–. II. Title.

G155.C2N56 2004   338.4'791   C2003-900692-1

0-13-120126-3

Vice President, Editorial Director: Michael J. Young
Executive Editor: Dave Ward
Sponsoring Editor: Andrew Winton
Marketing Manager: Toivo Pajo
Supervising Developmental Editor: Suzanne Schaan
Production Editor: Joel Gladstone
Copy Editor: Gilda Mekler
Senior Production Coordinator: Peggy Brown
Page Layout: Carolyn E. Sebestyen
Art Director: Mary Opper
Cover and Interior Design: Gillian Tsintziras
Cover Image: Getty/Christoph Wilhelm

1 2 3 4 5   08 07 06 05 04

Printed and bound in Canada.

Dedicated to my parents,

Gordon and Ethel Kerr

Contents

Preface ix

PART ONE   INTRODUCTION TO TOURISM

1   Understanding Tourism 1
The Canadian Tourism Product: An Overview 2
Reasons for the Growth of Tourism 6
Talking the Same Language 10
Historical Avenues 13
Tourism As a Career 17
Tourism Industry Associations and Organizations 18
The Buchanan Report on Tourism 20

2   Tourism Guests 24
Impact of Terrorism on the Guest 25
Classifying the Guest 26
Why Travel? 31
The Barriers to Travel 34

3   The Tourism Host 39
Tourism Illiteracy 41
A Brief History of Canadian Tourism 44

The Federal Government and Tourism 47
Training the Tourism Host 52
Marketing Tourism Products 56

4 *Planning and Development 64*
The Five Components of a Tourist Destination 65
The Life Cycle of a Destination 67
Tourism Planning 67
Tourism Development 74
Tourism Planning: A Provincial Approach 77

PART TWO COMPONENTS OF TOURISM

5 *The Transportation Sector 83*
Airlines 84
Automobile and Recreational Vehicle Travel 97
Rail 101
The Motor Coach Industry 107
Cruise Industry 110
Public Transportation 118
Selecting a Mode of Transportation 120

6 *The Accommodation Sector 126*
Lodging History and Trends 127
Lodging Ownership and Organization 131
Classifications within the Accommodation Sector 137
Marketing the Accommodation Sector 144

7 *The Food and Beverage Sector 153*
History of the Food-Service Industry 154
Trends in the Food and Beverage Sector 156
Restaurant Ownership 159
The Major Divisions of the Food-Service Industry 161
Marketing the Restaurant Business 169
Tourism and the Food-Service Industry 171

8 *The Attractions Sector 177*
Canadian Heritage 178
History in Brief 179
Public and Nonprofit Attractions 183
Private/Commercial Attractions 190
Niagara's Six Key Factors to Success 195

9   The Events and Conferences Sector 202
Special Events 204
Conferences, Conventions, and Meetings 210
Managing Events 217

10   The Adventure Tourism and Outdoor Recreation Sector 222
Parks and Crown Lands 223
Adventure Tourism 225
Outdoor Recreation 230
Tourism's Impact on the Environment 236

11   The Travel Trade Sector 247
The History of Tours 248
Wholesaling 249
Travel Agencies 259
Incentive Travel 265

12   The Tourism Services Sector 271
Governments and Tourism 272
Tourism Associations and Organizations 279
Marketing Services 280
Research and Consulting 281
Miscellaneous Services 282

PART THREE   THE FUTURE OF TOURISM

13   Challenges and the Future 287
Issues Raising Concern in the Industry 288
Terrorist Threats 290
Ethics and Tourism 291
Technology and Its Impact on Tourism's Future 291
Trends in the Tourism Industry 292
Tourism Challenges 297

Appendix: Tourism Education Councils 301

Glossary 303

Index 315

Preface

Recent events around the world have had a significant effect on tourism. The world that North Americans knew prior to September 11, 2001, is gone forever. Terrorism is now front and centre in our lives. Not that terrorism is a new phenomenon—it has been around for centuries—but this time it struck at home. Many prospective tourists now perceive travel to be dangerous and have opted to stay close to home. This third edition of *Snapshots* looks not only at the events of September 11 but also at terrorism in general and its impact on the global tourism industry.

September 11 clearly illustrated how one sector of tourism depends to a degree on the other sectors for economic growth. The airline industry lost much of its business in the last quarter of 2001, and it is still trying to deal with that enormous loss of revenue. Fewer travellers meant hotel rooms went empty and restaurants saw fewer diners. Conferences and conventions were cancelled, while major attractions, such as the Smithsonian Institute and the Statue of Liberty, added strict new security measures. At our border crossings, police and security personnel remained on high alert. Travel agencies and tour companies were forced to lay off personnel, and companies such as Boeing and Bombardier had contracts for new aircraft cancelled.

The only sector that did not suffer greatly was adventure tourism and outdoor recreation. Since much of this sector's activities occurs in more remote areas of the country, perhaps its enthusiasts see terror attacks as less likely. Canada has been fortunate; it is seen by much of the world as a safe place in which to travel. Tourism growth in Canada over the next few years appears likely to be strong in comparison with other destinations.

Most tourism textbooks tend to focus on one or two areas of the tourism industry, such as hospitality, travel, events planning, or marketing. This book divides the highly diverse tourism industry into eight easy-to-identify sectors and examines the tourism industry as a whole, balancing one sector or grouping of businesses equally with others.

The text is divided into three parts. Part 1 addresses the common components of tourism, such as reasons for the growth of tourism, theories of travel, motivation, planning and development, and marketing concepts. It is important that students first understand the basic concepts of travel before exploring the eight sectors of tourism. Part 2 takes a close look at each of the eight tourism sectors: transportation, accommodation, food and beverage, attractions, events and conferences, adventure tourism and outdoor recreation, travel trade, and tourism services. The last part looks at the issues, challenges, and future of tourism in Canada.

New to This Edition

Key revisions in this edition include the following:

- Expanded coverage of events and conferences (Chapter 9)
- Expanded coverage of adventure tourism (Chapter 10)
- A new focus on technology and how it has affected the travel industry
- Discussions of travel in a post-September 11 environment of heightened security and risk
- Updates to travel statistics throughout

Text Contents

Part 1 includes four chapters. Chapter 1 is an introduction to the tourism industry and provides the student with general knowledge of the industry as a whole. Chapters 2 and 3 discuss the intricacies of dealing with the people factor of tourism—guests and hosts. Included in this section are theories of motivation that affect travel, a summary of the positive and negative effects of tourism on a city, region, province, or country, and a brief introduction to tourism's unique product characteristics and how we use these features to help sell our product. Chapter 4 considers the importance of good planning and development strategies. A synopsis of a report from British Columbia provides students with a working example of how provinces approach the planning and development of their products.

Part 2 looks more closely at each of the eight sectors of tourism. Chapter 5 discusses travel by land, sea, and air. It reviews the organizations, legislation, and trends that create the transportation industry, as well as the theory of travel choice. Chapter 6 explores the lodging industry, including its variety, its organization, and its marketing techniques. Chapter 7 reviews the food and beverage industry, examining full-service restaurants, fast foods, and the contract food-service business. Chapter 8 deals with attractions, both private and public. In this chapter marketing plans are discussed in greater depth. Chapter 9 enters the world of special events and conferences. It describes the mushrooming business of conferences and conventions, the role of meeting planners, and future trends in business travel. Chapter 10, Adventure Tourism and Outdoor Recreation, takes a closer look at ecotourism, cultural/heritage tourism, recreational sports, and the value of environmental protection. The development of Canada's national parks system is also an integral part of this chapter. Chapter 11 discusses the important role of the travel trade—tourism's channel of distribution. In Chapter 12, support services for the tourism industry are studied. The roles of the Canadian Tourism Commission, provincial tourism boards, chambers of commerce, tourism organizations, professional associations, marketing and research businesses, and travel clubs are all included.

In Part 3, Chapter 13 examines the current challenges and issues facing the industry. What is the projected future of tourism in Canada and what role will it play?

I hope that the variety of teaching opportunities provided with each chapter will make this introductory course an exciting one for both the instructor and the student. Tourism is really the "land of opportunity," but it can only be fully accessed when the big picture is understood.

How to Use This Text

A historical timeline, located on the inside front cover of the book, shows the student milestones of an ever-developing tourism industry. Not all important dates are covered, so students should feel free to add dates identified by their instructors as significant. A series of short biographies interspersed throughout the book called "Snapshots" introduces students to the movers and shakers in the industry, focusing both on early pioneers of the tourism industry and on Canadians making a difference in tourism today.

"In Practice," practical applications that appear in each chapter, allows students to solve problems by combining their knowledge, common sense, and personal tourism experiences. The instructor and students can interact in small groups or as a class.

For those looking beyond the classroom, many chapters give practical information about working in the tourism industry. "Opportunities In" lists the kinds of jobs available in different tourism sectors and "Job Description For" has more detailed information about specific jobs in the industry.

In addition, each chapter contains an array of features that provide extra resources to both the instructor and the student. Learning objectives and key terms are set out at the start of the chapters, while a summary and list of weblinks end each chapter. There are also questions at the end of each chapter that are based on chapter material and can be used as out-of-class assignments, quiz questions, or small-group discussion questions.

Supplemental Materials

The **Text Enrichment Site** for *Snapshots* (www.pearsoned.ca/text/nickerson) will be of benefit to students and instructors alike. This resource Web site provides timely updates, self-assessment quizzes for each chapter, and links to other Internet resources.

The **Instructor's Manual**, provided free to adopters, includes lecture outlines, transparency masters, topics for discussion, recommended videos, and suggested projects and research assignments. This supplement is available online and can be accessed through the instructor link on the Text Enrichment Site or through Pearson's Instructor Central site at www.pearsoned.ca/highered/instructor.

The **Test Item File** includes multiple-choice, true/false, and essay questions for each chapter and is available in both print and computerized formats. The **Pearson TestGen** is a special computerized version of the Test Item File that enables instructors to view and edit the existing questions, add questions, generate tests, and print the tests in a variety of formats. Powerful search and sort functions make it easy to locate questions and arrange them in any order desired. TestGen also enables instructors to administer tests on a local area network, electronically grade the tests, and prepare the results in either electronic or printed reports. Issued on a CD-ROM, the **Pearson TestGen** is compatible with either IBM or Macintosh systems.

Acknowledgments

No author can work in a void: writing this text has been made possible by the help and support of friends and colleagues. Many thanks to the Canadian Tourism Commission, Jim Watson, and Judy Cameron, for their help and cooperation; to Ken Hovey of GAPC; to Lisa Clarke from Sam Jakes Inn; to my colleagues Debbie Wright, Liane and Ken Birch, Mike Tarnowski, Sylvia Densmore, and Celine Perrier; a special thanks to Jeff Jackson at the Algonquin Pembroke Campus, who guided me through some of the most difficult areas.

Over the years my greatest support, and a continued source of information, has been my family: John, Nancy, Wendy, and my nephew Tom Hadley. Thanks to my friend Glenor Bogard, who started me on my journey into the world of tourism. Many thanks to the staff at Pearson Education, in particular to Marta Tomins and Andrew Winton, with a special thank you to my copy editor, Gilda Mekler, for her perseverance.

A final thanks to those who reviewed this text and provided me with thoughtful insight. Your time and effort are greatly appreciated. Reviewers included the following:

- Michael Campbell,
  University of Manitoba

- Paula Carr,
  Camosun College

- Stephen Smith,
  University of Waterloo

- Margaret Walsh,
  Southern Alberta Institute of Technology

Paula Kerr
Algonquin College

1 Understanding Tourism

key terms

agricultural tourism	inbound tourist	same-day visitors
common currency	industrial tourism	tourism
cuisine tourism	leakage	tourist dollars
domestic tourist	"le grand tour"	travel deficit
excursionist	multiplier effect	trip
foreign tourist	outbound tourist	

learning objectives

Having read this chapter you will be able to

1. Discuss the importance of tourism to the overall economic well-being of Canada.

2. Identify and explain the importance of each tourism sector to the overall Canadian tourism product.

3. Discuss the reasons for the growth of tourism over the past 100 years.

4. Discuss the impact of terrorist attacks on the tourism industry.

5. Define the terms *tourism*, *trip*, *domestic* and *foreign tourist*, *inbound tourist*, *excursionist*, *travel deficit*, *leakage*, and *multiplier effect*.

6. Identify prominent tourism organizations and their roles in the tourism industry.

7. Explain the benefits of choosing a career in tourism.

No matter where you are in the world today, "**tourism**" plays an important role in the life of your community. Much of the world's population has had a tourism experience, and many nations depend on tourism to be one of their biggest revenue generators. Tourism is considered the number one industry in the world: "Worldwide, tourism is a $3.75 trillion industry. It employs more people than any other single industrial sector, and it makes a significant contribution to the economy of virtually every country on nearly every measure." This trillion-dollar industry is booming around the world even in times of recession, military conflicts, natural disasters, and energy problems. Nearly every country in the world is scrambling to lure tourists because tourism brings outside dollars into the country, stimulating the local economy.

Tourism is Canada's fourth-ranked export industry, behind motor vehicles, automotive parts, and business services. In 2001, foreign and domestic visitors spent a record $54.6 billion in Canada. That means tourism earned nearly $640 000 every hour of every day. Tourism revenues have more than doubled over the past 10 years. Tourism accounts for 2.3 percent of Canada's gross domestic product (GDP).[1] Why are these figures important to Canadians? These dollars become part of the revenue used to help balance the budget and reduce the deficit. Canada retains almost 3 percent of the global tourism market share and is ranked eighth in the world for the tourism revenue it generates. The future of tourism in Canada promises to be exciting and very profitable.[2]

The Canadian Tourism Product: An Overview

What is this exciting, dynamic, and challenging industry? Although all people use the products of tourism, Canadians are often unaware of the magnitude of the industry. They do not fully understand how important tourism is to their community, region, province, or country. In fact, people actively working in the industry are often unaware that their industry is called tourism and that they are working in just one of its eight sectors. For example, if you ask your local bartenders if they work in tourism, many will say no. Yet they will all agree that they work in food and beverage, which is the largest single sector in the tourism industry. How would people survive on vacation without food and drink? Although bartenders may serve mostly local customers and very few tourists, because they belong to the food and beverage sector, they are considered to be an integral part of the tourism industry in Canada.

Tourism, according to the World Tourism Organization/United Nations Recommendations on Tourism Statistics, "comprises the activities of persons traveling to and staying in places outside their environment for not more than one consecutive year for leisure, business and other purposes."[3] Put more simply, the tourism industry includes the transportation, lodging, feeding, and entertainment of travellers. This textbook further subdivides the four core elements into eight sectors: Transportation, Accommodation, Food and Beverage, Attractions, Events and Conferences, Adventure Tourism and Outdoor Recreation, Travel Trade, and Tourism Services. In this book, we will discuss each of these sectors in detail, but let's take a quick visit to each of them (see Figure 1.1).

FIGURE 1.1
The Eight Tourism
Trade Sectors

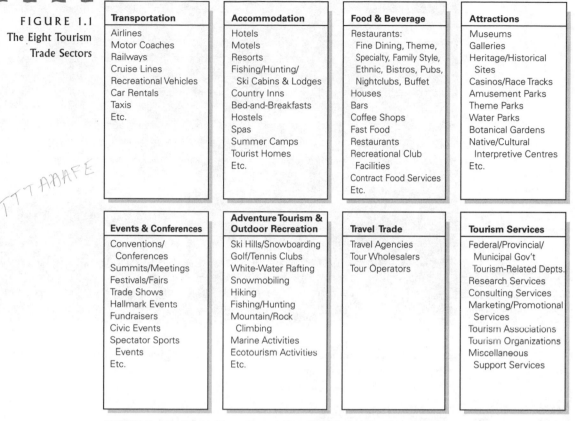

Transportation	**Accommodation**	**Food & Beverage**	**Attractions**
Airlines	Hotels	Restaurants:	Museums
Motor Coaches	Motels	Fine Dining, Theme,	Galleries
Railways	Resorts	Specialty, Family Style,	Heritage/Historical
Cruise Lines	Fishing/Hunting/	Ethnic, Bistros, Pubs,	Sites
Recreational Vehicles	Ski Cabins & Lodges	Nightclubs, Buffet	Casinos/Race Tracks
Car Rentals	Country Inns	Houses	Amusement Parks
Taxis	Bed-and-Breakfasts	Bars	Theme Parks
Etc.	Hostels	Coffee Shops	Water Parks
	Spas	Fast Food	Botanical Gardens
	Summer Camps	Restaurants	Native/Cultural
	Tourist Homes	Recreational Club	Interpretive Centres
	Etc.	Facilities	Etc.
		Contract Food Services	
		Etc.	

Events & Conferences	**Adventure Tourism & Outdoor Recreation**	**Travel Trade**	**Tourism Services**
Conventions/	Ski Hills/Snowboarding	Travel Agencies	Federal/Provincial/
Conferences	Golf/Tennis Clubs	Tour Wholesalers	Municipal Gov't
Summits/Meetings	White-Water Rafting	Tour Operators	Tourism-Related Depts.
Festivals/Fairs	Snowmobiling		Research Services
Trade Shows	Hiking		Consulting Services
Hallmark Events	Fishing/Hunting		Marketing/Promotional
Fundraisers	Mountain/Rock		Services
Civic Events	Climbing		Tourism Associations
Spectator Sports	Marine Activities		Tourism Organizations
Events	Ecotourism Activities		Miscellaneous
Etc.	Etc.		Support Services

SOURCE: Canadian Tourism Human Resources Council, *The Student's Travel Map*, 1995, p. 8.

Transportation

This sector gets the traveller going! Transportation (travel) has often been mis-named as tourism. In fact, it is just one piece of the tourism puzzle. Jobs in this sector vary according to the mode of travel, but, more so than in any other sector, skills developed in one area of the transportation sector are easily transferred to an-other. A reservation agent for an airline could work for a cruise ship or a railroad with little additional training. Some of the jobs you will find in this sector are pilot, reservation agent, cruise director, car rental agent, customer service agent, purser on a train, ship, or plane; and captain of a charter boat.

Accommodation

This sector provides visitors with a place to sleep and includes any type of lodging available to the travelling public. Its products range from deluxe hotels in major cities to fishing camps found in the Yukon Territory. About 1.2 percent of the Canadian work force earn their wages in this sector.[4] Because travellers have many different needs and wants in a lodging facility, properties must provide a wide vari-ety of products and services. The business traveller in Vancouver requires a comfort-able room with full service; a family travelling on vacation may require a room that sleeps four; and the fisher wants a rustic cabin near a lake that promises good fish-ing! Some of the jobs you will find in this sector are front-desk clerk, hostel man-

ager, health-club manager, valet, camp counsellor, night auditor, groundskeeper, concierge, and housekeeper.

Food and Beverage

This is the largest sector of the tourism industry, with perhaps the greatest opportunity for the entrepreneur. About 5.1 percent of the Canadian work force are employed in the food and beverage sector.[5] This sector includes all food and beverage facilities such as restaurants (quick service, takeout, family style, specialty, theme, private clubs, pubs and taverns); food service in lodging facilities; contract/ institutional food service; catering firms; and deli and gourmet shops. Most of these facilities are small, owner-operated establishments.

Some of the jobs you might find in this sector are wine steward, banquet chef, baker, bartender, night club manager, food-service director, catering manager, and food and beverage server.

Attractions

The attractions sector entertains and educates the visitor. Attractions may be a natural part of our geography or they may be manufactured. Canada's geography provides many world-class natural attractions, such as Peggy's Cove in Nova Scotia, Magnetic Hill in New Brunswick, Niagara Falls in Ontario, and the West Coast Trail in British Columbia. Manufactured attractions provide an even broader choice for the tourist; they include historical sites, museums, theatres, casinos, water parks, gardens, and zoos. Unique products have developed to serve emerging special interests such as culinary, agricultural, and industrial tourism. Examples of **agricultural tourism** would be a visit to the granaries of Saskatchewan or a vacation on a working ranch in Alberta or a farm in rural

Ontario. **Industrial tourism** includes such activities as a visit to the oil fields of Alberta or to the salmon fisheries of British Columbia. **Cuisine tourism** would include enjoying a tour of the vineyards in Southern Ontario, attending a culinary seminar at one of Canada's culinary schools, or visiting a sugar bush. The Attractions sector employs 1 percent of the Canadian work force. Some of the jobs you will find in this sector are concessions attendant, casino dealer, heritage interpreter, attraction facility guide, amusement park supervisor, sales manager, and public relations manager.

Events and Conferences

The ease of travel and the new globalization of work places have created opportunities for tourism that promise an exciting future for workers. Festivals, conferences, sporting events, conventions, and meetings provide a growing number of Canadians with employment. Canada hosts more than 50 000 meetings annually. Events and Conferences provide business for all of the above sectors of tourism. Professionals in this sector need good organizational skills, strong people skills, and the ability to focus on details. Some of the jobs found in this sector are destination services representative, program specialist, registration supervisor, catering coordinator, special events manager, trade show operator, meeting planner, exhibit designer, and convention centre manager.

Adventure Tourism and Outdoor Recreation

Adventure Tourism and Outdoor Recreation is the sector providing hands-on, physical activities for visitors. This rapidly growing sector employs 0.5 percent of the total Canadian work force.[6] Much of the growth of this sector is based on the desire of North Americans to stay fit and healthy through exercise. The ski industry alone generates more than $5 billion in revenue yearly. Tennis and golf, hiking, fishing, and hunting are all popular with the tourist. Choices for a Canadian trip packed with adventure are as diverse as the country's landscape. There is also a growing desire among tourists to try a new sport, or simply to have an adventure such as a white-water rafting trip on the Fraser River. One of the more interesting areas of travel in this sector is called ecotourism, and Canadian geography makes ecotourism an important part of the overall Canadian tourism product. Some of the jobs you might find in this sector are local tour guide, ski lift operator, park warden, avalanche control trainee, lifeguard, tennis pro, recreation director, and marina manager/owner.

Travel Trade

Who sells the industry? Who creates that neat package of flight tickets, hotel reservations, and attractions? The Travel Trade sector! This sector employs 0.3 percent of the Canadian work force. There are more than 5000 travel agencies in Canada and hundreds of tour operators. A love of travel, an interest in geography and cultures, and a love of people all combine to create the perfect job for someone who wants the best of both worlds—a chance to travel and still work in the hometown. Some of the jobs available in this sector are reservations agent, tour guide, sales representative, incentive travel specialist, tour planner, package tour coordinator, destination development specialist, tour operator, and travel agency owner/operator.

Many tourist come to Canada to enjoy our climate and recreational activities.
(Photo courtesy Canadian Tourism Commission.)

Tourism Services

This sector provides support services for the tourism industry. It includes the federal, provincial, and municipal governments; tourism education councils; associations; research, marketing, consulting, and education professionals; as well as small businesses providing services to travellers, such as information centres, gift shops, travel insurance agencies, and duty-free shops. Some of the jobs found in this sector are tourism teacher, tourism specialist, tourism researcher, customs official, travel reporter, and writer.

Reasons for the Growth of Tourism

Tourism has experienced phenomenal growth over the past 100 years. Much of this growth has taken place during the past 50 years. With the baby boomers reaching retirement age, predictions are that the tourism boom will continue for the next 15 to 20 years. Here are some of the reasons for the growth of tourism over the last 100 years:

Technology Most things that we do today have in some way been affected by the technological advancements seen over the past 100 years. The following four areas of changing technology have had the greatest impact on and will continue to influence tourism growth.

1. **The advancements made in our transportation systems.** Clearly, the way in which we travel today is very different from the beginning of the twentieth century. Humans had not taken their first flight in 1900, but in 1971 the Concorde (the first British/French supersonic passenger jet) travelled from London, England, to New York City in just under 2.5

hours! Planes are bigger, faster, safer, and more comfortable than they have ever been. Cruise ships are larger, with new designs and technologies that provide more entertainment and amenities for customers, helping to make rough seas smoother and the trip more comfortable. Cars, which the majority of North American families now own, are also faster, safer, and more spacious. European and Japanese trains can travel at speeds of more than 350 km an hour. Modern tour buses boast of large viewing windows, snack bars, and television sets, allowing passengers to watch movies or educational videos during their trip. Continued improvements to modes of transportation make travel less expensive and more accessible to tourists, adding to the growth of tourism around the world.

2. **The advancements made in media coverage.** Our media systems have become global and instant through the use of satellite technology. Now, as events happen around the world, we watch them unfold live on networks like CNN. Televised sporting events such as the Olympics, the Super Bowl, and the Kentucky Derby allow those of us who cannot be there to experience the thrill of the event. The excitement generated on the screen helps create a desire to experience the event in person.

3. **The introduction of computer systems.** The introduction of the computer in the 1960s heralded a whole new way of doing business throughout the world. Tourism has benefited enormously from this technology. From how we check guests in and out of a hotel to how we prepare their meals, from how we purchase an airline ticket to how air traffic controllers track the flights landing at their airport, computers have aided the traveller. It would take an entire textbook to describe the ways in which computers have changed world business practices. In today's world, lifelong learning is essential, and you will need to stay current in the field of computer technology if you wish to remain competitive.

4. **The Internet.** The most significant advance in computer technology has to be the Internet and the World Wide Web (WWW). The Internet/WWW in years to come will be the major tool we use to exchange information. Today, a business that does not have a Web page or is not otherwise accessible to its marketplace via the Internet is losing customers. Using the Web, tourists can not only "visit" a destination in advance to look at the variety of available entertainment and recreation facilities, but can also check out their hotel options, look at the variety of restaurants in the area, and then make bookings! Airlines can have last-minute sales on flights that are scheduled to leave within a day or two. This allows the airline to book seats that would otherwise have been empty, recouping at least a portion of a fare. Web sites have been developed for many museums, attractions, and other tourist facilities in Canada and around the world, making the dispersal of information fast, efficient, and inexpensive. The uses and possibilities of the Internet are so vast, it is impossible to list all the benefits it brings to the tourism industry; but knowledge of the Internet and how to use it is essential for any student entering the industry. At the end of each chapter you will find several Web sites that you might wish to explore yourself.

Will this technology replace existing means of information dispersal? Experts believe that new technologies in the foreseeable future will be used to enhance, not replace, the way information is distributed. Although the younger generation is comfortable using these new technologies, tourism's swelling baby-boomer market still enjoys looking through glossy travel brochures and magazines, with the personal attention of a travel counsellor. It is clear, however, that tourism companies not using the Internet and the latest technology will be left behind.

Better Educational Systems Higher education has become the norm for many young adults. The value of continuing, lifelong learning in today's technologically oriented work place cannot be ignored. Research shows that the more education people have, the more willing they are to travel. Learning broadens one's perspective and creates a curiosity that often motivates a person to travel in search of new personal experiences.

More Disposable Income The amount of disposable income has increased because of the rise of two-income families. With both parents working, even in recessionary times, vacation means travel. In discussions about disposable income, the emerging market of retirees comes to mind. Not only the baby-boom generation, many of whom have chosen early retirement, but also the generation that precedes the boomers will have a dramatic effect on tourism sales. These two markets are in good health, have money to spend, and have already travelled more extensively than any other senior group in history. With their mortgages paid off and their children educated, they are ready to continue their travel adventures. These two generations will have plenty of time and disposable income to spend on tourism.

What will this market be looking for? David Foot, a professor at the University of Toronto and author of the book *Boom, Bust and Echo*, has this to say about the "other" generation:

> These young seniors, born in the 1930s, they really had a rough beginning. They were pre-teens in the Second World War...[they] really did pay their dues up front but they didn't have to serve. Then they entered the job market in the post-war reconstruction of the 1950's. Did they ever have to worry about getting a job? No. They had their choice of jobs...[and] did better than they ever expected to do.... The richest people in Canada today are in their late 50s and 60s, and these are people who are now retiring.[7]

A More Stressful Lifestyle Even though new technologies are meant to reduce the amount of work we do, it seems that the pace of modern life has actually accelerated. Stress, the by-product of this faster pace, creates the physical and emotional need to get away. In addition, as companies attempt to keep costs down, benefit packages often include longer vacation periods, and overtime work is repaid, not with dollars, but with additional time off. Although the extended vacation seems to be disappearing, the long weekend and 10-day holiday provides vacationers with the opportunity to travel more often.

The Declining Cost of Travel The cost of travel has declined, making it more accessible to everyone. Modes of transportation vary from the least expensive (private vehicle or bus) to the most expensive (air). Deregulation has allowed new transportation companies to compete for business. Low-cost carriers have given the consumer an alternative to the major airlines. The Open Skies agreement has provided North Americans with a wider choice of flights and destinations as well as lower-cost tickets. Frequent traveller plans and the partnerships that have developed between destinations and the airlines have resulted in better packaging, which reduces the overall cost of the vacation.

Better Marketing and Promotion Products sell better when they have strong marketing programs, and all sectors of the tourism industry have become more active and creative in this area. New tourism advertising campaigns focus on fun, education, activity, and information. Electronic marketplaces bring up-to-date information not only to agents and operators, but also to clients. From the federal government's perspective, lack of promotion has hurt tourism in the past, giving the Canadian Tourism Commission its primary mandate of promoting the Canadian experience. Accordingly, the CTC launched five new promotional campaigns in 1996–97, addressing the needs of Canada's five major markets: the domestic market, U.S. leisure travellers, business travellers, Asia/Pacific, and Europe. Across Canada all levels of government are forming partnerships with local tourism operators to produce proactive marketing plans that feature state-of-the-art promotional materials.

A Common, Worldwide Currency Travel also flourishes when a **common currency** exists. Since the Second World War, the introduction of credit cards, travellers' cheques, automated banking, and currency exchange machines has created easy access to money and credit while on vacation. Nowadays, currency can be easily obtained using the Interac banking machines located in just about every major destination around the world. American Express, Visa, and MasterCard all focus on the pleasures of tourism as they promote the use of their cards.

Political Stability Peace and tourism go hand in hand. The world has been, for the most part, peaceful over the past 50 years. Only recently, with the terrorist

Shopping is usually a part of every tourist's vacation, and it is made even easier by the fact that credit cards serve as a common currency. Here tourists enjoy the shopping arcade at Jasper Park Lodge.
(Photo: Paula Kerr.)

attack on the World Trade Center, September 11, 2001 (9-11), have physical threats been a big concern for North American travellers. The impact of this event on tourism has been enormous and throughout the text, we will look at how it has affected each tourism sector. In countries where terrorism is a daily threat, tourism seldom plays a significant economic role. Countries such as Israel, for which tourism is a significant revenue generator, have seen this industry decimated. Analysts predicted, and tourism statistics show, that the fear of terrorism coupled with a weakened world economy drove international tourism spending down for 2002.

We have been fortunate in Canada to have earned a reputation as a safe and peaceful country and although we have felt the backlash of the terrorist attack on the World Trade Center with falling tourism revenues, Canada remains a country that inspires confidence in the traveller. Thus, Canadian tourism analysts believe that we will rebound more quickly than other parts of the world.

The tourism system itself has become user friendly, providing travellers with access to many sectors of the industry with a single phone call. Transportation systems are linked with accommodations, accommodations are linked with the food and beverage sector, and the food and beverage sector links itself to all parts of the tourism system. The industry is beginning to see the benefits of working together as a single tourism unit.

Talking the Same Language

To begin our discussion on tourism, we need some common, basic terminology. In order to understand the value of tourism, researchers gather statistics on all aspects of tourist activities, such as how travellers reached their destination, the type of accommodation and services they used, and how much money they spent. To make these figures understandable to any person reading and using them, parameters needed to be set that excluded activities obviously not related to tourist visits, such as going downtown to shop or travelling to school. It is important that you understand the following key terms: *trip, foreign tourist, domestic tourist, excursionist, travel deficit, multiplier effect,* and *leakage*.

In Canada, a **trip** is defined as "any travel that takes a person 80 km from their place of residence for any reason other than a commute to work or school, travel in an ambulance or to a hospital or clinic, or a trip that is longer than one year."[8] This definition eliminates both the trip downtown (if fewer than 80 km) and the student's trip to school.

In 1937, the Committee of Statistics Experts of the League of Nations defined **foreign tourists** as "persons visiting a country, other than that in which they usually reside, for a period of at least 24 hours." Foreign tourists may also be called **inbound tourists** (likewise, Canadians who visit other countries may be described as **outbound tourists**).

Although foreign tourists are an important part of our tourism business, more than 75 percent of all tourism revenues are generated by Canadians travelling in Canada, known as **domestic tourists**. Domestic tourists are "persons travelling in the country in which they reside, staying for a period of at least 24 hours, and travelling at least 80 km from their home."

Here are some guidelines the United Nations uses to clarify the term "tourist."[9]

You *are* a tourist if

- you are travelling for pleasure, for family reasons, to learn more about the world in general, for health or religious purposes
- you are travelling for business reasons other than direct remuneration by the country you are visiting
- you are visiting the country as part of a sea cruise or travel package

You *are not* considered a tourist if

- you are actively going to take up an occupation at your destination
- you are establishing residency in the country
- you are attending an educational institution and establishing a residence or
- you are staying less than 24 hours

As travel has become faster and easier, people often travel 80 km from their home for recreation or entertainment, but they do not stay overnight. By definition, they cannot be called "tourists" because they are not away from home for a long enough period. The tourism industry calls these travellers **excursionists**, or **same-day visitors**. In Canada, an excursionist is "any person who travels at least 40 km from the place of residence (round trip of 80 km), stays less than 24 hours, and is not commuting to work, school or operating as part of a crew on a train, airplane, truck, bus or ship."[10]

Canadians love to travel and they like to travel outside Canada. Here are some of the reasons why: (a) the cold winter weather makes sunny, warm winter climates popular; (b) many Canadians have relatives who live outside the country, so they must travel to visit them; (c) foreign countries promote their attractions more efficiently than Canada; and (d) Canadians are not aware of the tourism treasures within their borders. However, every time Canadians leave the country, their tourism dollars are lost to Canada. Canada had a **travel deficit** of $3.4 billion in 1996. (That is, Canadians spent $3.4 billion more outside the country than foreign tourists spent here.) In the last decade, the Canadian government has increased its support of the tourism industry by providing the Canadian Tourism Commission (CTC) with $50 million a year for promotion and advertising. The tourism industry, partnering with the CTC, has matched that dollar figure. Together, with the use of strong promotional campaigns, they cut the travel deficit by 44.7 percent, to $1.3 billion in 2001. How has Canada been able to reduce its travel deficit? More Canadians are choosing to vacation in Canada and more Americans, who view Canada as a safe destination, are taking advantage of the U.S. dollar exchange rate, choosing to travel in Canada. Although the number of Canadians vacationing outside the country has not dropped, they are spending less money in foreign destinations. Figure 1.2 shows the types of travel that bring foreign tourists to Canada, while Figure 1.3 shows the types of travel that draw Canadians to other countries. As you can see, they are very similar.

Tourism is a revenue producer and much of this revenue goes back into the local economy. The **multiplier effect** of tourism dollars has a beneficial effect on nearly everyone in the community. For example, when tourists stay in a Ramada Hotel, they pay the hotel for their room. The Ramada takes the **tourist dollars** and uses them to pay for salaries, supplies, mortgage payments, and electricity.

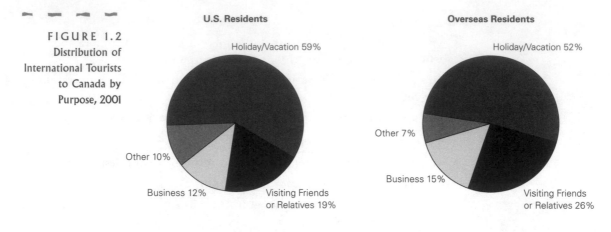

FIGURE 1.2
Distribution of
International Tourists
to Canada by
Purpose, 2001

SOURCE: Canadian Tourism Commission, *Canadian Tourism Facts and Figures 2001.*

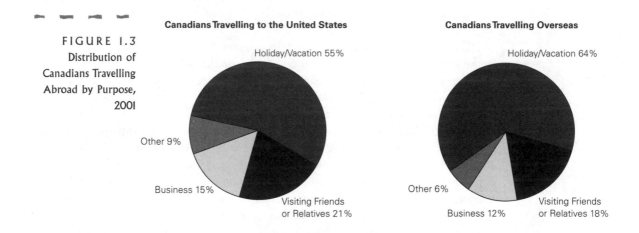

FIGURE 1.3
Distribution of
Canadians Travelling
Abroad by Purpose,
2001

SOURCE: Canadian Tourism Commission, *Canadian Tourism Facts and Figures 2001.*

Sally Hyung is a front-desk agent at the Ramada. She uses her salary to pay for rent, food, entertainment, transportation, dry cleaning, and so on. The grocer takes the money he receives from Sally and uses it to pay for his rent, buy supplies, and pay his salaries. Thus, tourist dollars have a ripple effect, benefiting just about everyone in the community.

The last term is **leakage.** Leakage occurs when the community cannot support the influx of tourists and must import workers and goods in order to sustain the industry. For example, the town of Banff does not have enough residents to support the throngs of tourists who arrive each summer. Every year, Banff's hotels, restaurants, and shops must hire workers from outside the community. Banff also needs to purchase supplies from larger centres like Calgary. Bill James, a college student from Oshawa, Ontario, is working in a Banff hotel for the summer. The tourist dollars spent in his hotel are used to pay for salaries, supplies, and the mortgage. Bill uses some of his salary to pay for his living expenses in Banff, but he is saving some of his pay to use for his last year at college. Part of what he makes is not being spent in Banff; it will be spent in Oshawa. This is an example of leakage. When leakage occurs, the community that hosts the tourist does not get the full benefit of the revenue generated. Leakage is particularly harmful in countries such as the Bahamas, an island with few resources to support its large tourism industry, where many workers and products must be brought in from other countries.

Historical Avenues

The history of travel is as old as the human race itself. In the early days of civilization, people travelled by foot and were exposed to many dangers. They seldom travelled for pleasure but rather to find new food sources, to follow climatic changes, or to escape other stronger, threatening tribes. Yet historical research suggests that people in early civilizations, often linked by marriage and common ideals, did travel occasionally for the purpose of business and pleasure. Archeologists have unearthed artifacts from digs in North and South America, Europe, and Asia that indicate that tribes would meet at certain times of the year to perform religious celebrations, to conduct tribal business, to trade, and simply to dance and socialize.

As civilizations developed, the strongest tribes would seek to control the resources of an area. Armies of warriors conquered entire regions, enslaving the inhabitants and taking their possessions. This activity increased not only the conquering tribe's influence, but their wealth as well. Two peoples of ancient times who became noted as traders, not warriors, were the Sumerians and the Phoenicians. They focused on industry to increase their wealth, and they established early trade routes in the African/Southern European corridors. The Sumerians were the first nation to develop coinage, used as payment for goods. The Phoenicians, noted sailors, were responsible for creating some of the first maps, showing their system of water routes, to help guide others.

Three major empires dominated between 4800 B.C. and A.D. 300: the Egyptian, the Greek, and the Roman. In its own way, each empire provided advancement for travel activities. Over this period of time, people travelled frequently to conduct trade, to complete government business, and for educational and social reasons. The Egyptians developed strong central governments and large flourishing cities, which attracted travellers. As many of their cities were built along the Nile River, with its northward currents and southward breezes, travel by boat was easy and safe, making these urban centres accessible.

By 900 B.C., the Grecian empire had emerged. Researchers, discoverers, and philosophers, the Greeks made travel a part of their education and way of life. Their cities flourished, becoming destinations in themselves. The Greek civilization developed strong community lifestyles. As tourists do today, the Greeks loved to shop, eat, and drink. They loved the theatre and spectator sports, and they travelled great distances to partake of these forms of entertainment. Of course, one of their gifts to modern civilization has been the Olympic Games. Over the past 100 years, athletes from around the world have gathered every four years to compete in the modern Olympic Games, replicating the ancient Greek tradition of honouring the best in each sport.

By 400 B.C., a new nation was on the rise and it was to become one of the most successful empires in the history of the world. The Roman Empire lasted a relatively short 800 years, but its influence is still felt in many parts of the world. Great conquerors, the Romans spread out across Europe, bringing under their influence colonies that ranged from Portugal and Spain to Gaul and Great Britain. Wherever they moved, they built roads—more than 80 000 km of them! Many of these roads are still found across Europe and England, and this allows the modern tourist to literally walk on ancient paths. Wherever they went, the Romans brought with them their culture, their language, and their way of life. They established a strong, central system of government, and Roman laws provided peace and security for the empire for many years. Roman coinage became the universally accepted currency. During this period of peace and prosperity, travel became both easy and safe. Inns and taverns sprang up in the towns and along the roads to care for travellers. Restaurants, bars, and a wide variety of entertainment flourished in the cities. The Romans developed spas to look after their physical well-being, and they devised the first "fast-food" style of restaurants (serving foods such as pickled fish and eggs, bread, and fruit). They loved to learn and to be entertained, and their cities became destinations sought after by many travellers.

More than any other ancient civilization, the Roman Empire clearly illustrates the conditions under which tourism may flourish. Peace and prosperity are the cornerstones of tourism. Travel modes must be easily accessible and safe. Common currency, a common language, and a well-established legal system are essential. As long as these conditions exist, people will be encouraged to travel. If any of these conditions are missing, the growth of travel will be diminished. As Roman society began to break down, its government allowing immoral and illegal behaviour to become common, its strength waned. By A.D 400. the Roman Empire lay in ruins and few people risked travel for any reason. It would be nearly 800 years before the world would see a true re-emergence of travel.

By the turn of the millennium, the Roman Catholic Church had gained dominance over people's lives. Wishing to free the Holy Lands from the rule of "infidels," the Church was able to raise large armies of knights and warriors from faithful parishioners. Wars, called the Crusades, took place between 1096 and 1291. The knights who fought in these "holy wars" brought back many interesting stories of different lands and cultures. During this time, much of the known world was being carved up into kingdoms, with strong families establishing their kingdoms by uniting their lands under one rule of law. Merchants, less fearful for their safety than most, began to venture farther into the countryside. One of the best known of the early travelling merchants was Marco Polo. Travelling from Europe to the Far East, he brought back spices, silks, and merchandise that created great interest in foreign lands and cultures. Slowly, humanity emerged from the "dark ages" with renewed curiosity and a desire for knowledge, which in turn led to a re-birth of travel and laid the foundations for the modern tourism industry.

In the seventeenth and eighteenth centuries, England's nobility, recognizing the lack of educational opportunities at home, began to send their sons to the

Continent to be educated. This event, dubbed **"le grand tour,"** prepared the heirs of their estates for the future by teaching them languages, financial skills, and a knowledge of religion and legal institutions. The trip lasted several years and included stays in Paris, Florence, Rome, Zurich, and Vienna.[11] It is interesting to note that "le grand tour" is still part of tourism today, but modern tourists complete it in days, not years.

Perhaps the greatest event to change the tides of tourism was a bloodless revolution—the Industrial Revolution. It changed the way people worked by providing them with machines, and it changed the focus of our lives from an agrarian philosophy to an industrial one. A growing industrial economy saw the emergence of a true middle class—people with enough discretionary time and money to make travel and vacation a common element of their lives.

Between 1800 and 1939, there were many major changes in modes of travel. Steamships and steam trains made crossing the oceans and continents easy. The invention of the automobile provided a means for people to travel independently, choosing their own time and destinations. Finally, in 1903, the era of air travel was born. By the late 1920s and early 1930s, air routes had been established and travel across the oceans had been reduced to days instead of months. With fast and accessible modes of travel now available, tourism was growing.

In 1939, with the outbreak of the Second World War, safe travel once again became unattainable. Those who travelled for pleasure were few. Canadian men and women, pulled from their Prairie homes, from the fishing fleets of British Columbia and the Maritimes—people from across the country, representing all ages and occupations—were shipped overseas to fight in this great war. Many did not return. Those who did brought back experiences of other cultures and lands to share with the folks at home. In the shadow of world war, the age of modern tourism had begun. During this brief period of war, great advances were made in modes of transportation. Bigger, faster planes and automobiles, faster and more comfortable ships and trains were necessary to the Allied victory. After the war, these modern machines fuelled a new growth in tourism. Industrialized nations became prosperous, and with that prosperity came more discretionary income and time. Time, money, peace, safe and accessible transportation systems, and common currency—all of these things have helped to build today's tourism industry.

No history of tourism will ever be complete without mentioning the terrorist attack on the World Trade Center (WTC) and the Pentagon on September 11, 2001 (9-11). More than 2800 people, representing 86 different nations, were killed. Twenty-four Canadian lives were lost. The visual impact of watching two American Airlines jumbo jets hit the twin towers and explode, followed by the collapse of the World Trade Center, stunned the world. Commercial airlines have been hijacked in the past. Bombs have been placed on commercial airliners causing midair explosions, as with Pan Am's flight 101 over Lockerbie, Scotland, in 1992. However, the deliberate use of fully fuelled jumbo jets with paying passengers aboard as guided bombs to attack a specific target made 9-11 even more brutal. Innocent travellers and innocent workers were caught up in a war that was never theirs to wage. Heroes emerged from this disaster, including the 43 passengers and crew of United Airlines flight 93. Attempting to recapture the aircraft from its hijackers, they chose to die in a field in Shanksville, Pennsylvania, rather than see more innocent people killed. Their actions may very well have changed the way airline passengers react if faced with a similar airline hijacking. Perhaps the

Conrad Hilton

First truly international hotelier, first to "gold dig" in his own hotel lobbies, first to set job and safety standards, first to set pricing programs for his properties, and the list goes on. Conrad Hilton, hotelier extraordinaire!

Conrad Hilton began his career in 1907, when he started to work as a hotel operator to help his family face some very hard times in his hometown of San Antonio, New Mexico. But it was not until after the First World War that Hilton bought his first hotel. He had been a soldier, a politician, and a banker, and in 1919 Hilton went to Sisco, Texas, intending to buy a bank! Instead, he purchased the Mobley Hotel. The oil boom had just begun and the hotel's owner had caught oil fever. He sold his property to Hilton, and left to strike it rich. Had he realized the Mobley Hotel would be the first stepping stone to wealth and fortune for one of the largest hotel tycoons in America, he might have charged more!

By 1929 Hilton had seven properties, but instant riches were not his destiny. The Depression found him penniless and in debt. At one point, his bellhop loaned him $300 for "eatin' money." It was during this phase of his career that he learned to operate economically and this lesson served him well. In 1946 Hilton Hotels Corporation was formed, and in 1949 Hilton International was established with its first operating contract at the Caribe Hilton in Puerto Rico. In 1954 he acquired the Statler Hotel chain. It was not until the 1960s that Hilton saw the advantage of franchising, and in 1967 he sold Hilton

International to Trans World Airlines. In 1969, Hilton began a partnership with the University of Houston. To honour his support, the Houston school changed its name to the Conrad N. Hilton School of Hotel Management.

What did Hilton give to the hotel industry?

- He was the first hotelier to insist that each hotel prepare daily year-to-date reports summarizing all the financial actions of the day such as revenues, expenses, and profit and loss.

- He set up one of the first computerized hotel reservation systems.

- He was a master at identifying lobby space that could be revenue producing; he would rent it to shop owners or develop a new bar or restaurant.

- He had an instinct for finding "white elephants"—hotels that had not been financially productive—buying them at bargain prices, and creating profitable properties just by implementing simple cost controls.

What kind of a man was he really? He was energetic, he loved beautiful women, he learned quickly, he was an incurable optimist, and he believed strongly in equality. He believed in working hard and playing hard. At age 90, he still held the position of chair of the board of Hilton Hotels Corporation. A giant in his time, Hilton is still recognized as one of the world's leading hoteliers.

next time tourists become pawns of terrorists, they will weigh their options and choose to fight back. As tourists we may be caught in the violent struggles of warring factions in a foreign destination. Three Canadians travellers, enjoying a night out in the Philippines, were killed in September 2002 when terrorists bombed the nightclub. In Russia, terrorists trying to force the Russian government to submit to their demands commandeered an entire theatre audience as they were about to enjoy a play. Tourism is now a target for terrorists, and, in the future, tourists will choose destinations with greater concern for their personal safety.

Despite these events, the United Nations and the World Tourism Organization still hold to the belief that one of the ways to build a peaceful world is to let people from different nations meet and learn more about each other. Tourism can provide a formula for friendship that no amount of government legislation can match. There is no better umbrella under which to foster such friendships than that of tourism.

Tourism As a Career

Why is tourism a good choice of career for you?

1. Tourism is one of the major industries in the world, employing more than 112 million people. Recent figures estimate tourism's dollar value at $54.6 billion in Canada and $3.75 trillion worldwide. It pays to get involved with this industry!

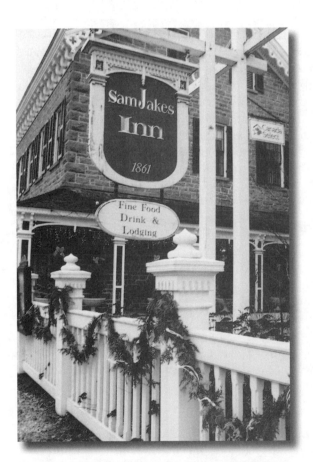

Good food and drink and a place to sleep are an essential part of a trip. Tourists have a wide variety of accommodation choices from elegant hotels through country inns to local campgrounds.

(Photo: Paula Kerr.)

2. Tourism is growing fast! With the projected growth of Canadian employment numbers estimated to be 1.6 percent per annum, tourism's projected growth is 2.5 percent per annum, with the greatest growth occurring in Food and Beverage, Adventure Tourism and Outdoor Recreation, and Events and Conferences.

3. Tourism is a global industry and the skills learned in one country are readily transferable to another. Not only are the skills international in nature, but basic entry-level skills may also be carried over into all of the eight Canadian tourism sectors and their many differing occupations.

4. Every day is different and the challenges of each day provide an interesting and exciting work place. Feedback on how well you are doing with your daily work is immediate. If you use your skills effectively, you can easily have the satisfaction of turning an unhappy customer into a contented one.

5. Innovation in this industry is welcome and can be highly profitable! The great diversity of this industry, the new business it generates, and the constant learning process all benefit a tourism worker.

6. Learning good people skills and discovering how to deal with people from different ethnic backgrounds are bonus skills that are needed in all Canadian industries. These skills will be valuable to you, no matter what else you choose to do in life.

Steps to Success

Career ladders have changed since the 1960s. In the past, graduates of hotel school expected to enter the hotel business and end their careers in management, as hotel managers, chief executive officers, or owners. Nowadays, it is not unusual for people working in the tourism industry to work in three to four sectors during their careers. For example, the core skills of communication; knowing how to serve customers; knowledge of your region, province, and country; and a love of service provide you with the basic ability to work at an information centre, on an airline, in a ski school, or at a local pub. Each position will require some additional training, but once you have the basic skills, knowledge, and attitude, the rest is easy.

Tourism Industry Associations and Organizations

There are many tourism associations and organizations responsible for (a) legislation/control of the industry, (b) research, development, and marketing, and (c) professional development of workers. Some of these groups will be highlighted in chapter 12. Listed below are five international organizations and six Canadian organizations that will be referred to throughout the book. You should be able to recognize their names and initials. Some will represent one or more industry sectors and many have more than one role to play. Some are strongly supported by government funding while others support their activities using funds received from their membership base.

International Organizations

World Tourism Organization (WTO) The WTO is the official consultative organization to the United Nations on tourism. Its fundamental aim is the promotion and development of tourism with a view to contributing to economic development, international understanding, world peace, prosperity, and universal respect for and observance of human rights and fundamental freedoms for all, without distinction as to race, sex, language, or religion. Activities of the WTO include international technical support, education, and training to member states; facilitation of tourism by removing obstacles to tourists; security and protection of tourists; encouragement of environmentally sound planning; and marketing and promotion of global tourism.

International Civil Aviation Organization (ICAO) ICAO is another consultative organization to the United Nations. Its members are governments that have a vested interest in the safe, orderly growth of the world's airline industry. Its mandates include encouraging development of safe airways and airports, discouraging unreasonable competition among the airlines, and meeting the needs of the global community by providing safe, regular, efficient, and economical air transport.

International Air Transport Association (IATA) Established in 1919, and completely reorganized in 1945, this major organization has been responsible for much of the ease of air travel in the last 50 years. The airlines themselves created and run IATA. IATA is responsible for the one-ticket/one-trip concept, and it takes an active role in the safety and security of global air travel. Additional information on IATA is also found in chapter 5.

World Travel and Tourism Council (WTTC) Established in 1990 and headquartered in London, England, this private organization works with governments around the world, helping them to realize the full economic impact of tourism. Its members are executives representing all eight sectors of tourism. The department that focuses on tourism's human resources, headed by Canadian Brian White, is located in Vancouver, British Columbia.

Pacific Asia Travel Association (PATA) Founded in 1951, PATA is a good example of countries uniting for the benefit of the tourism industry. Its members come from all sectors of the tourism industry, and its mandate is excellence in travel and tourism through promotion, research, education, development, and marketing. It represents 34 countries in the Pacific/Asia area and it meets annually to present research papers, discuss common problems, and examine and adjust its long-range activities to meet changing needs.

Canadian Organizations/Associations

The following organizations are just a few of the many that contribute to the smooth operation and the future development of Canada's tourism industry. Organizations and associations are part of tourism services.

Canadian Tourism Commission (CTC) The CTC is a working partnership among tourism businesses and associations, provincial and territorial governments, and the government of Canada. It plans, directs, manages, and implements programs to generate and promote tourism in Canada. The CTC was established in 1994 and is discussed in chapter 3.

Canadian Tourism Human Resource Council (CTHRC) The CTHRC provides a national forum to facilitate human resource development activities that will support a globally competitive and sustainable Canadian tourism industry. This organization brings together under a national framework the work of the provincial tourism education councils (TECs). You will learn more about these organizations in chapter 3 and chapter 12.

Tourism Industry Association of Canada (TIAC) TIAC was founded in 1931 to encourage tourism in Canada. It is a nonprofit industry association representing tourism-related businesses, associations, institutions, and individuals. TIAC provides representation at the national level and up-to-date information on tourism-related issues. TIAC works closely with the CTC and in 1996 was given the responsibility of running Canada's largest tourism trade show, Rendez-Vous Canada. It also works with customs to improve reception of all travellers, is a member of the CTHRC board of directors, lobbies the federal government on tourism issues, and supports research in cooperation with the Canada Tourism Research Institute. TIAC will be discussed again in chapter 12, The Tourism Services Sector.

Association of Canadian Travel Agents (ACTA) ACTA is the not-for-profit trade association for much of the travel industry in Canada. The name was changed from the Alliance of Canadian Travel Associations to its current name in June 1997. Retail travel agencies, tour operators, as well as any travel or tourism-related companies provide a broad cross-section of tourism-related member groups.

ACCESS ACCESS (**ACTA/CITC C**anadian **E**ducational **S**tandards **S**ystem) was formed in 1987 and is jointly owned by two professional associations: the Association of Canadian Travel Agents (ACTA) and the Canadian Institute of Travel Counsellors (CITC). Its mission is to improve the quality of the Travel Trade through education and professional development of its members. ACCESS conducts entry and advanced national examinations, certifying successful entry-level candidates as Certified Travel Counsellors (CTC). Working with the CTHRC, they have produced a training guide and set of skill standards for national certification of travel counsellors. ACCESS recognizes travel programs that meet or exceed the standard for travel training recommended by the association.

Canadian Tourism Research Institute (CTRI) The CTRI is an integral part of Canada's foremost research institute, the Conference Board of Canada. CTRI is privately funded and engages in extensive research on the tourism industry followed by reports written to inform other tourism organizations, the industry, and the public on tourism's past performance and its anticipated future.

In addition, each province and territory of Canada has an organization comprising government workers and sometimes private industry members. The focus of their work is the development, growth, and promotion of tourism at the provincial level with one main goal: to make that province the number-one destination choice in Canada. For example, Tourism Saskatchewan is a unique partnership that is industry led, market driven, and dedicated to all aspects of tourism in the province.

Municipal Organizations

The smallest but perhaps the most active tourism organization in your own community will be your local convention and visitor bureau (CVB). Much of the support the local tourist industry receives is from the city's chamber of commerce or its CVB. These groups are responsible for developing and promoting local events, bringing large tours or conferences to the city, and marketing a community's tourism products to a broader regional audience. Municipal organizations are part of the tourism services sector (chapter 12).

The Buchanan Report on Tourism

In 1993, the federal government commissioned a report on the status of tourism in Canada, headed by Judd Buchanan. This report dramatically changed the relationship between the tourism industry and the Canadian government. Although the report is not new and the numbers have changed, the general overview of tourism and its value to Canada remain unchanged. The full report may be seen on the *Snapshots* Web site. The following is a brief summary of Judd Buchanan's findings.

In his report, Buchanan acknowledges that tourism was a rapidly growing industry, both globally and domestically. In Canada it employs more than half a million workers and comprises more than 60 000 businesses, both entrepreneurial and corporate. Tourism is particularly important to the Canadian work force because it hires more young Canadians, Aboriginal people, visible minorities, and people with disabilities. In fact, tourism often provides the first work opportunity for young people, recent immigrants, and people returning to the work force (such as women who worked at home while their children were young). In addition, a higher proportion of women move into supervisory and management positions than in other Canadian industries. In 1993, tourism provided more than $26 billion dollars to Canada's gross domestic product. For every billion dollars in revenue, municipal governments received $60 million, provincial governments received $160 million, and the federal government received $230 million.

Buchanan maintained that Canadian cultural, heritage, and natural tourism products are undervalued not only by government, but by Canadians as a whole. He found fault with government policies of the early 1990s, when the tourism industry was neglected and funds to promote Canadian tourism had virtually disappeared. In the mid-1990s the government was spending only $16 million marketing dollars per year while Australia was investing $100 million. The Canadian tourism industry not only lost much of the domestic market, but also failed to promote the U.S. dollar advantage to American travellers and ignored the overseas markets. As a result, more Canadians chose to travel outside Canada, raising our travel deficit to an all time high of $7.9 billion. On the international front, Canadian tourism faced stronger competition than ever before.

On a positive note, Buchanan discovered that tourism professionals were anxious to participate in a recovery program. His suggestion was the creation of a totally new body, to be directed by a board of federal/provincial and private sector representatives. The Canadian Tourism Commission would work in partnership with the various sectors of the tourism industry, providing a strong, united front for the industry. Marketing programs would be developed and implemented jointly by this group, and funding for promotional activities would be shared on a 50/50 basis.

The creation of this working partnership between the tourism industry and the Canadian Tourism Commission has been a success. In 2001, the tourism industry made $54.6 billion, and the travel deficit has been cut by $6.6 billion.

summary

Tourism is one of Canada's largest industries and one of its largest exports. In Canada the industry is defined by eight sectors: Transportation, Accomodation, Food and Beverage, Attractions, Events and Conferences, Adventure Tourism and Outdoor Recreation, Travel Trade, and Tourism Services. All of these sectors interact to provide tourists with the lodging, food service, entertainment, and travel experience that best suit their needs.

Tourism has seen many changes over the past 100 years, from the method and speed with which we travel to the wide variety of new destinations and activities available to the average citizen. Although travel is still an important part of our lives, the threat of terrorism will change some of our travel patterns. There are many terms in the industry that should be understood before beginning to study the subject. Tourist (domestic and foreign), excursionist, visitor, trip, leakage, multiplier effect, and travel deficit are just a few of the terms you will need to know.

In 1994, Judd Buchanan, then a special advisor to the prime minister, reviewed the tourism industry and its impact on the lives of Canadians so that he could advise the government on how to approach this particular industry. His findings clearly identified the value of tourism to Canada and caused the government to create a new agency, the Canadian Tourism Commission, to promote the tourism product to Canada's many tourist markets.

A career in tourism is both challenging and exciting. It provides the entrepreneur with the opportunity to own a profitable business. Because of its nature, you can be assured that no two days are alike.

questions

1. Explain the interrelationship of the eight tourism sectors as they will affect

   a) a tourist

   b) your career ladder

2. a) List 10 reasons for the growth of tourism.

   b) Using any five of the growth factors, explain how you believe they will affect tourism over the next 20 years. Defend your answer using examples.

3. Summarize the Judd Buchanan Report on Tourism under the following headings:

   a) the Canadian tourism work force

   b) financial effects of tourism on Canada's financial well-being, both present and future

   c) the purpose and goals of the Canadian Tourism Commission (CTC)

4. Have recent terrorist activities changed your desire to travel? your destination? Why or why not?

5. Define, in your own words, the following tourism terms: *tourism, trip, domestic tourist, foreign tourist, excursionist, leakage, multiplier effect.*

6. Canada's travel deficit has been lowered over the past five years. Explain "Canada's travel deficit" and the measures taken by the CTC and the tourism industry that have significantly helped to lower it.

7. a) Discuss four global tourism organizations and four Canadian tourism organizations that you feel have the greatest impact on our tourism products, explaining why you have chosen them.

   b) In which sector of tourism would you find these organizations? Why?

weblinks

www.hospitalitynet.org

Hospitality Net bills itself as "All of Hospitality on the Net" and includes news, job links, and a discussion forum.

www.canadatourism.com

The Canadian Tourism Commission's Web site (see p. 19 for a description of the CTC).

www.world-tourism.org

The World Tourism Organization is the United Nations' official consultative organization on tourism issues (see p. 18).

www.wttc.org

The World Travel and Tourism Council is made up of chief executives from all sectors of the tourism industry (see p. 19).

notes

1. Canadian Tourism Commission, *Canadian Tourism Facts and Figures 2001.*

2. www.canadatourism.com, Canada's World Position as a Tourism Destination.

3. www.worldtouristm.org, Research/facts&figures.

4. Dr. M. Mohan, G. Gislason, and B. McGowan, *Tourism Related Employment: An Update* (Ottawa, Ontario: Canadian Tourism Human Resource Council, 1998.

5. Ibid.

6. Ibid.

7. Tourism Industry Association of Canada conference proceedings, 1996 National Conference on Tourism, Jasper, Alberta.

8. Statistics Canada, cat. no. 87-4023, p. 140.

9. Robert W. McIntosh, Charles R. Goeldner, and J.R. Brent Ritchie, *Tourism Principles, Practices, Philosophies,* 7th ed. (New York, NY: John Wiley & Sons, 1995), p. 9.

10. Statistics Canada, cat. no. 87-403, p. 141.

11. Roy Cook, Laura J. Yale, and Joseph J. Marqua, *Tourism: The Business of Travel* (Upper Saddle River, NJ: Simon & Shuster, 1999).

2 Tourism Guests

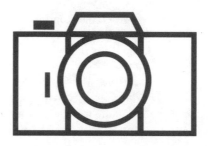

learning objectives

Having read this chapter you will be able to

1. Explain the differences between business and leisure tourists.

2. Identify the four business market segments and describe how they differ.

3. Define MNEs and apply them to specific guests.

4. Define family life stages and explain how life stages affect travel decisions.

5. Explain the use of demographics and psychographics in understanding travel motivators.

6. Identify and explain theories of travel as they relate to studies by Maslow, Plog, and Fiske and Maddi.

7. Discuss seven major barriers to travel.

In the study of tourism, it is important to understand the psychological and sociological composition of guests and hosts. **Guests** are the outside **visitors** who have come to be entertained by the people, community, or region. **Hosts** are individuals, communities, or regions who entertain the visiting guests. Hosts also refer to the members of the community or region that the guest is visiting. The correlation between host and guest is an interesting one. When we are guests, we expect to be treated with dignity, respect, fairness, and honesty. We generally will not accept anything but considerate treatment. However, when we are hosts, do we sometimes forget how a guest should be treated? For example, how many times in our hometown have we impatiently driven behind an obviously lost tourist whose brake lights flash on much too frequently and suddenly? Have we honked, cursed, and wished the tourist would learn to drive? How many times have we gone to our favourite local restaurant and become upset that the waiting line is much longer than expected because of all those tourists? We want good treatment when we are guests. We sometimes forget, however, our role as members of a host community or region, particularly when our role is passive.

This chapter will focus on the guest. Guests are as diverse as humankind. Trying to define and understand the characteristics of guests is like trying to put together a giant jigsaw puzzle with pieces missing.

Impact of Terrorism on the Guest

Tourists travel only when they feel secure in taking the trip, as September 11 clearly illustrated. On September 1, occupancy rates in the Rockies were at their normal 95 percent, but by September 15, they had fallen 30 percent. Cross-border travel also fell dramatically, forcing border towns like Windsor to lay off staff in hotels, the food service industry, and even in the casino. Business travel around the world dropped by 45 percent in the weeks that followed the attack.

Friendly greetings and information about the area can provide tourists with a positive start to their vacation. Sam Jakes Inn, Merrickville.

(Photo: Lisa Clarke.)

The world's global tourism organizations quickly formed a coalition to deal with the problems of falling revenues, prompting Jean-Claude Baumgarten of the WTTC to appeal to governments "to work together in partnership to ensure that measures to strengthen security are effective, harmonized internationally and applied globally. This will help restore consumer confidence in travel and tourism, the economic health of our industry and the livelihood of all those who work in it."[1]

It is interesting to note that the impact of September 11 on travellers with Canadian Adventure Tourism and Outdoor Recreation (ATOR) packages was minimal. Although some ATOR travellers did change their destinations, they still travelled.[2] In 2002, travel to Canada rebounded more quickly than anticipated. Our country has a reputation for being a friendly, safe place to travel and, using this core image, the CTC invested $20 million in advertising during the latter part of 2001. A mild resurgence of tourism revenues resulted, including a rebound of 3.8 percent in U.S. visitors and 11.3 percent in European guests.[3]

Classifying the Guest

Guests may be classified in different ways, depending on the purpose and the study source. Guests are most commonly grouped in three ways:

- by their **motivators** (business or pleasure)
- by their **demographics** (age, occupation, education and income level, marital status)
- by their **psychographics** (personality, behaviours, likes and dislikes)

Business Guest

Business travel is generally nondiscretionary travel, in that the guest has few choices of where, when, how, and how long to travel. **Business guests** constitute nearly 35 percent of all airline seats and are usually members of one or more frequent flier programs. Meetings and conventions continue to be the two main reasons for business travel, as they have been for many years. Consulting, sales, operations, physical functions (maintenance), and management are other reasons for business travel, but even combined they do not equal the number of convention and meeting trips.

Four major segments make up the business market:

1. Frequent business traveller: These guests stay in the hotel often, and the hotel offers them specialized service, such as instant check-in. In addition, staff members are encouraged to remember the guests, addressing them by name whenever possible.

2. Luxury business traveller: Desiring the best of travel experiences, these guests are not concerned with cost but consider service attitude extremely important.

3. Female business traveller: In 1970, only 1 percent of business guests were female. In 2000, women made up 50 percent of the business tourism market. The female guest is more concerned with safety issues and, if alone, is more likely to ask for room service rather than venture outside for meals.

4. International business traveller: Travel in this segment is down due to higher costs, a weakening global economy, and the threat of terrorism. Many international companies are using Internet conferencing as a viable option to travel.

An interesting trend that appears to reflect the state of the economy is that business travel is being consolidated; that is, travellers tend to stay on the road a little longer to maximize accomplishments while minimizing cost. The implications of this trend, if it continues, will be significant to travel industry suppliers.

Pleasure Guest

Pleasure travel is very different from business travel and is affected by discretionary time and income, as well as family life stage.

Discretionary time is time away from work and other obligations. Vacations obviously fit this definition. Reduced discretionary time might be the reason people are taking fewer pleasure trips of one week or longer but are taking more weekend trips: two-income families may be unable to coordinate long trips but can manage more minivacations.

Discretionary income is the money people may spend as they please. The relative value of personal income has grown sluggishly in the last decade, which has tended to slow the growth of personal travel.[4] Still, it is important to the tourism industry to convince people to spend any discretionary income on travel rather than, say, on a health-club membership or a new TV.

Family life stage refers to a person's position in his or her life. The basic pattern, and some common variations, are shown in Figure 2.1

An important aspect to note is the amount of discretionary income and time that accompanies each life stage. Generally speaking, people in the young single and the **empty-nest** stages have more discretionary income (with neither mortgage nor children to support) and time (with fewer family obligations) than do those in the other stages. In addition, empty nesters who are still working have more vacation days than younger workers. Family **pleasure guests** generally spend their time and money differently than single pleasure guests do. Children have different needs, but if the children are happy, so are Mom and Dad. Therefore, family vacations are normally child-oriented.

Discretionary income and time will dictate how much a guest can spend and how long a guest can be away. Family life stage, however, is the best predictor of what guests will do on particular pleasure trips. The following examples illustrate the influence of family life stage:

Example 1: Jon is taking a vacation in Nova Scotia's Kejimkujik (ked-gee-ma-coo-jic) National Park. He is 24 years old, single, and has one week of vacation. He packs his camping gear and flies from Winnipeg to Halifax. There he meets two friends from college and they rent a car. The three of them spend the next five days camping and hiking in the park.

Example 2: Jon and his wife, with their two young children, decide to visit Nova Scotia for their vacation. They have some family they wish to see and they want to take their children to experience the wildlife and beauty of Kejimkujik National Park. Jon has two weeks of vacation and spends a total of four days driving from Toronto to Nova Scotia. Jon is pulling a tent trailer and they will camp during most of the trip. Once in Nova Scotia, they will visit family and then spend the rest of their vacation camping at the edge of Kejimkujik Park, taking advantage of the wonderful summer activities the Park has to offer.

FIGURE 2.1
Life Stages

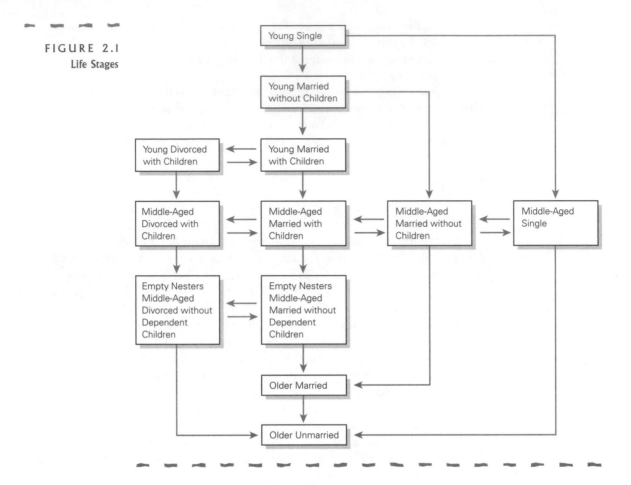

Example 3: Jon and his wife are recent empty nesters. They have chosen to take four weeks of time to test out their new recreational vehicle. They will be driving to Nova Scotia to visit family and intend to stop and see historic Quebec City. Then they will take the ferry across the Bay of Fundy from Saint John, New Brunswick, to Digby, Nova Scotia. From there they plan to see sights they have missed on previous trips, such as Lunenburg, Canada's first UNESCO World Heritage Site, and Peggy's Cove. They are also looking forward to travelling around Cape Breton on the Cabot Trail, visiting national historic sites such as the old fortress at Louisbourg, and perhaps doing a little whale watching on the side.

As you can see by the preceding examples, Jon's vacation habits change depending on life stage, income, and time. This behaviour is common for middle-income families in the United States and Canada. Upper-income families have more discretionary income, so the scenario would change. Lower-income families might not be travelling as far or might not be travelling at all.

Demographics

In addition to classifying travellers as business or pleasure guests, many travel industry personnel like to know more about their guests. Most demographic data suggest that generally travellers are more highly educated than average and represent the white-collar worker more than the blue-collar worker. Beyond that information, guest characteristics vary widely. Tourism businesses should be aware of a guest's domicile, age, occupation, income, marital status, education, and sex, as this demographic information can then be used to further categorize the guest. This in turn helps the business determine the type of facilities and services that best suit a guest's needs. Knowledge of where guests come from may suggest where advertising might be most effective. Depending on the choice of strategy, advertising can be placed in the cities and regions of current guests to continue to attract these visitors, or in other cities and regions in an attempt to expand market areas.

Psychographics

Using motives or behaviour to categorize travellers is also useful. Psychographics helps hosts to understand the activities, interests, opinions, personalities, and likes and dislikes of guests. It is clear that guests at golf and tennis resorts come because of the activity provided. What is not as clear are the reasons guests come to a particular city with many different activities available to them. Psychographic data help cities or regions determine in what categories their guests may be grouped.

The use of personality as psychographic data was first introduced by Stanley Plog.[5] Plog uses a continuum from psychocentric to allocentric to describe vacation travellers, with definable groups of near-psychocentric, midcentric, and near-allocentric between the two extremes (see Figure 2.2). The **allocentric** is a risk-taker. These travellers prefer to go where no foot has trod before. They are willing to go without the normal conveniences of life in order to gain a fuller travel experience. Allocentrics, often referred to by marketers as "innovators," are the first to try a new travel destination. Once a destination has been established with a broad market base, the allocentric moves on. At the other end of Plog's spectrum is the **psychocentric** traveller. *Psychocentric* is a derivative of words that suggest a centring (centric) of thoughts and actions on the self (psyche). These "armchair travellers" are often reluctant to travel at all. When they do travel, they prefer places that feel like home. The host community will speak the same language, food will be familiar, and the mode of travel they choose will be one with which they are comfortable. For example, they will drive to their destination whenever possible and will choose to eat at a McDonald's while in Germany; often their motivation to travel is to be with friends and family. A travelling psychocentric makes a great repeat customer. The majority of travellers fall between these two extremes. **Midcentrics**, according to Plog, travel to obtain a break in their routine. Although they enjoy the change of pace, they are not likely to choose a vacation that deprives them of the basic comforts of life.

Nickerson and Ellis[6] extended Plog's theory and Fiske and Maddi's[7] personality theory to generate the activation model of travel personality, which describes guests in terms of four personality dimensions: activation, variety, extroversion or introversion, and external or internal locus of control.

Activation is the guest's level of excitement, alertness, or energy, which is either high or low. **Variety** is degree of desire for change or novelty, which the guest either seeks or avoids. In addition to these two dimensions, the traveller is categorized by extroversion or introversion and external or internal locus of control. An **extrovert** is an individual who is outgoing and uninhibited in interpersonal situations. An **introvert** is more concerned with personal thoughts and feelings than with those of others. People with an **internal locus of control** believe that they are

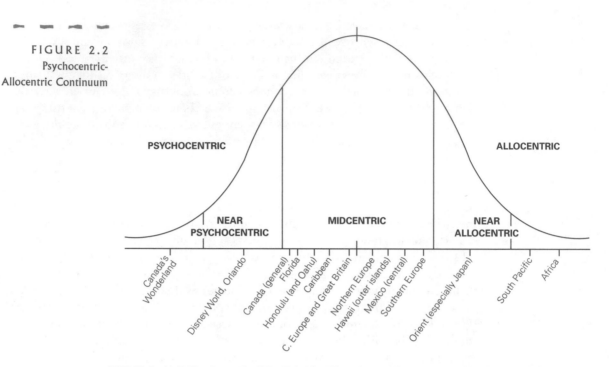

SOURCE: Stanley C. Plog, *Leisure Travel* (New York: John Wiley & Sons, 1991), p. 83. Reprinted by permission of John Wiley and Sons Inc.

in charge of what happens in their lives. People with an **external locus of control** believe that events are determined by other powerful individuals, fate, or chance.

Combining these dimensions of personality with travel produces a model that can be described in terms of destination preferences, travel companions, interaction with local cultures, degree of participation in activities, and other distinguishing characteristics. For example, consider a high-activation extrovert with a need for variety and an external locus of control. High activation means that he wants lots to do. The need for variety means this guest would prefer to see a number of different places on a trip. Extroversion leads this tourist to prefer cities or popular campgrounds to remote cabins, and to prefer travelling with companions. An external locus of control makes this traveller wary of risk. The package tour, which combines all these elements, is designed for just such a guest, sometimes called a voracious tour-taker.

in practice

Identify yourself in the following terms:

- psychocentric, midcentric, or allocentric
- high or low activation or energy
- seeker or avoider of change
- introvert or extrovert
- internal or external locus of control

Based on how you identify yourself on each of these personality dimensions, choose your dream vacation and justify your choice.

Why Travel?

Demographics and personality have a great bearing on where a person travels and the activities they do while at the destination. But what actually motivates a person to travel? A motivator is a "promoter of action" and its purpose is to fulfill a need or a want. We know a business guest is motivated to travel to conduct business away from the office. Motivators for pleasure travel are very different.

The reasons people travel vary from deep psychological needs to simple needs for escape or relaxation. The psychological need to travel is theoretical and may be difficult to pinpoint in an individual. It does, however, lead to a better understanding of the superficial reasons for travelling.

Maslow's Hierarchy of Needs Abraham Maslow first developed the theory of motivation based on a hierarchy of needs or motivations. Five levels of need are specified, from lowest to highest order (see Figure 2.3). According to Maslow, an individual will satisfy the lowest motivational level (that is, physiological needs) first. Once that has been satisfied, a higher-order need will emerge to generate behaviour. Thus, it is the unsatisfied need that leads to action. In advanced economies such as those in Canada and the United States, most tourists' physiological and safety needs have been met. According to Maslow, however, few people satisfy their social and ego needs sufficiently to move to the fifth-level need, self-actualization. Therefore, the most important motivating forces in travel are social and ego needs.

To apply these principles to tourism, let's look at each step and how it might affect the traveller. *Physiological needs* are simple and generate motivations such as escape from a cold climate, getting away from the stress of work to allow physical relaxation, or choosing a trip with frequent rest stops, good food service facilities, and a comfortable place to sleep at night. *Safety needs* must be met in order for travel to take place. Few tourists would knowingly make a travel choice that would endanger their lives. Safety for the traveller rests with governments, with those who provide police, medical, and similar services, and with individual tourism businesses. Nothing brings tourism to a halt faster than war or the threat of terrorism. News of a plane crash, fatal food poisoning from a restaurant, a fire in a hotel, or a theme park ride that has malfunctioned, throwing passengers to their death, has an immediate negative impact on that business. *Social needs* are by far the most common motivators. Visiting friends and relatives (VFR) is the number-one pleasure motivator. The need for companionship and belonging may be identified by the choice of a trip. For example, a tour package offers group activities with other people who share similar interests, and a sense of belonging may be fulfilled by a trip to trace

FIGURE 2.3 Maslow's Hierarchy of Needs

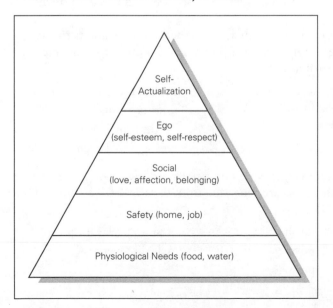

a person's ancestral roots. *Ego/self-esteem* deals with a person's need to feel important and special. Included in these motivators might be a trip to see special events such as the Olympics or a Barbra Streisand concert, incentive travel vacations (awards for high performance), and the need for special services such as gold memberships or first-class service. This category includes the need to "keep up with the Joneses" or the "all my friends have been there" motivator. Finally, *self-actualization needs* focus on achieving one's full potential as a human being. These motivators might see a tourist choosing a self-guided walking tour through the vineyards of Bordeaux to learn the language and discover more about French wine, travelling to Toronto to help build homes for the charity Habitat for Humanity, or climbing Mount Everest.

McIntosh and Goeldner have looked at motivators from a different perspective.[8] They have divided motivation into four basic categories: physical motivators, cultural motivators, interpersonal motivators, and status and prestige motivators.

1. **Physical motivators** are directly related to health. Sports participation, relaxation, and recreation are preventive health maintenance motivators, whereas medical exams, health treatments, or "fat farm" attendance are curative health motivators. Both types are seen as tension releasers through physical activity or attention to a health problem.

2. **Cultural motivators** are a desire to know and learn more about the music, architecture, food, art, folklore, or religion of other people. These motivators stem from a curiosity to experience another way of life through travel rather than just through books or television.

3. **Interpersonal motivators** include two extremes: escaping from family and friends and wanting to visit family and friends. People who live close to family sometimes feel a need to get away from the family influence even if only for a short time. Those who live far from family sometimes feel a need to get back in touch through vacation time experiences.

4. **Status and prestige motivators**, which were discussed earlier in this chapter as social and ego factors, concern the need for recognition, attention, appreciation, and good reputation.

To further explain motivation, Epperson[9] devised a model based on **push** and **pull factors.**

The pull factors, external things such as scenic beauty, draw guests to a destination and continue to be an important reason for travel. Pull factors include people, places, and activities such as the following:

friends	scenic areas	cultural events
relatives	historic areas	sports events
celebrities		educational events
public figures		recreational events

Push factors are those forces, needs, motivations, and ways of thinking that come from within us. Push factors are generated from our inner selves and include such factors as

adventure	kinship	rest and relaxation
challenge	novelty	self-discovery
escape	prestige	

Table 2.1 shows what tourists actually do in Canada. For a variety of reasons, people do want to travel. They look forward to their next trip and talk about previous trips. Reasons for travelling always exist and lead to actual experience.

Motivation, Needs, and Expectations (MNEs)

All guests arrive at their destinations with a specific purpose for the trip, special needs to be fulfilled, and certain expectations with regard to how these needs will be met. Whether they come back is determined by how well the destination meets

TABLE 2.1 *Top Activities Participated in* by Tourists in Canada, 2001*

	Canadian Residents %	U.S. Residents %	Overseas Residents %
Visiting friends or relatives	66	31	55
Participating in sports/outdoor activities	37	31	29
Shopping	36	63	85
Sightseeing	27	54	78
Going to a bar or night club	15	22	30
Visiting a national or provincial nature park	12	23	51
Visiting an historic site	8	29	43
Boating (motor, sail, kayak, canoe, other)	8	9	10
Attending a sport event	7	6	10
Visiting a museum or art gallery	6	21	40

*More than one activity may be participated in while on a trip.

As tourists attempt to enter the gates of Louisbourg (Cape Breton), they are challenged by the guard to identify "anglais" spies.
(Photo: Paula Kerr.)

Tourists travel to Canada from around the globe to experience the awesome natural beauty of such destinations as Athabasca Glacier, Banff National Park.
(Photo: Tom Hadley.)

their motivations, needs, and expectations (**MNEs**). Obviously, the motivation for business travellers is to conduct business. Depending on the kind of business and the segment of the market, needs will vary. For example, if business guests plan to spend a week in your city, they will need some form of transportation, a hotel that offers valet service, and good dining facilities on premises. Another common need is the ability to easily hook up a personal computer or fax machine and to access Internet services. Guests will expect the room to be quiet, check-in and check-out to be quick and efficient, and the staff to be friendly and aware of their needs. For pleasure guests, MNEs vary according to life stage, personality, and likes and dislikes.

The Barriers to Travel

We've just talked about the reasons people choose to travel. What, then, stops them from making the decision to travel? Seven common barriers to travel are very difficult to overcome. You will note that often one factor influences another. Time, cost, and distance are often interrelated. If you live in Halifax, a trip to Sydney, Australia, will not only be costly, but also will include a long airline journey. In a typical two-week vacation, you will likely spend at least 20 percent of your vacation on a plane!

Cost At no point can the average Canadian avoid considering the cost of a trip. In times of economic difficulty, destination, length of stay, and travel method will all be modified by the amount of discretionary income people have to spend on their vacations. Occupation and education may determine whether someone can afford the trip because they are often related to wage scale and time off the job. Two other factors that affect cost are the number of people travelling and the price structure at the destination. A family of four interested in learning more about French culture may find a trip to Paris too expensive, while a trip to Quebec City provides them with a similar cultural experience at a fraction of the cost.

Lack of Time No matter where you decide you want to go for vacation, travelling takes time. If you have a three-day weekend and live in Halifax, you may be going to Sydney, Nova Scotia, to see family, but you will not be visiting family in Sydney, Australia. Time limits the choice of destination and, often, the mode of travel. The further the destination is from home, the more likely you are to take a plane rather than a car. This allows you maximum time to spend *at* the destination rather than travelling *to* it.

Accessibility or Distance Can you reach your destination easily? Do you have to fly or can you drive? Many tourists who come to Canada to fish are looking for pristine lakes, like those you will find in northern Quebec. These lakes are exactly what the fisher wants, but they are inaccessible by car. Why? There are no roads! To reach these fishing camps, you must use a small float plane. Because distance and time are so closely related, they can stop travellers from picking their first-choice destinations.

Travel Tastes and Experience Your personality and age affect this barrier. For instance, psychocentrics are not fond of travel at all. In fact, if they take a trip, it will likely be within their own province. Border crossings, a foreign language, and strange food are not on their agenda.

S N A P S H O T

J. Willard Marriott

J. Willard Marriott was a man of vision who valued people above profit. He lived a life that reflected his Mormon heritage and his great love of country. Marriott began his career in hospitality in 1926, when he invested in a franchise to sell A&W root beer. His first summer was a busy one, but by fall, sales of the ice-cold drink had fallen off. Initially, he and his partner attempted to divest themselves of the quickly failing business, but buyers could not be found; so they added chili and tamales to the menu. Overnight they transformed their small restaurant into a counter-style food-service outlet called Hot Shoppes. Within the year, Bill Marriott bought out his partner and began to envision

his next step. Together with his employees, he built one of the first drive-in restaurants, and the concept caught on. By 1930, there were five Hot Shoppes. With the Depression looming ahead, Bill and his wife, Alice, managed to stay afloat, continuing to provide customers with value for their dollar. In 1933 Marriott was diagnosed with what was believed to be Hodgkin's disease and was given only a year to live. Fearful of the future, Marriott took a year off and a much needed vacation. When he returned, the doctors announced he was miraculously cured. It was at this time that he recognized the value of good employees, friends, and family. This belief in the importance of relationships was to guide him throughout the rest of his life.

By 1934, his Hot Shoppes menu included full-course meals, and in 1937 he moved into contract food services. He was the first to recognize the airline industry's need for catering services, and began supplying American and Eastern Airlines with box lunches. By 1980, Marriott Flite Services had a total of 80 domestic and international flight kitchens. During the war, Marriott moved farther into the contract food-service business, running the cafeteria for the naval communications annex as well as the lunch wagons that provided daily service for plant workers in the area. After the war, Marriott continued his quest for the takeout market, opening a chain of fast-food restaurants called Pantry Houses. He also expanded his Hot Shoppes.

The Marriott Company did not enter the hotel business until 1957, with the purchase of a 360-room hotel in downtown Washington, D.C. Since that time, the company has grown to include more than 180 000 hotel rooms, servicing three distinct markets: commercial and contract food services, theme parks, and a cruise line. In the past 15 years, the company has slowly divested its interest in these various tourism sectors and intends to concentrate on its contract food-service operation, Host Marriott, and its hotel properties.

The Marriott Company has always believed in a strong centralized operation. It runs its food-service facilities from Fairfield Farm Kitchens, where the central commissary, kitchens, warehouses, and offices are located. The central office for its lodging facilities is found in Washington, D.C. The company has always espoused family values and believes that employees should be hired for life, not just a five-year stint. It encourages employee participation in stock options and was one of the first to offer a company profit-sharing plan. It established an employee credit union and continues to offer incentives for long-term employment.

What kind of a man was Bill Marriott? He believed in strong central management. He had the vision to foresee the future of takeout and fast foods, contract food service, the expansion of accommodations, and the diversification of the recreation sector. Most of all, Bill Marriott lived by a code of ethics that valued the human resources of a company as highly as its profits. He treated his employees, guests, and community with the same care he showed for his own family.

Education also influences the travel decision. Generally speaking, the more education you have, the greater your knowledge of the world and the more likely you are to seek out new experiences.

Finally, the old saying "try it, you'll like it" holds true for travel. If your past experiences have been good, you'll try it again.

Age When we are young, travel is an exciting adventure. As we age, it becomes more difficult to handle change and, eventually, travel stops altogether. A 96-year-old woman in a wheelchair is highly unlikely to travel at all. If she does, it is with great preparation and usually with a younger travelling companion.

Health Poor health also hinders a person's ability to get around, although there are travel companies that specialize in programs for clients with health disorders.

Fear The most difficult barrier to overcome is that of fear. Fear of new places, fear of water, fear of flying, fear of terrorism. Fears can paralyze activity and are seldom based on concrete experience. Fears may be real or imagined. For example, the beautiful beaches in Israel sit empty because of continued terrorist activities in that region. Perhaps tourists are right in avoiding this destination. However, if you are flying from Toronto to Winnipeg, it is unlikely that your aircraft will be hijacked and turned into a bomb. The vast majority of flights safely carry passengers to their destinations; in fact, flying is still considered to be the safest mode of transportation. Unfortunately, knowledge does not always overcome fear.

summary

Guests and hosts are the people factors within the tourism industry. Guests are the people we entertain. Hosts are the entertainers. In a broad sense there are two types of guests. The pleasure guests are, by choice, visiting the area on vacation. The business guest is on nondiscretionary travel or visiting for the purpose of meetings, sales, or conventions. Beyond the business and guest profile, the guest can be categorized by demographics and psychographics. Demographics provide basic information about where the guest is from, family income, age, occupation, and education level. A psychographic profile provides more insight into the motives, behaviours, interests, and personalities of the guests. An understanding of personality dimensions such as activation, variety seeking, and degree of introversion or extroversion allows a destination area to provide the experiences the tourist seeks. Understanding why people travel and the barriers they face when they choose to travel can help the host provide a satisfactory travel experience.

questions

1. Plan a trip to your hometown for a business guest and a pleasure guest by explaining how their motivations, needs, and expectations (MNEs) differ and providing examples of the tourism products they will use during their trip.

2. a) Compare the needs and expectations of pleasure travellers at four different life stages.

   b) Does life stage affect the business traveller? Justify your answer using examples.

3. Define the following terms in your own words: *demographics, psychographics, motivators, locus of control, push and pull factors, discretionary money, nondiscretionary time.*

4. Explain how your tourism region can best fulfill the needs of

   a) a psychocentric

   b) an allocentric

   Compare the needs and expectations of each. Justify your answer by defining the terms and choosing an activity that would match their individual personalities/needs.

5. Arrange the barriers to travel in order of difficulty, starting with the one you consider most difficult to overcome. Justify your answer.

weblinks

www.checkin.com

Checkin: The Internet Tourism Database includes databases on airlines, airports, and hospitality.

www.hotelschool.cornell.edu

The Web site for the School of Hotel Administration at Cornell University in Ithaca, New York, one of the major research institutions in hotel and restaurant management.

www.tourismcollege.com

Vancouver's Canadian Tourism College educates students aspiring to a career in tourism.

notes

1. Canadian Travel Press, October 11, 2001. CTX article 32609.

2. Tourism Canada, Tourism Monthly Jan-Feb 2002, p. 13

3. CTX news, October 18, 2002. US Travellers Drive Tourism Numbers Up in August 2002.

4. *1994 Outlook for Travel and Tourism* (Washington, DC: U.S. Travel Data Center, 1993), p. 6.

5. Stanley C. Plog, "Why destination areas rise and fall in popularity." Paper presented to the Travel Research Association Southern California Chapter, Los Angeles, CA, October 1972.

6. N. Nickerson and G. Ellis, "Traveler Types and Activation Theory: A Comparison of Two Models," *Journal of Travel Research* 29 (1991): 26–31.

7. D. Fiske and S. Maddi, *Functions of Varied Experience* (Homewood, IL: Dorsey, 1961).

8. Robert W. McIntosh and Charles R. Goeldner, *Tourism Principles, Practices, Philosophies*, 6th ed. (New York: John Wiley & Sons, 1990), p. 131.

9. Arlin Epperson, "Why People Travel," *Journal of Physical Education, Recreation and Dance*, 31 (April 1983): 53–54.

3

The Tourism Host

- -

key terms

certification
channel of distribution
demand
elastic demand
inelastic demand
marketing
marketing mix
marketing plan

market segmentation
national tourism office
  (NTO)
niche/target marketing
occupational standards
people resources
place
price

product
promotion
supply
tourism education
  council (TEC)
tourism illiteracy
trinketization
value

- -

learning objectives

Having read this chapter you will be able to

1. Define the term *tourism illiteracy* and discuss its effect on a community.

2. Give a brief analysis of nine barriers that discourage tourism in a community.

3. Identify and evaluate 10 positive effects of tourism on a community.

4. Identify the role each of the six federal government departments plays in the tourism industry

5. Identify 10 human resource issues facing the tourism industry today.

6. Analyze the new initiatives of governments and industry as they relate to the human resource issues identified in the 1980s.

7. Discuss the roles of the following private and public organizations: tourism education councils, Canadian Tourism Human Resource Council, National Capital Commission.

8. Summarize the unique characteristics of the tourism product.

9. Discuss the importance of *value* in today's marketplace.

10. a) Explain what is meant by the terms *marketing* and *marketing plan*.

    b) Explain how a tourism business sells its products by using the marketing mix (product, price, place, promotion) and the criteria for niche marketing.

- -

With the completion of the Canadian Pacific Railway in 1885, Canada began its transformation from frontier country to industrial nation. Vast lands were united by a safe and comfortable mode of transportation. The West was being settled. Canadian industries prospered and, along with this industrial growth, a fledgling industry emerged called "tourism." It was a surprise to see visitors flow into the tiny town of Banff because it was just another stop on the new rail line. However, Banff's allure came from the beauty of its majestic mountains, the hot sulphur water that poured into a natural rock cavern, and the warm, hospitable people who lived there. The guests loved it, and the residents (now tourism hosts) had found a new line of work!

Ever since that time, the number of communities benefiting from tourism has steadily increased. However, amidst this growth, a current of discontent has tarnished the vision of a prosperous tourism industry. Much of the ill feeling toward tourism comes from a lack of understanding of the industry and its powerful, positive effects. What is "tourism illiteracy"? Does your hometown have it? This chapter deals with both tourism illiteracy and the wide variety of tourism hosts who

Mounties are part of Canada's cultural heritage. One of our most popular events is the musical ride, performed by the RCMP.

(Photo courtesy Canadian Tourism Commission.)

work together to make Canada a friendly, exciting place to visit. It looks at how the federal and provincial governments, regions, and communities affect the quality of the tourism product. It describes recent moves on the part of business and government to work together to develop a more professional tourism product for Canada. Finally it explains how the host markets this unique product called tourism.

Tourism Illiteracy

A host's attitude toward tourism can be positive and open or negative and closed. Two neighbours on the same block can have divergent feelings about tourism and both will be partly correct. Trying to get an entire community to be good hosts is like trying to convince people in a political party to agree on all issues. Part of this difficulty stems from **tourism illiteracy**, an educational deficiency about tourism. People can be illiterate in the sense that they

- do not plan for tourism
- do not see tourism as a benefit to the community's economy
- do not understand how to the use the tourist dollar for expansion (e.g., a "bed and booze" tax that would tap tourists rather than locals and would generate revenue that residents would be able to use to fund community improvements)
- feel that tourists should not intrude on their way of life

The problem is that tourism illiteracy is hard to overcome. People who are illiterate about tourism have probably had a bad experience with tourism and, therefore, label all tourism as bad. These people express their negative feelings to others in the community or directly to tourists to encourage an anti-tourist sentiment. Such a sentiment spreads easily.

Barriers to Tourism Acceptance

Some barriers to the acceptance of tourism are based on fact; others are based on suspicion. Detrimental effects on a host community include the following:

1. **Crime and unwanted behaviour.** Tourists come to a destination with money, credit cards, and other valuable belongings. In any host society, there are those who wish to take advantage of people who are unfamiliar with the customs, the area, or potential dangers. For example, Miami, Florida, experienced a rash of very violent crimes in the late 1980s. *Crime against tourists has no national boundaries.* Protection of the tourist is an important part of maintaining a safe image to the rest of the world. Also disturbing to the host community is unwanted behaviour such as prostitution and drunkenness, which often become more prevalent in a town that focuses on tourism as its main source of revenue.

2. **Air, water, land, and noise pollution.** Adding a million additional people to a region during a short tourism season puts a strain on the ecosystem. Banff is one of the best examples of "people pollution." In order to control this damage, tighter controls have recently been established, limiting

new development and the number of visitors and reinforcing regulations to ensure that the ecosystem is safe.

3. **Congestion of roadways, parks, shopping areas, recreational centres, attractions, and restaurants.** Although a region may benefit greatly from tourism revenues, it creates a feeling of ill will when locals are forced to deal with competition for their favourite restaurants or recreational activities.

4. **Local resentment.** Tension may develop when differences exist between guests and their hosts. For instance, resentment may occur if tourists do not follow the social or cultural norms of the host country, or if young residents begin to question the values of their cultural traditions. Some members of the community may also resent guests' extravagant lifestyle.

5. **Inflation.** Inflation increases when tourists hit the town. During high season, hotels charge full rates, shops are less inclined to offer bargains, and the cost of lodging workers is higher.

6. **Seasonality.** Regions like Cape Breton that experience a seasonal tourist influx will also experience high unemployment once the season is over.

7. **Leakage.** When demand for the tourism product is greater than the destination's local resources, leakage occurs (chapter 1) and the community does not get the full benefit of tourism dollars.

8. **Increases in the cost of services.** Most tourism events require additional police service and may require onsite paramedics. During World Youth Day in July of 2002, the hot weather required additional staff to hand out bottles of water, paramedics to deal with sunstroke victims, and police to ensure the event proceeded in an orderly fashion.

9. **Diversion of government funds.** Tourism may divert government money and attention from needed projects in order to build and renew a country's tourism products. For example, when a major hurricane smashed into the east coast of Mexico in 1987, the coastal villages and resort towns like Cancun and Cozumel were destroyed. The initial effort in rebuilding was focused on the tourist resorts because they provided work and revenue for the local people and the government. A year later, Cancun and Cozumel were completely restored, but many of the villages still lay in ruins.

Benefits of Tourism

To overcome negative feelings toward tourists, it is important to outline the benefits of tourism to local people.

1. **Economic diversification.** A wider variety of both full-time and part-time jobs are available.

2. **Cultural preservation.** One motivation to travel is the chance to learn about other nations and ways of life. The Canadian culture has been influenced by many different nations. This diversity gives tourists a mosaic of experiences to enjoy while on vacation. Canadian Heritage oversees the protection and development of Canadian culture and historical sites.

3. **Better choices in entertainment, shopping, and food service.**

4. **Enhanced travel.** More roads, airports, ports, and public transportation are built or improved.

5. **Area beautification.** Tourists choose Canada as a destination because of the image of a clean, natural, and healthy environment. Destinations take care to ensure that their region is planted with trees, flowers, and lawns; that towns and roadways are cleared of waste; and that, through municipal legislation, the area maintains its attractive appearance.

6. **Tax revenues.** For every billion dollars of tourism income earned in Canada, $230 million goes to the federal government, $160 million to provincial governments, and $60 million to municipal governments. That money helps keep our taxes down.[1]

7. **Foreign capital.** When an international company invests in Canada, its foreign dollars help to build the Canadian product. Jobs are created and revenue is produced for Canadian tourism workers, with less investment needed from the region or municipalities.

8. **Recreational and educational facilities.** Many public universities and colleges would have financial difficulty were it not for government support, and most hospitality schools have had some form of government financing. National and provincial parks, historical sites, and attractions are also funded in part by tourism dollars.

9. **Modernization.** Better infrastructure helps public service departments, such as police and sanitation crews, do their jobs.

10. **A favourable world image.** For five days in July 2002, the city of Toronto welcomed more than 250 000 young pilgrims who came to attend World Youth Day celebrations with Pope John Paul II. Vancouver still reaps the benefits of the World Trade Fair it hosted in 1986. Events such as these strongly support the global vision of Canada as a safe, clean, and friendly country to visit.

Effects on Societies Tourism's effects on a culture or society are often mixed. Mass tourism can undermine even the strongest, most defined societies. In the early 1960s, large numbers of U.S. tourists crowded the streets, stores, and restaurants of Paris demanding hot dogs instead of moules marinières and milkshakes instead of wine; they demanded that English be spoken and openly criticized the French way of life—their coffee, their cigarettes, etc. The term "ugly American" was coined and the elders of French society fought against the Americanization of traditional French culture, with little success. Today tourists can eat at McDonalds just off the Champs-Élysées, and Sanka coffee may be on the menu.

Yet tourism may also play a role in the survival of a culture. Over the past 200 years, Aboriginal societies such as the Inuit, Cree, and Haida nations have struggled to survive in a world that focuses on white, industrial ways of life. The modern tourist, however, is searching for real knowledge and experiences, and, to this end, countries are recognizing the importance of sustaining the knowledge base, languages, and customs of their Aboriginal peoples. Today we are seeing the revitalizing of some of these tribal societies, with elders teaching the young the ways of their ancestors. Granted one underlying reason may be to bring in the tourist dollar, but if the end result is the preservation of a fading society, is it not just as valuable?

Tourists enjoy buying souvenirs to remind them of their holiday, and many want the real thing, not a mass-produced trinket.
(Photo: Grace Vigneron.)

The goal of cultural support, however, will not automatically be served if care is not taken in setting up tourist experiences. Using Aboriginal guides and interpreters, producing handmade, traditional artifacts locally for purchase and maintaining the rigid standards of the culture provide both the producer and the consumer with something of value. But too often tours are planned and conducted by outsiders, and guests are offered a cheapened version of traditional artifacts, in a process called **trinketization**. Dream catchers, for example, are beautifully handcrafted by many Aboriginal nations; they are also mass-produced in China and sold at a fraction of the price at flea markets. This approach means that the host community reaps few of the benefits of tourism revenue, and tourists are denied the valid interchange they seek with another culture.

Lessons of the past and a new attitude among industrialized nations have made beneficial tourism possible in many Canadian destinations that were inappropriate for development only a few years ago. Destinations that allow the visitor to experience the beauty of the Canadian wilderness are gaining in popularity. Travellers intent on experiencing the true life of northern Canada may now be welcome in small villages scattered across the Yukon and Northwest Territories. These allocentric travellers embark on a quest for knowledge and truth, with a sensitivity for the needs of each unique destination. The interactions that occur teach visitors a new-found respect for lifestyles that differ so greatly from their own.

in practice

If you were placed in a leadership role in your hometown and were trying to convince residents of the benefits of tourism, who would be your strongest allies and who would represent your toughest barriers? How would you try to sway the opinion of those opposed to tourism?

A Brief History of Canadian Tourism

The Canadian government's involvement in tourism can be traced back to the completion of the Canadian Pacific Railway in 1885. As visitor traffic increased in the Banff/Bow River region, Parliament became concerned that the influx of visitors might harm the wildlife and terrain. In 1887, it established Canada's first national park, Banff, and hired a small group of park rangers to patrol the area. This group was called the Rocky Mountains Park Branch, and its formation marked the beginning of federal tourism policy. For the next 35 years, this unit represented the federal government's only involvement in regulating Canada's tourism industry.

During the 1930s, when the Great Depression swept North America, Prime Minister Mackenzie King established a new federal branch to deal with tourism—the Canadian Travel Bureau. It was launched in 1934 with a budget of $100 000 and a staff of three. This move was not a recognition of the tourism industry, but strictly an attempt to fight the Depression by creating new jobs. Its staff focused on promoting fishing and hunting in Canada. Its budget increased over the years, as did the staff, and it was later renamed the Canadian Government Travel Bureau.

In 1939, the Second World War broke out across Europe, and Canada quickly became involved. As would be expected during a time of world conflict, tourism almost came to a halt. Men and women from across North America did travel, but they travelled to fight in Europe and the Pacific. Most of these young men and women experienced their first Atlantic crossing on an ocean liner, their first airplane ride, and often their first sight of Europe, home of their ancestors. Many brave Canadians were killed in action. But those who did return had gained an experience that would change their lives and the face of tourism forever. They had seen the Tower of London, the lowlands of Holland, and the beauty of Italy. They had walked down the Champs-Elysées in Paris. They had used fast, efficient transportation and had developed an interest in places other than their home communities. These experiences helped lay the foundations of a new age for tourism.

After the war, a new market emerged. The Canadian government saw an opportunity and opened its first **national tourism office (NTO)** in New York City. The year was 1951. NTOs followed in Chicago and San Francisco, but it was not until 1963 that Canada took a serious look at the international markets in Europe. The first overseas NTO was opened in England, followed by offices in Paris, Zurich, and Rome. As Canada geared up for its Centennial Celebration in 1967, 14 additional offices were opened across both the United States and Europe.

What a year 1967 turned out to be! Birthday celebrations for Canada were hosted from St. John's, Newfoundland, to Victoria, British Columbia. Montreal hosted Expo 67. A record 40.5 million visitors from around the world arrived to help celebrate. In the aftermath of 1967, one very clear conclusion was reached: Canada, despite its natural attractions, exciting cultural experiences, and warm hospitality, was poorly equipped to handle such a large number of tourists. Facilities and services were underdeveloped, and if Canada was to enter the tourism industry, hard work lay ahead.

In 1973, the Canadian Government Travel Bureau was reorganized and renamed the Canadian Government Office of Tourism (CGOT). Canada was finally looking beyond fishing and hunting as tourism generators. In 1982, the CGOT was renamed Tourism Canada. Tourism Canada was a part of the Department of Regional Industrial Expansion (DRIE). DRIE was responsible for development in the areas of manufacturing and resource processing, tourism, and small business. Tourism Canada was given responsibility for the research and development of tourism products and for creating new promotional programs. It created and hosted two major tourism expositions: Visit Canada—a showcase that introduced writers from around the world to the Canadian tourism product; and Rendez-Vous Canada—a trade show that brought together Canadian tourism products/suppliers and international tour operators. The Tourism Industry Association of Canada (TIAC) has taken over the production of this very important showcase.

Tourism Canada was to become one of the most recognized, highly regarded, and sought-after tourism organizations in the world. With the United Nations, Tourism Canada assisted third-world countries that wanted to develop a tourism trade. In 1994, Tourism Canada was replaced by the Canadian Tourism Commission (CTC). The purpose of this organization is to promote Canadian tourism both at home and abroad, and it does so by joining forces with the tourism industry. Together, they have created a highly successful partnership. Since its inception, the number of tourists visiting Canadian tourism destinations has increased, tourism revenues have more than doubled, and our travel deficit has been cut in half.

How has 9-11 affected U.S.–Canadian borders? Although our borders were never closed entirely, border controls were tightened on the U.S. side, with the National Guard called on to help monitor border crossings. Air marshals were strategically placed on specific U.S. air routes in and out of Washington and all foreign carriers were denied access to the U.S. capital. In November 2001, a WTTC report estimated that globally, more than nine million jobs would be lost. Business travel fell off by 63 percent and vacation travel patterns changed. Tourists chose to travel by car, motor coach, or train and stayed closer to home.

What was Canada's role in the days just after the disaster? During the first 12 hours of the 9-11 attack, we welcomed more than 35 000 unexpected visitors. With airports and airspace across the United States closed, inbound airliners had little option but to land at Canadian airports. The small town of Gander, Newfoundland (population 10 500), is a good example of how communities put on their "host hats" for these stranded travellers. In fewer than 10 hours, this town alone received 6600 tourists needing lodging, food, and comfort. Because of the volatile situation in the United States, airline officials decided to leave passengers on board their aircrafts for 24 hours, while they monitored the situation. Meanwhile Canadians were working to ensure that when passengers disembarked they would have clean blankets, fresh food, and beds. The warm hospitality of Newfoundlanders helped passengers cope with the horrors of 9-11. New friendships were forged all across Canada, and American passengers left knowing that their Canadian friends would willingly step forward in their darkest hours with unconditional kindness and support. Gander, along with many other cities across Canada, earned the title of "Best Host."[2]

After 9-11, the Canadian government and the CTC quickly announced a one-time $20 million cash infusion for the promotion of tourism. This allowed the CTC to quickly put together a new marketing plan reflecting recent events and assuring travellers that Canada was still a safe destination. It paid off. In the first quarter of 2002, there was a surprising global resurgence of tourism. In Canada, seven of our top 12 foreign markets (other than the United States) rebounded with a higher numbers of visitors (up 11.3 percent). U.S. tourist counts are up by 3.8 percent and more Canadians are choosing to vacation at home. Despite the turmoil created by September 11, 2001, Canada saw a marginal increase in tourism in 2002.

The Federal Government and Tourism

There are six federal government departments that directly affect the tourism industry.

- **Industry Canada** is responsible for the overall well-being of the tourism industry. Working as a Crown corporation under the auspices of this department is the Canadian Tourism Commission.

- The **Department of Foreign Affairs and International Trade** is responsible for issuing Canadian passports and visas for non-Canadians (see chapter 12).

- **Canada Customs and Revenue Agency** handles Canada Customs (see chapter 12).

- **Citizenship and Immigration Canada** verifies the travel documents of returning Canadian travellers and foreign visitors. Both Immigration and Customs officials play an important role in creating a positive first impression for tourists. Sensitivity to the tourists' needs, a polite manner, and good communication skills are essential. (see chapter 12)

- **Canadian Heritage** is responsible for Parks Canada, National Historic Sites and Battlefields, National Museums and Archives, and the National Capital Commission (see chapters 8 and 10).

- **Transport Canada** oversees the regulation of our transportation systems and helps with the building and maintenance of the transportation infrastructure (see chapter 5)

A Crown Corporation: The Canadian Tourism Commission (CTC)

The most significant change for our tourism industry has been the establishment of the Canadian Tourism Commission (CTC). Originally under the federal department responsible for tourism, Industry Canada, it has recently become a Crown corporation. The CTC provides a good example of how the federal and provincial governments can partner with an industry to ensure its growth and success. This partnership provides a unique opportunity to develop and coordinate programs that benefit the industry and the country as a whole. The industry matches government promotional funding dollar for dollar. This 50/50 formula has allowed the advertising budget to increase from just under $20 million in 1993 to $100 million in 2001. Some of the activities that the CTC supports include gathering and maintaining data on potential markets, analyzing international and domestic marketplace opportunities and issues, market research and analysis, advertising, public relations, promotional projects, and travel trade activities.

One of the most successful CTC ventures has been the creation in 1995 of product clubs: consortia, or groups of independent businesses who work together with a common purpose in mind. Some of the products are new to the marketplace, some are well established; some are similar businesses (ski operations) and others are clustered by region. Members support one another by sharing information and helping to make their products market ready. Their promotion funds are matched by the CTC. An example of a regional cluster is the Gardens and Green Spaces Product Club, which helps develop garden tourism packages to

Mandate and Mission Statement for the Canadian Tourism Commission

Vision
Canada will be the premier four-season destination to connect with nature and to experience diverse cultures and communities.

Mission
Canada's tourism industry will deliver world-class cultural and leisure experiences year-round, while preserving and sharing Canada's clean, safe, and natural environments. The industry will be guided by the values of respect, integrity, and empathy.

Strategic Objectives
The main thrusts of the commission are to market Canada as a desirable travel destination and to provide timely and accurate information to the industry to assist in their decision making.

appeal to the 4.5 million U.S. and Canadian visitors who enjoy horticulture-related activities. Members could include ornamental gardens, nurseries, and inns set among native plants, trees, shrubs, and flowers. In September of 2002, the CTC announced the creation of seven new product clubs: Canada by Rail, the Okanagan-Shuswap Bioregion, Aerotourism, Explorers of the Western Canadian Wilderness, the Snowmobile Product Club, Boreal Wilderness Adventure and the Gardens and Green Space Product Club.[3]

The CTC does not lobby government or provide direct subsidies or grants. Those activities are performed by tourism associations, organizations, and provincial and municipal governments. An interested Canadian may judge the performance of the CTC by looking at the yearly results in five areas: overall tourism revenue increases, growth in visitor volumes, reduction in the travel deficit, market share changes, and job creation.[4] Certainly the five-year results shown in Table 3.1 are encouraging.

TABLE 3.1   *Canada's Tourism Industry Numbers, 1995–2001*

	Revenues 1995 in Billions	*Revenues 2001 in Billions*	*Percentage Change*
Total tourism revenues	$29.2	$54.1	Up 85.2%
Domestic tourism revenues	$21	$39.9	Up 80.2%
International tourism revenues	$8.2	$16.2	Up 98.3%
Canada's international travel deficit account	$3.3	$2.1	Down 34.4%
Canada's international ranking by arrivals	11th	9th	
Canada's international ranking by tourism revenues	12th	9th	

SOURCE: Canadian Tourism Commission.

A Crown Corporation: The National Capital Commission (NCC)

The capital of a nation always holds a special position, for it is the heart of a country. As such, it hosts the central government and it is the site of many historical events that help to shape a country's culture and heritage. A capital city is the showcase of a country's vitality, talent, creativity, and accomplishments. There were many reasons for Queen Victoria's choice of Ottawa as Canada's capital: the natural beauty of the region with its rolling hills and waterways; its inherent bilingual nature due to the closeness of its neighbour, Quebec; and the distance from the U.S. border, which provided the new capital with military security.

In 1884 Sir Wilfrid Laurier, later Canada's prime minister, wrote of the nation's capital, "I would not wish to say anything disparaging of the capital but it is hard to say anything good. Ottawa is not a handsome city and does not appear destined to become one." Determined to eradicate this perception of Ottawa, William Lyon Mackenzie King, after he was elected prime minister, hired French architect Jacques Gréber to design a capital city that would be a showcase for the young Canadian nation. In 1933, Ottawa was still a lumber town—the Ottawa River was clogged with logs floating downstream to the mill, and centretown was a maze of more than 56 km of railroad track. Gréber's work was interrupted by the Second World War, but he returned to complete his design for the capital. In 1955, plans were placed before Parliament detailing large green spaces and parks, parkways, and wide streets leading to downtown Ottawa, a city centre that focused on the canal and locks and clean, free-flowing rivers. The plans were approved and the transformation of Ottawa into one of the world's most beautiful capital cities began. To oversee the work, the federal government appointed a new Crown corporation, the National Capital Commission (NCC).[5] The NCC is an independent legal entity created by Parliament to ensure that public policies pursued on behalf of the National Capital Region benefit all Canadians. The NCC has the broad goal of maintaining the integrity and beauty of the Capital region, which extends over a large area of Gatineau and western Quebec and the Ottawa area. It has the following mandates:

- to make the Capital Region Canada's meeting place and to support national reconciliation by encouraging active participation of Canadians in the evolution of their capital
- to use the capital to communicate Canada to Canadians and to assist in developing and highlighting the Canadian national identity
- to safeguard and preserve the capital's physical assets and natural setting for future generations

The NCC began this task by redesigning the centre of Ottawa itself. In 1958, Ottawa was a maze of railroad tracks. The NCC's first task was to remove most of the train tracks and relocate the train station outside the downtown core. Many of the abandoned track beds were transformed into expressways and parkways.

To preserve the natural beauty of the area, an aggressive plan for parks and green space was developed. Today more than 35 000 ha of land on the Quebec side have been preserved for Gatineau Park, the largest wilderness park in the Capital Region. It provides visitors with paths and nature trails for biking and walking, downhill ski areas and cross-country ski trails, and beaches for swimming and picnics. One of the Capital Region's largest tourist attractions is the autumn colours of Gatineau Park. The NCC has also created green space that rings the city and maintains the natural beauty of the region, while providing additional outdoor experiences for visitors and residents alike. It is responsible for maintaining that portion of the Rideau Canal that lies within the city. This historic canal is one of the longest artificial waterways in the world. It donates the land on which many new museums and cultural centres are located and acts as a guardian for heritage treasures such as the Aberdeen Pavilion at Lansdowne Park. It is impossible to walk through the older neighbourhoods of Ottawa without stumbling across unique buildings or sites designated by the NCC as part of Canada's history. The NCC helps sponsor events in the region such as the Tulip Festival and Winterlude. The board of directors for the NCC consists of 14 appointed members: seven represent the National Capital Region and seven represent the interests of all other Canadians. It meets several times a year but has come under criticism for its lack of an open forum. NCC meetings are now open to the public, but there are still concerns regarding expenditures on projects such as the Confederation Steps ($1.5 million), redevelopment plans that ignore the historical perspective of Ottawa's downtown core, and plans to sell protected green space to developers.

in practice

Why should a country's capital city be a showpiece? List the capital cities of five foreign countries. What sites do they have that create a cultural/historical ambience or a positive world image? Are Ottawa's pull factors competitive with the foreign capitals you have chosen? Why or why not? Should the NCC continue to make decisions for the City of Ottawa, or should the citizens of Ottawa be given the sole power to shape Ottawa's future tourism development? Justify your decision.

The National Capital Commission is responsible for maintaining the Capital Region—its parks, waterways, and grounds. Pictured here: the National Art Gallery.
(Photo: John B. Kerr).

S N A P S H O T

Judith Cabrita

When Judith Cabrita walks into a room, her energy quickly spills over into conversations. Here is a woman who has a love of tourism, and it has guided her career and life over decades of endeavours. Judith epitomizes the new tourism professional, successfully manoeuvring her career through three tourism sectors: accommodation, food and beverage, and tourism services. No one knows better the flexibility and transferability of tourism skills. A native of Toronto, she is Nova Scotian at heart. Judith was educated at Ryerson University, where she became active in the Student Association, serving as its secretary and graduating as a silver medallist. Her career began in the accommodation sector. Working first in the hotel business and then the resort business, she gained skills in a variety of different positions. Looking for additional challenges, she then accepted the position of chef manager at the Voyageur Restaurant in Halifax. The next step for Judith was into the tourism services sector where she worked her way up to vice president of a hospitality consulting group. Her quest for continued challenge then turned her career path toward education and innovation. Teaching a class for youth with special needs, she took over the management and training of these students and successfully turned their classroom into a small, profitable dining room, which provided them with valuable hands-on skills. Judith then worked as a consultant to the Government of Nova Scotia, helping design and implement a hospitality curriculum. Her last positions in the field of education were industry coordinator and co-op coordinator at Mount St. Vincent University. As with many female tourism workers, she also managed to raise a family while pursuing her ever-changing career!

"Learning is a lifetime experience" has been Judith's personal mission statement. She not only believes in education and training, but she has also used her strong convictions to improve the tourism product of Nova Scotia through the development of skills upgrading and training for the province's tourism workers. Judith was one of the original members of the Tourism Industry Standards and Certification Committee (TISCC) and in 1989 she initiated development of the Education and Training Department branch of the Tourism Industry Association of Nova Scotia (TIANS), now its Human Resource Council. In 1995, Judith was appointed director of TIANS, Nova Scotia's tourism education council. Under Judith's leadership, it is one of the most active councils in Canada. Judith strongly believes in the power of people and investing in tourism employees by providing them with continual educational opportunities and training based on industry standards. Nova Scotia has helped in the development and implementation of 14 occupational standards for the industry, including Responsible Beverage Service and Gambling.

Today, TIANS operates the largest tourism industry trade show in Canada and works with the industry to establish environmental guidelines to ensure that tourism remains a viable, sustainable product. Judith remains active in many different industry associations, such as the Canadian Food Service Executive Association and the Halifax and Nova Scotia chambers of commerce. She sits on the board of directors of both the Canadian Tourism Human Resource Council (CTHRC) and the Tourism Industry Association of Canada (TIAC).

Ask Judith Cabrita what she believes life's most important lesson is and her quick response will be "lifelong learning." Most of her working life has focused on education and training and there is no higher compliment she can give to you than "a job well done." This focus on excellence has driven Judith all her life and she has passed her energy on to those around her, helping develop Nova Scotia into one of Canada's most successful tourism destinations. In 1993 she was awarded the Canada 125 medal. Judith's work with TIANS, the CTHRC, and occupational standards is helping the industry develop a more professional work force—making an imprint that will last well into this century.

Training the Tourism Host

Over the past 20 years, the tourism industry has become a major revenue producer for Canada. The fact that there is such a variety of small, independently owned and operated businesses creates problems that are not faced when an industry produces just one product—such as the auto industry. This fragmentation hinders united efforts at improving the quality of the product; however, this same diversity allows the industry to offer a broad-based market appeal. Measuring the dollar value of tourism is easy, but the real economic importance of tourism to Canada also involves the number of jobs it creates. Tourism is a very labour-intensive industry. Tourists do not drive home in the product. When they purchase a trip to Prince Edward Island, they are purchasing experiences and services. Departing for home, they must leave behind the island's beautiful beaches, historical sites, and entertainment. So what *do* they get for their money? Memories. These memories may be warm and friendly or they may be easily forgotten. No machine or technological advancement will ever replace the warm and caring interpersonal communication that takes place between a tourist and a professional tourism host. For this reason, when Canada began a review of its tourism industry product, its focus was on **people resources.**

Human Resource Challenges, Issues, and Concerns

Tourism illiteracy is just one challenge the industry faces. Between 1983 and 1990, a series of studies by government and industry identified 10 critical human resource issues.

1. **Industry image:** Tourism has never been viewed as a true profession by the majority of Canadians. The public perceives tourism workers as hamburger flippers or bed makers working long hours in a dead-end job with low wages and few benefits.

2. **Unskilled labour:** In some areas of Canada the shortage of trained workers is so great that employers are forced to hire applicants who have little or no training.

3. **Poor training practices:** As training is often regarded as an expense, employers often do not take the time to provide their new employees with the skills needed to accomplish the job. Although training does take time and money, professionals know that trained staff will not only be

more productive, they will also provide customers with a positive experience which, in turn, increases revenues.

4. **Poor attitudes/self-image:** When workers have not been trained, they not only lack the skills to perform their job well, but also are often unsure about what they are supposed to do. This leads to frustration and negative responses from both customers and management, and can culminate in feelings of inadequacy or apathy on the part of the worker.

5. **High turnover:** The poor attitudes described above lead to discontent, causing workers to quit.

6. **Poorly trained managers:** Many managers have been placed into their positions without the benefit of having any training themselves. They have not developed the skills to deal with personnel problems and do not understand the value of training.

7. **Lack of recognition for institutional training:** Business operators, who themselves may lack formal training, often do not recognize its importance.

8. **Shrinking labour pool:** Tourism has always depended on the labour pool that is less than 35 years of age. Although the demand for labour is increasing, the numbers of younger workers and unskilled immigrants are declining.

9. **Language barrier:** Tourism is a business that deals with many cultures and languages, both in the marketplace and in the work force. Language problems will always require additional attention from businesses wishing to maintain a competitive advantage in tourism.

10. **Declining profits/increasing competition:** Although overall revenues for tourism are up, the problems faced by the industry have caused profit margins to decrease. In addition, as newer products enter the marketplace, competition for the tourist dollar increases. To succeed, any business/tourism operator must understand all of the above problems and have a plan in place to deal with them effectively.

How will tourism continue to grow if it is unable to find qualified workers? How does an industry that undervalues training and education and yet requires long hours from a dedicated work force stay in business? How does it attract and keep the best staff? The answer is, it doesn't. For today's managers, and for those training to be tomorrow's managers, understanding the problems we have just discussed is essential. The federal and provincial governments are doing their share to help solve these problems by developing industry-based training programs and national certification for employees who have demonstrated their competence in specific tourism occupations. Now owners and managers must take a proactive stance and put real solutions in place for tourism workers. It is up to the industry to develop and use reasonable, scheduled hours, appropriate pay scales, and advancement opportunities for their staff. Without this, growth in the tourism industry faces what may be an unbeatable challenge.

Tourism Education Councils (TECs)

Many of these studies recommended that government, industry, and education cooperate to restructure the current education and training practices in the industry. In addition, several of the studies advocated the development of occupational standards and a system for the certification of qualified tourism professionals.

In June of 1986, Tourism Canada invited six national industry associations to consider ways in which all parties could work together to resolve the human resources issues.[6] The Tourism Industry Standards and Certification Committee (TISCC) included representatives from

- Tourism Industry Association of Canada (TIAC)
- Canadian Restaurant and Foodservices Association (CRFA)
- Hotel Association of Canada (HAC)
- Association of Canadian Travel Agencies (ACTA)
- Canadian Institute of Travel Counsellors (CITC)
- Canadian Federation of Chefs de Cuisine (CFCC)

These six organizations were charged with developing job standards for five management positions in the industry. Employment and Immigration Canada provided the funding, with Tourism Canada coordinating the effort.

The provinces themselves were already taking steps to deal with these very important human resource issues. In 1987, Alberta established the first **tourism education council (TEC)**, which was quickly followed by TECs in British Columbia and the other provinces. Industry driven, tourism education councils were given provincial mandates to stimulate and coordinate the development of tourism education in their provinces. The TISCC committee recognized that provincial TECs needed to be major players in TISCC, and in 1988 the committee expanded to include

- Alberta Tourism Education Council (ATEC)
- Pacific Rim Institute of Tourism (PRIT)
- Tourism Industry Association of Nova Scotia (TIANS)
- Ontario Tourism Education Corporation (OTEC)
- Tourism Industry Association of Saskatchewan (STEC)
- Hospitality Newfoundland and Labrador (HNL)
- Tourism Industry Association of Prince Edward Island (TIAPEI)
- Tourism Industry Association of the Northwest Territories
- Tourism Industry Association of Manitoba (MTEC)
- Tourism Industry Association of New Brunswick
- Associations touristiques regionales associées du Québec
- Educators and other tourism professionals

During the next six years, this group identified more than 400 jobs in the tourism industry for which occupational standards could be developed. To address concerns of duplication by the provinces, they created a strong, united front. Considering the mobility of the tourism work force, the provinces also recognized that the value of certification was tied to its portability. In other words, if you are a certified front-desk agent in Vancouver, you need to be able to transfer your credentials to a similar position in Saskatchewan.

In January of 1993, the groundwork was laid for an expanded, permanent council to deal with developing, validating, training, and certifying tourism workers, and TISCC was disbanded. This new, quasi-independent branch of the government is called the Canadian Tourism Human Resource Council (CTHRC). Members of TISCC became the founding members of the CTHRC. The CTHRC serves as a national forum to facilitate human resource development in the form of training programs, providing leadership and support for provincial TECs. Both governments and the tourism industry firmly believe that a trained work force is the best way to ensure that the Canadian tourism product is both sustainable and globally competitive. (For more details about TECs, see the Appendix.)

Occupational Standards

Occupational standards are documents that outline the skills, knowledge, and attitudes that an individual must demonstrate and practise to be deemed competent in a given occupation. The process of developing occupational standards ensures that industry members from across the country identify and validate the skill, attitudes, and knowledge components outlined in the standards and that the documents are relevant to industry.

Once developed, the standards are used as a basis to develop certification programs and training resources for learners, educators, and trainers. Individuals have the opportunity to acquire standards-based training and to complete a testing process based on those standards. Completion of the practical and written testing results in either a provincial or national certification by the Canadian Tourism Human Resource Council (CTHRC). **Certification** provides industry recognition of individuals who have demonstrated their competencies. National certification is granted to any standard that has been validated by seven or more provinces.

Standards-based training resources have been designed in a modular format to facilitate training in the work place, in the classroom, or in independent study. Standards have served as the basis for the development of training products by the

Training for tourism workers helps maintain professional standards in the tourism workforce.
(Photo: Paula Kerr).

CTHRC and may influence curriculum development for secondary school, college, and university programs.

College programs that use CTHRC training products or have a curriculum that is based on the standards give their students the opportunity to acquire the skills, knowledge, and attitudes the industry demands. With experience, students will be well prepared to enroll in certification for their chosen occupation. Certified individuals gain an edge in an increasingly competitive job market. Whether you are training to work as a front-desk agent or front-office manager, your awareness of occupational standards will become increasingly important.

Standards serve the industry: they help with the development of job descriptions; they streamline the recruitment and selection process; they result in a well-trained work force that is committed to the industry; they provide recognition of the value of tourism occupations; they increase service levels, thereby meeting or exceeding client expectations; they serve as a basis for training programs; and they address the issues identified by the Tourism Industry Standards and Certification Committee.

Marketing Tourism Products

Part of the hosts' responsibility is to promote and market their destination. If a host community is to stay competitive it must learn how to market its products effectively. Communities will use destination marketing organizations (DMO) and must be willing to invest the required dollars so that effective promotions for their region and product may be created. The federal government in the late 1980s learned this lesson the hard way. Canada as a destination was performing well in the mid-1980s, and it rested comfortably in the WTO's list of top 10 tourist destinations. Confident that Canadian tourism was in good shape, the government greatly reduced the tourism marketing budget during the late 1980s. By the early 1990s, Canada's place as a world tourism destination dropped to 14th place. The Buchanan Report clearly identified this problem and stated that funds needed to be allocated to support a strong marketing program. From a low of $20 million, the federal government and the tourism industry now spend nearly $100 million on a marketing program, sharing the cost on a 50/50 basis. It has paid off! In 1998, the WTO reported that Canada had regained its position in the top 10 tourist destinations and is currently sitting in the number eight spot.

Many books have been written on the subject of marketing, and most Canadian colleges and universities offer diplomas or degrees in this subject. In this short space we will only touch on the subject, but if you are intrigued by the marketing process, further education in this area is readily available. What is **marketing**? According to Morrison, "Marketing is a continuous, sequential process through which management plans, researches, implements, controls and evaluates activities designed to satisfy both customers' needs and wants and their own organization's objectives."[7] It is the bringing together of products, the seller, and the purchaser. However, tourism is not like manufactured products. We sell service, experiences, and time.

When you purchase a car, you begin by researching different car manufacturers. Then you go to a dealer who sells the kind of car you want, and you look at the different types and styles available. You sit in the car, kick the tires, and take it for a drive. If the product suits you, then you make your purchase. If the colour you desire is not available on the lot, the dealer will get it for you. That car is your property and sits in your driveway until you determine it is time for a new one.

Compare that purchase to the purchase of a two-week holiday in Barbados. Although you do research on your destination, you are unable to physically see or handle any of the components you are purchasing. No one can package and send it to you; you must physically go to "pick it up." Finally, when you finish using the product, you must leave it behind, coming home with only memories and a scrap book. The product you purchased, "Barbados," is still available to be sold to the next customer!

What are some of the other unique characteristics of the tourism product? Let's take a look.

Understanding the Unique Tourism Product

To be able to sell a product well, salespeople must first understand it. The tourism product is complicated, not only from the standpoint of its diversity, but also from a marketing perspective. Here are some of the characteristics that make a tourism product different from other products such as a car, a television, or a bottle of shampoo:

1. **Tourism is intangible.** The tourism product does not sit on a shelf. It cannot be handled, examined, or tried prior to purchase because tourism sells experiences and memories. Although most consumers would not purchase a sound system without first testing it out, they willingly spend $1500 on a cruise package without ever having stepped on a ship! Therefore, the person who is marketing and selling the product has been granted a high level of trust by the consumer and must represent the product accurately.

2. **Travel is a costly product.** Vacations are something the working public saves for all year. Although people do not mind spending money on their vacations, they do expect value.

3. **Tourism products are highly perishable.** Tourism professionals sell time, and time is a perishable commodity. For example, communications, travel technologies, and information systems made the New Year's Eve that ushered in the new millennium into the biggest party the world has ever seen. The tourism industry wanted to cash in on the excitement. Cities planned huge celebrations. Some of the hotels around Times Square in New York City were booked long in advance. Cruise lines planned special trips, taking reservations without providing their customers with the 1999 price! Yet, how long does it take to change from one century to another? A second in time.

   Every day hotel rooms are vacant, planes leave with empty seats, and attractions are not filled to capacity. Each one of those empty "units" means lost revenue for the business. An airline cannot sell a seat on an aircraft that departed 10 minutes ago. The seat is still there, but the customer with the money is waiting at the airport for the next flight. The tourism industry must sell its product or lose the revenue it can generate.

Marketing has come up with some interesting approaches to this problem, such as seat sales and last-minute discounts.

4. **The tourism product cannot be stored.** If a business understands the demand of the marketplace, it can often take advantage of periods when demand for its product is high. For example, if Christmas is a time when many people purchase television sets, then the manufacturer can produce and store enough televisions to handle the Christmas rush. However, in tourism, even though demand for a product may be high during the summer, businesses are unable to store up unused "units" from February to sell in July; so some people who wish to purchase may have to go without.

5. **There is a fixed supply of the product and it cannot be easily altered.** Because of the immense cost of building hotels, aircraft, cruise ships, and resorts, and because of the length of time construction takes, tourism cannot quickly add to its size. If a hotel has 250 rooms, it cannot increase the number of rooms to 350 for July without bearing the cost of empty rooms in January. Airlines that seat 200 passengers cannot suddenly increase their capacity to 300 during spring break. The demand is there; the capacity is not.

6. **The tourism product is highly seasonal.** Tourism experiences periods of great demand (peaking of demand) and periods of very low demand. For example, many Canadian resorts close for the winter. During the season they are full to capacity, but the cost of carrying empty rooms over an extended period of time reduces profit margins. Closing is one of the ways in which the industry deals with seasonality. Others prefer to reduce their rates during the off-season or create a product for a different market altogether. For instance, a Canadian resort may promote golfing packages during the summer and convention or cross-country skiing packages for the winter. All these money-generating ideas have come from a creative marketing mind!

7. **The use of the product is curbed by time constraints.** Few people have endless vacations. They are given a week or two once a year. Planning a trip to Australia for a Canada Day long weekend may not be impossible, but it is impractical. A two-week tour of the Cabot Trail is not possible if a tourist has only one week of vacation.

8. **The quality of the individual product often depends on factors beyond the control of the producer or seller.** Tourism consists of many components, all separate entities run by different businesses. Although the hotel may be wonderful, a rude reception by the customs official or by a taxi driver may overshadow the entire stay. A bout of food poisoning from a local restaurant ruins the memories of the perfect resort. A hurricane in the Caribbean leaves cruise passengers disgruntled with their trip. A delayed aircraft could mean that an important business negotiation cannot be completed. A good tourism experience depends on so many factors that marketing the product is a real challenge. When working with a marketing firm, a professional needs a knowledge of the marketing process, an understanding of the tourism product, and an honest and creative approach in order to succeed with this unique product.

Tourism's Elasticity of Demand Added to the list of constraints on the tourism product, marketing agencies must also consider the tourism product's high elasticity of demand. What is *elasticity of demand*? First, it is necessary to understand the terms **supply** and **demand**. Demand (in the marketplace) is created by the need or desire for goods and services, that is, the number of purchasers wanting to buy a product. Supply is the amount of product available. Ideally, supply should equal demand. If a product has an **inelastic demand**, people will purchase it no matter what the price. Gasoline is a good example of a product with an inelastic demand. Car owners must buy gasoline, no matter what it costs per litre. On the other hand, products with an **elastic demand** are price sensitive. With every price change, there is a corresponding change in demand: the lower the price, the higher the demand and vice versa. The tourism industry learned this lesson with the new millennium celebrations. Overpriced products remained unsold, hotel rooms were left vacant, and huge parties were cancelled due to poor sales.

Why do most tourism products have an elastic demand? Travel is a luxury, not a life-sustaining product. It is bought only when the purchaser has the discretionary income available. The higher the price of the vacation, the lower the demand. There are a few tourism products that have created inelastic demand. They usually appeal to an elite clientele and offer a product or service that is unique or unmatched. A destination that is in vogue, popular with movie stars, royalty, and millionaires, may enjoy a period when people will pay any price for the chance to mingle with the rich and famous!

The First Four P's of the Marketing Mix

All products have a **marketing mix**—controllable factors that may be selected to help satisfy customer needs or wants. There are eight controllable factors that may be used to create an organization's marketing mix: product, price, place, promotion, packaging, programming, people, and partnership. These eight P's are the foundations upon which a marketing plan is created. Only the first four P's are discussed here: product, price, place, and promotion.

1. **Product: What do you sell?**

   We have already discussed the generic tourism product and its unique characteristics, but our **products** also have a physical and service component. Each of these components is developed based on specific market needs: for example, the type of hotel, its rooms and amenities, and the level of services it provides for guests. From a marketing standpoint, these qualities are the most important. How does the location and physical layout of your hotel differ from other hotels in your area? What services are offered that sets it apart from similar hotels?

2. **Price: How much do you charge for your product?**

   Many factors help you decide on the **price** of your product, including location, time of year, and quality of service. Of course your pricing strategy must cover basic costs and expenses and include a profit margin. The elasticity of demand for a tourism product must be considered as well as the competition's pricing structure. Knowledge of your clients and their purchasing power is also an important factor. Did you think the pricing of your tourism product would be easy?

3. **Place: Where are you going to sell your product?**

Place is also called the **channel of distribution**. Many businesses have sales departments within the organization that handle marketing and sales. One of the best venues for selling the tourism product is the travel agency system. The Travel Trade sector is the sales force of our industry and can be effectively used by the smart businessperson. When the Cruise Lines International Association (CLIA) first organized the modern cruise industry in 1960, they used travel agencies as their sales force. It was a system and a sales force that was already in place and it brought the cruise lines immediate success. Ninety-five percent of all cruises are still sold through travel agencies.

4. **Promotion: How will you advertise your product?**

What is your advertising budget and how can those dollars be most effectively used? Which media format is most likely to be seen or heard by your target market? The choices are vast and the cost of advertising varies widely. Businesses must know who their clients are and how best to reach them. Large international businesses might opt for national newspapers or TV promotions, but the small business must focus on using community news, radio, brochures, mail-outs, or their own Web site. In today's world, if you are not on the Internet, chances are you are losing customers!

There are two important trends in how we approach **promotion**. Tourism is made up of a variety of small, often unrelated businesses. Individually, they have very little ability to market themselves effectively to tourists before they actually arrive at the destination. The Internet has changed all that! For a very low cost, Web sites can be created to introduce your product to travellers long

Colourful brochures with beautiful views of destinations help give substance to the intangible tourism product prior to purchase.
(Photo: Paula Kerr.)

before they even anticipate their trip. As people become more comfortable with using the Internet, as computers and the Internet become more user friendly, this method of promotion will become essential to business survival. The second important trend in our industry is packaging. With less discretionary time, consumers are looking for one-stop shopping opportunities. By linking our tourism products in tour packages, whether they are designed for individuals or groups, each product enjoys the strength of joint marketing initiatives.

Customer-Oriented Marketing

In order to effectively sell our products, we create and implement marketing plans. A **marketing plan** is simply a written short-term plan that details how your product will use its marketing mix to achieve its goal (financial or other) over a specified period.

How does a business develop a customer-oriented marketing plan? First, the business must understand its products and services. It must have a clear understanding of the needs and expectations of its customers, and, finally, it must be able to determine whether the product is fulfilling customers' MNEs. Customers come to a business with specific expectations. They have preconceived ideas as to what your product is and how well it will fulfill their expectations. A good marketing plan identifies these expectations and is able to provide value for the customer's dollar. **Value** is the customer's mental estimate of the worth of a product. For some, value is price-sensitive: the cheaper the better; but for others it is the total experience that matters—the friendliness of service and the quality of the experience! It does not matter that different customers have different views of value, because as long as the exchange of dollars matches their own perception of what the product is worth, they will be satisfied.

Can one product fulfill everyone's needs? Will a tourism product that satisfies one traveller's need for hard adventure also satisfy the traveller who wants the comforts of home life? Obviously not. Market segmentation is one way to deal with the wide variety of personalities, life stages, and motivations our products must satisfy. **Market segmentation** is simply the division of the overall market into groups of people who share common characteristics or have similar needs. Club Med Resorts provides a good example of how one company handles a diverse marketplace. Originally Club Med was created to provide vacations for single, young adult travellers. Their resorts provided a full range of recreational activities and social functions, as well as the companionship of other single travellers. After several years of operation, Club Med discovered that its first set of loyal customers had moved on from the family life stage "single/newly married without children" to "married with young children." To satisfy this market's changing needs, Club Med designed new child-friendly resorts. This **niche** or **target marketing** is essential to our industry because of the diversity of clientele and their needs and expectations. The wide variety of tourism products available make this kind of marketing strategy easy. A career in tourism marketing (see chapter 12) could be an exciting career option for you. As each destination creates additional attractions, the role of the marketing consultant will be even more important.

summary

The host is the second half of the "people factor" of tourism. Members of a community may not understand their role as host, nor may they understand the important role tourism plays in their community's welfare. These "tourism illiterate" people, including many political leaders, usually do not support tourism initiatives, seeing only the negative impacts of the tourism industry on their neighbourhood. In fact, such people can make the tourists' visit rather unpleasant. It is important that the industry continually educate residents about the benefits of tourism, including its role in bringing employment opportunities to the community as well as greater revenue in the form of additional tax dollars and wage earnings. Many community concerns could be alleviated through this education process.

One of the hosts' responsibilities is to market their destination. In order to do this effectively, they must understand the unique characteristics of the tourism product. They must have a good knowledge of the marketing mix and how to use it effectively to attract an increasing number of tourists. They must also be able to identify target markets and provide these groups with the products and services that best suit their needs.

Both federal and provincial governments play an active part in creating a positive experience for the tourism guest. Industry and government have identified 10 problems that exist in the human resource component of the industry. To overcome these problems, the industry acknowledges that it needs trained professionals delivering both products and services. TECs and the CTHRC, working together with industry, have created certification programs and training products that are fast gaining international respect for their thoroughness and validity. CVBs and chambers of commerce have become an integral, proactive part of the tourism product. Canada has strong new tourism initiatives in place.

questions

1. Is your local government "tourism illiterate"? Define the term and justify your answer, using local examples.

2. Tourism has both negative and positive effects on a region/country.

   a) List nine negative effects of the tourism industry and ten positive effects.

   b) From each list choose the three effects (total of six) that you believe are most important in your region, and explain why you have chosen them.

3. In the federal government, there are six departments that affect tourism. Arrange these departments in order, beginning with the one you believe has the greatest impact and ending with the department that has the least effect on tourism in Canada. Explain your reasons for their placement.

4. a) What is the NCC and why was it established?

   b) What criticism has recently been voiced regarding the NCC's activities?

c) Should Canadians from across the continent have input regarding the development of the National Capital Region (Ottawa)? Why or why not?

5. List with a brief explanation the 10 issues and concerns identified by the tourism industry regarding its human resources.

6. Tourism Education Councils (TECs) work to improve the quality of front-line staff in the tourism industry.

   a) What are occupational standards? Who develops occupational standards? What is the difference between a national standard and a provincial standard?

   b) Will you take advantage of the certification process? Why or why not?

7. Marketing the tourism product can be difficult because of its unique characteristics. List eight of these characteristics, explaining them in your own words and providing examples.

8. Define the following terms as they relate to marketing: *product, price, place, promotion, elastic demand, inelastic demand, marketing mix, target market.*

9. Describe a tourism product (e.g., a hotel, a restaurant, a tour, a cruise ship) by using the first "four P's" of the marketing mix.

---

weblinks

www.canadatourism.ca

The Web site for the Canadian Tourism Commission. It provides up-to-date information for the entire tourism industry.

www.capcan.ca

Canada's National Capital Commission is a Crown corporation that manages tourism in the Ottawa–Hull region.

www.worldweb.com / ParksCanada-Banff / index.html

The official Web site for Banff National Park, Alberta (discussed in this chapter). There are also Tourism Education Councils (TECs) in the various provinces and territories, though not all have a Web site. See Appendix, page 301, for a complete listing.

---

notes

1. J. Judd Buchanan, "Report on the Tourism Industry," in *Report From the Honourable J. Judd Buchanan*, October 1994.

2. www.airport.com, October 2, 2001.

3. *Tourism—Canada's Tourism Monthly,* September 2002.

4. www.tourismcanada.ca/en/ctc.

5. National Capital Commission, *A Capital in the Making,* 1991 brochure.

6. *Canadian Tourism Human Resource Council Handbook,* 1995.

7. Alistair M. Morrison, *Hospitality and Travel Marketing* (Albany, NY: Delmar Publishers Inc., 1998), p. 4.

4 Planning and Development

- -

key terms

balanced development	infrastructure	rapid development
catalytic development	integrated development	revenue performance
centralized development	interdependency	secondary developers
coattail development	isolation	suprastructure
destination life cycle	market performance	transportation systems
forecasting	natural resources	trend
functional form	product capacity	trend analysis
higher-value tourist	qualitative forecasting	visitor use
hospitality of host	quantitative forecasting	

- -

learning objectives

Having read this chapter you will be able to

1. Describe the five essential components of a tourist destination.

2. Explain how the life cycle of a product affects tourism destinations.

3. Identify the five priorities the Canadian government uses to help plan future tourism growth.

4. Identify and explain the eight steps of the planning process.

5. Explain why communities differ based on type of development.

6. Explain the differences in the three types of development.

7. Describe the role of communities and regions in tourism planning and development.

8. Show how five global trends relate to the future of tourism in Canada.

9. Identify eight constraints on the future growth of Canada's tourism industry.

- - - - - - - - - - - - - - - - - - - -

Cities, regions, communities, and resorts do not become tourist destination areas (TDAs) overnight. An abundance of formal and informal planning is required before an area is known well enough that people make it part of their vacation plans. A century ago, tourism developed with little knowledge of the residents. In today's marketplace, with access to communications available to a community, it is usually a planned venture. Planning is an essential component of a profitable tourism destination. This chapter will focus on the processes used to forecast, plan, and develop future tourism destinations and products. The concepts involved can be used by any business or region, from a small entrepreneurial tourism business to an entire country.

The Five Components of a Tourist Destination

To understand the development of a tourist destination area (TDA), it is first necessary to understand the components or pieces that must be in place. When a community has already been developed, the first four components will likely be in place. Undeveloped communities may be lacking some of these components and still appeal to the risk-taker or allocentric traveller who wishes to experience the destination in its first, "unspoiled" stage. However, all of these components must be in place in some form or another if the site is to be a viable tourist destination.

1. *Natural resources:* A destination needs to have the physical means of supporting the tourist. It will need land and agriculture, a habitable climate, a water supply, and natural beauty to attract the tourist. Hawaii is an example of a destination that has many **natural resources** available— soft sands, beautiful waters, and flora and fauna that have intrigued people from early times. The Jasper and Banff valleys are good examples of spectacular Canadian scenery, and although they lack the warm temperatures of Hawaii, the majestic snow-capped mountains, the unique wildlife, and the changing seasons have created a huge tourist market. Not all destinations need such a dramatic backdrop to entice the tourist, but they must all have the natural resources available to support life and the tourist's needs.

2. *Infrastructure:* **Infrastructure** has been called the "guts of the city." It is the first component put in place in any area that is being developed for habitation. What makes up the infrastructure? Roads, telephone wires, electric wires, sewage and drainage pipes, docks, railroad tracks, runways—all those essential services that are unseen or built into the ground.

3. *Suprastructure:* **Suprastructure** consists of all the buildings found at the destination, in other words, structures that are built up from the ground. Lodging facilities, restaurants, terminals, sport complexes, stores—these are all examples of the suprastructure of a site.

4. *Transportation systems:* The **transportation system** consists of the actual vehicles that use the infrastructure. What good are the runways of an airport if there are no planes? Infrastructure and the transportation systems are completely dependent on each other and provide the guest (and host!) with access to and around the destination.

5. *Hospitality of the hosts:* **Hospitality of the host** destination includes the social and political climate, but involves much more than laws and culture; it is the genuine warmth shown by the local population—the smiles and greetings, the willingness to tolerate the changes that tourism brings. The host city may have the finest hotels, the best restaurants, the most modern methods of transportation and yet not attract the tourist market because of a less than welcoming attitude.

As an example of how these components fit into an area that has already seen some development, consider Newfoundland and Labrador, which is gearing up for tourism growth. This province has an abundance of natural beauty to attract the tourist. Gros Morne National Park on the west coast is a UNESCO (United Nations Educational, Scientific and Cultural Organization) World Heritage Site. True to its nickname, "the Galapagos of the tectonic plate," the park has an abundance of wildlife, spectacular mountains, and fiords carved by glaciers from a distant time. Infrastructure and transportation systems are already in place. Newfoundland and Labrador has many beautiful scenic roads to travel. Airplanes and ferries connect cities on the island to one another and to the mainland. Gros Morne National Park offers the tourist a unique infrastructure—more than 65 km

Planning for tourism means providing wide, clean walkways and streets with accessible local transportation.
(Photo: John B. Kerr.)

of hiking trails! Newfoundland and Labrador's suprastructure intermingles the modern hotel with bed-and-breakfast inns, historical forts with state-of-the-art museums, craft stores with shopping centres, and ski lodges with golf courses. The hospitality offered by Newfoundlanders makes this province an exciting tourist destination.[1]

The Life Cycle of a Destination

The life cycle is a familiar pattern. People are first conceived, then born; they then develop to maturity and finally grow old. Every product, like every person, has a life span. In a **destination life cycle**, the first stage is called *conception*. This is when the creative entrepreneur comes up with a new concept that is different and exciting. Ideas flow, plans are made, and research is done to ensure that there is a demand for the product. The second stage is the actual building of the product. If the product is a new destination, this stage may interest the allocentric. The area is undiscovered, and there will be few if any tourists visiting. The further along development moves, the more tourists the product may attract. The third phase is maturity. During this phase, all components of the destination are fully developed, the product is being marketed successfully, and visitor use is high. Once a site has enjoyed several years of high activity, it begins to lose visitors as they move on to newer destinations they have not yet experienced. This phase is called decline. The product itself may be well used and beginning to look a little run-down. At this point of its life cycle, the destination can choose to close, become a second- or third-rate activity, or rethink the product—returning to the conception stage, reinventing and renewing the destination to attract a new set of visitors and bringing past visitors back again.

The Disney theme parks provide good examples of how tourism products avoid the decline phase. Every few years, they add a new attraction or site, such as their new Animal Kingdom in Florida. They continually upgrade the older sites. They focus some of their marketing efforts on themes that send the message "come back and see us through different eyes." While their grown-up children sit at home wondering why their parents went back to Disney World, Mom and Dad are having a great time enjoying the adult Disney. The message here is that no product is free from its life cycle. Tourism professionals must be constantly looking to improve and renew their product and excite their target markets if they wish to stay competitive in this global world of tourism.

Tourism Planning

Planning, in a broad sense of the word, is organizing the future to achieve certain goals. In tourism, we attempt to foresee the future by

- using historical data (information collected from past experience)
- looking at current and future needs as determined by experts (people who have knowledge and experience in the subject area)
- choosing a plan that will provide us with the greatest level of success with the fewest problems[2]

Essential to tourism planning is determining who needs to do it. On a broader scale, countries plan for tourism by modernizing their system of customs, visas, and passports, as well as developing national tourism policies. The Canadian government is concerned with the growth of tourism and strongly supports careful, planned development. Here are five priorities identified by the government as important when new TDAs are planned on a national level:

- products that satisfy market demands
- safe, reasonably priced transportation
- development of human resources to improve service to visitors
- an integrated marketing plan to increase the number of visitors annually to Canada while providing packages that ensure their needs are met

Long-term growth and prosperity will only be achieved by balancing the development and maintenance of the physical and cultural environment.

Most of us, however, will not be dealing with tourism planning on a national level, but rather on a provincial, regional, or local level. Even then, we are more likely to be involved with community or business planning. The planning model presented in this chapter focuses on community planning but can be adapted to any type of tourism business.

Each community will need to develop goals specific to its interests. The goals of tourism development and planning in a community should include the following:

1. Provide a framework for improving residents' quality of life by developing infrastructure and suprastructure for residents and visitors alike.
2. Improve residents' standard of living through the economic benefit of tourism.
3. Provide a guideline for appropriate development within the city limits and within a certain radius of the city.
4. Design a tourism program that fits with residents' economic, cultural, and social views and attitudes.
5. Formulate a yearly evaluation policy for the tourism plan.

As seen in Figure 4.1, the planning model is cyclical. Once the original cycle is completed, it starts over again. The eight steps in tourism planning are basic to almost any planning process. The process begins with an inventory of what exists and ends with an evaluation of what has been accomplished. The intermediate steps identify the specifics required in good tourism planning.

Step 1—Inventory

The first step is to conduct a thorough inventory of the community's social and political atmosphere and its physical and economic environment.

a) **Political atmosphere:** Assess the political atmosphere of the community, indicating attitudes of local politicians and community leaders toward tourism that need changing or reinforcing. How do they feel about the tourism industry, and do they understand the benefits it will bring to their constituents?

b) **Social atmosphere:** Outline the political and cultural history of the region. Note festivals and special cultural events. Assess community

FIGURE 4.1
The Planning
Process

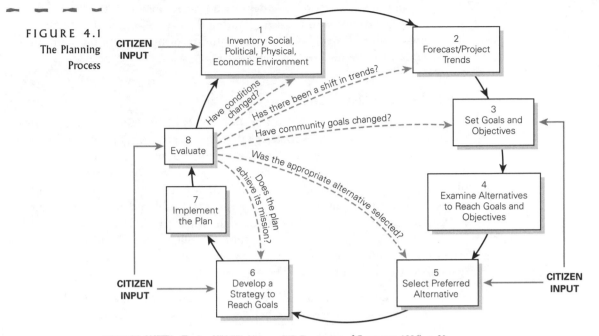

SOURCE: USTTA. *Tourism USA* (Washington, DC: Department of Commerce, 1986), p. 20.

awareness of the value and benefits of tourism. If the region is found to be tourism illiterate, it is important to inform residents of the tourism planning process and the value of the industry to their region. This can be done in a variety of ways: town meetings, television or radio talk shows, newspaper articles or editorials, and a general education campaign. It is also important to identify the "people resources" in the area: individuals with artistic abilities, those with a knowledge of local cultures, and those with training in the industry who are willing to get involved. Using local talents during the development process helps to eliminate opposition and encourages a sense of pride and commitment in the community as the plan proceeds.

c) **Physical environment:** Consider the region's geography: its location, natural resources, climate, and natural history.

d) **Infrastructure and suprastructure:** Will transportation systems to and around your destination support an influx of visitors? What improvements are needed? Will additional infrastructure be required and who will be responsible for its development and cost?

List the accommodations, restaurants, attractions, and conference facilities available for the tourist. Can a tourist play a round of golf? take a swim? go canoeing or biking? Are any facilities geared toward the adventure tourist?

e) **Economic environment:** If a community has a strong economy, then it may not see a need for tourism development. If this is the case, it might be useful to focus on diversification of the economy and employment for students, those returning to the work force, and new immigrants. If a community is economically depressed, then it may lack the financial resources to invest in tourism. Finding the capital to help fund development will provide a much-needed infusion of money and jobs and can help solve the region's economic woes.

Step 2—Forecast Trends

Forecasting trends is important in our industry. It identifies opportunities for regions or developers and helps to keep a destination and its tourist activities on the cutting edge of what is popular. The word **trend** means "a current style or preference." However, people are fickle and what is trendy one year may not be so popular the next year. Quick change is difficult for tourism because much of the infrastructure and suprastructure is expensive to build and permanent. Tourism entrepreneurs must recognize the trends that will last for a long time.

Forecasting means looking to the future. It allows us to look at the potential growth of the community and the surrounding region, and to see how that growth will enhance or hinder tourism. There are two basic techniques used in forecasting:

1. **Qualitative methods:** the use of experts and their accumulated experience and knowledge to predict the likely outcome of events.

2. **Quantitative methods:** the analysis of numerical data (current and historical) to help determine the future.[3]

One form of **qualitative forecasting** is the Delphi technique: a systematic survey of tourism industry experts, who are asked a series of questions developed by a panel of community members. The experts' collective opinions are sent back to the panel, which reviews the answers until a consensus on the timing of future events is reached. This structured method is particularly useful for analyzing medium- and long-term changes in demand and in weighing less tangible factors such as motivation. Qualitative approaches usually require less data and money than quantitative approaches.

Quantitative forecasting employs rigorous mathematical and statistical models. The results are generally more accurate and useful. Quantitative forecasting requires an adequate database, to which a range of numerical techniques can be applied. **Trend analysis** plots historical data over a number of cycles. For example, tourist arrivals at some future date are estimated by analyzing past arrivals and projecting these numbers into the future.

One difficulty is the scarcity of reliable data. Although hotels and restaurants have been collecting and using information such as occupancy percentages and average guest cheques, only in recent years has the tourism industry as a whole has been concerned with such data. Timely and reliable data are needed to make tourism strategies more effective and less risky.

Step 3—Develop a Mission Statement and Goals

A mission statement should provide an overall vision of the destination, site, or activity. A good mission statement reflects not only the purpose of the development, but also how it will improve the quality of life in the region. Suppose the community of Dartmouth, Nova Scotia, has hired you as a developer to build a family entertainment centre to attract tourists: the Wahoo Virtual Reality Centre. Its mission statement might read: *"To provide a unique opportunity for family entertainment and education using cutting-edge computer technology and virtual reality experiences in order to foster a better understanding of the latest advanced technological innovations and their impact on our lifestyles."*

After the mission statement has been written, you should then identify specific goals. Goals should be clearly stated, identifying your purpose in developing the product and the results you will be looking for to indicate success. Goals should be measurable whenever possible. An example of some of the goals that might be developed for our Wahoo Centre are

1. to provide a state-of-the-art entertainment centre that allows the public to interact with and use the newest developments in high-tech computer features and virtual reality games

2. to help educate young people and encourage them to become more innovative and to consider a career in the high-tech field

3. to provide wholesome entertainment for people of all ages

4. to provide employment for 150 full-time and part-time staff

5. to welcome 100 000 people to our facility the first year of operation

6. to make a 10 percent return on investment the first year of operation

Goals must give clear direction. Most important of all, goals must be realistic and achievable.

Step 4—Study Alternative Plans of Action

Rather than identifying only one method to achieve your goals, it is important to brainstorm as many alternatives as possible. It is okay to be a little silly or outrageous when suggesting alternatives. Sometimes the silly suggestions are changed a bit to become the most achievable method. At this point public discussion or the use of experts may once again become important. Each alternative should be looked at from both a positive and negative point of view. Here are some examples of alternative plans we might suggest for building our Wahoo Virtual Reality Centre:

Plan # 1 **Hire a team of computer specialists to design the centre.** Many tourism entrepreneurs have good ideas but lack the expertise to properly develop them. Hiring and paying experts is one answer. Forming a partnership with them that links financial success to their plans is an alternative course of action.

Plan # 2 **Choose to use Paramount's Virtual Reality Centre franchise.** Franchising is always worth considering because it provides the purchaser with a product that is already a success. It has a brand name and tourists are often more comfortable purchasing a familiar product. (See chapter 6.) But the wise investor researches the company, its contract, and the product before making any commitments.

Plan # 3 **Convince a large high-tech company such as Corel, Apple, or Microsoft to invest in and help design the centre.** Any time you can find funding from an alternate source of funding, you should look into this option. It may be a private firm interested in helping you to realize your idea and, in the process, promoting their own products; or it may be government funding. With banks still largely unwilling to help finance tourism products, alternate sources of funding are most welcome.

Plan # 4 **Using the company's expertise, develop your own Wahoo Virtual Reality Centre. Hire an architect and construction company to build it. Approach a variety of computer software companies and convince them to invest in the Centre, providing you with their latest, most innovative products.** Private ownership has the advantage of allowing the entrepreneur flexibility in the creation and operation of the business. The inherent risk is failure and bankruptcy, a strong possibility in the tourism industry.

Step 5—Select Preferred Alternative

Once you have thoroughly examined all possible ways of building or achieving your goals, then decisions must be made. Which alternative makes success most likely? If you have identified the strengths (pros) and weaknesses (cons) of each method, then this part of the process will be easier.

After consultations with the City of Dartmouth and a review of the various options, a decision must be made regarding the plan best suited to the community. Plan #1 requires finding either local citizens with expertise who are available to work on this project or qualified people willing to relocate. It also requires a project leader with knowledge about planning and developing tourism attractions. Plan #2, to purchase the franchise from Paramount, is the easiest to implement. It provides the centre with an established name and a product that is already successful. But the franchise fees are high, and this plan does not allow Dartmouth to gear the centre to local needs or to make any changes without Paramount's approval. Plan #3 requires that a computer/software company recognize the value of this project and be willing to spend time and money helping to design and build it. Of course, should it be a great success, both the town and the computer company will be winners. On the other hand, failure will have the reverse effect. Plan #4 is possible only if some of the partners have the high level of knowledge required for such a specialized attraction. In addition, they must be able to find partners and funding. In the end, the developer reaches an agreement with Apple Computers to help fund and design the Virtual Reality Centre. This provides the project with some funding, expertise, and a name-brand product.

It is important to build rest areas into the design. Butchart Gardens is not only one of Victoria's main attractions, but also a great spot to relax in.
(Photo courtesy Canadian Tourism Commission.)

Step 6—Develop a Strategy to Reach Goals

At this point, you need to outline specific objectives that must be met if you are to reach your goals and a detailed plan that allows any community member to see exactly how the goals will be achieved. The plans should consider all community components, address varying levels of services provided, and identify when, where, and how each objective will be met. A timeline showing deadlines for each objective helps individuals focus. A timeline might look like the following:

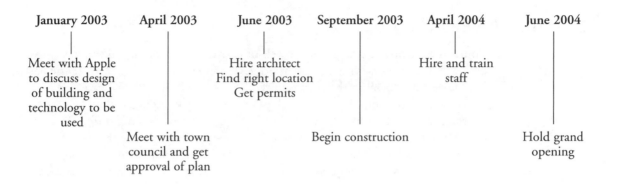

| January 2003 | April 2003 | June 2003 | September 2003 | April 2004 | June 2004 |

Meet with Apple to discuss design of building and technology to be used

Hire architect
Find right location
Get permits

Hire and train staff

Meet with town council and get approval of plan

Begin construction

Hold grand opening

Step 7—Implement Plan

This is the action stage. All the planning to this point must be implemented. Because many hours have been spent developing the plan, it is important to carry it through.

During the implementation stage, setbacks will occur. Unexpected developments will require a change in thinking and possibly in planning. When considering these changes, always refer to the mission statement and original goals.

Community support, through the chamber of commerce, the city council, and other businesses, is a prerequisite for success in a community-planned business. The grand opening should be a gala affair with many community members present.

Step 8—Review, Evaluate, Revise, and Continue with Plans

Does the plan work? Without an evaluation, the attraction might be going off in the wrong direction. It is imperative, therefore, to judge both the factors that contribute to the program's progress and those that detract. Are the goals being met? Are the time requirements and quantity and quality of work adequate? Is the alternative working? Evaluation must be ongoing to be effective. Early detection of problems allows for changes while they are still feasible.

In summary, the planning process should include as many people in the community as possible. The more participation, the more likely the plan is to develop into a successful tourism project. Participants usually include business and political leaders and residents. Planning enables tourism to be a positive and integrative force in the community. After the planning stage, actual development takes place. The next section outlines different types of development strategies.

Choose a community in your area that could benefit from a tourism plan. Write a brief description of the social, political, physical, and economic environment in that community. Based on this information and your knowledge of the area, design a mission statement with goals and objectives for tourism planning for the community. Write strategies for two of the goals.

Tourism Development

Tourism development ranges from well-organized areas that are ultimately pleasant to visit, to areas with such haphazard development that anyone can see the past and current upheaval in the community.

One classification of tourist development, defined by Douglas Pearce,[4] is based on the division of responsibility in the development process. **Integrated development** implies development by a single promoter or developer. **Catalytic development** occurs when a major promoter encourages complementary development by other companies or individuals. **Coattail development** occurs when visitors are enticed to an area of natural or unique qualities, and development takes place to provide the facilities and amenities they desire.

Integrated Development

Disney World is a classic example of integrated development. Integrated development occurs when an individual or company possesses a large parcel of land and develops the property to the exclusion of all other developers. The resort can usually stand alone, with all the tourist necessities and amenities. The following factors are characteristic of integrated development:

1. *One developer.* The entire resort is built by a single developer who has all the financial and technical resources. As a result, local participation is largely excluded from the development process.

2. *Balanced development.* Because the entire property is under the same owner, one portion of the resort can operate at a deficit that is offset by a more lucrative portion. For example, at a ski resort the sale of ski tickets and the operation of chairlifts may not be very profitable, but these low margins may be offset by large margins from condominium sales and rentals, creating a **balanced development.**

3. *Rapid development.* Once approvals are given to build, one entity generally will not encounter roadblocks caused by other groups or the community. Because it is private, the company can move quickly in the building phase, resulting in **rapid development.**

4. *Functional form.* An individual developer has the power to build an entire resort community based on a cohesive theme. This theme requires all buildings to adhere to a **functional form:** to look a certain way, to be located in the most convenient spot, and to enhance the recreational activities of the tourists.

5. *Isolation.* Complete freedom is necessary to develop such resorts. As a result, these resorts are commonly located away from existing settlements. Eventually, community development may occur nearby, but generally, this type of development remains in **isolation**.

6. *High prices.* This type of resort is generally first class in all aspects and attracts those who can afford the high prices. The increased costs of developing an integrated resort are usually offset by the high price of staying at the resort. In fact, the isolation of the resort may enhance its status.

Catalytic Development

Whistler, British Columbia; Banff, Alberta; and Mont Tremblant, Quebec, are examples of catalytic development, in which initial development stimulates other projects. The catalytic development process is characterized by the following steps:

1. *Centralized development.* Initiating **centralized development** is a single, large promoter who provides the basic facilities such as the ski lifts, major accommodation units, and promotion. Again, the developer usually has a large parcel of land to develop but is basing the success of the resort on the added facilities others can provide. In a general sense, the developer is providing the infrastructure for the other facilities.

2. *Secondary developers.* Based on success in the initial years of the resort, **secondary developers** build complementary facilities such as nightclubs, movie theatres, restaurants, shops, accommodations, and additional recreational activities such as miniature golf or swimming. These developments require less capital investment, which permits active participation by local companies and individuals.

3. *Interdependency.* The success and increased expansion of this type of resort depend on the entrepreneurial activities of others, creating a condition of **interdependency**. If the initial resort development does not succeed, other developers will not proceed with their projects. Conversely, if the other developers do not succeed, it could lead to the demise of the initial resort. In some cases, the principal promoter will pressure municipalities to block secondary developments that it doesn't consider compatible. Additionally, the local government may intervene to control growth.

Coattail Development

Niagara Falls is a good example of coattail development, which tends to occur around national parks, historic sites, and unique natural attractions. People are so drawn to these areas that entrepreneurs jump at the opportunity to ride on the coattails of the original site. Some of the characteristics of coattail development follow:

1. *No common theme.* Without a central organizer, there is no effort to have a common theme. Businesses develop because the tourist is readily available in the area. Initially, the nearby community observes little or no reason for a common theme. As tourism evolves, however, a community may develop a theme to fill a niche or create a sense of uniqueness in order to compete with other coattail communities in the area.

Juan Trippe

In the airline industry, no one has achieved the status accorded Juan Trippe. Born to a wealthy New York banker and educated at Yale, Trippe's vision of the future of aviation was right on target. He forged his Pan American empire with little regard for the risks. At its peak, Pan American controlled hotels, missile ranges, business jets, a midtown office building, and the mightiest international airline in the world. In the 1960s, Trippe was on top of a billion-dollar conglomerate.

Trippe fell in love with airplanes at the age of 10 and by the age of 18 he had learned how to fly. During his first year at Yale, the United States entered the First World War, and Trippe left university to join the naval air corp. He learned to fly early bomber planes but never got the chance to fight. Victory belonged to the small, light aircraft. When Trippe was 21, his father passed away, and the family bank failed, leaving the Trippes bankrupt. However, during his university years Juan had become fast friends with sons of the wealthiest families in America—the Rockefellers, the Vanderbilts, and the Whitneys—and these friendships were to help fund the dream of owning his own airline.

By age 23, Trippe had started the first of many airline companies—Long Island Airways. After it went bankrupt, he looked for business elsewhere. He landed a lucrative contract with the United Fruit Company and transferred his aircraft to Honduras, where his planes flew between Central American cities delivering goods. Politically astute and persuasive, Trippe soon forged many links with foreign countries and eventually had financial interests in airlines across Central and South America, China, Alaska, and New Zealand. However, his U.S.-based airline, Pan American, was his first love.

Pan Am first began operations by flying international mail routes. Soon Trippe was selling a few passenger seats on his mail flights. In 1935, Trippe and Pan Am made history by flying the first trans-Pacific passenger flight from San Francisco to the Philippines. By 1938 Pan Am had been granted a trans-Atlantic route, winning concessions for landing rights from Canada, Ireland, and Great Britain. Trippe and his company became experts at quickly setting up operational airports, and during the Second World War, they contributed both personnel and financial support to the U.S. government by building more than 25 new airports in South America and Africa. In return, Trippe asked for the flight routes to these destinations.

On the international scene, Trippe was a powerful negotiator, wearing his opponents down with his determination. He seldom lost his temper or raised his voice. He had an intuitive sense of the negotiation process and did not back away from his position. However, he had little patience when it came to negotiating with his own government and refused to support one political party over another with large cash donations. He had no friends in Washington, and in 1938, unable to sway political policies, his company, Pan Am, started looking for a new president. Pan Am had had two major air crashes and, using them as "just cause," the board of directors fired Trippe. For two years he sat in the wings as the world faced the threat of Hitler and the rising threat of the Japanese. By 1940, because Pan Am needed his strong leadership, Trippe was rehired.

After the war, when Trippe petitioned the U.S. government for domestic routes, he made two mistakes. First, he focused on improved service rather than the fact that although he could fly passengers from Australia to France, they were forced to use a U.S. domestic airline between San Francisco and New York. Second, he underestimated the animosity he had aroused over the years with his negotiating style. As a result, his petition was declined. Unfortunately, this refusal for domestic service rights was the first of many.

In 1955, while addressing an IATA conference in New York, Trippe announced that jet travel would change the destiny of the world. By 1958, Pan Am had led North America into the jet age of travel, flying the Atlantic in Boeing's new 707 jet. In 1971, Pan Am ushered in another era—the era of the jumbo jet. Believing that the supersonic jet Britain and France were developing was not the direction

air travel would take, Trippe invested Pan Am's money in a larger payload. This payload would reduce the cost of air travel so that flying could become more accessible to everyone. In 1968, Juan Trippe retired from his position as president to become Pan Am's chair. By 1991, the world's largest airline flew its last flight, finally forced into bankruptcy by years of poor decisions and disasters.

What kind of a man was Juan Trippe? He was a man who kept to himself—a visionary who saw the future of commercial airlines and then, almost single-handedly, proceeded to create it. He trusted his intuitions and never backed down from adversity. Juan Trippe did not stop until his dream became a reality.

2. *Duplication and redundancy.* Because no single promoter dominates this area, no guidelines or regulations are established stating what type of business is needed. Many entrepreneurs build similar businesses. Consequently, the variety of motels, restaurants, and shops is limited.

3. *Greater competition.* An offshoot of duplicated effort is increased competition in the area. If tourists have four T-shirt shops from which to choose, they are more likely to compare prices and variety before making a purchase. This competition among retailers produces a healthier business atmosphere.

4. *Late community involvement.* Most coattail development is piecemeal, which means development occurs as the need arises, without an organized plan. Many communities are now seeing the need to create consistency in the look and atmosphere of the town. But because most of the tourism businesses were established years ago, it is difficult to convince the business leaders of the need for change. Communities are starting with Business Improvement District (BID) approval, which encourages the improvement of downtown areas. Through a BID or other form of regulatory process, the community can influence the types and appearances of new businesses and promote the area as a unified group of shops, restaurants, and motels. The Niagara Region, for example, has worked hard to redevelop the destination and today Niagara serves as a model of tourism planning.

Tourism Planning: A Provincial Approach

British Columbia (B.C.) has consistently planned well for its tourism industry. As it looked to the new millennium, Tourism BC set a new goal of increasing tourism revenues by $9.9 billion annually, which translated into an additional 16 million visitors yearly. The next step was to begin the rigorous process of reviewing existing tourism capabilities to determine the feasibility of this goal. Two consulting firms, PricewaterhouseCoopers and the ARA Consulting Group Inc. were hired to produce a report, called *Tourism Industry Product Overview*, for Tourism British Columbia and the Council of Tourism Associations of British Columbia (COTA). The report is a thorough examination of the current product; an evaluation of each product area regarding prospects for growth; a look at the opportunities and constraints that may affect growth; and a plan of action that will take the province into the next decade.

The tourism groups opted to look at two sectors—accommodation and transportation—and seven product areas—skiing, sport fishing, golf, outdoor recreation, touring, urban tourism, and conventions/meeting business. With the help of hundreds of professionals representing these areas, data were collected and the products analyzed. The analysis focused on

1. **Product capacity:** the number of facilities, accommodations available, and transportation system capacity.
2. **Visitor use:** the total number of visitors or the number of visitor days or nights. In some areas, these data were just not available; in others there were good supporting statistics. (It is critical for the industry to begin to keep valid data if it will be making long-term decisions on product growth.)
3. **Market performance:** global product trends, growth rates, and past and current demand for the product.
4. **Revenue performance:** past and projected growth levels and estimated future revenues from each product sector.

To assess the viability of improving and expanding the seven tourism product areas, global trends for each area were studied. For example, when examining urban tourism trends, the report identified a strong visitor market for both Victoria and Vancouver, with a high visitor demand for greater choice in sites and services. It noted, however, that other cities, such as San Francisco, provided strong competition for B.C.'s tourist industry.

What were the conclusions after the data had been collected and analyzed? In 1998, the world began to experience an economic downturn with stock values fluctuating and world money markets suffering. Japan's economy suffered more than most, and this was one of the major market segments B.C. looked to for additional tourism revenues. Bearing this in mind, it was decided that the original goal of $9.9 billion by 2000 was unrealistic and a new goal of $7.5 billion was set. Goals that are not achievable need to be reassessed. The impact of September 11 on the world's tourism numbers and revenues coupled with new terrorist attacks of a smaller scale and the continued drop in financial markets has made it essential for communities and countries to reassess all their tourism plans.

The next series of studies and workshops dealt with creating a vision for tourism in B.C. Five criteria helped define this vision:

1. **Sustainability:** The group looked at the natural environment, the community, and economic implications.

2. **Quality of the visitor experience:** The group focused on the level of service that B.C. was providing to tourists, the quality of the setting (surroundings), the quality of the attractions, and the variety of experiences that the visitor could have while in B.C. Of course, if a region offers a wide range of activities, the tourist may stay longer or plan a return visit. Either way, additional revenue will be generated.

3. **Seasonality:** Seasonal products need to determine how to entice tourists throughout the year, thus creating four-season products.

4. **Financial benefits:** The benefits of tourism must be shared among all regions of B.C. Victoria, Whistler, and Vancouver are thriving, but the outlying communities, especially on the lower mainland, have yet to reap the benefit of tourism. Future planning should consider ways to distribute tourism products and revenue.

5. **Type of tourist:** B.C. tourism has opted to focus on "higher-value" tourists (tourists looking for upscale destinations and experiences) rather than the mass tourist population. Products already in existence need to be upgraded, and service must meet the expectations of the wealthier clientele.

Keeping these criteria in mind, all seven product areas were examined for current volume, capacity, and utilization. Tourism B.C. wants a development plan with maximum growth potential and minimal negative impact. Tourism sites and activity should be designed to ensure minimum destruction of the resource base and environment. For example, a new ski hill must provide the quality of experience the **higher-value tourist** wants, with little or no damage to the environment and the ecosystem. Advice is needed from experts in wildlife maintenance. Political or social problems should be handled with care to minimize the impact of tourism on residents' lifestyle. Many communities react negatively, so their concerns should be addressed through an educational program that focuses on the value of tourism to the region. Community leaders and citizens should be included in the planning process to ensure their needs are met.

During the planning process the expectations of the higher-value tourist were identified. They expect service to be friendly, timely, and professional at all times. To achieve this, the industry must hire and train workers with outgoing, professional attitudes. A wide variety of services and activities ensures visitors will spend more money and be more willing to return.

The value of tourism reaches its full potential for a province only when all communities benefit from its development and revenue stream. Except for Vancouver, Victoria, and Whistler, most of British Columbia has a distinct seasonality and is underused during off-season periods. Encouraging shoulder and off-season usage can increase revenues without major additional tourism development. Year-round products should market their services for slow activity periods. Optimal use is only possible if tourists can move around the province efficiently and at reasonable cost.

Hoping to maximize expenditure per visitor, B.C. charted average daily expenditures of visitors from the various product areas. For example, hunters pay upward of $1000 per day, but licences are limited and so is the revenue stream. Golfers spend only $125 per day, but the golf season is longer and the province has the capability of providing more than one and a half million rounds of golf to the consumer! For this reason, focusing on golf vacations produces a greater annual revenue than hunting. In addition, golfers could be encouraged to spend more if they were offered new local attractions such as restaurants and shops.

Constraints on B.C.'s Tourism Growth

Representatives from all sectors of the industry met to discuss the new Tourism Growth Management Strategy. They identified the following constraints to provincial tourism growth:

1. *Concern for B.C.'s delicate ecosystem.* Opportunities for new tourism land and resources are declining. Future tourism development in wilderness areas must be sustainable and minimally affect flora and fauna.

2. *Financial concerns.* Developing new projects is expensive. Where will the money come from? Although financial institutions lend money to major city regions, they are often reluctant to provide capital to outlying regions. In addition, financial institutions have a negative perception of the industry, often basing their decisions on the poor performance of old products without acknowledging the tremendous success of modern tourism products, such as the cruise lines.

3. *Tourism illiteracy.* Not all communities see tourism as beneficial. Education may be needed before starting any tourism projects.

4. *Seasonality.* This continues to be a problem for most of the B.C. regions.

5. *A lack of trained personnel.* Strong training programs must be readily accessible to tourism workers at reasonable cost.

6. *Transportation costs.* Ferries and air travel within B.C. are expensive. The infrastructure suffers from lack of modernization, especially in areas outside Vancouver, Victoria and between Vancouver and Whistler.

7. *Lack of high-quality development.* Outside of Vancouver, Victoria, and Whistler, the province lacks quality sites and products. If financial benefits are to be better distributed, these outlying areas must realize their potential as tourism destinations.

8. *Poor product packaging and the lack of an integrated market plan.* Both packaging and marketing must be emphasized in any new tourism plan.

in practice

Although B.C.'s approach differs slightly from the eight-step process discussed in this textbook, the elements of good planning are clearly visible. Compare B.C.'s method with the planning process illustrated in Figure 4.1. What planning steps did B.C. complete and how do the two processes differ? Can you explain why?

summary

Although planning and development are separate entities, they must occur together for tourism to succeed on a local, regional, or national level. Canada has looked carefully at its goals and has developed a series of guidelines for developing and maintaining its tourism product.

Planning is a cyclical, eight-step process. In any situation it is important to begin with an inventory of the social, political, physical, and economic environment of the community or business. This inventory gives direction on what is needed, what can be accomplished, and what should not be attempted. The second step is to look at trends. Forecasting provides a basis for deciding whether to proceed with certain plans. The third step, which creates the guidelines, is to develop a mission statement, goals, and objectives. Steps four, five, and six require the community or business to study alternative plans, to select the preferred plan, and to design strategies to reach the goals. The seventh step is implementation, and the final step includes reviewing, evaluating, and revising the original plan. When a tourism plan is devised as a community document, support for the ideas makes the plan successful. Without planning, tourism development is a hit-or-miss operation. Usually it's a miss.

Tourism development refers to the type of development that takes place in communities. Integrated development is achieved by a single company or individual. Most communities do not develop tourism this way. Catalytic development occurs when a developer brings a major attraction to an area and encourages other businesses to build nearby, giving local and regional businesses the opportunity to participate and become successful. Coattail development occurs when visitors are drawn to an area because of its scenic beauty or natural qualities. Owners see the potential and start new tourism-related businesses. There is usually little guidance or planning at the initial stages of development. A community must organize itself and put together a planning document to avoid becoming a hodge-podge of buildings without a central theme.

British Columbia has a strong commitment to a tourism growth management strategy. A comprehensive study and planning process examined provincial goals and objectives, global trends and their impact on product development, and constraints. This initiative provided the province's tourism industry with a collective vision and a planned direction.

questions

1. Illustrate the effectiveness of your city as a tourism destination by discussing how it fulfills the five essential components of a generic destination.

2. Discuss the four stages in the life cycle of a destination.

3. Outline five goals that a viable tourism destination should meet in order to enhance the community.

4. a) Briefly explain in your own words the eight steps in tourism planning.

   b) Which of these steps do you feel is most important? Explain.

5. Define the following terms as they relate to tourism planning: *functional form, product capacity, qualitative analysis, quantitative analysis, market performance, revenue performance, higher-value tourist.*

6. a) Illustrate the differences among integrated, catalytic, and coattail development of a tourism destination area.

    b) Which style of development do you feel is best? Explain your answer.

7. List the eight constraints identified by B.C. Tourism. For each point, discuss whether it applies to B.C. only or to Canada as a whole.

---

weblinks

commercecan.ic.gc.ca

Canadian Business Map: statistical data, directories and research/development on Canadian businesses.

www.unesco.org

UNESCO (the United Nations Educational, Scientific and Cultural Organization) designates certain "World Heritage Sites" for preservation, from the Galapagos Islands in Ecuador to Alberta's Head Smashed In Buffalo Complex.

travel.bc.ca

This is Tourism B.C.'s Web site (discussed on p. 80). The provincial government's ministry responsible for tourism may be found at
www.sbtc.gov.bc.ca / programs / tourism.html

---

notes

1. *Newfoundland-Labrador* (St. John's: Tourism Newfoundland-Labrador, 1995).

2. Edward Inskeep, *Tourism Planning: An Integrated and Sustainable Approach* (New York: John Wiley and Sons, 1991), p. 25.

3. Robert W. McIntosh and Charles R. Goeldner, *Tourism Principles, Practices, Philosophies*, 6th ed. (New York: John Wiley & Sons, 1990), pp. 265–267.

4. Douglas Pearce, *Tourism Development*, 2nd ed. (New York: John Wiley & Sons, 1989), pp. 67–70.

5

The Transportation Sector

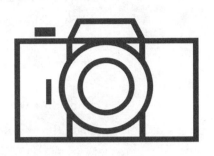

bilateral agreement
BritRail pass
bullet train
Canrailpass
charter
circle trip
corporate rates
direct flight
Eurailpass
fly/coach tours
Freedoms of the Air
gateway airport
high-speed transporta-
tion (HST) system
hub and spoke

interline connection
International Air
Transport Association
(IATA)
International Civil
Aviation Organization
(ICAO)
Jetway
kilometre cap
landing fee
load factor
loading apron
LRC (light, rapid,
comfortable)
motor coach package

nonstop flight
online connection
open-jaw trip
Open Skies
Orient Express
overnight/short tour
round trip
scheduled air carrier
Shinkansen
special interest cruise
sightseeing/day tour
taxiway
theme cruise
unlimited kilometres
VIA Rail Canada

Having read this chapter you will be able to

1. Summarize the effects of deregulation in Canada on the airline and tourism industry.

2. Describe the Canadian air transportation system.

3. Explain how the type of trip and flight affect the cost of a ticket.

4. Discuss Freedoms of the Air and how they affect flights in and out of Canada.

5. Compare and contrast the common perceptions of a tour by automobile/RV versus a motor coach tour.

6. Analyze the history of the rail industry in Canada to show its effect on tourism.

7. Compare foreign rail with domestic rail in terms of product and services provided.

8. Outline the advantages of taking a cruise as a vacation.

9. Explain the reasons that one mode of transportation is chosen over another.

10. Discuss the job opportunities available in each of the four transportation modes: air, rail, ground, and water.

11. Summarize current trends in the transportation sector of tourism.

Transporting a visitor from a place of residence to a chosen destination begins the tourism experience. Some people believe that travel and tourism are synonymous; they are not. The transportation system, along with the infrastructure that supports it, does play the most significant role in tourism: if visitors cannot reach their destinations, then none of the other tourism components are needed. Nearly 20 percent of the tourism labour force, and 2 percent of the total Canadian labour force, work in the transportation sector, and employment continues to grow.[1]

Travellers use many different modes of transportation, and why they choose one mode over another is an interesting area of research. This chapter reviews the common modes of tourist transportation, discusses some of the studies on travel choices, and looks briefly to the past and the future of this exciting sector.

TRAVEL BY AIR

Airlines

The History of Air Travel in Canada

The airline industry primarily brings together the businesses of airports, regularly scheduled flights, charters, reservations, customs, and the support services of food, car rental, and concessions. It provides services for millions of people as they traverse the world for business and pleasure.

From the very beginning of the Canadian airline industry, the government has controlled this transportation system carefully. In 1937, the government gave Canadian National Railways the right to operate a subsidiary called Trans Canada Airlines (TCA) and the sole right to air passenger service, domestically and internationally. TCA, now Air Canada, enjoyed this monopoly in the air until 1945. After the Second World War, the federal government awarded privately owned Canadian Pacific Airlines (CP Air) international routes to Asia, the Pacific, Australia, and South America. In 1958, CP Air was finally awarded a single transcontinental route from Montreal to Vancouver, to be flown on a daily basis.

In 1966–67, Canada passed several pieces of legislation that affected the transportation industry. The National Transportation Act provided guidelines for service in the passenger and freight business in Canada and gave CP Air domestic rights to 25 percent of the Canadian market. The 1970s were a period of "regulated competition." Liberalization of charter regulations saw new, small charter airlines emerge, like Wardair, based in Edmonton, Alberta. By the early 1970s Canada had several transcontinental airlines (Pacific Western, Time Air) as well as two international carriers (Air Canada, Canadian Pacific).

In 1978, the United States government made a daring move and deregulated the American airline industry. Prior to the Deregulation Act, travel by air had been viewed as a service industry, providing fast, efficient transportation to all parts of America. Opposing factions successfully argued that citizens would be better served if the airlines were open to competition, with real market forces, not the government, determining the cost of a ticket. Deregulation in the United States had devastating effects. Of the 36 carriers in existence in 1978, only 20 were still in operation 15 years later. More than 130 new airlines emerged in the first year of deregulation, only to go bankrupt or be swallowed up by the larger companies. Today, eight major U.S. airlines control nearly 95 percent of American airline traffic.

Canada, recognizing the need for change in the airline industry, also began the process of deregulation. In 1985, the federal government released a white paper called *Freedom to Move*, which put the framework for reform in place. This paper culminated in the new National Transportation Act of 1987. It had been 20 years since the last major piece of legislation for the transportation industry and the new legislation was far reaching. It affirmed that a safe, economic, efficient transportation network was necessary to meet the needs of Canadian businesses and travellers. It replaced the Canadian Transportation Commission with a new agency, the National Transportation Agency (NTA). Air Canada, which had enjoyed special status as the government-owned airline for more than 40 years, was privatized. With no more government subsidies, Air Canada finally faced the same marketplace with the same rules as Canadian and other airlines. Pricing regulations were eliminated and entrance into the scheduled airline business was finally open to all Canadian airlines.

Canada's National Transportation Act did not go as far as the U.S. legislation in deregulating. Recognizing the difficulties of serving vast, thinly populated areas, and wishing to avoid some of the problems that arose from the U.S. law, government continued to regulate northern routes.

Deregulation has not been all that it promised to be. Major air carriers dropped smaller, less profitable routes, especially if they were not on a major flight path. This left communities with no flight service or with poor scheduling and, in some cases, high ticket prices. A report released October 29, 2002, by the Organisation for Economic Co-operation and Development calls Canada's deregulation efforts a disaster for the consumer. Smaller companies that have tried to compete with the major airlines have gone bankrupt or merged with the larger carriers. These circumstances allowed Pacific Western Airlines to merge with Canadian Pacific Airways to become Canadian Airlines International (CAI) and then purchase Wardair.

There are, however, some benefits. Although the larger scheduled airlines were merging and fighting for their market share from major cities like Toronto and Vancouver, commuter or "feeder" airlines like Bearskin Airlines, Calm Air, and PEI Air started service to cities like London and Sudbury, Ontario; Sydney, Nova Scotia; and Yellowknife, Northwest Territories. These small airlines have been able to survive because they use smaller, more fuel-efficient aircraft, carry fewer passengers, and require fewer personnel. They service destinations with little or no competition from the other companies.

Another benefit is the emergence of "no frills" or discount airlines, which focus on shorter flights with limited services. Discount airlines can be strong competition for the major carriers because they control their costs so efficiently. Canada has several "no frills" airlines: CanJet, JetsGo, and WestJet, based in Calgary. WestJet has been serving cities in British Columbia and Alberta since 1996 and it has expanded its services eastward, establishing a headquarters (hub) in Hamilton. It now serves Ottawa, Toronto, Montreal, and points west. WestJet has a simplified fare structure with low ticket pricing based on the day of the week or time of the year. CanJet and JetsGo provide services for Eastern Canada under similar conditions. Competition with Air Canada is limited because these airlines have fewer aircraft and serve fewer destinations with limited schedules. Nevertheless, Air Canada has counter-challenged its competitors by establishing three no-frills services, called Jazz, Tango, and Zip.

Another outcome of deregulation has been the strengthening of airline systems through alliances. Air Canada has cooperative agreements with several international airlines to create more competitive fares though a process called "code sharing." For example, a passenger who takes a flight from Halifax to Denver flies Air Canada to Toronto, connects to United Airlines to Denver, and pays a fare that has been determined jointly by both Air Canada and United Airlines. On the departure and arrival screen, the flight will have both airlines listed, but in fact, only one plane carries the passengers. This allows the airlines to give the passenger a lower fare, as though it were the same airline all the way through, and it provides additional business for both members of the alliance.

Route structures also changed with deregulation. During the early years of the airlines, routes were linear. Planes flew from one destination to another, perhaps picking up passengers along the way. They returned via the same route. Linear routes are still common in international flight structures. With deregulation, the **hub and spoke** system emerged. Airlines concentrated their services at major airports, reducing costs by consolidating staff in one or two major centres. The larger aircraft (Airbus and Boeing 747s) now carry passengers between these major cities, then transfer them to smaller planes to fly to the final destination. Feeder/regional airlines are the link between the hub city and the destination. In Canada, our hub cities are Halifax, Montreal, Toronto, Winnipeg, Edmonton, Calgary and Vancouver (see Figure 5.1). Regional or feeder airlines such as Air Nova, Air B.C., and Air Ontario are affiliated with Air Canada. In July of 1999, the Canadian government created a furor by temporarily suspending the *Competition Act* for airlines. This allowed Onex, a private organization, to come forward with a bid to purchase Canadian Airlines, a company that had been struggling for survival since deregulation. The fight for Canadian became very intense, with Air Canada also putting in a bid, promising to run it as a separate company if the purchase were approved. In November, following a court battle, Onex withdrew its offer and Air Canada purchased and merged with Canadian, giving Canada only one international carrier.

No history of air will ever be complete without addressing the far-reaching impacts September 11, 2001, has had on not only the airline system, but also other modes of travel. In the late 1960's and 1970's, airlines were forced to deal with a rising number of hijackings. U.S. airlines carried armed sky marshalls, and passengers were used as bargaining chips to persuade governments to give in to the terrorists' demands. September 11 painted a whole different picture of terrorism, as jumbo jets became moving incendiary bombs. The World Trade Center was not only one of the great financial centres of the world, but also dominated the New York skyline making it an obvious target for the hijackers. American Airlines Flight 11 hit the North Tower at 8:46 a.m. At 9:02 a.m. United's Flight 175 slammed into the South Tower. The twin towers simply could not withstand the high heat levels, both collapsing in just under two hours. In Washington, DC, the same scene played out, with the Pentagon as the target. Once officials determined this was a terrorist operation, the Federal Aviation Authority (FAA) closed U.S. air space.

In two and a half hours, over 4500 aircraft nationwide were forced to land or were diverted. International flights with a U.S. city as their destination landed in Canada, flooding small and large airports with stranded, worried passengers. U.S. airspace stayed closed for a three-day period then slowly began operations again, but America's faith in its airline system was badly shaken.

Airlines suffered extreme financial losses, with United Airlines, the world's second largest carrier, losing over $5 million daily. Some governments provided one-time bail-out grants, with Air Canada receiving $5 million. Several airlines declared bankruptcy, including Scandinavian Airlines (SAS) in Europe and Canada 3000 in Canada. Unable to recover from lost revenues due to 9-11, United Airlines was forced to file for creditor protection under U.S. federal bankruptcy laws in November of 2002.

Air travel has not recovered fully, with travellers choosing to use the train, travel by bus, or use their own automobiles more frequently than before. Security at airports has increased, and for Canadian air travellers, it has meant an additional security surcharge of $24 per round trip. Airlines have reconfigured cockpit doors to provide a stronger barrier. Critics say airport security is still too lax. While passengers undergo close scrutiny, airport workers and their access points do not.

In January of 2003, the Canadian Air Transport Security Authority (CATSA) began operations at most Canadian airports. Its mandate is to ensure the safety of passengers, with improved screening processes for both airport workers and airline passengers, thus decreasing the risk of terrorist acts.

In March 2003, the U.S. and Britain, supported by a coalition of supportive countries, attacked Iraq to eliminate Saddam Hussein's regime. For the second time in two years, demand for air travel dropped dramatically. Airlines reacted quickly by implementing flexible rebooking policies, but by March 23, Atlantic air travel dropped by 25 percent with an overall global decrease of ten percent. Advance bookings fell by 40 percent in the Atlantic area and 30 percent in the Pacific.[2]

By April 1, 2003, Air Canada was finally forced to file for bankruptcy protection in both Canada and the United States. Addressing the current state of the air industry, IATA director Giovanni Bisignani, speaking to delegates at the ICAO conference in Montreal in the spring of 2003, urged the troubled industry to "look beyond the horizon and re-invent itself" and for countries to reduce restrictions on the industry allowing it to move away from its "national framework" to become a global industry.[3]

Understanding Canada's Air System

The federal department responsible for all of Canada's transportation systems is called Transport Canada. It sets the rules and regulations for licensing pilots, flight engineers, and airplane mechanics. It provides licences for each commercial aircraft and determines the number of hours a plane can fly between maintenance checks. It sets the appropriate weight loads allowable for each type of aircraft. For more than 60 years it operated the country's air navigation system.

In November of 1996, NAV CANADA (NAVCAN), a non-share, capital, private-sector corporation was given ownership and control over the country's air navigation system. NAVCAN currently provides aircraft with air navigation, air traffic control, flight information, weather briefings, airport advisory services, electronics and such services as training and electronic maintenance. Operating as a private corporation, NAVCAN charges users (primarily commercial airlines) service fees, which are, of course, passed on to consumer. Most of NAVCAN's employees worked for the federal government, and so the transition to a privatized air navigation system has been smooth. They have begun to streamline the system by consolidating the many regional offices operated by the government into two offices in Edmonton and Ottawa. NAVCAN is just one example of a trend toward privatization of services in Canada over the past decade. By putting the safety of airline passengers under one private corporation, the government hopes to save money and provide Canadians with a more efficient, safer air system.

Some of our finest wilderness experiences can be reached only with float planes.
(Photo courtesy Canadian Tourism Commission.)

Air travel is best described in terms of scheduled and nonscheduled service. In addition to commercial flights, general aviation includes corporate fleets for use by private corporations, small private planes for business and pleasure, and planes for special services such as fire prevention and law enforcement.

Scheduled Air Service Airlines that operate with published timetables, on defined domestic or international routes, for which licences have been granted by the government or governments concerned are called **scheduled air carriers**.[4] Scheduled services can be offered by private companies or public entities. Air Canada and WestJet are both scheduled carriers.

Charter Air Service Nonscheduled airlines or charter air services arrange to fly wherever a group plans to visit. A **charter** refers to the rental of a plane, bus, or ship to transport people, usually at lower rates than regularly scheduled service. Many times the charter service is arranged by a tour operator, although, since deregulation, the difference between scheduled and nonscheduled flights has become blurred. Many scheduled air service companies also offer charters, and charters have been opening their services to cities with scheduled flights. Charter operators have much more flexibility than operators of scheduled flights; they can fly on their own time, even cancelling the flight if necessary. Passengers, however, have less flexibility because the dates, times, and departure points are set by the charter company. One major difference is the space available for seating. Many charter carriers have changed the seating configuration to accommodate more passengers, resulting in crowded conditions. The savings in price, however, usually make up for the uncomfortable seating arrangements. Skyservice and Air Transat are examples of charter airlines.

Airports

Airports fall into two major categories: *air carrier* airports and *general aviation* airports. There are approximately 450 air carrier airports in Canada, and they serve both scheduled airlines and charter airlines. Many also have facilities for private aircraft, especially corporate jets. General aviation airports serve all types of flights except scheduled airlines.

Most of Canada's major airports are now leased from the government to a private company or airport authority. Since these companies are in business for profit, service charges have gone up. Increased landing fees, which of course must be passed on to passengers, have been a major concern to airlines. Airports currently under private management include those in Halifax, Montreal, Ottawa, Toronto, Winnipeg, Calgary, Edmonton, and Vancouver. Some airports are owned and operated by provincial authorities, and a few remain under the control of Transport Canada.

Many of our airports require extensive remodelling, new and longer runways, and improved services to stay competitive and to handle expected higher passenger volume. To cover these costs, most airports charge passengers departure taxes called Air Improvement Fees (AIFs), which may be added to the ticket at the time of purchase or collected when passengers go through security. Airports also make additional revenue from rental spaces, parking facilities, and other services.

Airport Components Airports consist of many different components: passenger terminals, parking lots, control towers, hangars, runways, taxiways, loading

Many airlines now provide their passengers with the choice of standing in line to check in or using the new express check-in. This means shorter lines for ticket agents and faster service for passengers.
(Photo: Paula Kerr.)

aprons, chapels, customs and immigration facilities, restaurants and bars, lounges reserved for first-class travellers, souvenir shops, car rental agencies, banks or money exchange services, administration offices, and any other service that the airport feels is needed by a traveller. Some airports have hotels as an integral part of the terminal, and others have direct access to subways or a train station. Each airport is a unique experience and can be a very enjoyable stopover. General aviation airports servicing private aircraft usually have a contractual agreement with a fixed base operator (FBO) who sells fuel, provides maintenance, leases airplanes and hangar space, and conducts flying lessons.

Airline Terminology You Should Know

landing fee	fee charged to an aircraft each time it lands at an airport, passed on to the consumer in the ticket price
gateway airport	an airport that receives a high volume of international flights
taxiway	paved strip of concrete or "road" aircraft use to move from one area of the airport to another, especially from the runway to the gate
loading apron	concrete area on which aircraft park to load and unload passengers and baggage
Jetway	movable hallway that connects the aircraft to the terminal
round trip	trip that originates in one city, takes passengers to their destination, and returns them to the originating city using the same airline
circle trip	a type of round trip in which the route taken to the destination differs from the route taken from the destination
open-jaw trip	trip that takes passengers to one destination, allows them to use another mode of travel to a second destination, and flies them home from there

nonstop flight	a flight that travels from one destination to another without a stop
direct flight	a flight that travels from one destination to another, making at least one stop but no change of plane
online connection	a flight that forces travellers to change aircraft to get to their destination
interline connection	a flight that forces travellers to change airlines to get to their destination

Airfares and Reservations

On average, deregulation and more efficient operations have dramatically reduced airfares. As implied earlier, when airfares drop, more people take to the skies. The airline industry is more affected by changes in oil prices than almost any other factor in airline management. During the Persian Gulf war, jet fuel prices nearly doubled.[5] The net loss to the industry was approximately $1 billion.[6] When fuel prices go up, airfares increase, causing fewer people to travel by air, which in turn creates hardship on employees through management cost-cutting decisions. To offset rising fuel prices, many airlines are adding a fuel surcharge to the price of a ticket.

Airfares Airfares are set according to two very broad markets: the business traveller and the discretionary traveller. Business travellers usually want to adhere to a relatively strict schedule, so they have fewer options on flight times. Because of this inflexibility, they pay the standard fare or even the higher business or first-class fare. Discretionary travellers, who can shop around for more convenient flights at the best price, are usually able to get discount fares because they are not locked into a specific schedule. Airline strategies in discount fares have led to multitiered pricing, with as many as 100 different prices for the same route. The difference in price between a standard fare and the discount fare can be considerable. An airline passenger might have paid hundreds of dollars more (or less) than the passenger in the next seat, for the same service and destination. The complexity of airfares goes far beyond the difference between business and pleasure travel. Fares are also based on the type of trip a passenger desires. For example, a round-trip airfare from Halifax to Toronto may be less expensive than one where the traveller flies into Toronto, then travels by rail or car to Ottawa, returning to Halifax from there (open-jaw trip).

The **load factor** is the average percentage of seats filled by paying or revenue-producing passengers. Load factors are one reason for multitiered pricing strategies. Airlines believe it is better to fly a full plane than a half-empty one. Once that plane leaves the terminal, empty seats will never produce revenue for that leg of the flight. Generally, the major costs of the flight, such as crew salaries, aircraft depreciation, and maintenance, are fixed. Incremental costs to carry one more passenger are minimal: one more prepared meal and a small amount of jet fuel. Therefore, revenue is maximized by pricing some seats at a lower rate to encourage additional passenger travel. This is true even though the airline nets a lower revenue per passenger-kilometre than it would if everyone paid the standard fare.

Reservations Computer technology has proven to be a great advantage for the airline industry. Nearly all travel agencies and all airport and airline ticketing agents are online with a computerized reservation system (CRS). The CRS used by travel agents has access to many major tourism products such as hotels, attractions, and car rentals, as well as the worldwide airline network.

The International Air Transport System: How It Works

Bilateral agreements are international agreements made between two countries. All countries have signed many bilateral agreements. These agreements cover a number of issues, including the number of flights permitted from each country into a specific airport, the size and capacity of the airplanes, and special fares. The **Open Skies** agreement of 1995 is an example of a bilateral agreement between Canada and the United States. It has "opened the skies" above North America, providing tourists with more options of carrier, destination, and type of flight. This new bilateral agreement has already benefited cross-border tourism, allowing Air Canada to serve many new U.S. destinations and U.S. airlines to provide some cross-border competition for Air Canada.

When Korean Airlines flight 007 was shot down in 1985, with a loss of 269 lives, immediate disbelief and outrage were aimed at the Russians. Although the aircraft had strayed into Soviet airspace, it was felt that the Russians had violated one of the unwritten agreements of the sky: the right of safe passage for civilian airlines. Most countries claim ownership not only of their land but also of their shorelines, waters, and skies. In the early years of aviation, this ownership caused some concern for aviators. To ensure the right of safe flight, the nations of the world sat down to write some very basic rules. These rules regulating air activity have been developed at worldwide conferences, through bilateral agreements, and by international organizations like the International Civil Aviation Organization (ICAO) and the International Air Transport Association (IATA).

Airline Associations

IATA The **International Air Transport Association (IATA)** was formed in 1919 and was reorganized in 1945. Its members currently include more than 200 of the world's scheduled airlines, with major flag carriers taking a leadership role. The principal function of IATA is to facilitate the movement of persons and goods from and to any point on the world air network by any combination of routes. IATA's mandates are to

- provide a forum for airlines to meet and discuss mutual concerns
- promote air safety
- represent the airlines in travel agency affairs
- encourage global air travel
- recommend fares and tariffs for government approval

Each country has absolute right to its airspace, and it can set any conditions it likes with regard to air travel, so to be effective rules or tariffs formulated by IATA must also receive approval from the appropriate government.

In 1919, IATA held its first world conference. By 1940, these multinational meetings had set up parameters for

- controlling aircraft registry
- issuing airline tickets

- setting liability of the airline with regard to lost luggage
- setting liability in the event of passenger injury or death

In the late 1960s, in response to a rash of airline hijackings, the global airline community agreed that under no circumstances would hijackers be given asylum by any country, including their chosen destination. They must be returned to the country of departure for prosecution. Although hijackings still occur, the numbers have been significantly reduced because of this agreement.

One of the more important accomplishments of these world conferences has been the development of rights called **Freedoms of the Air**. The first two freedoms deal with the rights of passage for an airplane. After the Bay of Pigs incident in 1963, in which the United States encouraged an unsuccessful invasion of Cuba by Cuban expatriates, Fidel Castro rescinded all Freedoms of the Air for U.S. airlines. Because Canada still has these rights, Canadian airlines may fly across the island, but U.S. airlines are forced to fly around it. The next four freedoms are called traffic rights. They deal with the dropping off and picking up of passengers. The last two freedoms are the newest. They give special rights to certain airlines under specific circumstances. The eighth freedom, called *cabotage,* gives a foreign airline the right to carry passengers from one destination within a country to another, allowing Delta Airlines, for example, to pick up passengers in Toronto and let them disembark in Vancouver. Canada does not currently give U.S. airlines the right of cabotage. Some believe that granting this right would prevent Canada's flight system from becoming monopolistic. However, this proposal has not met with much support because our Open Skies agreement gives considerable freedom to North American airlines to form partnerships and to share routes and fare structures. The following are the Freedoms of the Air:

First Freedom: right of transit (e.g., Air Canada departs Toronto and overflies the United States to reach Mexico City).

Second Freedom: right of technical stop (e.g., Cathay Pacific departs Toronto and lands in Anchorage to refuel en route to Hong Kong).

Third Freedom: right to discharge passengers in a foreign country (e.g., Air Canada boards passengers in Halifax and they disembark in London, England).

Fourth Freedom: right to pick up foreign passengers in their country and transport them to the airline's country of registration (e.g., Air Canada boards passengers in Miami, Florida, and allows them to disembark in Montreal).

Fifth Freedom: right to pick up passengers in one country, stop in another country to pick up more people, and then continue on to a third country (e.g., Singapore Airlines boards passengers in Singapore, stops in Seoul, Korea, to pick up more passengers, and allows them to disembark in Vancouver, Canada).

Sixth Freedom: right to carry passengers from the airline's country of origin, make a stopover in a gateway city in another country, and continue on to the final destination (e.g., Canada 3000 picks up passengers in Toronto, makes a stopover in Honolulu, Hawaii, with a final destination of Nadi, Fiji).

Seventh Freedom: right of an airline registered in one country to carry passengers between two destination points outside that country (e.g., Air New Zealand picks up passengers in Los Angeles and allows them to disembark in Sydney).

Eighth Freedom: right of an airline registered in one country to fly passengers between two points within another country. (Also called *cabotage.*)

ICAO The **International Civil Aviation Organization (ICAO)** is an agency of the United Nations and its members are representatives from U.N. member nations. ICAO was formed to ensure that the development of the airline system is both safe and orderly. ICAO is responsible for organizing world conferences, mediating disputes between members, and setting standards for aviation equipment and operations. Canada has played an active role in ICAO and recently promoted an international "no smoking" policy that would be observed by all international air carriers, making international flight a smoke-free experience. To date, this proposal has not received worldwide acceptance, nor has it been enforced.

The air system is dealing with another security problem, that of air rage. As life becomes more stressful, passengers are taking out their frustrations on cabin crew. In the United States, stiff penalties and jail terms can be given to any person disturbing the normal activities of the cabin crew. Canadian law is not as tough; however, crews today are more cognizant of their passengers, and the air crew are quick to respond when given an alert by the flight attendants. If trouble begins in the cabin, you can be sure the aircraft will land at the nearest airport and the perpetrator will be turned over to local police.

The Future of Passenger Flight

What does the future hold for air passengers over the next 25 years? Let's first examine supersonic air travel. The SST Concorde has been providing service for travellers between Paris or London and North America for more than 25 years. There are currently 14 in service, but the Concorde has never achieved the success the developers had hoped for. It is a costly airplane to operate and its payload is small. Even with a 25 percent surcharge to first-class fares, this aircraft has not been profitable for British Airways or Air France. On the drawing board is a new supersonic aircraft called the HSCT. It is being designed by Boeing/McDonnell, working with scientists from NASA. This new aircraft will fly at mach 2.4 (about 2400 km/h) and will hold 300 passengers. At this speed, the trip from New York City to Tokyo will be reduced to 7.5 hours! The pilots will be using a digital video camera, infrared images, and radar to "see," as there will be no cockpit windows. This external vision system is better than the human eye because it "sees" clearly through all weather problems, providing the pilots with good visibility in snow, fog, or rain. The supersonics fly at very high altitude and their exhaust puts deadly emissions into our stratosphere, which deplete the ozone layer. Many of our modern machines do the same thing, but not in space. Before the HSCT can be built and flown, scientists must solve this problem, ensuring that there is little or no environmental impact on earth's stratosphere.

A new subsonic jumbo aircraft is also in the development stages. The Airbus Consortium in Europe is working on the A3XX, which will carry 500 to 800 passengers and will be able to land, unload, and reload in just 90 minutes. Operating costs will be 20 percent lower than for current jumbo jets, which will provide higher yields and keeps ticket prices lower.

Another aircraft on the drawing board is the Bell 609. Developed with the support of the U.S. government, this aircraft is a combination helicopter and straight-wing craft. Time is money to a business traveller, and this aircraft will target business people in large urban centres. The aircraft is designed to land like a helicopter on a landing pad, which would be located in the heart of a large city. It carries six to nine passengers and can fly them to their destination at almost 500 km per hour (much faster than a helicopter). Passengers would be able to fly from downtown Toronto to downtown Montreal in just over one hour, eliminating travel time to and from the airport as well as much of the tedious check-in process.

Airports around the world are struggling with the increase in traffic, and major expansion is sometimes impossible or beyond the region's financial capabilities. Aircraft that can carry larger loads can reduce the number of flights into airports, and the Bell 609 could help handle the increasing needs of the travelling business world. Some experts claim these new aircraft will extend the life of our current airports by 50 years. Air travel in the next few decades promises to be very different from how we fly today.[7]

in practice

You have read about and probably experienced some of the ups and downs of the airlines. Make two lists. The positive list should consist of all the world and national changes that have benefited the airline industry in the past. The negative list should indicate the changes (temporary or permanent) that have had a detrimental effect on the airlines. Now add predicted future changes to each list. What do you think are some of the good and bad things that could happen to the airline industry in the next 25 years? How could the airline industry minimize negative effects?

S N A P S H O T

Max Ward

Maxwell William Ward was born to fly! "Max," as he is affectionately called by Canadians in the tourism industry, lived and slept with dreams of flying throughout his childhood. Those dreams became a reality in 1940 when, at the age of 18, he enlisted in the Royal Canadian Air Force as a pilot. His first flight was marked by "poise, courage, and breakfast," as Max quickly found out that he was prone to airsickness! But dreams overcome many of our weaknesses and Max went on to get his wings and graduate at the top of his class. As did many young fighter pilots, Max itched to get into the Second World War, but it was not to be. He spent his years in the RCAF training other pilots for action. At the end of the war, Max left the Air Force to work for Northern Flights Limited, but he soon discovered that he was not interested in flying for someone else—he wanted to be his own boss. The trials and tribulations Max Ward

dealt with over the next 43 years clearly reflect how the federal government "hogtied" Canada's commercial airline industry until deregulation. In June of 1946 Max began his first airline, called Polaris Charter Company Limited, and with the help of family and friends he bought his first aircraft, a single-engine biplane called a Fox Moth. His career as an airline owner/operator did not start off auspiciously. His first commercial flight ended with a crash! Then his company was forced to fold when the Air Transport Board (ATB) discovered Max had not applied for a commercial licence.

By 1949, after a series of mishaps and a broken partnership, Max decided to give up his airline dream and returned to Alberta to build houses. Within three years, he realized that his life without flight would be no life at all, and he applied to the ATB for a commercial charter licence. He was turned down the first time, but his persistence finally paid off, and Wardair was officially launched. He chose a deHavilland Otter as the company's first aircraft, and he flew gold miners and equipment into the northern territories. It was tough going for the little airline as every new plane it bought required that Max cut through the mass of red tape needed for government approval to fly commercially. Every new route it applied for was initially turned down. However, in that negative, restrictive government climate, Wardair beat the odds and survived. By 1961 Wardair was making a profit and Max changed the name to Wardair Canada Ltd. Within a year, Wardair had flown its first passenger charter from Calgary to Ottawa and its first international charter to Denmark. In 1966, Wardair took delivery of its first jet, a Boeing 727, the first one of its kind in Canada. It looked as if the little airline that Max had built finally had its wings.

Trouble followed hard on the heels of his first success. Back in the early days of charter flights, only groups or associations could charter an aircraft and the rules defining a group were very restrictive. Max tended to define his clients in the loosest sense of the word "association," and soon the Air Transport Board of Canada had expelled him for breaking the rules of charter flights. To add to his difficulties, the government set new, tougher guidelines for charter companies, called the "charter affinity rule." This made it even harder for private airline companies to compete with the newly renamed national carrier, Air Canada. Max Ward refused to give up. Lobbying Ottawa against its restrictive, unfair air transport policies, Max succeeded in having the affinity rule abolished. Max was invited back into Air Transport Association of Canada, given a lifetime membership, and named "Transport Man of the Year"!

In 1975, Max Ward was awarded the Order of Canada, and he was running Canada's third-largest airline! In 1978, after the United States deregulated their airline industry, Max went back to Ottawa to demand more freedom in the charter airlines business. He was successful and Wardair was finally given permission to fly domestic charters. He booked his first Advanced Booking Charter. Wardair International expanded aggressively, and its high-quality service earned it the title of "world's best charter airline." As the Canadian government began to consider deregulation, Wardair was granted its first scheduled route between Canada and the United Kingdom. Max had achieved the success he had strived so hard for, and his little airline entered the big leagues.

In 1988, deregulation in Canada went into effect; to meet the demands of the marketplace, Ward bought 12 Airbuses and 16 McDonnell-Douglas MD-88s. Wardair was not only recognized as one of the best in the world, but its aggressive, creative marketing placed the airline in a favourable position against the two big carriers—Air Canada and Canadian International. In the real world however, Jack seldom beats the giant, and so it was with Wardair. Max Ward had not invested wisely in computer reservation systems, and he had overextended the company in purchasing new equipment. Unable to compete effectively with Canada's two major carriers, Max sold his beloved company to Pacific Western Airlines Corporation, and Wardair merged with Canadian Airlines International.

Max Ward is one of tourism's most beloved pioneers: he created a fine airline, he fought continually to reduce government red tape and overregulation, and, in the end, rather than see his employees out of work, he made the hard decision to sell his company before its competition, Air Canada, bankrupted it. "I don't think he would consider himself totally a success in business; he didn't beat them," his son Blake once said. Those of us who have known Max see him for what he was—a giant in the Canadian airline industry, a fighter who never quit, a man who stood for excellence in service and helped create the Canadian air system as it exists today.

Automobile and Recreational Vehicle Travel

Transportation's transition from horse-drawn carriages to private automobile changed domestic travel habits and abilities more than any other factor in tourism, giving families more freedom of movement. No longer were people tied to rail and coach schedules. Before the automobile, travel patterns were very predictable, and resorts and hotels were built along rail lines and in ports. The automobile introduced a more random, unstructured pattern of travel movements. Motor hotels, motels, and attractions sprang up along the highways and enjoyed success.

The automobile will continue to be a popular mode of travel as long as its benefits continue. People travel by car rather than public transportation for the following reasons:

1. low cost, especially for three or more people
2. convenience
3. flexibility in departure and arrival times, route, and stops
4. enhanced trip experience
5. easier luggage transport with less restriction
6. assured transportation on arrival at the destination
7. opportunity for a relaxing and private atmosphere different from everyday business

Recreational vehicle (RV) travel has all the advantages of the automobile plus the convenience of carrying one's home along on the trip. RV travel eliminates the hassles and the expense of hotels and restaurants. The traveller can experience the great outdoors without really leaving the comforts of modern-day life, thus enjoying the best of both worlds.

Trends in Auto and RV Travel

Automobile travel in North America has the highest share of all domestic travel and this share continues to rise. However, it would be incomplete to discuss private automobile and RV travel without discussing family vacation trends. The family vacation market accounts for about 80 percent of all vacation travel in both the United States and Canada.

According to the American Automobile Association (AAA), family travel destinations are closer to home and shorter than other vacations. The weekend mini-vacation is popular and growing, even though the weeklong vacation is still the cornerstone of the auto travel market. Families are being drawn to camping, educational excursions, and theme parks as well as adventure trips like white-water rafting and ecotourism trips. The back-to-basics theme has increased travel to rural areas and communities. It has drawn the traveller off the beaten track to lesser-known areas. Scenic byways have become popular transportation routes for family travellers and have increased tourism dollars in rural communities. This trend holds true for Canadians as well.

According to the Recreation Vehicle Industry Association (RVIA), 10 percent of all families who own a vehicle own either a motorized or a towable recreation vehicle. RVs are categorized by RVIA as travel trailers, motor homes, tent/fold-down camping trailers, truck/slide-in campers, and van/multi-use vehicles. RV ownership is expected to continue surging in the twenty-first century because of the aging of baby boomers. The prime RV-buying years are ages 45 to 54, and this age segment will nearly double in the next 15 years.

The growth in RV ownership and travel is directly related to the growth in private campgrounds, RV franchise parks, and RV caravan companies. A private-membership RV campground requires an initial fee to join plus annual fees, which entitle the member to visit numerous locations and enjoy the amenities and security of the campground. It is a way to guarantee a highly desired camping spot during the prime camping months of the year.

The Car Rental Industry

The car rental business can be traced back to the early twentieth century. Recognizing that not everyone could afford a car but might need one for a day or two, some wise entrepreneur decided to offer them for rent. Hertz started renting his cars in 1918 and his company is now the largest and the oldest car rental agency in the world. Tilden, Canada's largest car rental firm, began operation just six years later, in 1924. It has been purchased by National Car Rental, a company with whom they have been affiliated for some time. Car rental agencies did not see a real boom in the business until the age of jet travel. Expansion was rapid once business travellers found that although the airplane could bring them long distances in a short period of time, they needed a car at their destination. Warren E. Avis, recognizing a business opportunity, conveniently established his car rental business at airport locations. However, while Avis does try harder, it has never been able to overtake Hertz, the leader in the business.

Business travellers still make up the greatest percentage of renters, but in recent years the leisure market has expanded dramatically. Combining a car rental with another mode of transportation provides a leisure traveller with the freedom to get around at the destination, a convenience that is becoming increasingly more popular. The fly/drive packages are good examples of how the industry has learned to package products.

There are more than 5000 car rental locations across North America. The top four rental agencies in North America are Hertz, Avis, National, and Budget. In Canada, Tilden/National has approximately 365 locations.

Car rental agencies also have in-town and suburb locations, even though 75 percent to 80 percent of all car rental business takes place at airports. Rental prices change depending on the agency's location. Car rental agencies pay more to lease counter and parking spaces at airports, so a driver will pay more for a car rented at an airport location than for one rented from the same company in town. Some car rental agencies avoid the high price of the airport location by providing a free shuttle bus service to an off-airport location. The extra time spent by the traveller to get to the location is offset by reduced rental rates.

Car Rental Business Dynamics The car rental business is highly competitive. Like airlines, car rental companies do not have a fixed capacity. When the demand is high in one location, it is just a matter of moving the fleet to the high-demand area. Car rental companies can change fleet size, structure, and price on demand, allowing them to react quickly to competition.

The car rental business is dynamic. Managers must have an understanding of economic conditions and tendencies nationwide. When gas prices increase sharply, consumers want to rent compact cars, which have a record of excellent fuel consumption, whereas a fleet of standard or deluxe cars will remain idle. If the manager has anticipated fuel price fluctuations, the fleet will resemble a compact-car factory lot. New additions to a car rental company's fleet often mirror new styles of automobiles that have gained popularity because customers often feel more comfortable driving a vehicle similar to their own. So for example, most rental businesses now have vans and SUVs available.

An interesting component of the car rental business is the used-car selling business. Most car rental companies sell a car, either directly to a consumer or to a used car dealership, after it has been driven 28 000 km to 40 000 km to avoid the cost of major car repairs and the risk of breakdowns. Thus, one major factor in purchasing cars for a fleet is the type of car people will want to buy 18 months later.

To the possible annoyance of customers, car rental companies glean their revenues from a variety of sources, including the rental fee and add-on charges that the rental agent either tries to convince the consumer to purchase or simply adds onto the base rental price. Add-ons include insurance, gas, drop-off, and lost-key charges. Insurance covers collision damage waiver and personal accident. When renting a car, customers should be aware of the personal insurance they carry on rented vehicles. A gas charge is added if the car is dropped off with less than a full tank. The rental car company fills the tank at a premium price, which may exceed the going rate of gasoline by 50 percent. If the vehicle is dropped off at a location other than where the driver picked it up, substantial drop-off charges are assessed. Lost-key charges are obvious.

Although these extra fees may be irksome to consumers, they do represent costs incurred by the car rental business. One reason add-on fees are itemized apart from the standard rental fee is so companies can advertise more competitive prices. To remain competitive with larger firms, small agencies may not charge some of these fees.

Marketing Strategies   Marketing strategies in the car rental business are coveted information. Because demand can change so quickly, most companies are not willing to provide information on fleet size, structure, or marketing ideas. However, basic product, price, and location strategies are visible to everyone.

The product varies from company to company. Even though each company offers a variety of cars, one type may predominate. Some companies offer vehicles with wheelchair lifts and special seating for customers with disabilities. In mountain regions rental cars are more likely to be four-wheel drive vehicles with ski racks. Some companies rent recreational vehicles. Cars may be equipped with car phones for the business traveller or restaurant and attraction coupons for the leisure traveller. The type of vehicle and any extras offered depend on the market position the car rental company desires. Some rental companies will pick clients up at their home or business, and "Frequent Renters Programs" are often a part of a company's marketing strategy.

Another marketing strategy is the fly-and-drive vacation package. This combination of airline travel and car rental is negotiated with airlines and tour operators but sold through travel agents. It usually involves a substantial savings in transportation costs and may include entry fees and discount coupons. Both the cruise lines and railroads offer rail-drive and cruise/rent-a-car packages, taking advantage of a tourist's desire to extend their trip by car.

The price factor in car rental has been creative and very competitive. A program called **unlimited kilometres** allows the traveller to drive as many kilometres as desired for a flat fee. Even though the major car rental companies began this program, they are now trying to ease themselves out of it because of the substantial difference it makes in revenues. Many smaller companies continue the strategy to remain competitive. A **kilometre cap** allows a certain number of kilometres for a flat fee each day, imposing an additional charge for every kilometre put on the vehicle over the cap. **Corporate rates** are reduced rates given to companies with a high rental volume. In addition to the corporate rate, some rental companies have separate check-in areas for their corporate customers. The major car companies have frequent-driver programs similar to airlines' frequent-flier programs to encourage consumers to stay with the same company each time they rent a car.

Location is a major factor in the car rental business. Airport or nearby locations with free shuttle service to and from the airport are coveted. The ease and speed with which a business traveller can get off a plane and into a rented car weigh heavily in selecting a car rental company. As nearly 80 percent of the car rental business is from airport locations, the marketing strategy of car rental companies is to be located in or near the airport.

Recreational Vehicles in Action

With so many North Americans enjoying the luxury of home-away-from-home travel, modern recreational vehicles have emerged to capture this market. Companies selling RV tours, rallies, and caravans have created new ways to enjoy an RV.

Most RV tours balance organized movement of a group of RVs from point A to point B with flexibility, so that the individual RV traveller can enjoy a family vacation without feeling it is a military exercise. Everyone meets at point A (a campground). Directions for where to go are provided, with dinners and evening entertainment furnished for part of the trip. Attraction and event tickets are included in the overall tour price.

RV tour and rally companies are successful because they allow travellers to meet each other in a semischeduled atmosphere. Lasting friendships are made and new areas of the country are explored. The company takes care of the logistics of the vacation so the RV traveller can simply follow the road and enjoy the countryside. Once at a campground, the RV customer is treated royally, with hassle-free camping arrangements, a chartered bus trip to the evening's entertainment, and a guaranteed comfortable bed for the night. An RV rally or caravan is one method of getting the type of pampering most people want. The following excerpt from a brochure gives an idea of what RV tours can be like.

> Woodall's World of Travel will conduct a Nova Scotia RV tour starting July 12th in Canaan, Maine, and ending July 25th in the unforgettable splendor of Cape Breton Island. Along the route the Woodall's World of Travel RV families will come to understand why Nova Scotia has been charming visitors with scenery, history, hospitality and a unique way of life for more than 100 years. The tour will begin with an evening hog roast "welcome dinner" followed by an orientation meeting in which the tour leaders will go over in detail the day-to-day activities of the 14-day RV vacation.

In the brochure describing the trip, each stop along the way is enticingly detailed. The cost includes all camping fees, welcome dinner, bus tour of Saint John, bus tour of Prince Edward Island, dinner at The Bonnie Brae, tour of Halifax, lunch at the Citadel, tour of the Fortress of Louisbourg, lunch at the Hotel de la Marine, bus tour of the Cabot Trail, lunch at Cheticamp, farewell dinner, identification badges, itinerary booklet, daily hospitality refreshments, and the services of the Woodall wagon masters throughout the tour.

Rail

History of the Train in Canada

"All aboard" rings out along the station departure area. For the baby boomers (as well as other folk), those two words invoke the romantic thrill of travel by train. In 1836, when Canada's first train roared over the tracks between Laprairie and Jean sur Richelieu at a breathtaking 20 km per hour, a love affair began between Canadians and the train. Not only was the new form of transportation fast (a trip of 23 km could be made in just 43 minutes) it soon became the most convenient form of transportation for Canadian travellers. Quick to follow was the first Maritime railroad, connecting the coal mines of Nova Scotia to Pictou Harbour. By 1856, all the major centres in Upper and Lower Canada were connected by this mighty new mode of transportation. The *Dorchester*, the earliest of Canadian-built locomotives, soon steamed its way from Montreal to Toronto and on to Guelph and Windsor.

As the United States promoted settlement of its western territories with the offer of free land, British politicians worried about maintaining control over their North American colony. With the addition of Manitoba and British Columbia, construction of the Canadian Pacific Railway from Montreal to Vancouver finally began. The line was completed in November of 1885, with the last spike driven into the ground at Craigellachie, British Columbia. Canada was united from sea to sea! In June of 1886, the first transcontinental train, called the *Pacific Express*, left Montreal and arrived in Port Moody, just east of Vancouver, a short six days later. Canada had moved into the golden age of rail.

Over the next 20 years, many small entrepreneurial railroad companies emerged, and their trains reflected a life that was full of all the modern conveniences of the day. They had electric lighting, washroom facilities, fine dining rooms, and comfortable sleeping cars. With the large numbers of immigrants flooding the west, rail companies prospered. Trains not only linked the Canadian provinces, but also extended their services into the United States. Two of the more famous international routes were the *Allouette* (Montreal to Boston) and the *Maple Leaf* (Toronto to New York). Because this method of travel was safe, efficient, and comfortable, it continued to be the major form of land travel until the 1930s.[8]

The first glimpse of trouble for Canadian railroads emerged as the immigration and settlement of Canada slowed during the first Great War of 1914–1918. By 1923 many of the smaller railroads were financially unable to continue operations, so their companies were united under the government-owned Canadian National Railways, providing direct competition for Canadian Pacific Railway. The Great Depression of the early 1930s caused massive financial ruin for many, and the railway suffered along with the rest of North America. There was a brief resurgence of popularity for rail transportation during the war efforts of the 1940s, but the golden age of rail was over.

In 1976, the Canadian government reviewed the future of rail transportation. It concluded that Canada could not support two passenger railroad companies and called for the merging of the passenger services of Canadian National Railways and Canadian Pacific Railway. This new Crown corporation, **VIA Rail Canada**, was to be responsible for all passenger traffic. For a period of time, there were few changes to the system, but in 1981 a VIA Rail downsizing took place, eliminating 20 percent of Canada's rail system. Gone was the *Super Continental*, the train that travelled from Montreal to Vancouver via Edmonton/Jasper. Only one transcontinental train remained, *The Canadian*, whose route passed through Calgary/Banff as it headed to Vancouver. Since 1990, however, *The Canadian* has operated on the CN route through Edmonton/Jasper.

Three factors contributed to the decline in rail travel. First, the automobile provided freedom of travel in terms of time and place. As more people came to own cars, the need to travel by train diminished. Second, the convenience and speed of airline travel, its relatively low cost, and the easy connections between cities made flying a desirable way to travel long distances. Finally, the cost of maintenance, equipment, and labour was high compared with other types of surface travel. Moreover, freight travel was competing with interprovincial trucking.

In 1985, when the *Freedom to Move* paper was published, a close look at transportation in Canada was taken and recommendations regarding the future of these systems were given to the government. Based on this paper's recommendations, the revised National Transportation Act was passed in 1986. In this legislation lay the seeds of demise for the Canadian railroad system. In 1990, a second massive downsizing of the passenger rail service occurred, reducing service by 50 percent, cutting the number of passenger trains in Canada from 810 to 396, and leaving only 20 of 38 routes in operation. *The Canadian* was cut to three scheduled departures a week. VIA kept the northern route through the Rockies using the Edmonton, Jasper, and Prince Rupert route and abandoned the southern route through Calgary and Banff.

Seizing the opportunity, a team led by former motor coach operator Peter Armstrong established a luxury rail company, Rocky Mountaineer Railtours. Leaving Vancouver with an overnight stay in Kamloops, B.C., passengers experience the best of the Rockies during daylight hours in complete luxury. During the winter, guests enjoy the glittering beauty of Rockies' snowfalls and can participate in a variety of winter sports on their arrival in Banff. In 2002, the Rocky Mountaineer welcomed its 500 000th passenger.

The Acadian Railway company is Canada's newest network of international railway tours and provides guests with luxury train travel in the eastern regions of Canada and the United States. Your trip may begin in New York City, Boston, or Montreal and carry you through the pristine wilderness to Moosehead Lake, New Brunswick, or along the shores of Nova Scotia through historic towns like Peggy's Cove. Tours vary from season to season and focus on the beauty and history of our eastern provinces and of the northern U.S. states.

Train lovers lost one of Canada's most historic trains in the spring of 2002. *The Royal Hudson*, whose route carried passengers along the coast of British Columbia between Squamish and Vancouver, was one of our last working steam trains and a special era of train travel in B.C. came to a close.

Over the past few years, VIA Rail service has focused on the Quebec/ Montreal/Toronto/Windsor corridor. Newer trains travelling this route are called **LRC (light, rapid, comfortable)**. Both VIA 1 Service and economy service are provided on these trains, giving a choice of service level and price. Over the past several years, there has been discussion regarding the addition of a **high-speed transportation (HST) system** or a train similar to the Maglev. The Maglev uses a magnetic levitation system and can travel at 250 km per hour. At that speed, the Ottawa/Toronto trip would take just over two hours! The problem is twofold: these new fast trains usually need special track, creating a prohibitive cost for VIA; and cold Canadian winters, combined with hot summers, cause these rails to buckle and break. A fast train, designed to use the old style rail, is on the drawing board in Europe.

Many business travellers do choose the train over the plane. Here is the reason: The train from Ottawa to Toronto takes four hours. Passengers arrive at Union Station, right in the heart of the city. Seats on the train are comfortable, meals are available, and there is time to get some work done. Weather has little effect on the trip or the arrival time. At first glance, a four-hour train ride seems long compared to a one-hour flight. However, check-in at the Ottawa airport is now one hour prior to departure, and arriving at a destination in downtown Toronto will take an additional 60 minutes. That two-and-a-half hours of travel time easily increases with traffic or weather delays. The price of the trip by train has no surcharges and is competitive with the cost of air. With the new, faster locomotives coming on line, it seems that the train may be a good option after all!

In 2000, the transport minister persuaded the federal government to inject $400 million over the next five years to rebuild, refurbish, and renew VIA Rail. By the end of 2003 VIA expects to have 139 plush new cars and 21 new locomotives. Seasonal rail travel has risen dramatically, and after the September 11 attack, the train experienced a 63 percent gain in ridership. Unlike its American counterpart, Amtrak, Via Rail has been relatively free of fatal accidents. Although the number of passengers has declined over the past year as faith in the air system is renewed, many travellers still view the train as a safer method of transportation.

Marketing Strategies

It's being awed by mountains towering above the train's glass dome. It's suburban gardens and the glow of the approaching city lighting up the sky. It's fishing shacks and a shoreline so close you could throw out a line. Or feeling you could lean out and touch the passing maple trees.

This is not 35 000 feet. It's not highway hassles. It's huge windows, wide seats and walk-about aisles. It's quick snacks and fine dining. It's unwinding over a drink on your way home between cities. Or curling up in bed, in your own cozy cabin.

And all the while, up close, the world moves silently by. Just as you, spellbound at the window, move just as surely towards your own destination across VIA's vast network.[9]

This excerpt is taken from a VIA Rail advertisement. In an attempt to convince travellers that the train is "the way to travel," VIA Rail's brochures show glossy photographs of families and businesspeople enjoying scenery, food, and comfort in a relaxed atmosphere. Comfortable accommodations, excellent service, and planned vacation packages can all be part of a railroad's marketing strategy.

VIA Rail's The Canadian *provides tourists with a spectacular transcontinental ride from Vancouver, through the Rockies, across the prairies, and around the tip of Lake Superior to Toronto.*
(Photo courtesy Canadian Tourism Commission.)

VIA Rail Accommodations   Each standard coach design found on VIA Rail trains has up to 76 reclining, turn-around seats fitted with adjustable footrests, overhead luggage racks, and tables. There are washroom facilities located in each car. VIA's *The Canadian* offers dome cars that feature skylights for better viewing, dining cars with table service and gourmet meals, and four types of sleeping accommodations: double berths, single bedrooms, double bedrooms, and drawing rooms. Double berths have both upper and lower berths, and privacy is obtained by simply pulling a curtain around the bed. Washroom facilities are found at the end of the car. Single bedrooms or roomettes accommodate a single passenger and contain a fixed seat, private toilet, and folding bed. Double bedrooms sleep two and have a variety of seating and sleeping layouts. Two bedrooms can easily be combined to sleep a family of four by removing the partition between them. Each room has its own set of controls for air conditioning and lighting, and can be adapted in the day to a private living space with large, comfortable armchairs that swivel to face a picture window. Drawing rooms are approximately 25 percent larger than the bedroom layout and can sleep three passengers. Bedrooms and drawings rooms are provided with the appropriate amenities and have private bathroom facilities. Not all trains have these sleeping configurations available, and surcharges are added to the larger bedroom/living quarters.[10]

Railroads are constantly trying new ideas to increase ridership. One such strategy is the auto/train option for people who want to have their cars at the destination. As on a ferry, the car moves onto a car carrier and rides the train. Between Washington, D.C., and central Florida, the auto train allows travellers to sit back and enjoy the scenery in the comfort of the train, yet have their own cars at the destination to use for further sightseeing.

The passenger railroad system has a unique challenge. Rather than just providing a means of getting from point A to point B, it is required to be a restaurant, a motel, and an entertainment centre. Unlike the airlines, rail travel becomes part of the vacation experience. In some instances, it may *be* the vacation. Therefore, the challenge is to provide quality accommodations, food, entertainment, and travel—a major feat for any company.

VIA Rail Service and Fares For a passenger travelling VIA 1 Service in the Quebec City/Windsor corridor, the fare includes the following:

- special check-in lounges and priority boarding
- complimentary magazines and newspapers
- hot meals with complimentary alcoholic and nonalcoholic beverages
- spacious, comfortable seats, reserved in advance
- complete nonsmoking cars
- a high standard of personal service

VIA fares have always been competitive with other forms of transportation. Here is a summary of the discounted fares offered:[11]

- the **Canrailpass**, which allows unlimited travel on VIA trains over specific travel periods (unlike the Eurailpass, this pass can be bought in Canada for domestic travel)
- 40 percent savings for space booked at least five days in advance
- discounted student fare with an International Student Identity Card
- special discount passes, such as the Commuter Pass, Corridorpass, and BizPak
- discounts for children between the ages of 2 and 17
- free travel for children under two years of age not occupying a separate seat
- seniors' discounts
- corporate fares
- special rates for groups of 20 or more on most VIA services

Foreign Railways

Although travel by train in North America has declined, in Europe it is one of the most widely used modes of travel. Here are some of the reasons travel by rail is so popular:

1. Rails crisscross most of Europe. As each country built their own railroad, they also connected their system to the neighbouring country's. This network of railroads is now called the International Inter-City Network.

2. Train terminals are conveniently located in the heart of the city.

3. Although many Europeans own cars, the cost of gasoline has made driving an expensive way to travel. Canadians, on the other hand, have difficulty moving at all without their cars!

4. The proximity of one country to another and the short distances between major towns and capitals make travel by train an efficient way to move from one destination to another.

5. Air travel in Europe is not only expensive, but also the weather often causes long delays.

6. Trains in Europe are noted for their on-time arrivals and departures.

7. Many railroads are still owned and operated by European governments.

8. European countries cooperate by marketing their trains as one rail system.

The **Eurailpass**, a good example of this marketing strategy, provides unlimited first-class travel in 17 countries. It is also valid on some ferries and intercity bus routes. The pass has a variety of validity periods ranging from 15 days to three months. It is very affordable and is sold only to non-European travellers. Note: Great Britain does not participate in the European network but offers a similar discounted fare for the British Isles—the **BritRail pass**.

Many tourists travelling in Europe feel that the train is the only way to go. It is a relaxing, comfortable travel experience that allows the tourist to fully enjoy the scenery while mingling with local residents. With the completion of the Chunnel, England was linked by rail to the rest of Europe. Travelling below the surface for almost 50 km, tourists now make the trip from London to Paris in a short time and without having to deal with seasickness! Many critics have noted the tunnel's outrageous cost, and some would prefer that the link had never been finished, but for the tourist it provides a convenient, fast, comfortable ride by train.

Trains of the World

Japan, on the leading edge of train technology, has the most advanced rail system in the world. The Japanese created the high-speed train and built the first **bullet train** in 1964. This train, known as the ***Shinkansen***, connects major Japanese cities at speeds of 200 km per hour. Their new Maglev promises to reach speeds of 480 km per hour and could revolutionize travel by train around the world.

The Russians have boasted the longest train ride in the world. The *Siberian Express* travels from Moscow to Mongolia during a leisurely 19-day trip. The *Blue Train* of South Africa provides a luxurious trip from Cape Town to Pretoria. The *Royal Scotsman*, staffed by servers in kilts, gives tourists a slow, comfortable trip through the Scottish Highlands in the true elegance of days long past.

But the true grande dame of the rails is the famous ***Orient Express***. In 1833, the *Orient Express* began service from Paris to Istanbul, carrying queens and kings, political leaders, the very rich, and the very powerful. The route was spectacular and the service fit for royalty. The train was also the focal point for many famous stories, including Agatha Christie's *Murder on the Orient Express*. Fame, in the end, could not save it. In 1977, tired, worn, and forgotten, the *Orient Express* made its last run. But one of the values of the tourism industry is its vision, which often leads to the restoration and renewal of disappearing cultures and history. Five years later, under the direction of James Sherwood, founder of Orient-Express Hotels, many 1920 vintage railcars were restored to their original splendour and a shorter version of the *Orient Express* was inaugurated. The Venice–Simplon Orient Express tour travels from Paris to Venice, passing through some of the most spectacular scenery in Europe. This tour has allowed many tourists a chance to travel back in time and ride the magnificent *Orient Express*. Sherwood has since added several luxury vintage train excursions in Asia and Australia, as well as a luxury train in the Andes mountains to complement his three new Peruvian luxury hotels.[12]

People ride trains for a variety of reasons including safety, comfort, cost, and the opportunity to view scenery en route. People fly mostly for the speed and the ability to reach an overseas destination.

in practice   Knowing why people travel by train and why they do not, what methods could VIA Rail use to increase ridership? In light of the aging of the population of North America, what future do you see for train travel? Why?

The Motor Coach Industry

Travel by bus has long been an alternate method of transportation for tourists when travel by car was not readily accessible. Buses are an important part our lives, beginning when we step onto our first yellow school bus. Buses provide transportation for class trips or to various sporting events. For those of us without cars, they transport us not only around our city and region, but between city centres as well. Most tourists are comfortable using a bus, but, surprisingly, people often have a negative perception of bus services. They believe that travel by bus necessarily means riding in an old, uncomfortable, dirty vehicle. These images could not be further from the truth. The new tour bus design includes more comfort, with a larger, reclining seat, footrests, and more leg space. Wraparound windows now provide a full view to passengers. Services on the bus include overhead storage bins, modern washroom facilities, video monitors, and CD/cassette stereo systems. Some executive coaches provide refrigerators, microwaves, and lounges with sofa-style seating. Experts predict that travel by bus will be an increasingly popular mode of transportation for the baby boomers as they retire.

In 1949, scheduled inter-city bus service peaked at 208 million passenger-kilometres. By 1996, a steady decline had reduced that number to just 18 million passenger-kilometres. The Canadian bus industry is still regulated in terms of entry and exit requirements, but both federal and provincial governments have indicated that they intend to deregulate it. As with many other tourism businesses, consolidation of the industry is inevitable. There will be fewer family-owned and operated bus operations. Today the key players in Canada's bus industry are Coach USA, which operates in 25 states and two Canadian provinces, Greyhound, Laidlaw, Brewsters, and Trailways. Most of these larger companies are focusing on the lucrative tour market rather than on scheduled, inter-city services.

The Advantages of Motor Coach Travel

There are many reasons a person chooses to travel by bus. As it is the least expensive of the travel modes (except for personal automobiles), cost is often cited as a prime factor. Scheduled inter-city bus service is particularly price sensitive. However, for small towns that have no infrastructure to handle rail and air, bus service is the only commercial transportation that links them to larger cities. If you choose to travel by car, the driver must concentrate on driving and may miss most of the sights along the route. In addition, the driver must know the route, have parking available at the destination, and, if moving from province to province, know how the traffic laws differ. Using the new hub and spoke concept, bus companies now book customers for several days in one hotel, which allows them to relax, unpack, and enjoy all the local sights and attractions. Fly/motor couch tours allow tourists to fly to their destination and then climb aboard a luxury bus for the ground portion of their tour. Buses are the most environmentally friendly and fuel-efficient forms of travel and, according to the Ontario Motor Coach Association (OMCA), the safest as well.

Charters versus Tours

A charter, whether it is using an aircraft, cruise ship, or bus, occurs when a pre-existing group secures the services of the transportation, usually at a reduced price. The group may be members of a particular club or organization, or may simply form through the common interest of travelling to a destination at a reduced cost. A bus tour, however, has very specific components. Depending on the duration of the tour and the level of service the operator wishes to provide, bus tours will contain one or more of these components: (a) transportation, (b) accommodations, (c) attractions, (d) sightseeing, (e) meals.

Categories of Tours

Tours using a bus are categorized as sightseeing/day tours, overnight/short tours, longer tours, and fly/coach. **Sightseeing/day tours** may be limited to an urban area such as Vancouver or they may be a day excursion to a special event or festival. For example, you might be travelling from Edmonton to see the Calgary Stampede, or from Ottawa to see the fall colours of the Gatineau Hills. The event may be a theatrical performance at the Shaw Festival in Niagara-on-the-Lake, or a sporting event, or the Symphony of Fire at Ontario Place. With day tours, the price of admission is usually included in the tour price. The second category is **overnight/short tours**. These tours will include accommodations. Tourists who must travel more than three hours to get to their destination are more likely to choose a short tour. Both day tours and overnight/short tours offer groups affordable short getaways, provide a restful drive to and from the destination, and eliminate parking problems. They may also provide the participant with a prepaid, guaranteed entrance to the site or activity.

The third category, longer tours, vary from three to thirty days and are usually referred to as **motor coach packages**. In this type of tour, a tour director accompanies the group to ensure that all goes well. Longer tours will include several major city destinations and may include some interesting off-the-track, local sights. Tours focus on a region: perhaps Calgary or Vancouver and Banff/Jasper

National Parks; Nova Scotia and Cape Breton; the wine region of Niagara; or a combined Ontario/Quebec visit with stops at Quebec City, Montreal, Ottawa, and Toronto. **Fly/coach tours** combine airfare with an escorted bus tour. This type of tour is essential when the visitor is travelling a long distance and it is particularly popular with Japanese tourists, who often fly into Vancouver, travel by motor coach through Banff and Jasper National Parks, and then fly out of Calgary. To complete the cycle, the tour company will then greet a second group in Calgary, reversing their trip and ending in Vancouver.

Grading Tour Packages

Tours in today's marketplace are graded as budget, moderate/first class, first class, and deluxe. The quality of the tour is based on several factors:

- quality of the accommodations—hotel grade, area of town, and proximity to restaurants and sights.
- attractions—the number and quality of sites and admissions covered in the price.
- meals (which may or may not be included in the price)—the type of restaurant and degree of menu choice. A set menu, ordered in advance, is less expensive as quantity and price are already agreed upon.
- the pace of the tour—How many kilometres are covered in a day? How many consecutive days does the group travel between stops?
- amenities: additional services and products offered.

In choosing a tour, travel agents and clients should carefully research the company and its past performance. The adage that you get what you pay for has particular meaning when booking a bus tour.

Tour buses are usually seen at attractions and are growing in popularity as a form of travel and entertainment.
(Photo: Norma Nickerson.)

Marketing Bus Tours

Marketing a bus tour is similar to marketing any other tourism product. Product, price, place, and promotion all play an important role. Niche or target marketing, however, is becoming increasingly important. The OMCA has identified several special markets. Focusing on education and learning experiences, the youth market provides an important and growing opportunity for tour bus operators. During the school year, school groups may travel to historic sites such as the forts of the Niagara peninsula to learn about history; they may visit a special museum to gain knowledge about a specific branch of science; or they may travel to participate in outdoor activities such as winter skiing. During the summer, exchange tours allow students to visit and learn about a new culture.

The seniors (55 and over) market has been a cornerstone for the bus industry in the past and it will continue to be a big market as boomers retire. How will seniors change the tour product? They are looking for a more active tour product, for soft adventure and learning activities that allow them hands-on experience. The boomers are more sophisticated, have a higher level of education and more disposable income, and demand good service. This will influence the choice of accommodations and food services included in a tour package. This market enjoys the companionship of a touring experience, likes a mix of ages, and prefers not to be called the "seniors market"! The needs of seniors must be met. They often retire and rise at an earlier hour. They like good lighting, large clear print, and a feeling of comfort and security. Romance is often renewed at the mature stage of life and, as long as their health and vitality lasts, seniors will be a strong market.

Finally, the growth of specialty markets over the past 10 years has been strong. Special-interest tours include theatre tours to Stratford, Ontario, attendance at special events such as the Stanley Cup Playoffs, and visits to the wineries in the Niagara Region.

No matter what type of tour a customer chooses, having a qualified tour director or escort is essential. Responsibilities may include paying all accounts during the trip; coordinating all activities, including handling of admissions and tickets for meals; keeping the tour on schedule; anticipating and solving problems; monitoring the activities of the bus driver and baggage handlers; being knowledgeable about the tour and the places it visits; and keeping the passengers happy, relaxed, and interested. If you love to travel and enjoy dealing with people, you might consider a career in the motor coach industry.[13]

in practice

Assume you want to start your own tour bus company in your hometown. To be successful, you will need to identify the potential markets in your region. List local clubs, groups, associations, businesses, and churches that might be interested in a group tour. How would you increase your likelihood of success? What marketing strategies would you use to gain business?

TRAVEL BY WATER

Cruise Industry

The History of Cruising

Although people have travelled by water from earliest times, it was not until the invention of the steam engine that travel for pleasure began. The first ocean crossing with tourists as the payload was in 1867, on a German ship called the *Quaker City*. These tourists travelled from New York City to the Holy Lands; on board was the celebrated author Mark Twain, who was to write about his trip later. Ships in those days carried passengers from one destination to another and were called ocean liners or passenger ships, not cruise ships. Ocean liners in the early 1900s focused their product on wealthy patrons who enjoyed travelling in high style and living in luxurious surroundings. However, hidden beneath the luxury on the lower decks was the real payload—immigrants trying to reach America to start a new life. This class of service was called "steerage," and conditions were squalid. In 1907, the Cunard Line developed and installed improved engines on their two newest ships—the *Mauritania* and the *Lusitania*. These ships still had the luxurious interiors but, more important, they provided passengers with a faster, smoother ride, reducing the time it took to cross the Atlantic from ten to four-and-a-half days. Not to be outdone, their rival, the White Star Line, launched its new boats in 1911 and 1912. The *Olympic* and the *Titanic* were slower than Cunard's ships, but what they lacked in speed they made up for in grandeur. The builders of the *Titanic* had provided the ship with new, innovative safety features and claimed that it was "practically unsinkable." Looking for a marketing edge, White Star eliminated the word "practically" and advertised the ship as "unsinkable." To prove their point, they did not provide enough life jackets or life boats to accommodate the passenger load. The rest is history. On April 14, 1912, the *Titanic* struck an iceberg, losing 1601 passengers and crew. It was the single worst disaster in the history of the industry. One of the passengers who died was the manager of Canadian Pacific's newest hotel, the Château Laurier, located in Ottawa; lost with him was the furniture that was being imported for the hotel. Despite the tragedy, ocean liners thrived until the end of the First World War.

In the early 1920s the industry was faced with its first big challenge. The U.S. government drastically reduced the number of immigrants it would accept and the industry lost half its revenue. To compensate, steerage class was converted into more comfortable cabins and called tourist class. They were sold at a reasonable price, targeting for the first time the middle-class American. During the prohibition years, when drinking alcohol in the United States was illegal, foreign ocean liners cashed in by providing a haven for Americans who opposed the legislation. Once in international waters, the bars opened and the "booze cruise" started.

With the outbreak of the Second World War, ocean travel became dangerous and many ocean liners were refitted as troop carriers. At the end of the war, tourism entered a boom era and so did the ocean liners' business. People wanted to experience foreign destinations; with increased disposable time and wages to spend, they flocked to the passenger ships.

In October 1958, the world of tourism changed forever. Pan American World Airways flew the first nonstop passenger jet flight from New York to Paris in just seven-and-a-half hours. In six months, ocean liners lost two-thirds of their business, and by 1960 they carried a mere 5 percent of the trans-Atlantic traffic. To survive, passenger lines were forced to redesign their product. Instead of Cunard's slogan "Getting there is half the fun," the slogan became "Being here is all the fun." Cruise lines had repositioned themselves as "resorts on water," not as a mode of travel. In 1971 the cruise lines carried half a million passengers. In 1998, they carried almost 5.9 million passengers and the industry is growing at a rate of more than 7 percent yearly. Estimated capacity utilization in 1998 was 91.6 percent, an amazing statistic for any tourism product. After September 11, 2001, the cruise lines saw a flurry of cancellations and a drop in bookings. Many passengers were afraid to fly to their departure point, unsure where and when the next attack might come. As these fears subside, reservations have returned to near-normal numbers.

An entirely new concept in cruising began in 2002 with the launching of *The World*. For sale, at $2.25 million – 7.5 million U.S., were 110 spacious, fully furnished luxury residences. With a full-time crew of 320, the ship combines the best of cruising, the comforts of a full-service resort, and the familiarity of home. Onboard facilities include a 2100-m Spa by Clinique of Paris, a jogging track and fitness centre, a full-size tennis court, two pools, a casino, eight different types of food and beverage service, and a "real grass" putting green! Although the condominiums are sold out, 88 smaller suites are available for rent. *The World* continuously navigates the globe and plans on stops for major events like the Cannes Film Festival, the 2004 Olympics, and the America's Cup.

The Cruise Line International Association (CLIA) announced in the late 1990s that between 1999 and 2004, more than 60 new ships would be launched. Some are mega-ships like Cunard's *Grand Princess*, which has 1300 staterooms and was built at a cost of $450 million. Others will be smaller ships, like those being built for the Crystal Cruise line, focusing on high-end travellers who wish a more intimate, luxurious setting. Some will be yacht-like, catering to more adventuresome travellers. Most will fall in between these categories. Surprisingly, only 6 percent of the North American population has taken a cruise, leaving an enormous untouched market available to the cruise lines.

The growth trends in cruises are a positive sign for the tourism industry. When cruise line passenger volumes increase, revenues increase for airlines, hotels, and restaurants. This positive correlation has encouraged cooperative arrangements between cruise lines and airlines, railways, resorts, and attractions.

In Canada the port of Vancouver has seen dramatic growth over the past 10 years. It is now ranked as one of the busiest ports in the world, serving more than 500 000 passengers a year. Most cruise companies are based in the United States, but an increasing demand for small-vessel cruising favours the Canadian cruise industry. Canadian cruise ships carry between 15 and 250 passengers on short trips ranging from 3 to 10 days. The Canadian cruising experience often focuses on historical sites, wilderness themes, or adventure and pampers the tourist with gourmet food and a professional, knowledgeable crew.

Industry experts predict that mergers and acquisitions will result in a few larger lines dominating the marketplace.

Cruise Types

The image of sailing on a large luxury liner like the *Love Boat* is only one aspect of the cruise line industry. Cruise lines are certainly the largest component of the industry, but smaller cruises on rivers, coastal areas, and lakes are also common.

Sea Cruises Sea cruises range from one-day "see nothing" trips to three-month around-the-world trips. One-day trips may cost as little as $70 per person, whereas a three-month world trip may cost more than $24 000 for two people. The typical sea cruise is three to seven days with stops at various ports.

A sea cruise is now promoted as a vacation in itself. The stops are an added luxury to an aboard-ship vacation of sun and relaxation, whether cruising in the Caribbean or Mediterranean, or viewing mountains and glaciers along the Alaskan and Canadian coasts. The ship is the entertainment centre, with swimming pools, onboard entertainers, 24-hour buffets, recreation centres, health spas, and themed special events.

Victoria is a favourite port of call on the Inside Passage cruise.
(Photo: John Kerr.)

The Caribbean and Mediterranean are the most popular warm-weather cruises. Other warm-weather destinations are Mexico and the Mexican Riviera, the Bahamas, Bermuda, San Juan, the Canary Islands, Morocco, and the Panama Canal. Other North American trips include cruises along the Pacific coast from Los Angeles to Vancouver or from Vancouver up to Skagway or Prince William Sound, Alaska. Like Alaska, northern Europe is popular for its scenery in and around Norway and Sweden.

The cruise lines have been very creative in marketing their product to new target groups. **Theme** and **special interest cruises** are gaining in popularity. The country-and-western cruise is an example. Top country-western singers are booked to perform nightly for the audience. The entire cruise offers a unique opportunity for fans to enjoy their favourite performers. Special-interest cruises fall into six distinct categories:

- recreation (e.g., sports, bridge, backgammon)
- culture (e.g., opera, theatre, music)
- education (e.g., history, religion, wildlife, financial planning)
- health (diet and exercise)
- hobbies (e.g., stamp collecting, gourmet cuisine, murder mystery)
- adventure (e.g., a trip up the Amazon, to the Galapagos, to Alaska)

The final type of sea cruise available to tourists is called the *repositioning* cruise. Ships that cruise the Alaskan routes or sail northern European waters have a limited season in their areas. As the weather grows colder and ice becomes a threat, these ships must change their home ports and destinations. For a tourist who loves to cruise, this trip offers an interesting set of ports, perhaps combined with an ocean crossing, often at a reduced cost.

River Cruises The river cruise, like the sea cruise, can be short or long. A short trip may be two to three hours, whereas longer river cruises last 12 days. The Delta

Queen Steamboat Co. carries passengers back in time to relive the past on the mighty Mississippi with its river gamblers and lush living. The *Delta Queen,* the *Grand American Queen,* and the *Mississippi Queen* are paddle-wheel ships designed to give the traveller a luxury cruise through history.

Many riverboats are used for company retreats, wedding receptions, and other group parties. One disadvantage for these companies is the seasonal aspect of the business. Many northern rivers freeze during winter months and, unlike a cruise ship that can head south to another season of tourist traffic, the riverboat must close down for the season.

In Canada, many rivers have short cruises available. The City of Winnipeg offers a variety of cruise options along both the Red River and the Assiniboine. The M.S. *Paddlewheel Queen* sails through the heart of the city offering an afternoon of sightseeing or an evening of dinner and dancing. Or you might choose the Splash Dash Water Bus cruise. These double-decker boats provide tourists and residents with a fun-filled 45-minute cruise along Winnipeg's two rivers. Finally, Winnipeg offers an exclusive luxury yacht for charter. The *Wendebee II* is a sailing yacht that will handle up to 32 people for cocktails and dining. Many large cities with navigable waterways close at hand offer similar cruise experiences. The St. Lawrence Seaway offers cruises that have gained worldwide recognition, such as the whale-watching cruise that departs from Tadoussac, Quebec, and sails up the Saguenay River. Finally, the Northwest Territories provides the tourist with a combination cruise/hiking vacation. Tourists cruise Great Slave Lake, live on board the M.S. *Norweta,* and explore the rugged terrain and wildlife habitat of this beautiful region.

Lake Cruises and Ferries   Lake cruises are common in some of the Great Lakes. Combined as a ferry and a cruise, the ship travels to a destination across the lake, then turns around for the return trip. Many vacationers take their vehicles across Lake Superior on these ferries to experience the cruising life, as well as to avoid the long journey around the lake, through Chicago. Ferries travel day or night across the lakes.

Ferries, which carry passengers and often their vehicles on board, are common around Seattle and New York, between Alaskan and Canadian islands and the mainlands, across the English Channel, and around other spots where people need to get across a body of water with their cars to work or play on the opposite shore. Ferries have managed to maintain ridership throughout the increased popularity of the plane and automobile because they go to areas where plane service is expensive or nonexistent and automobile access is limited or nonexistent. Ferries that travel short distances usually have informal seating and deck space. Long-distance ferries may have cabins, food service, and even recreation rooms.

Most ferry service in Canada is found along the coasts. On the east coast, ferry routes include Saint John, New Brunswick, to Digby, Nova Scotia; North Sydney, Nova Scotia, to Port aux Basques, Newfoundland; and Yarmouth, Nova Scotia, to Portland, Maine. In British Columbia, ferries connect Vancouver Island to the mainland and Victoria to Seattle. To go from Vancouver to Victoria, travellers can choose a large, comfortable catamaran. Aisles are wide, seats are comfortable, and no cars are allowed!

Freight Cruises   A small number of tourists can travel via freighter lines worldwide. Accommodations are similar to cruise lines, although there is little or no onboard

Tourists and B.C. residents may opt to use the high-speed catamaran that connects Victoria and Vancouver.
(Photo: John Kerr.)

entertainment. The advantage of going by freighter is the chance to see ports around the world that are never used by cruise ships, thus offering an authentic view of people and their customs. Freight cruises are for adventuresome travellers who do not need pampering and who like to view the world from a less touristic stance.

Freighters usually limit their passengers to 12 or fewer, because a doctor must be provided for a larger group. Because the passenger numbers are low, the chance of getting on a freighter is limited. Inquiries should be made well in advance to secure a spot on a freight cruiser. As more travellers look for adventure on their vacations, freight cruising may become more popular. The only limiting aspect is the length of time a traveller must set aside for the trip. Some freighters, however, are allowing passengers to disembark at destinations of their choice and then return by plane. New passengers embark where the others left, allowing more people to travel via freighter for shorter durations.

Charter Yachts, Sailboats, and Houseboats In the past, chartering a yacht, sailboat, or houseboat was considered an activity for the very rich. Now it is within the reach of people with middle incomes. Charters can be arranged for a few hours or an entire vacation. A charter can be rented with the sailor included, or to people experienced enough to sail the boat on their own. Many private owners are willing to charter their boats to keep up with maintenance costs. A new concept is the "yachtaminium," like the time-share concept of condominiums. The consumer purchases time on a yacht and can then trade for time on another yacht in another marina across the country. Houseboats provide family-style living on the water, a chance to get away from the hassles of travel while still enjoying a series of port calls.

Cruise Line Marketing Strategies

The cruise industry knows it has a great untapped market and is using a variety of strategies to win potential cruisers. The most successful strategy to date occurred when all North American cruise lines banded together to market cruising during February 1991, which they designated National Cruise Vacation Month. CLIA supported the campaign with a comprehensive media tour that crisscrossed the United States and Canada, allowing industry spokespersons the opportunity to talk about cruising on television and radio programs in more than 50 cities. CLIA-affiliated travel agencies were encouraged to transform their offices into cruise headquarters during February. The strategy generated so much awareness and new business that the cruise industry plans to repeat it.

Individual cruise line marketing strategies are trade secrets. Creative marketing is required to secure the return passenger and encourage new passengers. The following section discusses cruise line strategies based on the marketing concepts of product, price, place, and promotion.

Product   The product is the ship, the amenities and service on board, and the route. Each part of the product is provided with quality and service in mind. If the product is outdated, there is nothing that price, place, or promotion can do to keep customers coming. Each product segment is discussed in further detail.

A big sea cruise liner is physically laid out to accommodate a large number of passengers without feeling crowded. Each passenger has a cabin or stateroom for sleeping and relaxing. Cabins have berths or beds, which are either double, twin, or bunk bed arrangements. Larger cabins may accommodate up to four passengers, either families or the economically minded who want to share accommodations.

The rest of the ship is designed to entertain guests. It is the resort centre for the vacation. The cruise liner may be equipped with large multipurpose rooms for meetings, conferences, or dancing. Most ships have health spas, fully equipped gyms, swimming pools, and lessons available in anything from tennis to golf. The deck is laid out so that passengers can sunbathe next to the swimming pool, play board games in the sun, or simply lie back on a lounge chair and read a book. As the price of a cruise includes meals, food becomes a major source of entertainment. Elegant dining rooms serve a wide variety of North American and ethnic foods. Some dinners will have a theme, for example an Italian night, with fine Italian dishes and wines and perhaps strolling musicians. The walls that encircle the main dining room on Disney's new ship, the *Disney Magic*, are covered with animated figures that gradually come to colourful life as each course is served. Cruise ships have ventured beyond the more formal dining setting and are providing specialty restaurants like pizza and burger parlours, salad bars, and Italian bistros for customers wishing more casual dining. The midnight buffet and the captain's cocktail party are two of the favourite events. Food is available 24 hours a day and it is "free," so passengers can indulge in their favourite foods at no extra cost. Beverages, both alcoholic and nonalcoholic, are not included in the cost of a cruise and are an important method of increasing onboard revenues. These revenues help to keep the cost of a ticket low, and they can add up!

To maintain a high quality of service, cruises need a high ratio of crew to passengers. Labour costs are offset with the onboard revenues generated from a ship's casino, souvenir, clothing, and duty-free shops, and added services that help make the ship a total resort experience. These services usually include a spa facility, an exercise room with all the latest equipment, virtual reality centres, and special sports opportunities such as golfing and skeet shooting. Should a passenger get sick, a full medical staff with state-of-the-art equipment is available on board. Shore tours also add to the expense of a cruise and may cost upwards of $60–$100 U.S. A number of free activities often complement these services. For example, a seminar on how perfume is made encourages passengers to pick up a new scent at the duty-free shop; a seminar on care of the skin and face may encourage passengers to try the spa. Today ships have rock-climbing walls, ice-skating rinks, and in-line skating. As ships get taller and wider, the ability to provide customers with any trend-setting activity will become a reality. Imagine the opportunities for a ship designed for the conference and convention market.

The actual route and stops en route are also part of a key marketing strategy. As mentioned earlier, warm-weather cruises are the most popular. These cruises usually stop for several hours in one or more ports to allow passengers to shop and experience another culture.

In recent years, many cruise lines have added shorter trips to their schedules to provide cruising opportunities for people on fixed or lower incomes who otherwise would never get on board. The key to this strategy is obtaining repeat customers. Once people have taken a cruise, they are more likely to take another one of a longer duration. They have been bitten by the cruise bug, so to speak.

Price The price of a cruise varies according to cruise duration, season, ship age or profile, and cabin choice. Obviously, the longer the trip, the more it will cost. The season is an important factor in price. Most people want to get away from the cold north in the winter and bask in the warmth of a tropical climate. The peak season for the Caribbean is during the Northern Hemisphere's winter months, whereas the peak season for the Alaska trip is the summer months. Peak season correlates to peak prices.

The ship profile is a little confusing because the older ships, converted from point-to-point to cruise vessels, actually charge more than the newer ships and carry fewer passengers. The cabins of an older ship tend to be roomier, and other rooms also tend to be larger. "The space ratio for a ship can be calculated by comparing the gross registered tonnage (GRT) to the number of passengers carried. The GRT represents the amount of enclosed space on the ship."[14] The choice of cabin is a factor in the overall cruise price. Outside cabins with a view cost more than inside cabins. Cabins higher up in the ship are more expensive because they experience less ship movement. The price of single occupancy is considerably higher than two, three, or four people sharing a cabin.

Once the duration, season, ship, and cabin have been chosen, the price remains the same for the entire trip. Most cruises are popular because the passenger pays one price and receives the same amenities as everyone else on board. No one is treated with special attention because of a higher-priced ticket. There is a cruise that will satisfy even the most unusual interests or hobbies and a price that will suit any pocketbook!

Place In the world of marketing, *place* is channel of distribution, or where the product is sold. Cruise lines recognized that their channel of distribution was already in place—the travel agency network. Travel agents are trained by CLIA and the various cruise line companies to know the products available, identify the customer most likely to enjoy the facilities and amenities aboard the different ships, and effectively close the sale. For example, a family of four with young children might truly enjoy Carnival Cruises or the *Disney Magic*, but would probably be uncomfortable on a ship taking seniors for an ecotour along the Alaskan shore. Niche or target marketing will become even more important as the number of ships increases. Many travel agencies are beginning to specialize in cruise packages only. In recognizing the value of the travel agency and keeping the partnership alive and healthy, cruise lines will continue to prosper. Partnering is going to be the wave of the future for tourism success, and the airlines, rail companies, and rental cars have all begun to provide packages that meet all of the consumer's transportation needs. Cruise packages can include airfare to the departure point and a waiting rental car!

Promotion   Cruise line promotional activities are developed around product and price. Success in the cruise industry requires niche marketing, such as theme or business cruises. It also requires joint marketing efforts, like National Cruise Vacation Month, and creative strategies for selling to travel agents or directly to the consumer.

Because travel agents sell 95 percent of all cruise tickets, cruise lines depend heavily on travel agency loyalty and spend a great deal of their promotional efforts on a limited number of agencies that actively sell cruises. Other agencies are reached through direct mail, travel shows, and telemarketing.

Promotion directly to the consumer is usually through newspaper advertisements. Located in the travel section of most newspapers, cruise line ads emphasize price and relaxation but tell the consumer to talk to a local travel agent for further information. Some cruise lines have advertised extensively on television. For example, the Carnival Cruise Line is known for its "fun ship" slogan on television. Repeat Carnival ads have resulted in public awareness and the highest occupancy rate of any cruise line: full capacity on nearly every sail.

in practice   Are travel agents the best means of selling cruise vacations to the consumer? Why or why not? How is selling a cruise line ticket different from selling an airline ticket through a travel agent? In groups of four, try to design a new method of ticket selling for a cruise line.

Public Transportation

Public transportation is any organized passenger service available to the general public within a small geographic area. Visitors commonly use these transportation systems to see the city sights.

Most cities have some form of bus transit system, but the bright-red double-decker buses in London are a particularly popular choice among tourists. London and Edinburgh have special inexpensive and easy-to-use "tour" buses that carry passengers from one site to another with onboard guides who give a nonstop verbal description of the route. The service runs continually all day long and for the cost of a day pass, passengers make as many stops as they want. In the Philippines, visitors can ride the brightly decorated Jeepneys. The modern subway systems of

Sightseers enjoy a leisurely tour of Victoria in a horse-drawn carriage.
(Photo: John Kerr.)

Washington, D.C., and Paris have gained worldwide reputations for their user friendliness. If you are in San Francisco, the cable cars are a ride that cannot be missed. To travel between Victoria and Vancouver, you must use a ferry or an airplane! The list of public transportation methods is as varied as the number of cities a tourist visits. As a traveller, it is important to understand how an individual public transportation system works. For example, if you ride the GO Train in the Toronto region, you are responsible for validating your own ticket; if you fail to do so, you may be fined. In Tokyo, *white glove pushers* will literally push you on board the transit trains during rush hour. They are not being rude, simply doing their job by putting as many people on the train as possible.

Airports have a number of transportation options for the traveller: limousines, buses, and taxis. At Kennedy Airport in New York City, an alternative to the bus service is the "train to the plane." This special subway takes passengers on an express trip into the heart of the city, helping them avoid the heavy traffic delays on the expressways. Edmonton, Vancouver, and Calgary have light rail transit (LRT) systems that run on their own tracks, circumventing traffic. LRT systems are not only quick, but also environment friendly. Miami, Florida, opened its new monorail system in 1986, and passengers can now avoid traffic congestion by connecting across the city six metres above the ground! The world-renowned London cabbie makes a trip around the city a treat. But hold on, England, the cabbies of Halifax are ready for the challenge! They have all had special training developed by the Tourism Industry Association of Nova Scotia and other provincial TECs. Their knowledge of the city and their friendly, helpful attitude make a taxi ride in Halifax pure pleasure.

Information about the public transportation system in any destination city is available from many sources, but travel agents or a good guidebook on the city will provide you with the travel tips you need. Public transportation is usually the least expensive way to move around a town and provides the tourist with a bit of local colour that may otherwise be missed.

Selecting a Mode of Transportation

What causes a tourist to choose one mode of transportation over another? Here are the obvious reasons:

1. Cost, especially if more than one family member is travelling.
2. Time available for travel component. A business traveller will usually choose the fastest mode available to allow maximum time for business. For example, Mr. Jones has chosen to use the Concorde to return to Washington, D.C. His departure time from London, Heathrow is 11:30 a.m. and he arrives at Dulles Airport at 8:30 a.m., giving him a full day in the office. If a family living in Winnipeg has a week to visit friends and relatives in Red Deer, Alberta, the additional cost of airfare may outweigh time constraints.
3. The convenience of reaching the embarkation point, the check-in procedures, and parking availability. Is the bus station located in a safe part of town? Is there parking near the station? For this reason, long-term parking lots are often located near terminals.
4. Route structure. If a town is no longer serviced by the train, then the traveller must choose from other available modes. Passengers who once enjoyed the train must now choose between the bus or private vehicle.
5. Frequency of departures. Hourly flights from Ottawa to Toronto often make flying the better choice for a businessperson. Perhaps the train would have been an option, but it has only three departures daily.

In his research, Jagdish Sheth has found that psychological factors also influence the decision-making process: fears and prejudices formed during childhood will affect a person's choice of transportation. A child who grew up with a fear of water will not likely choose to travel by ship as an adult. Fear of flying may make travel so difficult as to impair a businessperson's ability to perform the job effectively. Stereotypes and perceptions are also difficult to overcome. For example, the motor coach industry has struggled for years with the "retiree" image.

Performance of a mode of transportation may influence a traveller's choice. Does it consistently depart/arrive on time? Does it provide for easy access? Are the service personnel friendly and professional? These factors create a positive or negative perception in clients' minds that may change their travel decisions. For example, it is common knowledge that the demand for air travel slows for a brief period after a major airline crash. Finally, our self-image and our desire for status may eliminate a method of travel that would otherwise serve us well. A person wishing to travel from Calgary to Vancouver may choose an airline over a bus, despite cost factors, simply because travel by air reinforces a personal image of success.

Transportation operators are aware of these many emotions, needs, and constraints, and their marketing programs address them in detail. To dispel the stereotype of retiree travelling, tour bus companies focus on the quality of their equipment, the ease of seeing the countryside without having to drive, and the friendliness and knowledge of their staff. Airlines promote fast, friendly, and safe travel, using images of qualified pilots and crew members and caring, concerned mechanics and ground personnel. In the end, the choice of how we travel is a very personal one. We use all of our experiences and knowledge to choose the mode best suited to our needs at a given time.

OPPORTUNITIES IN TRANSPORTATION

	AIR	RAIL	GROUND	WATER
OPERATION (FRONT LINE)	Flight Attendant Pilot (helicopter, plane) Customer Service Agent Sales and Service Agent—City Ticket Office Sales and Service Agent—Reservations Sales and Service Agent—Airport Sales and Service Agent—Cargo Cabin Services Attendant Aircraft Cleaner Sales Representative Clerk, Human Resources	Ticket Reservation Agent Customer Service Agent Onboard Services Attendant Seasonal Car Attendant Transfer Officer/Agent Traffic Agent Baggage Agent, Baggage Handler Step-On/Local City Guide Meet-and-Assist Guide Tour Production Coordinator Media Relations Coordinator Sales Representative	Rental Agent (car cr RV) Motor Coach Driver Service Station Attendant Ticket (Reservation) Agent Customer Service Agent In-Transit Attendant Taxi Cab Driver Transfer Officer/Agent Traffic Agent Baggage Agent, Baggage Handler Step-On/Local City Guide Meet-and-Assist Guide Sales Representative	Rental Agent (boat) Terminal Attendant (ferries) Ticket (Reservation) Agent Customer Service Agent Boat Charter Pilot Transfer Officer/Agent, Traffic Agent Baggage Agent, Baggage Handler Catering Attendant (ferries) Buffet Attendant (ferries) Steward (ferries) Step-On/Local City Guide Meet-and-Assist Guide Sales Representative
SUPERVISORY	**Customer Service Director/Purser** Station Attendant/Baggage Handler (Airport, Cargo, Ramp) Training Instructor/Developer	Purser/Dining Car Steward Sleeping Car Porter Onboard Customer Service Supervisor Market Research Supervisor Public Relations Supervisor Advertising Supervisor Training Representative	Road Supervisor Driver Guide/Step-On Guide Market Research Supervisor Public Relations Supervisor Advertising Supervisor Training Representative	Purser/Steward Head Steward & Night Steward (ferries) Bar Steward (ferries) Catering Supervisor (ferries) Deck Officer Market Research Supervisor PR Supervisor, Advertising Supervisor Training Representative
MANAGEMENT	Airport Service Supervisor—Passengers Airport Service Supervisor—Reservations Airport Service Supervisor—Cargo Airport Service Supervisor—Ramp Onboard Service Manager Cabin Services Manager Sales Manager Training Officer Human Resources/Training Manager Manager, Flight Attendants Reservations Manager Airport Manager Cargo Services Manager Operations Manager (airport) Terminal Control Manager Ramp Services Manager Cabin Services Manager	Conductor (Train, Sleeping Car) Operations Manager Public Relations Manager Human Resources Manager Reservations Manager Sales Manager Customer Service Director Regional Manager	Operations Manager Public Relations Manager Human Resources Manager Car/Rec Vehicle Rental Agency Manager Service Station Manager Motor Coach Director Sales Manager Tour Manager/Long Distance Guide Taxi Owner Motor Coach Company Owner/Operator Car/Rec Vehicle Rental Agency Owner/Operator	Recreation/Social Director (Passenger Ship) Operations Manager Public Relations Manager Human Resources Manager Pilot (ship) Chief Steward (ferries) Cook (chief cook, etc.—ferries) Product Development & Sales Manager Reservations Centre Manager Marketing & Public Relations Manager Charter Boat Owner Cruise Line Operator/Director
EXECUTIVE	Director Base Manager/Regional Manager Vice President Senior Vice President	Corporate Vice President	Corporate Vice President	Corporate Vice President

SOURCE: Courtesy of Canadian Tourism Human Resource Council, *The Student's Travel Map*, 1995.

JOB DESCRIPTION FOR . . .

CUSTOMER SERVICE DIRECTOR/PURSER

Industry Sector	Transportation
Division	Air, Rail, Ground, Water
Industry Setting	Airline companies, passenger rail companies, motor coach tour companies, ferry/cruise/tour boat companies and other tour/travel-related companies
Job Level	Supervisory
Description of Duties	Supervise activities of flight attendants and provide service to passengers during flight. In general, supervise attendants, arrange activities for passengers and conduct facility's business, such as signing on crew, maintaining payroll records, assisting passengers in preparing customs declarations, providing information about flight/route plans and schedules, and supervising baggage storage. Duties include attending to the comfort and safety of passengers aboard transportation facilities.
Working Conditions	Work in comfortable but sometimes cramped conditions and spend most of time during flight on feet. Serving meals can be strenuous and trying, especially during short or rough flights. Hours of work are irregular. In general, can expect to be away from home one third of the time. Only most-experienced attendants are permitted choice of base and flights.
Skills	Poised, tactful, and resourceful people who deal comfortably with the public in general and in emergency situations. Must be Canadian citizen or have landed immigrant status and pass medical examinations prior to hiring—excellent health and stamina are necessary. Well groomed with clear complexion, good teeth and body weight in proportion to height. May require minimum of 160 cm and/or a maximum of 186 cm height. Height specifications are set for safety reasons, not for physical attractiveness. Attendants must be tall enough to reach all safety equipment in the cabins. Vision requirements vary from 20/50 uncorrected to 20/30 corrected. Glasses and contact lenses are acceptable in most airlines. Must demonstrate willingness to relocate to any of airline's bases.
Knowledge	Fluency in English; knowledge of a second language is a definite asset. Good knowledge of travel/tourism-related geography and information, company policies and procedures.
Education	Grade 12 completion and certification for successful completion of a Department of Transport–approved company exam.
Industry Experience	Previous experience as flight attendant.
Career Paths	Training Representative, Human Resources Manager
HRDC Reference	NOC 6432 Pursers and Flight Attendants

summary

Trends and changes in the airline industry have increased the volume of traffic as well as the choice of destinations. Deregulation in the airline industry has opened the doors to more carriers, brought about a hub and spoke airport concept, and produced price wars and other marketing strategies beneficial to consumers. Deregulation left many medium-sized communities with very limited or no commercial air service. Since 9-11, travel by air has declined, putting even large airlines like United and Air Canada on the verge of bankruptcy.

The airline industry is divided into scheduled air carriers and charter air service.

Airfares for flights change daily. Computerized reservation systems allow airlines to respond immediately to a competitor's fare change. Discount tickets with restrictions have become a standard pricing technique to increase the load factor on the plane.

Airports are the backbone of the airline industry. NAVCAN now operates the air traffic system, and many larger airports are run by private companies. Airlines lease space from an airport to board and deboard passengers and park aircraft overnight.

The automobile and RV transportation segment represents the largest group of travellers. More kilometres are logged by private automobiles than by airlines. Family vacations by car account for 80 percent of all vacation travel in the United States. The trend is toward more minivacations for families with two working adults.

The car rental industry is volatile and competitive because of its ability to change fleet size and structure rapidly. Most major car rental agencies get a majority of their rental reservations through travel agents rather than walk-ins. Marketing strategies in the car rental industry include specialized vehicles, fly and drive programs, and pricing strategies such as unlimited kilometres for a flat fee.

Car rentals from airport locations make up nearly 80 percent of all the rental business, making location a prime concern in the industry.

The RV industry expects to see an intense growth period as baby boomers move into the prime RV-buying age bracket. RV caravans and rallies are becoming popular ways to spend prepackaged vacations with others.

Trains in North America have had their ups and downs in the history of ridership. Amtrak and VIA Rail are the result of a near-collapse of the railways in North America. These government-subsidized trains have slowly rebuilt the system by providing more comfortable seating and sleeping arrangements, convenient stops, speed, and package vacations at prices competitive with other means of transportation. Since 9-11, North American railroads have seen a growth in passenger revenues, as increased numbers of travellers are choosing the train over the plane.

The bus industry comprises scheduled bus service, charter service, and tour service. The bus system also uses a hub and spoke model. Convenience and price are often cited as reasons people travel by bus. Charter service is provided by bus companies that simply rent the bus and sometimes the driver to the interested group. The charter business is growing in segments like student, church, and social groups because it provides an opportunity for members of a club or organization to travel with friends and acquaintances with common interests. Motor coach packages are becoming more popular and will continue to grow as the baby-boom segment of the population ages.

The cruise line industry is the fastest-growing segment of the travel industry. Cruise lines were innovative in the 1960s and 1970s, switching to offering floating resorts after airlines took over the mass transportation market. Passenger numbers have increased 7 percent annually for the past few years and are expected to continue that rate of growth. The future looks promising for cruise lines as they band together to promote cruising as an alternative type of vacation. Theme cruises and business and convention cruises are the latest trends. Other methods of water transportation include ferries, lake cruises, freight liners, riverboats, and the chartering of yachts and sailboats. The love of water and the desire to see the countryside from a different perspective have transformed many communities into attractions. Casino riverboats on the Mississippi are the fastest-growing form of river transportation.

Public transportation is an important means of moving tourists from one site in a city to another. Many cities have their own system, providing the tourist with a unique cultural experience.

Choosing a mode of transportation is complicated by many factors, both practical and psychological. Time, cost, ease of access, route structure, and frequency are often the deciding factors. However, self-image and stereotypic views of transportation modes can complicate decision making. In the end, the method of travel chosen will often depend on the circumstances of the moment.

questions

1. Summarize briefly the impact of deregulation on Canada's transportation systems.

2. a) How does the role of IATA differ from the role of ICAO? Explain your answer.

   b) Why were the Freedoms of the Air developed and how do they affect Canada's air industry?

   c) What is the name of Canada's latest bilateral agreement regarding air travel, who is it with, and how has it affected our air transportation system?

   d) Why has Canada privatized its air transportation system. Who runs it? How has privatization affected airlines?

3. Three new aircraft were discussed in this chapter. Which one do you believe will have the greatest impact on future travel? Discuss your reasons.

4. Compare and contrast three advantages and three disadvantages of travel by automobile and travel by motor coach.

5. a) Using the four P's of the marketing mix discussed in chapter 3, discuss the following tourism products: (i) motor coaches, (ii) railways, and (iii) cruise lines.

   b) What is the greatest challenge faced by each of these tourism products? Explain how you, as a marketing consultant, might deal with each challenge.

6. Compare and contrast the following terms as they relate to the transportation sector (use examples where possible): *direct/nonstop flight; online/interline connection; scheduled/charter trip; open-jaw trip/circle trip; theme/special interest cruise; day/overnight tour.*

weblinks

www.aircanada.ca

Air Canada is Canada's largest and, now, principal airline, providing both domestic and international routes.

www.viarail.ca

VIA Rail runs passenger trains, particularly in Ontario and Quebec but right across the country.

www.omca.com

The Ontario Motor Coach Association represents Ontario's inter-city bus industry.

www.greyhound.ca

Greyhound Bus Lines has a presence throughout both Canada and the United States.

www.iata.org

The International Air Transport Association or IATA (p. 97), regulates international air travel and airlines.

www.cruising.org

Cruise Line International Association's latest information on new ships and cruising.

www.avis.com

Avis is one of the largest car-rental agencies and allows guests to make bookings online.

notes

1. Canadian Tourism Human Resource Council, *The Workforce Series,* 1998.
2. ctx_news@ctc-cct.ca Friday April 4, 2003.
3. cctx_news @ctc-cct.ca Wednesday April 2, 2003.
4. J. Christopher Holloway, *The Business of Tourism,* 3rd ed. (London: Pitman Publishing, 1989), p. 64.
5. David A. Swierenga, "U.S. Air Carrier Industry Outlook in 1992." *Outlook for Travel and Tourism* (Washington, DC: U.S. Travel Data Center, 1991), p. 67.
6. Karen Rubin, *Flying High in Travel: A Complete Guide to Careers in the Travel Industry* (New York: John Wiley & Sons, 1992), p. 161.
7. *The Airline Story,* "Speed Vision," aired February 9, 2000.
8. David W. Howell and Robert A. Ellison, *Passport* (Toronto: Nelson Canada, 1995), p. 139.
9. *Canada Up Close As Only the Train Can Show You, A Traveller's Guide to VIA Rail Services* (Montreal: VIA Rail, 1995).
10. David Wright, *Professional Travel Counselling, 2nd ed.* (Toronto: Canadian Institute of Travel Counsellors of Ontario, 1994), p. 208.
11. www.viarail.ca
12. www.orient-expresstrains.com
13. Ontario Motor Coach Association, *Trainer's Handbook,* 1999.
14. Howell and Ellison, *Passport,* p. 131.

6

The Accommodation Sector

key terms

American plan (AP)
back of the house
bed-and-breakfast (B&B)
Bermuda plan (BP)
campgrounds
cannibalization
chain ownership
condominium
conference hotel
confirmed reservation
continental plan (CP)
corporate rate
day rate
double
double double
dude or guest ranch
European plan (EP)

family plan
franchise
franchise advisory
 council (FAC)
franchisee
franchiser
front of the house
guaranteed reservation
hospitality suite
hostel
hotel
joint venture
management contract
modified American plan
 (MAP)
motel
occupancy rate

overbook
rack rate
referral system
REITS
resort
resort hotel
run-of-the-house rate
single
spa
suite
tentative reservation
time-share
tourist courts
turn down service
twin
walking
weekend rate

learning objectives

Having read this chapter you will be able to

1. Explain trends in the lodging industry.

2. Compare and contrast the four basic management systems within the lodging industry.

3. List the advantages and disadvantages of being a franchisee.

4. Identify and explain the different departments within a hotel.

5. List and describe the different types of lodging available to the consumer.

6. Explain the factors affecting the pricing structure of a hotel.

7. Understand the different career opportunities within the lodging industry.

8. Identify five Canadian lodging establishments.

- -

Lodging, one of the oldest segments of the tourism industry, retains many of the same principles today as it did hundreds of years ago. The development of a place for people to stay that provided specific services evolved as soon as people began travelling by land and sea.

Today, Canada has more than 359 000 rooms to offer the tourist, ranging from deluxe accommodations to rustic cabins on a wilderness lake. The accommodation sector generates at least $10.6 billion annually and employs more than 172 300 people in more than 6900 properties.[1]

This chapter discusses history and trends, lodging management systems, the departments within a hotel and their responsibilities, the variety of lodging choices available in today's market, factors that affect the pricing of this product, and career opportunities within this sector.

Lodging History and Trends

As long as people have had the desire to travel, they have had the need for lodging and food along the way. The history of the accommodation sector of tourism began long ago, but the earliest known "hotel" system belonged to the Roman Empire. Besides being great conquerors, the early Romans were also great road builders, and along their roads they built lodgings to house the traveller. When Roman soldiers journeyed to distant provinces to keep peace and order in the empire, they needed places to stop and rest. Roman citizens also loved to travel for education or relaxation. Because of the different needs of these travellers, the system had to provide a variety of accommodations ranging from simple huts for shelter to more elaborate dwellings with all of the amenities of the day. In the city of Pompeii, Italy, frozen in time by the eruption of Mt. Vesuvius, you can still see two examples of ancient hotels—the hospitium (full-service inn) and caupona (budget inn). When the Roman Empire collapsed, travel became a rare and dangerous undertaking and this early system of lodgings disappeared.

By the year A.D. 1000, the Crusades into the Holy Lands had begun. Religion, for a brief period, was the cornerstone of the accommodation industry. Monasteries and other religious institutions provided lodging because it was their holy duty to offer shelter to the weary traveller. However, soon the flow of knights, with their troops and pilgrims looking for redemption in the Holy City of Jerusalem, became greater than these religious institutions could handle. To meet the increased demand for lodging, townsfolk along the route began to offer rooms and meals in their homes, for a price; so the industry we call hospitality was born. The first major evolution of this new industry occurred in 1282. In order to protect their interests, the merchants of Florence, Italy, formed a guild that controlled the licensing of the city's innkeepers and ensured that each inn received its fair share of business.

The early inns of North America were established along water routes, especially in seaport towns. The first inn was built in Jamestown on the Virginia coast in 1607.[2] The early American inns typically provided family-style meals, a large common room (known today as a lobby), a number of private bedrooms, and a stable for guests' horses. The inn also became a meeting place for local politicians, clergy, and other citizen groups.

Roadside inns began to appear throughout the eastern states as horse-drawn coaches became a familiar sight. But the roadside inn gave way to early types of city hotels with many more amenities for guests. The first U.S. hotel, built in 1794, was the 73-room City Hotel in downtown New York City. In fewer than 30 years, hotels outnumbered inns in New York and provided such amenities as single and double rooms, locks on doors, soap, towels, bellhops, and room service. These hotels became the pride of the city and the standard for other cities.

In Canada, the first building specifically designed as a hotel opened in 1831 in Aylmer, Quebec. Upper Canada Village, a living museum located near Morrisburg, Ontario, invites tourists to wander through an exhibit of two of Canada's earliest inns.

The hotel era boomed in the days of the railroads' expansion and domination of transportation. As railroads crisscrossed regions, towns sprang up along the route with hotels to accommodate the rail passengers. Railroads made accessible many national parks, which offered accommodations to adventuresome tourists. The Yellowstone Lodge, built by the railroad company in the late nineteenth century, is still one of the most popular lodges in the park. Located within a buffalo's snort of the Old Faithful geyser, the lodge provides modern accommodations in a near-wilderness setting. Fairmont's Banff Springs Hotel is one of Canada's best-known examples of a lodging built in a national park specifically for the pleasure tourist market.

The hotel industry grew in the early twentieth century but experienced a devastating blow during the Great Depression, when people did not have the money for travel. Between 1930 and 1935, nearly 85 percent of all hotels in the United States went bankrupt.[3] The lodging industry quickly rebounded during and after the Second World War. In the 1950s there was a period of rapid expansion, when lodging chains discovered a different way to finance their new properties, a method called franchising, which will be discussed later in the chapter.

In the final analysis, inventions of humankind have had the greatest impact on the development of the hotel industry, beginning with the new technologies that evolved from the Industrial Revolution in the early nineteenth century. Besides providing accommodations with innovations such as the elevator, this "bloodless revolution" dramatically changed both the modes of travel and the tools used to conduct a hotel's business. Accommodations have evolved over the years, based on the needs of both the transportation system and the traveller. For example, prior to the early nineteenth century, courtyards with stables for a guest's horse were an integral part of any inn or hotel. When railroads became a major form of transportation, hotels were built along the rail routes. Many hotels were constructed directly beside or over the train station. The Château Laurier in Ottawa and the Royal York Hotel in Toronto, linked to the train stations by underground tunnels, are excellent examples of old railroad hotels. With the emergence of the automobile as a major form of transportation, the design of a hotel changed. Mom-and-pop **tourist courts** provided the customer with a small cabin and a parking space. Soon the tourist court evolved into the motel. Motels differ from hotels because they provide not only free parking, but also access to a guest's room directly from the parking lot, eliminating the need for large lobbies. In the 1960s, the jet age of travel saw new hotel development cluster around the local airport. Airport hotels have evolved into highly specialized facilities that provide unique services to fulfill the needs of their transient guests. As these hotels are not located in the heart of a city's business district, they must be able to provide many services that might otherwise be supplied by merchants in the downtown core.

No new modes of transportation have evolved since the jet age, but hotels have continued to evolve, moulded not by new transportation systems but by new technology, global economies, and changing consumer needs. In the 1970s, when economic difficulties arose because of a gas shortage, hotels focused on an inexpensive, no-frills product. In the 1980s, as global business boomed, city hotels were built in the downtown core and older hotels in this area underwent massive restorations. Convention and conference facilities became the focus of their new product offerings. Over the past 30 years, the resort hotel has emerged, with recreation and entertainment as the major part of its service. It meets the needs of the vacationing family and is usually built where large tracts of land permit the development of extensive recreational facilities. In the late 1980s, the last accommodation trend of the twentieth century emerged—the all-suite hotel. The rooms in these facilities resemble an apartment, and guests may choose to make their own meals or eat out.

Technological changes in hotels have significantly altered the way most properties do business. Check-in/check-out is streamlined with the use of computer systems. Daily reports are available to managers, summarizing the day's activities. Heating and cooling systems are tied into some computerized systems, only functioning when the guest is actually registered in the room. Even the keys used in many major hotels have changed. The big old brass keys of the past are collectors' items now. In their place, electronic cards open the door. Finally, it seems the lodging industry has come full circle, for in today's market, townsfolk are again offering food and lodging in their homes, this time calling their units "bed-and-breakfasts."

During the past decade, hotels have faced some difficult times. The overbuilding of the 1980s, coupled with a recession in the early 1990s, caused **occupancy rates** to drop drastically. Luxury properties and certain regions of Canada seem to have been hit hardest. Today, in the highly competitive lodging industry, major hotel chains are forming alliances and focusing on buyouts to strengthen their product. Brand names are becoming more important in all sectors of our industry. For the future, tourism products must reflect an understanding of the impact the retiring baby boomers will have on the marketplace. These travellers are knowledgeable, and they demand good service. To survive in the future, businesses must control their costs and ensure that the appropriate services are offered and delivered in a timely, professional manner.

The start of the twenty-first century was full of promise for tourism and the accommodation sector was experiencing steady growth. But the year 2000 proved to be a difficult one as sales in the high-tech industry slowed and profits fell. Falling profits hurt investments and stock markets around the world. Investors lost billions on falling stock prices, the industry laid off thousands of high-tech workers, and business travel declined. A final blow to business travel came with the September 11 tragedy. In some areas, business travel fell by almost 60 percent as firms tried to deal with both issues. Yet a more normal state of business travel seems to be returning. In the meantime, businesses depending on travel suffered the fallout; many hotels were forced to lay off employees or reduce hiring.

Finally we have the story of a little hotel, snuggled between the two towers of the World Trade Center and credited with saving many of those who managed to escape from the burning wreckage—the Marriott, 3 W.T.C. At 8:46 a.m., people working in the Marriott were startled to see the huge landing gear of American's flight splash into the swimming pool. This, coupled with other falling debris, triggered the hotel's alarm system. Employees, following their standard emergency drills, met at the concierge desk in the lobby. Two Marriott employees began a room-to-room search, while a third, using the last guest registry printout, phoned hotel rooms to ensure guests had left the building safely. Firefighters raced to the roof to inspect damage and the lobby, because of its strategic position, was used as a central command post for the firefighters. The front entrance of the North Tower (1) had been blocked by fire and falling debris, so the lobby of the hotel, which was linked to the North Tower, became the main escape route for those who worked in Tower 1. Mr. Keller and Mr. Fetter, managers in the hotel, worked in the lobby, directing people to safety through the door of the Tall Ships Bar and Grill. When the two towers collapsed, so did the hotel. Most of those working in the lobby area, including Keller, were killed. Fetter managed to escape in the company of several firefighters. To its credit, of the 940 guests staying in the Marriott, only 11 have been unaccounted for. Two employees died in the rescue attempts and the staff at the Marriott is credited with saving hundreds of lives by staying in the lobby to direct escaping workers from the North Tower to safety.[4]

The Château Laurier in Ottawa is one of the "grandes dames" of Fairmont Hotels. The first general manager was sailing home on the Titanic *with the furnishings for the hotel when the ship sank. The opening of the Château Laurier was delayed for several months.*
(Photo: Paula Kerr.)

Lodging Ownership and Organization

Owner and *manager* do not necessarily refer to the same person. In smaller, independently owned properties, the owner often acts as the manager; however, in larger hotels and within chains, different people normally carry these titles. Up to the time when chain motels became prevalent, ownership by individuals was common. Today, with the diversity of the lodging industry, establishments are managed in four ways: by an individual (private ownership), by a company, by a franchise, or by a management contract. A description of these methods of management along with a brief discussion on referral systems and REITS in the lodging industry follows.

Individual Ownership

Nearly half of all lodging establishments in North America are operated as individual proprietorships. These small hotels, including mom-and-pop motels, inns, and bed-and-breakfasts are an important component of the lodging industry. In fact, a majority of people spend more nights in the smaller hotels than in the larger, well-known lodging establishments.

The chief advantage of individual ownership is that the owner has full control over policies and operating procedures. Add to that the potential for individual profitability and a decision-making process free of bureaucratic red tape and it is clear why people enjoy owning their own property. The major disadvantage is that the owner/manager assumes full risk for the property. In bad times, the owner usually lacks the financial resources of a big company to hold on. Furthermore, the individual owner does not have the advantage of national advertising and reservation systems—a serious shortcoming when competing with national chains and franchises. Finally, independents have trouble raising capital to expand or add new properties.

Sometimes hoteliers may opt to form partnerships with investors. These **joint ventures** work because one partner supplies the expertise in the hotel business and the other partner provides the financial investment needed for a new property.

It is probably safe to say that individually owned hotels/motels exist in most communities that have lodging facilities. To compete with large, familiar franchised or chain properties, these privately owned hotels become affiliated with organizations such as the American Automobile Association (AAA), the Canadian Automobile Association (CAA), Independent Motel Association (IMA), or the Hotel Association of Canada (HAC). AAA/CAA approval gives small businesses the associations' equivalent of the "*Good Housekeeping* seal of approval." Travellers generally feel more comfortable staying in a lodging facility that has met certain standards. In addition, both the CAA and the AAA recommend their approved hotels/motels when designing itineraries for members.

Referral Systems How does a property owned by an individual compete with the large franchise chains? They use a marketing strategy called a **referral system**. The most widely known referral company is Best Western. If a hotel becomes a member of a referral system, it receives instant brand-name recognition, along with access to a worldwide reservation system as well as national and global advertising campaigns. As an example, when one of the family-owned hotels in Ottawa wanted to expand its clientele, the owners chose this option. It allowed them to operate their hotel as they liked while instantly linking them to a global market. A large percentage of their market had been VFR (visiting friends and relatives), but within a year of becoming a referral system member, the owners saw an increase in their business of more than 15 percent, directly attributable to their new affiliation. Service fees charged by companies such as Best Western are similar to those charged by a franchise operation, and the quality of the hotel is monitored.

Company Chains

Chain ownership is not as common as it was in the early twentieth century because of the tremendous expense of multiple hotel ownership. Four Seasons Hotels is a good example of the chain ownership category. The company operates a number of properties, all reporting to corporate headquarters. All major management decisions are generated from headquarters, making changes to management, services, and décor much simpler to implement. The Four Seasons has created a niche in the luxury end of the lodging industry. Yet, although the level of service does not vary, each Four Seasons hotel has its own unique ambiance, capturing the local culture. In Japan, the Four Seasons has a Japanese feel; the property in Bali is not a hotel building but cottages with private pools, porches, and fans. Although ownership is centralized, hotels in a chain have more operational independence than franchises; while customers are seldom aware of ownership structures, they can sense the distinctive feel of a hotel.

Franchises

The third type of operation is the **franchise**. The franchise relationship consists of two parties: a name brand company, called a **franchiser**, and the property owner, called the **franchisee**. Those who opt to purchase a franchised business are usually buying a proven business formula. Franchising offers the advantages of a brand-name product, while leaving ownership and most management control in the owner's (franchisee's) hands. The franchisee agrees to follow all franchiser's management policies, to pay an initial development fee, and to pay a monthly franchise. This fee usually falls between 3 percent and 6 percent of the total gross room sales. All the hotels in a franchise have the same décor and image; unlike the varied Four Seasons properties, a Ramada hotel is always a Ramada. The advantages of the franchise system include the following:

1. Use of a nationally known name attracts travellers.
2. National and international advertising and reservation systems are available.
3. Borrowing costs are lower because lending institutions are more willing to lend to a mortgagee affiliated with a nationally recognized franchise organization.
4. Professional managerial assistance is provided by the franchiser.
5. Group buying or central purchasing offers many supplies at much lower costs. Franchises provide architectural plans, layout, decoration, and other critical development components at substantial savings.
6. Employee training is available at little or no cost to the franchisee.
7. Common décor and a familiar atmosphere are comforting to a weary traveller in an unknown place.

However, a franchise does come with a number of disadvantages:

1. Initial franchise fees are generally quite high.
2. Franchise fees usually include a percentage of the monthly gross revenues.
3. Each owner is adversely affected by other franchise owners who do not live up to customers' expectations.
4. If the franchiser becomes financially insolvent or does not provide the management assistance required, the franchisee suffers.
5. Policies and procedures of most franchises are set by the main office and require strict adherence, with little or no flexibility for the individual owner.
6. The franchisee agrees to many terms set by the franchiser. If at any time the franchisee does not follow the agreement, a clause in the agreement allows the franchiser to buy back or cancel the franchise.

To buy into a franchise requires a significant investment. A person or group must be willing to invest in the building, pay the franchise fee, and contribute to the ongoing operation of the business. Most franchisers work to make the investment as simple and straightforward as possible. For example, the Super 8 Motel franchise has an eight-point program that makes it easy to join the economy segment of the lodging industry. The following excerpt appears in Super 8's "Come Grow with Us" document aimed at gaining new investors:

> Begin by purchasing a Super 8 motel franchise for a specific area. The franchise is a 20-year agreement. Monthly royalty fees will consist of 4 percent of your property's gross room revenue. You will also pay a 2 percent marketing fee along with a 1 percent media advertising fee. That's all! No reservation fee, no training school fee…nothing else!

Super 8 Motels guarantees to keep all its motels far enough apart to avoid competition within the franchise, sometimes referred to as "**cannibalization**." It will assist in city and site selection, market studies, architectural plans, and interior design and will provide the financial package, a list of lenders, and counselling on financing programs. Finally, Super 8 Motels will share company contacts for construction as well as recent cost information for similar projects.

Franchising does not always result in a happy partnership. It is important to research the company with which you are investing to ensure that they manage a quality product in an ethical manner. In the 1950s and 1960s, when hotel franchising mushroomed, many disputes about interpretation of franchise agreements arose between franchisers and franchisees. To create a better working relationship, **Franchise Advisory Councils (FACs)** were started. These bodies represent the franchisee and provide a forum through which to address concerns and solve problems. If you are thinking about investing in a franchise, find out whether the company has a working FAC. Most large franchise companies work well with their FACs, recognizing that their success is dependent on the success of their franchisees.

Management Contract

The fourth type of management system is the **management contract**, which separates hotel ownership and operation. The Delta Hotel chain, owned by Fairmont Hotels, is a good example of a management contract company. This agreement can be made with individual properties or with hotel chains. The owners (the investors in this relationship) contract with a professional management team to operate the property (the investment) for a fee or a percentage of gross revenue. It is the preferred method of management when the owner has limited knowledge of the hospitality business. Furthermore, lending institutions are more likely to step forward with financing if they know a professional team is managing the investment. International hotel chains use the management contract system to establish a hotel in a foreign country, especially if the country does not permit outside ownership or is politically unstable. When a chain takes on the role of the manager, they often place their name on the property, allowing the hotel to access their brand name, international reservations system, and professional marketing plans. However, the contract chain may also operate as a silent management team, with only employees aware of who pays their salaries.

The disadvantages of a management contract are similar to those of any large company, especially when communication between upper management (owners) and lower management (management contractor) is not good. Some owners believe that they are not kept adequately informed about the managers' business activities. Owners may disagree with some of the operational decisions made by the property's management, but generally owners do not have control over those decisions. In addition, the owner must pay a guaranteed management fee of 1 percent – 3.5 percent of gross revenues. Finally, as with the franchise, management contract companies may lack an understanding of the local culture when operating a foreign property. To be successful, any business must have a good knowledge of and working relationship with local cultural traditions.

Variations on these four systems are sometimes implemented, such as an individual or company buying the franchise and a management contract. Employees need a clear understanding of their property's ownership and management structure to follow company politics.

Hotel Real Estate Investment Trusts (REITS)

Many traditional hotel companies, such as Fairmont, are using **REITS** as a new form of ownership. REITS emerged as hotel companies searched for new ways to fund development using sources other than financial institutions. Hotel REITS are companies that buy hotels and hotel resort properties worldwide. They then sell shares in their company, trading them on the stock market like any stock. From an ownership perspective, REITS are used to gain funding for acquisitions, new construction, and renovations. The remarkable success of REITS is generally attributed to their terrific performance for investors. They provide hotels with liquidity in the capital marketplace and the financial support they need to expand in this growing industry.

Organization and Functions

The organization of a hotel or motel depends on its size and ownership. Owners of small, individually owned motels may hire only maids, performing most of the other work themselves. Most hotels, however, require a fairly large staff to function properly. The hotel staff is divided into those who work in the "**front of the house**" and have direct contact with customers: front office, food and beverage, housekeeping, and customer services; and those who have little contact with the guests and work in the "**back of the house**": administration, sales and marketing, accounting, engineering, and security.

Administration The administrative staff includes the general manager, an assistant manager, and all the department heads. The general and assistant managers are responsible for the overall operation of the hotel. They assist and direct the other managers and keep all departments informed on the day-to-day business of the hotel. The department managers are responsible for their departments' success and the direct supervision of their employees. They must all work together, normally meeting weekly to report on their progress and share information. For example, all managers need to be aware of the needs of any group booked by the sales managers, as well as specific promises made by the sales managers.

Sales and Marketing This department is responsible for four different areas: sales, advertising, research, and public relations. Sales include both group and convention sales—promotions, rate setting, and travel trade sales (group bookings from travel agencies and tour operators). The sales staff spend most of their time bidding for conventions, corporate meetings, and other multiple reservations. Public relations involves creating a favourable image for the property by cultivating contacts with travel writers and editors or becoming involved as a sponsor with a major event such as the Festival of Fire, held each summer in Victoria. News releases, press kits, and promotions are part of public relations. The marketing component includes learning about the competition, researching customers' wants and needs, and designing a product and service that meets those needs. Marketing is a relatively new concept in the tourism industry, one introduced within the past 50 years. The term itself carries a double meaning—one naming the specific department and the other describing the actual functions of the marketing staff in dealing with customers, sales, and promotions. A company that seeks first to satisfy the wants and needs of its clientele is one that has a marketing management style.

Front Office and Guest Services These are the people who have direct contact with guests. They are normally both the first and the last people to be in touch with the guest. The image, attitude, and professional standards they convey set the tone for the guest's total experience. The responsibilities of front-office personnel include check-in and check-out, providing information, answering telephones, and cashiering. The service staff include the concierge, bellhops, bell captain, lobby porter, and doorperson. Although most of these positions are entry level, the guest will judge the hotel through encounters with these people.

Accounting The accounting staff is responsible for tracking all financial information. In some instances, the control function is separated from other management functions by having the comptroller or financial officer report directly to the home office rather than to the general manager of the hotel. This method decreases the possibility of perpetuating ineffective accounting procedures and allows the general manager to concentrate on guest relations rather than on financial issues. Under this arrangement, the comptroller becomes a key financial advisor for the hotel. Other positions within this department may include auditors, accounts receivable supervisor, payroll supervisor, cashier, and purchasing agent.

Food and Beverage When a hotel has restaurant, cocktail lounge, and banquet facilities, the food and beverage department can generate up to half of the hotel's revenue. Career positions include the food and beverage manager plus a manager for each of the other areas, such as restaurant, catering, and lounge. The department needs to be aware of reservations in order to forecast food and beverage and staff requirements. For example, a large conference will require extra servers for banquets and socials; a full house of independent travellers will require extra workers in the restaurant and lounge. Open communication with other departments ensures effective cost management, resulting in increased profitability. In addition to serving guests, many hotel restaurants and lounges offer incentives for community residents to eat and relax at their property. This service requires a knowledge of the community and marketing and promotional schemes to encourage local use.

Food preparation may be part of the food and beverage department, or it may be a department on its own. The executive chef and assistants are responsible for maintaining an enticing menu, experimenting with new recipes, and supervising all kitchen staff. Chef positions are often held by people with culinary talent but no experience in personnel management. Havoc ensues when the chef is good at food preparation but delinquent in hiring, motivating, and maintaining a staff. A good chef provides the meals, works on budgets and menu planning, supervises staff, and maintains working relationships with other departments in the hotel. There is some disagreement as to whether this department belongs to the accommodation sector or to the food and beverage sector. It will be discussed further in chapter 7.

Housekeeping This department is responsible for the guests' comfort by ensuring that individual rooms and public areas are kept clean and neat. In most hotels, a head or executive housekeeper is responsible for supervising all room attendants, floor supervisors, serving specialists, and housekeepers. When a guest needs an extra towel or an iron and ironing board, housekeeping delivers. This one-on-one interaction with the guest requires well-trained and pleasant employees. However, housekeeping is usually seen as a dead-end department for people with little education; jobs are low paid, providing few reasons to give extra effort. Most hotels now pay housepersons per room, allowing them to set their own pace and encouraging speed and efficiency. This method does put additional burden on room checkers, who must ensure that each room is cleaned to the hotel standard. Some properties will provide other incentives for fast efficient work such as a free ski pass from mountain properties, meal tickets, bonus points for gift shop purchases, or bonuses.[5] Whatever the incentive, hotels are constantly challenged to hire good employees for the housekeeping department.

Engineering This department, sometimes called maintenance and operations, focuses on the physical structure of the hotel. All problems in air conditioning, sound systems, electricity, equipment breakdown, and outside maintenance are sent to the engineering department. A director of engineering must have considerable knowledge of building maintenance and equipment. Although guests have little contact with engineering personnel, their importance cannot be overemphasized. Any problems with the physical structure of the hotel will mean inconvenienced or uncomfortable guests.

Security For many larger hotels, especially in downtown areas, a security department is essential. This department is responsible for protecting guests and property. Some, but not all, security officer positions may require police training. Generally, the presence of a security officer at the entrance to a hotel makes a statement that the property is safe for the guest. Hotels usually prefer to have security personnel in street dress rather than uniforms because the presence of uniformed security guards can upset guests, who wonder whether there are security issues of which they are not aware. Because security officers need an understanding of law enforcement rather than of hotel operations, these positions are not usually stepping stones to hotel management.

in practice How do a Super 8, an independent motel, and a Sheraton differ in terms of management and ownership? Which would you prefer to work under and why?

Classifications within the Accommodation Sector

The two main categories in the accommodation sector are the hotel and the motel. A **hotel** differs from a motel in several ways: it has a central lobby, rooms are accessed from the lobby, and guest parking may or may not be provided. Hotels can be classified by location, room rate, purpose of the guest's stay, level of service provided, or length of stay. Table 6.1 shows Canada's top five hotel and motel chains.

Hotels may be classified by *location* as downtown, suburban, airport, town, highway, or "resort" (located in a natural setting such as near the seaside, a mountain, or a lake). Travellers who choose to stay in a *downtown* location are willing to pay for the convenience of being near all the attractions, their corporate headquarters, or their place of business. These visitors often fly into a city and prefer to use public transportation rather than rent a car. Looking to the upscale business traveller, a new hotel product in the marketplace is the bistro hotel. The atmosphere is one of old-world wealth, a quiet understatement of lavish luxury. Guests receive highly personalized treatment, right from the greeting at the door down to individualized amenities. On the other hand, a family taking a touring vacation could very well prefer a *suburban* location. They might want to be near family who live in the suburbs, or they may be concerned with cost. These visitors often drive

TABLE 6.1 Top Five Hotel Companies in Canada by Revenue, 2000

Company	Revenue in Millions	Company Type
Four Seasons Hotels & Resorts	$2400.0	Management
Fairmont Hotels & Resorts	$1769.6	Management, Ownership
Starwood Hotels (eight resorts worldwide)	$677.5	Management, Franchise, Ownership
Best Western International Inc.	$495.8	Non-profit association
Westmont Hospitality Group	$439.2	Management, Franchise, Ownership

SOURCE: Hotel Association Directory, 2001–2002.

Downtown hotel properties fill the needs of the business market, upscale pleasure traveller, and conventioneer.
(Source: Fairmont Hotels and Resorts.)

their own car and look for inexpensive lodging with free parking. It does not matter how far they are from the attractions because they have the convenience of their own transportation. *Airport* hotels generally target the air traveller. Stays are short, often overnight, and many hotels offer day rates for travellers forced to spend a full day waiting for a specific airline connection. Many airport hotels will offer 24-hour valet service and food service. Quick check-in and check-out is particularly important because planes must be caught and weary travellers have little patience. Some hotels offer television channels that provide travellers with information on the weather at their next destination (pack the raincoat or wear it?) or provide updated departure and arrival times for local airline companies.

Hotel Terminology You Should Know

single	one person staying in the room, no matter how many beds
twin	room with two twin beds
double	two people staying in one room
double double	room with two double beds
suite	accommodation with two or more rooms combined—one set up as living room
hospitality suite	room that has a bar and sitting area, often provided to the executive of a conference to be used for informal meetings
rack rate	standard daily rate
weekend rate	discount rate charged for weekend stays
run-of-the-house rate	discount rate for block bookings
corporate rate	discount rate given to members of an organization, usually negotiated ahead of time based on anticipated volume of business
family plan	special family rate that allows children to stay with parents at no additional charge
day rate	rate charged for short stays during the day, often at airport hotel locations: usually 9:00 a.m.–9:00 p.m.

Even *small towns* require some type of accommodation for the traveller. Many of the smaller towns located near major tourist destinations provide lodging at a more reasonable cost and happily accept the tourist who has been unable to book a hotel near the site. Many towns will have historic buildings converted into inns or hotels. These provide opportunities for entrepreneurs who are able to use the local culture and history to advantage. *Highway* motels are familiar to truckers and those who venture to cross our country using the TransCanada Highway or to drive north to the Yukon on the Alaska Highway. These lodgings exist purely because of need and may be found in the middle of highway wilderness, a welcome stopping place for the long-distance driver.

Finally, **resort hotels** usually promote a specific destination. Even in ancient times people needed to escape the cities, the summer heat, or the winter blues and so they travelled to the seaside, health spas, or mountain resorts for relaxation, recreation, and entertainment. Summer **resorts** offer golf, tennis, swimming, horseback riding, boating, fishing, and canoeing. Winter resorts add skiing, snowboarding, snowmobiling, skating, and sleigh rides. Using the many beautiful sites and destinations found across Canada, our resorts have gained fame around the world. Jasper Park Lodge, Chateau Whistler, Chateau Montebello, and St. Andrews by the Sea are just a few of the spectacular resorts from the Fairmont Hotel and Resort chain. A resort may stand alone as a destination or, like Whistler Resort in British Columbia, it may support additional businesses. Nestled in the coastal mountains of British Columbia, this carefully planned resort community offers shopping, a variety of dining options, evening entertainment, as well as other amenities such as babysitting and day care, church services, fitness centres, laundry and dry cleaning, medical and dental clinics, a public library and museum, video rentals, and movie theatres. Every province has a variety of resorts that fulfill the needs of vacationers ranging from luxury travellers to those seeking a more rustic vacation. However, in today's world of tourism, seasonal resorts are having a difficult time remaining profitable and are looking to expand their business throughout Canada's four seasons.

Classification by *room rate* includes *economy/budget* hotels such as Super 8 and Comfort Inns; *moderate or midscale* hotels such as Holiday Inn and Ramada Inn; *upscale* hotels such as the Westin, Fairmont, and Delta Hotels; and *luxury* hotels such as the Ritz-Carlton and Four Seasons. All-suite hotels such as Novotel Canada and Embassy Suites may also be considered within this classification. Companies such as the Marriott Corporation and Ramada Canada designed their properties by targeting markets based on a specific room rate and scale/level of service (See Figure 6.1).

Another way we classify hotels is based on the *motivation or purpose of a visitor's trip. Business hotels,* usually found downtown area or near major airports, provide specific services for the business traveller such as airport limousine service, computer hook-ups with working space, room service and mini-bars, valet services, and easy check-in and check-out. Many business hotels provide a check-out system that may be accessed from the room using the TV screen as a monitor. Business travellers are important because they use nondiscretionary money and are thus less concerned with cost and more concerned with service. A strong business clientele provides revenue for a hotel even during the off season and recessions. The newest, and one of the fastest-growing groups of visitors, are those from the *convention and meeting market.* **Conference hotels**, usually found in larger cities with strong "pull power" or in resort-like settings, must provide large meeting

FIGURE 6.1
Marriott
Corporations Hotel
Operations

SOURCE: Marriott Corporation.

spaces and smaller meeting rooms, and have a portable food service available. These hotels are turning into high-tech conference centres that house audio and video recording facilities with equipment such as slide projectors, overhead projection units, and portable computer systems. Group meetings can now be held in special audiovisual rooms designed to record the meeting from a variety of angles with up to 10 different video cameras! Also available are in-house TV channels that broadcast to all sleeping rooms and meeting facilities, along with satellite uplink and downlink capabilities for people who cannot attend the conference in person. Large convention hotels may have an audiovisual staff and even in-house experts to help conference presenters, all on short notice. All these services are needed for hotels to succeed in the very competitive convention market. The convention hotel is discussed more fully in chapter 10.

The final grouping in this classification is the *pleasure/vacation guest.* They are often more concerned with price and location than with special services such as valet and room service. They do, however, appreciate information from a concierge desk, knowledgeable front-desk staff, or a brochure rack.

Hotels may also be classified by *level of service,* which is determined by the needs of the hotel's target market. *Budget hotels* are designed to provide clean, safe, low-cost rooms. They offer very few services and may not have in-house food service. Instead, budget hotels may choose a location near a restaurant strip or provide a menu in each room from a local restaurant that is willing to deliver. They will not have a pool area but usually provide televisions in the rooms. An example of a budget hotel would be a Comfort Inn. A *midscale hotel* will have a coffee shop on premises, may have a swimming pool or exercise room, and may or may not provide airport service. An example of a midscale hotel would be a Ramada Hotel. *Upscale hotels* are far more service oriented. They will provide a wide variety of services such as room service, a concierge desk, a dining room and lounge area, pool and exercise areas, a gift shop, or perhaps a mini-mall for shopping. *Luxury properties* take service to a higher level. They are located in a prestigious area of the city or countryside, and their lobby is often large, spectacular (for example it might include a waterfall or an indoor garden area), with elegant furniture and lighting. Service is discreet and efficient. Luxury hotel chains like the Four Seasons cater to travellers who can afford the expense and expect their every want and need to be fulfilled.

Length of stay is the last category we will discuss. Not all hotels cater to *transient guests*, that is, those who spends a short period of time at the property. *Residential hotels* provide guests with long-term accommodations, sometimes for a year or more. Most of these hotels are midscale to upscale, and all their services are provided to the resident guest. A transient hotel may opt to also provide residential rates. In Ottawa, where a great many politicians spend six months of the year representing their hometown constituents, hotels providing residential rates are more common than in Calgary. You may have already noted that hotels will fit several classifications. For example, an upscale hotel might be located downtown and cater to business clientele and the conference market.

Motels and Motor Hotels As previously mentioned, motels and motor hotels came of age in the 1950s with the establishment of the interstate/interprovincial highway system and the advent of chain motels. A **motel** refers to a lodging property that has free parking available to travellers. Most motels have doors to the parking lot from each room. As a result, motels generally have little use for large lobbies. A motor hotel also offers parking facilities, but because it is located in a downtown area, it has a lobby and more of a hotel atmosphere. Motels started out as an offshoot of tourist cabins built along the roadways. The basic idea of a simple room for sleeping close to the highway has changed into motels with pools and restaurants.

Motels offer simple, clean, and inexpensive accommodations to tourists travelling by car. Some motels may provide swimming pools and restaurants, but many choose to eliminate extra services in order to keep the cost of the room low. Chains and franchises choose simple room plans that translate into savings in design and construction costs. Rooms are usually limited to one or two double beds, and cots are available when needed. Many motels look to the family or seniors market, a market whose priority is a clean, safe, and comfortable room with few amenities. A traveller usually chooses a motel over a hotel based on two factors: cost and convenience of location. Because more people are self-employed and because corporations are working within tighter financial constraints, the market for economically priced lodging establishments is predicted to be on the rise. Canada's largest motel chain, Choice Hotels of Canada, owns Comfort Inns, Sleep Inns, Econo Lodges, Quality Inns, Rodeway Inns, Friendship Inns, and Clarion Hotels.

Other Lodging Options

Condominiums and Time-Shares Condominium and time-share units are also resort accommodations. A **condominium**, meaning "joint domain" in Latin, allows an individual to have full ownership over one unit in a complex. In many cases, the owner uses the condominium a few weeks each year and rents it out through an independent management agency for the remainder of the year. The management agency maintains the grounds, roads, and recreational facilities and provides security and cleaning services for a percentage of the rental fee. Resort condominiums in places like Florida, Hawaii, and ski locations in Colorado allow the traveller to have apartment-style accommodations in an area filled with recreational amenities.

Time-sharing is the concept of buying a vacation segment, usually of two weeks, in a condominium unit. The purchaser owns only the two-week segment,

Country inns may provide guests a fireplace, interesting antique furniture, and perhaps a four-poster bed.
(Photo: Lisa Clarke.)

not the entire unit. The segment is scheduled so that only one owner may use it at a time. Some time-share companies encourage their owners to swap segments, allowing them to go to a new resort each year. The popularity of the resort determines how easy it is for the owner to exchange segments.

Dude Ranches Another form of resort destination is the **dude or guest ranch**. The ranch is usually family owned and operated and offers the guest a western experience. With the desire to get back to basics, the dude ranch is becoming a popular choice for city dwellers.

A dude ranch may be a working ranch where guests assist the owners in day-to-day operations, or it may be a luxury resort with swimming pools, horseback riding lessons, and rodeo shows. Dude ranches include guest ranches, resort ranches, working cattle ranches, fly-fishing ranches, hunting ranches, and cross-country skiing ranches. Most ranches are located in the western United States, British Columbia, and Alberta. The movie *City Slickers* stimulated demand for working ranch vacations.

Foreign and domestic tourists are also opting to spend a week working on a farm in rural Ontario, helping out an egg farmer in Nova Scotia, or joining the harvest on a wheat farm in Saskatchewan. Guests pay for their lodging and meals, enjoying some of Canada's agri-tourism products.

Bed-and-Breakfast Bed-and-breakfast (B&B) inns can be found in every state and province. The B&B industry has increased in North America because of the high cost of foreign travel, the desire to be in a home away from home, and the need to escape the city and familiar motels. People have decided to explore their own backyards and hidden communities. Staying in a B&B allows the traveller to experience the daily life of the local people. The guests are pampered by the innkeeper, who enjoys sharing local folklore while recommending points of interest and good places to eat. B&Bs may be restored older homes in rural settings,

The Train Station Inn at Tatamagouche, Nova Scotia. Old railroad cars have been renovated as bedrooms, providing unique sleeping accommodations.
(Photo: Paula Kerr.)

scenic waterfront estates, cozy Gothic cottages, train stations, converted school-houses, or old mills or plantations.

Because these lodgings have been converted from homes, many do not have private washroom facilities for each guest. The communal bathroom down the hall is an acceptable alternative for vacation and business travellers. The parlour is the place for guests to mingle and make new friends. Most B&Bs serve family-style breakfasts; some offer dinner as well.

A B&B is usually family owned and operated. In a small B&B, the staff may be strictly family members; larger properties hire extra help. Checking in guests, cooking breakfasts, baking snacks, cleaning rooms, performing accounting procedures, designing advertising campaigns, and acting as tour guide could all become part of a daily routine at a B&B. It is a unique and fun way to learn about the motel business on a small but comprehensive scale.

Spas The ancient Romans knew the value of rejuvenation. Their spas, frequently located by the seaside, had many of the services the modern spa offers: mud baths, massage, exercise programs, and healthy food. In fact, **spas** have thrived in many cultures throughout the ages. Focusing on the body and mind as one, they pamper and work the human body back to health. Spas are found all across the accommodation sector of the industry. Resorts and hotels may offer a "Spa Weekend." Bed & breakfasts have joined the trend, and even cruise ships promote spa cruises. Their staff include certified professionals who deliver the spa program and chefs with a solid knowledge of nutrition who prepare healthy gourmet food. Facilities allow the client to achieve complete relaxation. Hot tubs, saunas, and exercise rooms become a necessary component of the lodging facilities. The price tag for a week at a spa may be higher than for other lodging vacations, but for those who want to feel rejuvenated, spa vacations provide a healthful alternative.

Hostels Generally known as a youth hostel, a **hostel** is a lodge with communal washrooms and bedrooms designed for four to twenty people. Hostels may be found in specially constructed buildings or in older homes, YMCAs, and even churches. In most cases, guests prepare their own meals or assist in meal preparation and cleanup. The low cost makes travel feasible for students and others on limited budgets. The hostel has been popular in Europe and many other countries for decades. Its recent growth in popularity in North America indicates a need for more hostel development.

An organization of hostellers called the American Youth Hostel, Inc. (AYH) is open to all ages. Membership in AYH provides discounts on already inexpensive overnight stays and offers different types of organized tours, including hiking, bicycling, canoeing, and skiing. Hostelling International–Canada (HI-Canada) provides similar services in Canada and represents more than 80 different hostels across the country.

One of the most interesting hostels found in Canada is the Ottawa International Hostel. This old stone building, located on Nicholas Street in downtown Ottawa, served as the Carleton County Gaol from 1862 to 1971. In 1972, it opened its doors to the public as a youth hostel called Nicholas Gaol. The colourful history of the building attracts many travellers. The prison was the site of Canada's last public hanging, and it is said that over the years, many evil deeds occurred there. During renovation, a mass grave was discovered in the courtyard. A few visitors have claimed that on dark nights they hear ghostly prisoners moan their stories of mistreatment. Today the cozy surroundings show few traces of the past, and the hostel has been renamed the Ottawa International Hostel. At a hostel, the guest does not reserve a room, simply a bed. (Beds at the old Nicholas Gaol can be reserved for as little as $15 a night.)

Travelling in Europe can provide the tourist with interesting accommodation options. You may decide to rent a room in an English castle, a chateau in Burgundy or a room in a quiet monastery. In Greenland, you can rent an igloo. Quebec City builds an ice hotel every winter. In Switzerland, farmers take their cows to alpine meadows for the summer, clean out their barns, and replace the old straw with fresh hay. For a very reasonable price, you can rent a stall! The variety of lodging facilities is limited only by the ingenuity of the owner and the tourist's desire to try something new.

Campgrounds As a form of accommodation, **campgrounds** have been popular with cost-conscious travellers, outdoor enthusiasts, and RV owners who simply want to enjoy an area with the comforts of their own belongings. In the past, campgrounds offered a piece of grass to set up a tent and possibly a lake for fishing and rock throwing. Such campgrounds still exist in the forests of North America, but many people are demanding more than a spot to set up camp. Camping has increasingly become a sophisticated art, with first-class RVs and programs at the campground for all ages. Many campgrounds have hot showers, coin-operated laundries, electrical and sewer systems to accommodate RVs, playgrounds, swimming pools, and recreation rooms. Campgrounds may have small grocery stores for the convenience of the traveller, and some even have gift shops.

in practice   How do campgrounds and dude ranches fit into the hospitality industry? What differentiates an economy hotel from a luxury hotel? Name three different hotels for each service level: economy, moderate, upscale, and luxury.

Marketing the Accommodation Sector

Marketing a nationally known chain or franchised hotel differs greatly from marketing a small family-owned inn or bed-and-breakfast. The larger hotels have the

Cesar Ritz

Ritzy and *putting on the ritz* are just two phrases that highlight the master of graciousness and quality—Cesar Ritz. He was born into a family with no wealth, yet the mere mention of his name conjures up visions of glamour, prestige, and elegance. Who is Cesar Ritz and why is he an important part of tourism's past?

He began his career as an apprentice at age 15 in Brig, Switzerland. At age 19, he moved to Paris to pursue his dreams. By the late 1860s, he had become a restaurant manager—not an easy feat for one so young. However, Cesar knew that his education was far from complete. He left his managerial position to become an assistant waiter at the most famous restaurant of the day, Le Voisin. Here he learned everything possible about service, such as the correct and genteel fashion in which the wealthy enjoy dining. It was not long before he had developed such a knack for pleasing his customers that they would insist on having him as their waiter. He knew their likes and dislikes, their vanities and their habits. Cesar Ritz had learned the finer points of service by understanding one of the basic needs of people: to be recognized and made to feel special.

At age 27, he became manager of one of Europe's most elegant hotels, the Grand National in Lucerne, Switzerland. The hotel was facing the prospect of bankruptcy. He sent out letters to all his famous former patrons, announcing that the hotel was now under new management. Soon they were staying at the Grand National under Cesar's care. For 11 years, Cesar Ritz managed this hotel. He joined forces with Georges Auguste Escoffier, a man who had learned to cater to a client's palate in the same careful, luxurious manner as Ritz used in his service style.

In 1887, Ritz was asked to take over the management of London, England's grand new hotel, the Savoy London. Barely open six months, it was losing money at an enormous rate. Ritz was given carte blanche to operate the hotel. Soon he had created a dining room that boasted fine culinary treats and live bands playing Strauss. He designed lights that would flatter the complexion, and he instituted a dress code, making evening wear mandatory.

By 1898, he opened his first hotel in Paris, called the Ritz. Once again, Escoffier and his team prepared the food. Every other detail was handled by Cesar, from the lighting down to the wallboards, from the fresh flowers to the fine china and glassware. He reduced the size of the lobby to discourage those who were just passing the time of day. He personally taught the maids how to make a proper bed! Service was silent, prompt, and dignified. The hotel was a tremendous success.

Once his hotel in Paris was up and running, Ritz returned to London and the new Carlton Hotel. In 1907, the Ritz Development Company franchised its name, and New York City's Ritz-Carlton was opened. It has since closed, but in special cities around the world, such as Montreal, Quebec, you will still see a luxury hotel property bearing the name Ritz-Carlton, a legacy from one of the world's finest hoteliers.

Cesar Ritz was a man who believed in excellence. He felt that his customers' wants, needs, and expectations should be fulfilled in a prompt, courteous, quiet manner and that their surroundings should be elegantly comfortable. Service, he stated, was the key to satisfied, repeat business. In memory of his steadfast devotion to beauty and charm, a new word became part of the English language. *Ritzy* means elegant, luxurious, and grand; *putting on the ritz* means living, behaving, or dressing in a refined and fashionable manner.

finances to hire prominent advertising firms to create high-profile ad campaigns. They are able to present their messages in a full range of media: television, radio, newspapers, and magazines. But for both the major hotel chains and the small, privately owned lodgings, skill and knowledge of advertising and promotional techniques is becoming more and more essential. How can any lodging facility best use the four P's of marketing? Let's take a look.

Product

What is the lodging product that we sell? Is there more to a hotel than a simple place to sleep? The answer to this question is yes and no. Some no-frills hotels pride themselves on simply providing an inexpensive, clean, comfortable place to sleep. At the other end of the scale, luxury properties have a wide variety of facilities, provide special services such as "turn-down service" (folding down the bedspread, placing a chocolate on the pillow at night), and take great pride in the friendly expertise of their staff. Although the hotel room is intangible to the customer at the time of purchase, very tangible elements of a property need to be properly conveyed. Décor and ambiance, facilities, and services may be illustrated through colourful pictures and written words. This may be done in a brochure format and mailed to prospective clients. However, the most important new technological development in sales and marketing is the Web page. Tourism businesses not taking advantage of the Internet will lose out. For a small investment, any business can promote its facilities to a global marketplace. Some Web sites simply show a picture of the hotel and provide basic information. But many businesses are creating interactive sites that allow the visitor to look at the rooms, the dining facilities and menus, and special features such as their indoor pool and hot tub. In addition, they link their site to the Web sites of local attractions, providing even more incentive for a customer to visit. Reservations are easily made over the Internet; the site also lists phone numbers for those who wish to speak to a representative in person.

How do prospective clients determine the quality of your product? As mentioned earlier in this chapter, organizations such as the CAA provide a rating scale for lodging properties and nine of our provinces share a common rating system developed by Canada Select Accommodations Rating Program (Table 6.2). In addition, some provinces such as Alberta go further and provide information on an accommodation's ability to provide services for people with disabilities. None of these ratings are mandatory for accommodations in Canada and are awarded only at the property's request. When marketing your property, it is important that you keep in mind the wants and needs of your target markets and that you focus on the aspects of your property that make it unique and set it apart from your competitors.

TABLE 6.2   *Canada Select Accommodations Program Rating Categories*

★	clean, comfortable accommodations
★★	clean, comfortable accommodations with some amenities
★★★	very comfortable accommodations with a greater range of facilities, guest amenities, and services
★★★★	the highest standard of accommodations with an extensive range of facilities, guest amenities, and services
★★★★★	exceptional properties that are among the best in the country in terms of their outstanding facilities, guest services, and quality provided

SOURCE: Canada Select Accommodations Program.

Price

Very few hotels have a single fixed price for a room. Prices vary depending on a number of factors:

- location (of the hotel and the room)
- the room size and its amenities
- the pricing expectations of target markets
- competitors' pricing strategies
- seasonality
- group purchase discounts (e.g., conference, tour, corporate)
- discounts given to special market segments (e.g., travel agents, seniors)
- available meal plans (Table 6.3)

All of these factors make the pricing of a room confusing, to say the least. Reservation agents need to be fully aware of all the pricing options and should provide the guest with the best possible price available to them. It is important to remember that the tourism product has a very elastic demand—the higher the price, the more difficult it is to sell. At the turn of the new millennium, many hotels were surprised to find they had overestimated what the public was willing to pay and were left with empty rooms and lost revenue.

Place

What are the channels of distribution for the accommodations sector? Hotels sell directly to the public using their own reservation systems. Large chains use a single 1-800 number for all properties, allowing clients to access reservations from anywhere within the country. Individual properties may choose to join a referral system. The main external channel of distribution is the travel agency and its resource materials, such as the *Official Hotel Guide*. Finally, the Internet has provided the accommodation sector with a global marketplace and reservation system.

Promotion

A **confirmed** or **tentative reservation** means that the hotel has a room waiting for a client, but can sell it to a waiting guest if the client does not show up by a specified time (usually 4:00–6:00 p.m.). Disney properties have a special desk that

TABLE 6.3	*Meal Plans*
European Plan (EP)	room only with no meals
Continental Plan (CP)	room rate that includes a continental breakfast: juice, coffee, and roll or pastry
Bermuda Plan (BP)	room rate that includes a full American breakfast: juice, coffee, eggs, sausage/bacon, toast
American Plan (AP)	rate that includes three full meals: breakfast, lunch, dinner
Modified American Plan (MAP)	rate that includes two meals, usually breakfast and dinner

deals solely with confirmed but unclaimed room reservations! A **guaranteed reservation** means the client has supplied a credit card number and must pay for the room whether or not it is used, unless the reservation is cancelled by a certain time and a cancellation number obtained. Most hotels have a high season and a low season. Because their product is so perishable, it must be sold daily. A room that goes unsold represents lost revenue. Sometimes hotels **overbook**, or sell more rooms than they have, anticipating that not all guests will show. Sometimes they are then left with too few rooms for the guests holding confirmed or guaranteed reservations. This is an unpleasant position for any hotel to be in, but it is the responsibility of the hotel to find the guests rooms at another property, called "**walking**" or "farming out." Usually the hotel will cover the guest's room charge and offer some additional compensation.

Advertising is important but not critical during high season. Low season, however, can be a challenge for any hotelier. Large hotels have a sales and marketing staff that creates packages that best suit the hotel's need. For example, a hotel in a downtown location with a large business clientele may be booked during the week but have rooms available on the weekends. Creating a package that provides local residents with "romantic getaways" or "stress relief weekends" may be part of the answer. Included in this type of package might be an overnight stay, use of the pool and exercise facilities, dinner for two in the hotel's elegant restaurant, and a champagne breakfast. Some hotels provide special floors for the higher-value tourist that offer limited access, open bars in a comfortable lounge, and free breakfasts. Still others may provide frequent-guest cards, airport limousine service, and instant check-in/check-out for corporate guests.

Public relations is also an important part of promotion. Supporting a special festival or event, raising money for local charities, and supporting local town improvements in association with a chamber of commerce or convention and visitor bureau all enhance a hotel's image in a very competitive business. Promotions can be as creative as the promoter, and understanding marketing principles and the needs and wants of the clientele are the best way to ensure that they are effective.

At the Inverrary Inn, Baddeck, Nova Scotia, guests have a choice of bedrooms in the main lodge, in two-room cabins, or in outlying buildings.
(Photo: Paula Kerr.)

OPPORTUNITIES IN ACCOMMODATION

	FRONT OFFICE & GUEST SERVICES	ADMINISTRATION	HOUSEKEEPING, MAINTENANCE, & FITNESS	FOOD & BEVERAGE
OPERATION (FRONT LINE)	Front Desk Agent **Guest Services Attendant** Switchboard Operator Concierge Reservations Clerk/Agent Sales Coordinator Valet Camp Attendant	Sales Coordinator Night Audit Clerk Human Resources Coordinator	Housekeeping/Room Attendant Linen/Laundry Attendant Night Cleaner Public Space Attendant Project Cleaner Health Club Attendant	Food Service Helper/Busperson Food and Beverage Server Doorkeeper/Bouncer Bartender Wine Steward Dishwasher/Potwasher Cook (1st, 2nd, Camp, Chef de Parti, Journeyman Cook, Garde Manger)
SUPERVISORY	Chief Concierge/Guest Services Manager Public Relations Manager Sales Representative Assistant Front Office Manager Night Manager Switchboard Manager Reservations Manager Camp Counsellor	Sales Representative Chief Night Auditor Human Resources Officer	Assistant Executive Housekeeper Linen Room/Laundry Supervisor Night Cleaning Supervisor Floor Inspector/Supervisor	Maître d'Hôtel Host/Hostess Catering Functions Supervisor Sous Chef Assistant Chief Steward
MANAGEMENT	Front Office/Rooms Division Manager Director of Sales and Marketing Executive Assistant Manager Convention Services Manager	Sales Manager Comptroller Human Resources Manager Purchasing Agent Director of Sales and Marketing Executive Assistant Manager Human Resources Director	Executive Housekeeper Fitness/Recreation Director Front Office/Rooms Division Manager Rooms Division Executive Housekeeping Director	Catering Functions Manager Beverage Services Manager Night Club Manager Room Service Manager Executive Sous Chef Executive Chef Chief Steward
EXECUTIVE	Resort/Leisure Operations Manager Hostel/Lodge Manager Accommodation/Facilities Manager Resident Manager General Manager Corporate Vice President Regional Manager of Chain	Resident Manager General Manager Corporate Vice President Regional Vice President	Corporate Vice President General Manager	Corporate Vice President General Manager

SOURCE: Courtesy of Canadian Tourism Human Resource Council, *The Student's Travel Map*, 1995.

JOB DESCRIPTION FOR. . .

GUEST SERVICES ATTENDANT

Industry Sector	Accommodation
Division	Front Office & Guest Services
Industry Setting	Hotels, motels, resorts and other accommodation properties, transportation-related companies, tour/travel-related operations
Job Level	Operational (Front Line)
Description of Duties	Carry luggage for guests, escort incoming guests to rooms, check rooms to ensure satisfaction, offer information regarding features of rooms, services of hotel, and points of interest. Transportation-related duties include convey luggage by hand or hand truck at airports or railway stations, hail or phone for taxicabs, and offer information or answer questions regarding features of rooms, services of hotel, and points of interest.
Working Conditions	Usually wear tailored uniforms and work in attractive and comfortable surroundings; must work shifts and holidays and take rotating days off; work can be hectic during peak travel seasons.
Skills	Must enjoy working with wide variety of people and possess pleasant, outgoing personality; neat personal appearance, tactful and courteous manner are essential; good English-speaking skills and ability to lift and carry luggage are required.
Education	No specific educational training is required.
Industry Experience	Previous experience is not required.
Career Paths	Guest Services Attendant, Concierge, Guest Services Manager, Assistant Front Office Manager, Front Office/Rooms Division Manager
HRDC Reference	NOC 6672 Other Attendants in Accommodation and Travel (except Airline Travel)

in practice   Write the names of 10 hotels or motels in your community. Identify their locations and what each is near. Does the location dictate the type of clientele of each motel or hotel? What type of marketing strategies do they use? Why does one facility do better than another in the same community?

summary

The hotel business has been around for centuries and continues to grow and change. From small roadside inns to time-shares, this sector provides a wide range of career opportunities.

Hotels are operated under four basic types of management. The individual owner usually has a small lodging property and single-handedly manages the business. Outside staff may or may not be needed. The owner has the privilege of operating the property in any manner desired. A company chain operates its own hotels from a single, corporate headquarters. Franchise properties are owned by an individual (sometimes a company) but fall under the guidelines of the franchise. The owner obtains the right to use the nationally known name and reservation system, which brings in more business. In some cases, a franchise dictates what the property should look like; in other cases, the name is the only link between one property and the next. The fourth method is the management contract, in which one company owns the property, but another company (usually a chain) manages it. This method is ideal in countries where foreigners are not allowed to buy property. A hotel company lets the local company own the building but runs it as if it is part of a chain.

The numerous types of hotels provide something for everyone. Hotels are classified as economy/budget, midpriced, upscale, and luxury. In addition to the various price ranges, there are motels, hotels, convention hotels, resort hotels, condominiums, time-shares, dude ranches, hostels, campgrounds, and bed-and-breakfasts. Each type of accommodation will have a different strategy for luring guests. Location is the key to determining who will stay where.

questions

1. a) Explain the difference in the way a hotel/motel is operated based on ownership/organization for (i) individual ownership, (ii) chains, (iii) franchises, (iv) referral systems, and (v) REITS.

   b) Which types of management are represented in your region? (Provide examples.)

2. a) Design an organizational chart for (i) a 50-room privately owned motel and (ii) a 300-room franchised hotel.

   b) Briefly describe the areas of responsibility of each department.

   c) Did you eliminate any departments in the smaller hotel? Justify your decisions.

3. How do the following hotel classifications determine the scope and quality of the hotel product? Back up your answer using examples.

   i) location

   ii) room rate

   iii) purpose of visitors' trip

   iv) level of service

   v) length of stay

4. Using a hotel advertisement taken from a newspaper, magazine, or the hotel itself, show how the property has used product, price, and place in its promotion.

5. Define the following terms as they relate to the accommodations sector: *AP, MAP, EP, walking, back of the house, cannibalization, guaranteed reservation, time-sharing, hospitality suite.*

weblinks

www.all-hotels.com

All-Hotels boasts that it is the world's leading hotel site, listing more than 60 000 hotels worldwide.

www.lodgingnews.com

Lodging News is geared to hotel executives and issues in the industry.

www.hotels.ca

This is the Web site of the Hotel Association of Canada.

www.ahma.com

Founded in 1910, the American Hotel & Motel Association (AH&MA) is the trade association representing the $93.1-billion lodging industry in the United States; its Web site is excellent for hospitality information.

www.hostellingintl.ca

Hostelling International-Canada provides information about youth and budget accommodation throughout Canada and around the world.

www.hilton.com

This is the Web site for the Hilton Hotel Corporation chain of hotels (see profile, p. 16) and has links to its hotels on five continents.

www.cphotels.com

Canada's famous Canadian Pacific Hotels, now called Fairmount Hotels and Resorts, operates many luxury hotels around the world including the Plaza Hotel in New York City.

www.marriott.com

The Marriott Company (profiled on p. 35) is a huge hotel and food company.

www.bbcanada.com

This site lists bed-and-breakfasts across Canada.

notes

1. Hotel Association of Canada Directory, *Hotel Industry Facts 2000*, p. 15.

2. David W Howell, *Passport* (Cincinnati, OH, South Western Publishing Co., 1989), p. 140.

3. Ibid., p. 141.

4. *New York Times,* September 11, 2002, p. 1.

5. *Worker Shortages in Accommodations, Food Service and Travel Agencies.* Prepared for the CTHRC by CS/RESORS Consulting Ltd,, 2002, p. 9.

7 The Food and Beverage Sector

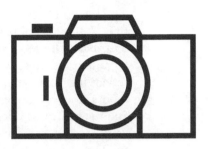

key terms

allergy awareness
bistro
buffet house
cafeteria
cash bar
coffee house
commercial food service
contract food service

couponing
ethnic restaurant
family-style restaurant
fast-food restaurant
fine dining
haute cuisine
independent
    restaurateur

menu
multi-unit corporate
    restaurant
open bar
pub
specialty restaurant
theme restaurant

learning objectives

Having read this chapter you will be able to

1. Explain briefly the history of the food-service industry and its current trends.

2. Differentiate between the two major divisions of food service: commercial and contract.

3. Explain the difference between the fast-food and full-service dining styles.

4. Describe seven styles of full-service restaurants and three styles of fast-food restaurants.

5. Discuss food service in the hotel industry and identify the problems that occur.

6. Apply the principles of marketing to the restaurant business.

7. Discuss the impact the food-service industry has on tourism and the tourist.

— —

The food and beverage sector is the largest sector in the tourism industry. More than 700 000 people work in the food-service industry, and the numbers are increasing.[1] The food and beverage sector is divided into two distinct divisions: commercial food service and contract/institutional food service. Commercial food service includes restaurants and fast-food outlets, private clubs, bars and pubs, and food and beverage departments within the hotel system, catering to both guests and the general public. Contract/institutional food service includes food and beverage services found in stadiums, museums, department stores, catering firms, the military, recreational camps, hospitals, nursing homes, and schools.

Tourism accounts for 21 percent of commercial food sales and although spending dropped after September 11, 2001, a recent Statistics Canada report shows that tourism spending is on the rise again and with it, food services revenues. In the second quarter of 2002, it reached an all-time high of $1733 million.[2] Although much of the food and beverage sector is not dependent on the tourist dollar, tourists are dependent on food service. Many commercial operations in the downtown core of a city rely heavily on tourist traffic. Part of the pleasure of travel is trying different restaurants and food-service options. Depending on the method of transportation and type of accommodation, tourists will use food-service establishments that best suit their needs at the time of a meal. If tourists are staying in a hotel, they can order breakfast in the room (if the hotel offers room service), they can buy muffins from the corner store and make coffee in the room (many hotels now provide coffee makers for guests' convenience), or they can eat in a coffee shop or dining room in the hotel or in the area.

Tourists need information regarding local eateries, but where can they find it? Each city, through its convention and visitor bureau, provides an information booklet for visitors describing local sights and attractions, services, shops, and restaurants, and hotels will often leave a booklet in each room. Visitors might also ask the front-desk attendant or concierge for advice on where to eat. Many restaurants in the downtown core of a city will put menus in the window to entice customers into their establishments. Tourists will often look for a unique dining experience, one that reflects the culture of the region. Tourists must eat out, and wise entrepreneurs in the food-service business have learned that tourism helps to pay their bills.

This chapter deals with both commercial and contract food service. It explores current trends, ownership styles, types of food-service facilities, how we market the industry, and the importance of food service in the tourism industry.

History of the Food-Service Industry

Food has always been a necessity, but from the early days of civilization it has also been associated with celebration, cultural rituals, and a show of friendship. Dining out has a long history. As early as 1700 B.C., the Egyptians were meeting in public places to share simple meals of fish or fowl, olives, grains, fruits, and vegetables. However, it was the ancient Romans who were the first to create truly lavish banquets with live entertainment, portable food services (for their troops), as well as fast-food outlets and snack bars. Food used for entertainment was elaborately prepared and garnished. One description of a feast includes hummingbird pie, made from the tongues of 10 000 hummingbirds. As the Romans were very superstitious by nature, they developed rules of etiquette based on these superstitions. They felt it was unlucky to enter a house or a room with the left foot. The host never placed an uneven number of guests along the sides of a table and always made sure that the number of seats was divisible by the lucky number three! In the ruins of Pompeii are remains of tabernae (bars), thermopolia (snack bars), and popinae (the world's first fast-food restaurants). As the Roman Empire flourished, the commonsense origins of the nation dissolved into an unrestrained lifestyle that would eventually cause the empire to collapse. Roman festivals became food orgies and would last for days. Entertainment changed from jugglers and musicians to bloodier sports, which included battles performed by slaves who fought to the death in front of feasting guests. With the collapse of the Roman Empire, and the start of the period of history referred to as the Dark Ages, the refined lifestyle developed by the Romans disappeared.[3]

By A.D. 1100, the world had emerged from the Dark Ages. Travel became safer, and public entertainment and food services were again part of community living. The peasants ate simple foods made from grains and seldom had meat, fish, or fruit to put on their tables. The diet of the aristocracy was slightly more varied and included roast meats, fresh salads made from bitter, leafy greens and onions accompanied by a strong vinaigrette dressing, and sweet puddings.[4] Utensils for eating were not common, even in the large courts of England and France. The fork was introduced to the French court when Catherine de Medici was betrothed to King Henry II of France in 1573. Desolate at having to leave the comforts of the Italian court for the more barbaric ways of France, she agreed to the marriage only when her father promised to send his chef and kitchen staff with her. So it was in the roots of Italian cuisine that the world-renowned French culinary tradition arose. As travel increased, so did the number and the variety of food-service establishments. The tradition of elegant French dining out began with the French Revolution in 1789. As the royals rode to the guillotine, their talented chefs suddenly found they were out of jobs. Many of them became entrepreneurs and opened small, fine-dining establishments that catered to the new upper class.

In the United States, the first true full-service restaurant opened in New York City in 1827. It was called Delmonico's and was operated by three brothers— John, Peter, and Lorenzo. They began with simple fare, such as small cakes and breads, but at the height of their business, their menu listed more than 300 different items.[5] Tourists visiting New Orleans today often make a point of dining at Antoine's, which has an excellent reputation for fine dining. Antoine's opened its doors in 1840, and has the longest continuous service history in North America.

The restaurant business in North America fell upon hard times during the 1920s and 1930s. First, the United States passed the Prohibition Act. Restaurants were no longer allowed to sell liquor. Many owners who adhered to the law were forced into bankruptcy. The Great Depression was the second blow to the industry, bankrupting many restaurants that had been lucky enough to survive prohibition. By the middle of the 1930s, restaurants had made a comeback.

Fast food was not a new concept, but as North Americans fell in love with the automobile and took to the roads, a new kind of fast-food restaurant emerged. It differed from earlier eating establishments because it provided plenty of parking spaces. The restaurants also started serving a "new" food, the all-American hamburger. The hamburger as we know it was first served at the St. Louis Exposition of 1903. In the 1930s it emerged as the number-one seller in the new fast-food business. In the 1950s franchising began its rise to prominence in the food-service industry. Companies such as A&W, Kentucky Fried Chicken, and McDonald's sprang up on many neighbourhood corners. A&W developed the "drive-up" restaurant. Cars pulled into parking spaces and servers, often on roller skates, took orders and delivered the food to car windows. In the 1970s fast-food operators cashed in on a more mobile, busier lifestyle and, taking advantage of a time period during which the restaurant had previously been closed, created the "McBreakfast." By the 1980s competition had become extremely fierce. The era of the great haute-cuisine restaurants was coming to a close. Profits were undermined by labour and equipment costs, a faster lifestyle and a clientele with changing needs, and concerns with liability for table-side flambées. As a result, many haute-cuisine establishments evolved into the fine dining category, allowing these restaurateurs to maintain their quality of service and eclectic, gourmet cuisine. With equipment costs and labour costs now under control, fine dining in America had come of age. Fast-food franchises began linking their product with children's television programs like *Sesame Street* or with newly released children's movies and toys became a drawing card for the younger generation. The 1990s saw a growth in family-style restaurants such as East Side Mario's and Red Lobster. These restaurants catered to busy families with parents looking for friendly, quick service and reasonably priced food served in a more relaxing atmosphere than fast food could provide. But the toys remained a big drawing card. Today much of a movie's hype comes from the promotion of toys given by major restaurant chains.

Among the devastation of September 11, 2001, was the ruins of one of the world's most famous restaurants. Located on the top floor of the World Trade Center's North Tower, Windows on the World was a New York City tourist attraction. Its reputation for an outstanding view of the New York skyline and for its excellent food and service made it one of the busiest restaurants in the city. While 220 staff and guests were enjoying the breakfast hour, the first aircraft plunged into the north tower. No one survived. Restaurants in the shadow of the World Trade Center that survived the collapse of the towers opened their doors to rescue workers, providing them with food and water during the first few days. Over the following months, as grieving New Yorkers shunned their daily luncheon and dinner outings, many small restaurants were forced into bankruptcy. Only recently have New York restaurateurs seen some business rejuvenation.[6] Canadian restaurateurs also experienced lower revenues as the number of business and pleasure travellers dropped over 2001–02, but as tourism in Canada begins to rebound, so do revenues in our food and beverage industry.

Trends in the Food and Beverage Sector

According to B. Hudson Riehle of the National Restaurant Association, North Americans are looking for more variety, more menu choices, and more casual dining. Other trends include a greater concern for nutrition, a desire for good service, and the continuing impact of legislative controls.

Casual Dining As more people stretch their financial resources to make ends meet, the luxury of fine dining is being replaced by a more casual dining atmosphere. Use of plants, natural woods, and earth-tone colours have replaced the formal look of starched white linens, crystal goblets, and sterling silverware. Restaurants are becoming smaller and more intimate. Menu choices have an ethnic flair to them, and unless a restaurant is using frozen-food products, there are fewer menu items from which to choose. Value-driven consumers are setting the trend for restaurants to provide lower-priced menu items. Pasta, pizza, and bistro fare are all popular. A new interest in back-to-basics cooking is spurring interest in reasonably priced regional fare.

Takeout Takeout and delivery are an important driving force behind the restaurant industry's growth, with off-premises traffic representing nearly 50 percent of the industry's total. As lifestyles continue to become busier and more stressed, with both parents working, takeout food offers a family the chance to sit and eat together in the comfort of their home. Grocery stores are finding that less of the food dollar budgeted by a family is being spent purchasing groceries and more is being spent for takeout foods. To recapture this lost revenue, grocery stores are offering more ready-to-eat foods. Fried chicken, roasted chickens, and ready-made salads are part of their product lines already. Smart restaurateurs will have their own products readily available as takeout. Taking advantage of this trend toward takeout meals may offer another key to financial success for Canadian restaurants.

Dining out with Children Restaurants will have to continue to cater to the children of the baby-boom generation, some of whom are still young. Children influence how much can be spent on a meal away from home as well as where to go for that meal. By providing a children's menu with hamburgers, french fries, hot dogs, and chicken, restaurants can cater to nearly every child's palate and put parents at ease. A child's menu that serves as a game or colouring page with crayons given to each child as well as child-friendly play areas help attract families with small children.

Service Service tops the list of reasons consumers return to a particular restaurant. Restaurants that provide a good meal with a pleasant atmosphere (décor and personnel) will outshine the competition. In the past there has been a large discrepancy between management perceptions of customer satisfaction and the actual level of satisfaction customers expressed. This gap indicates that restaurants need to look more closely at their customers. Restaurant surveys and customer contact are the only methods of appraising satisfaction levels, but these methods require extra time and money and, therefore, get put on the back burner until the restaurant is desperate to find out what is wrong. By that time, it is often too late, and the restaurant cannot recover its losses.

Canadian restaurants face a particular challenge because of legislated wage levels. Canadians working in this industry are paid better wages with better benefits than counterparts in the United States. Although this is good for workers, it adds additional financial stress to a fragile industry. To survive, restaurateurs must be able to do more with less. That means controlling food and labour costs carefully, simplifying menus, being innovative in production methods, and providing customers with the products and services they demand.

Nutrition For more than a decade, nutrition and health have been national issues, reflecting the consumer's desire to reduce intake of foods high in saturated fat and cholesterol and to increase consumption of complex carbohydrates and fibre. Fat-free and low-fat foods inundate grocery stores and appear on restaurant menus. Even fast-food and family restaurants have responded by using all-vegetable oil or shortening for frying and have expanded their menus to include pita sandwiches and salads. McDonald's is testing the McVeggie burger, appealing to the growing number of vegetarians in our society. It has also reduced the fat in its regular burger from 30 g to just under 7 g.[7] Although good nutrition remains a top concern, it does not entirely translate into menu choices. Many people who watch their diets while at home choose to "treat themselves" when dining out, perhaps figuring they can always go back to their diet the next day. Many menus reflect the desire for nutritious foods by identifying vegetarian items or those with low fat or low salt content, but the reality is that less than 5 percent of sales are derived from these nutritionally sound choices. Some restaurants will use the nutritional content of their menu to target specific markets. People who eat out often are more likely to consider nutritious alternatives. Restaurateurs must be aware of their clienteles' needs and continue to provide the type of food offerings that are most in demand.

Allergy Awareness The issue of **allergy awareness** continues to plague the industry as more of our population appears to be developing allergies to foods. What was once a rarity is now a major concern. One of the problems faced by the industry is the growing use of ready-to-cook/ready-to-eat foods. Because they are not prepared from the raw ingredients, kitchen staff often do not know their ingredients. Consumers are asking for a list of the ingredients that have gone into creating the dishes they order, and in many regions, they have a legal right to know. MSG (monosodium glutamate), peanuts, nut oils, preservatives—all of these products must be identified for a customer on request. It is the responsibility of restaurant staff to identify all ingredients in a dish, whether or not that dish has been prepared on the premises. This simple courtesy to the customer may help prevent a tragedy and legal action. "Secret ingredients" are no longer a selling point!

Legal Issues Legal issues have become a great concern to Canadian restaurateurs. New laws enacted over the past 20 years dealing with alcohol consumption and smoking have changed revenue generation and owner liability. Prior to drinking-and-driving legislation, many full-service restaurants could expect beverage sales to be at least 50 percent of the total bill. Today alcohol consumption accounts for less than 25 percent of the revenue generated. Restaurants and alcoholic beverage producers are addressing this problem in a number of ways. Restaurants are offering to sell all their wine by the glass, allowing customers to enjoy their favourite wine with the meal. The cost of the bottle is recovered with just two glasses of wine sold. Servers are then made aware of recently opened wines that can be promoted to customers. Half bottles of wine are sold whenever they are available. For champagne lovers, Piper Heidsieck has introduced the Baby Piper, a 200 mL bottle. In British Columbia, patrons who don't finish a bottle of wine are now being permitted to carry the open, partial bottle home in a doggie bag. To make up for the loss of drink revenue, restaurants must also generate more money from the sale of food. This is difficult because the number of seats is static and cannot easily be changed. Servers are trained to use upselling techniques, such as suggesting a soup or salad before the meal or a dessert with coffee. Upselling should never be aggressive, but should consist of helpful suggestions. Another concern for customers is the amount of taxes added to a bill; often more than 15 percent of the total cheque is accounted for by goods and services tax (GST) and provincial food and beverage taxes.

But the biggest legal issue facing restaurants today is that of smoking. In 1998 the Workers' Compensation Board in British Columbia imposed a wide ban on smoking, which included all food service establishments. However, after two months, a study revealed that nine businesses had gone bankrupt, 730 jobs had been cut, and $16 million in revenue had been lost. B.C.'s Supreme Court overturned the ban and a second piece of legislation was abandoned. B.C. now has one of the most reasonable smoking bans in Canada. Effective May 1, 2002, restaurants and bars may dedicate 45 percent of their floor space to a separate smoking room. The air must be redirected outside or cleaned through a ventilation system; employee work stations may not be located in the smoking area; and workers cannot spend more than 20 percent of their shift in the smoking room. B.C. municipalities may pass their own, stricter smoking legislation. In Ontario, smoking legislation varies dramatically from one municipality to another. Ottawa has the strongest legislation, allowing no smoking in any public area, including restaurants, bars, bingo halls, and Legion Halls. Alberta, Saskatchewan, Newfoundland and Labrador, P.E.I., and New Brunswick either have less restrictive smoking bans or are struggling to come up with legislation that balances the needs of both residents and restaurants. Food service industry professionals have argued that heavy-handed interference by governments hurts only the operator and that smoking policies should be market driven, not legislated. Their requests for a middle-of-the-road approach that allows properly ventilated smoking areas has met with little success and the government refuses to address the core issue—that tobacco is still a legal substance. A study by the Ontario Restaurant Hotel and Motel Association shows that the air quality of properly ventilated smoking rooms is equal to or better than that in no-smoking establishments and argues that the zero level of tobacco smoke demanded by health authorities is prejudicial. Douglas Needham, president of the Canadian Restaurant and Foodservice Association, has stated that "society would grind to a halt if chemical standards were set to absolute zero. The lowly potato contains 150 different chemicals including arsenic but Health Canada continues to allow its consumption."[8] The battle over second-hand smoke will remain a costly and difficult issue for restaurateurs.

Restaurant Ownership

Restaurants may be owned or managed in three ways: as independents, under a single corporate structure, or under a franchise agreement. Unlike hotels, the majority of restaurants are owned independently.

Independents

In the food-service business, the majority of restaurants are owned by one or two individuals. These are flexible businesses that allow the owners to change menu

Many restaurants are owned and operated by chefs and the reputation of a restaurant is often based primarily on its food.
(Photo: Lisa Clarke.)

items at will, or redecorate to tailor their establishments to the needs of the community. However, such independence can be risky because it requires such a huge personal investment of time and money. Within five years, statistics show that 80 percent of these businesses will be bankrupt. For this reason, franchised units are taking over the market that once belonged to **independent restaurateurs**.

Multi-Unit Corporate Restaurants

Just as in the hotel business, it is possible for a single corporate headquarters to run a series of restaurants in one city or across Canada. For a **multi-unit corporate restaurant**, corporate headquarters provides the leadership, control, and planning for each restaurant. Managers are trained by the corporation and given freedom to operate as a single unit as long as company policies are adhered to and the profit quota is met. These companies may own and operate restaurants that are very similar, such as Lone Star, based in Ottawa, or Boston Pizza International, a chain from Vancouver. If this is the case, their expansion will usually be provincial, perhaps national. Other corporations own and operate restaurants that are very different. These corporations will focus on a region or a city, keeping their locus of operational control small and easily handled. An example of the latter model is SIR Corp., based in Burlington, Ontario. One of Canada's fastest-growing restaurant companies, SIR operates Jack Astor's Bar and Grill, Armadillo Texas Grill, Walt's Grill, Al Frisco's, Alice Fazooli's, Moose Winooski's, Far Niente, Soul of the Vine, Canyon Creek Chop House, and Leone's Italian Kitchen. Many times, larger corporations, seeing the success of a corporate chain, will purchase it, adding a new but established product to their business. In the past several years, Cara Operations has purchased Kelsey's Corporation of Oakville and added Milestone's from the Spectra Group.

Franchises

Are you interested in owning your own restaurant but feel you need more training and experience? Then you may be looking at a franchised restaurant. Franchising was discussed in chapter 6, and the same pros and cons apply to restaurant franchising. Two important benefits are national advertising and a well-known name such as McDonald's, Swiss Chalet, Boston Pizza, or Tim Hortons. Banks and lending institutions are more willing to lend money to a restaurant when a name brand makes success more likely. Other advantages include assistance in finding the right location; a proven layout and design; training procedures for all levels of staff; group purchasing power; food and beverage labour cost control systems; and managerial support. Of course there are disadvantages. It is costly to purchase a good franchise restaurant, and a given percentage (usually around 15 percent of gross revenue) must be paid yearly to the franchiser. The franchisee has no say in how the business is run and cannot adapt to serve local needs, to use local food products, or to take advantage of trends in the restaurant business. For tourists, a franchised restaurant means a familiar menu and décor no matter which province, state, or country they are visiting. Familiar foods in a foreign country provides a level of home-style comfort that is often a treat for a traveller. Franchising is becoming the major form of ownership in the commercial food-service business. Some popular Canadian franchises include Tim Hortons, Swiss Chalet, Le Bifthèque, Boston Pizza, and Second Cup. These franchises may fall under the corporate leadership of one of Canada's food conglomerates. Cara Operations, Canada's largest food corporation, now owns Swiss Chalet, Tim Hortons, Kelsey's, Montana's, Milestone's, and the Canadian franchise rights to Taco Bell and the Outback Steakhouse, and Cara's in-flight services.

The Major Divisions of the Food-Service Industry

As discussed at the beginning of the chapter, the food-service industry is split into two very distinct divisions: commercial food service and contract/institutional food service. The distinguishing factor is the clientele, not the type of food. **Commercial food service** serves the public and is available to anyone wishing to eat out. **Contract food service**, however, is found in a location that serves a "captive audience." Often this type of food service is found in institutions whose primary purpose is not food. For example, a hospital's primary goal is to help patients get well; however, since patients, staff, and guests must be fed, hospitals have well-developed food services. The customers in an institutional setting usually have little choice in who prepares their food, how it is prepared, and where it is served. Consider a sports arena where fans have come to watch a game. If they are hungry, they will choose to eat on the premises, so as not to miss any of the action. Their choice of food is dependent on the variety of restaurants found in the building. Contract/institutional food service is a growing area of the food and beverage sector, and it can provide a lifestyle for its workers that is very different from that of a restaurant.

Commercial Food Service

Commercial food service is a much larger division than contract food service, and it is further subdivided by the way in which guests are served. Full service provides customers with a chance to sit down, have their orders taken, and then be served. How the actual food is prepared, plated, and served greatly depends on the style of restaurant and the philosophy of the owners. Self-service, on the other hand, has little or no table service. Customers order and pick up their own food and are often responsible for clearing the table before they leave. This style focuses on quick meals for the person on the run. Full service restaurants comprise a range of styles, although differences may be somewhat blurred as many restaurants combine aspects of more than one style.

Haute Cuisine This very elegant and expensive style of restaurant is noted for its opulent décor, highly trained staff, method of service, table settings, and clientele. The **haute cuisine** restaurant has beautiful silverware, crystal goblets, fine linen tablecloths and napkins, and fresh exotic flowers. Wait staff are exceptionally well trained and include positions such as commis (busperson), chef de rang (chief server), maître d' (head waiter), and sommelier (wine steward). The food is fresh, cooked daily by the chef and sous-chef, and the menu often includes signature items, dishes that have been created specifically for the restaurant. The food is often prepared tableside on a gueridon (cart) and may be flamed in front of the guest by the chef de rang. The wine cellar is stocked with a wide variety of excellent, vintage wines. The entire dining experience is elegant, a true adventure into the world of gastronomy. These restaurants were popular at the turn of the century, when those who dined out were wealthy. In order to survive in a very competitive world, many of these restaurants have had to reduce their costs by eliminating the finer touches, such as the sterling silver placeware and the crystal goblets. The quality of service, wine list, and foods have not been changed. The Georges Cinq Hotel in Paris boasts one of the finest haute cuisine restaurants in the world.

Fine Dining Many restaurants today still provide elegant service, although they have dispensed with the many levels of wait staff and the costly table settings. The food remains unique and exciting, and the staff still requires a high level of skills. Few of these **fine dining** restaurants continue to flambé food because of high liability costs. The food is prepared from fresh, raw ingredients. It is plated in the kitchen, and great care is taken to ensure that the food is a wonderful collage of exciting colours and tastes. The wine cellar is extensive and well chosen to suit a variety of clientele tastes and price ranges. One example of this style of restaurant is North 44 in Toronto. Specializing in Canadian dishes, it has one of Canada's largest, most complete wine lists and is recognized as one of the outstanding restaurants in this region.

Dining This category includes a wide variety of dining experiences and is the largest grouping of full-service restaurants. These restaurants range from a good local eatery to the greasy spoon around the corner. What distinguishes this style of restaurant from the fine dining/haute cuisine is the more casual approach to the guest, the menu, and the price. Remember that all restaurateurs bring their own philosophy of food and service to the marketplace, but successful restaurateurs understand their clientele's needs and are able to fulfill their expectations. **Bistros**, cafés and trattorias show how the restaurant industry has responded to the demand for more casual dining combined with the fresh, eclectic food served by fine-dining establishments. Although décor is simple and the restaurant is small, the food from the kitchen features unusual pasta dishes, pizza from a wood-burning stove, exotic lettuces, oils and vinegars, homemade desserts, and specialty coffees. **Pubs** are another form of casual dining that try to recreate the ambiance, menu items, and types of beer and whiskey typical of an English, Irish, or Scottish bar. The Prime Restaurant Group based in Mississauga have developed not only the Irish pub concept (D'Arcy McGee's, Slaínte), but have also added a new concept with Esplanade Bier Market in downtown Toronto, which boasts of having Canada's largest beer list.

The **family-style restaurant** is found in the suburbs, where family lifestyle is common, or near tourist attractions. This type of restaurant designs its service to be fast, its food to be "comfortable," and its décor to be suitable to the younger customer. As customers walk through the door, they will see a supply of highchairs and booster seats along the wall. Children's menus are provided and the décor can handle spills and messes. The servers are not required to handle complicated menu items, but they need to be friendly, fun loving, and ready to serve young customers. These restaurants attract families by using many different marketing techniques such as activities for the children, a "kids eat free" policy, or family specials. Another style of restaurant that often caters to the family market is the **specialty restaurant**. This differs from the family style because it serves one kind of food. For example, Red Lobster is known for its seafood, St. Hubert and Swiss Chalet for chicken, and Tony Roma's for ribs.

With the tremendous immigration Canada has seen over the past 40 years and the numerous cultures that have become part of the Canadian way of life, restaurants specializing in national dishes have sprung up across the country. These restaurants are called **ethnic restaurants**. French, British, and American foods have always been available in Canada, but today, customers can choose from a global marketplace of restaurants. There are three main reasons for the growing desire for foods with a foreign flair. First, Canadians are travelling to more exotic places or learning more about foreign foods by watching television. Second, the population of Canada has become more diverse, and immigrants have brought their own culinary cultures. Finally, grocery chains and frozen-food packagers are responding to these trends with sauces such as "Memories of Singapore," dishes like moussaka, and products such as arborio rice, fresh figs, and papaya. Canadians are now willing to try something new in the dining experience, making ethnic restaurants a viable alternative to standard Canadian fare.

With the emergence of theme parks came **theme restaurants**. These restaurants transport a customer to a time and place beyond the mere meal, often providing entertainment before, during, and after the meal. Theme is carried through to the menu, choice of foods served, and description, with the theme often becoming more important than the food. Theme restaurants do not have to be big, but because of the expense involved in creating the theme, many are quite large. They are located in major cities with good tourist traffic, appealing to the conference and convention market as well as the general public. Medieval Times, located in Toronto on the Exhibition grounds, is a good example of a theme restaurant. This U.S.-based company opened its first restaurant in Orlando, Florida. It owns the largest breeding farm in the world, raising and training Andalusian stallions

Theme restaurants reflect a special time or place. Gad's Hill Place tucks its menu between the pages of a Charles Dickens book and dresses servers in nineteenth-century costumes.

(Photo: Paula Kerr.)

for its shows. The Toronto site was developed in 1990. During the meal, the audience watches a program that includes an illustration of how the Andalusian stallions are trained and a spectacular drama recreating a battle between the Knights of the Kingdom and their archrivals, the Visigoths. In this theme restaurant, the servers are dressed in costumes that reflect medieval times, and the menu items are appropriately named. Medieval Times has the capacity to serve 2500 customers at a time, focusing on large groups that come to the Toronto area for conferences and conventions.

During the 1980s, North America saw the re-emergence of the **buffet house**, a concept that is centuries old. A buffet is a wide assortment of food, both hot and cold, held in a serving line. Customers help themselves to the foods they want in portions they desire. These all-you-can-eat restaurants provide a customer with some table service, such as removal of empty dishes and service of drinks, coffee, or tea. They combine the speed of a fast-food restaurant with the attention of table service—a nice combination in a busy world.

Fast-Food Restaurants   The serving style of a **fast-food restaurant** is to let the customer do the work. Once the order has been received, the customer must locate the napkins, condiments, straws, and a place to sit, as well as clean up afterward. This style decreases the cost of the food, as servers and buspeople are unnecessary. The drive-through concept has helped lower costs and maximize revenues by increasing the output of food without adding seating. Fast-food franchises include McDonald's, Wendy's, Burger King, Kentucky Fried Chicken, Harvey's, A&W, Dairy Queen, Pizza Pizza, Taco Bell, Extreme Pita, Tim Hortons, and Made in Japan. Fast-food franchises have learned the secret of success by locating along busy highways and near resorts, theme parks, recreation areas, and malls, locations that provide convenient stopping places for the traveller. It is very common to see fast-food restaurants located within a few blocks of one another along a major travel route, on the hypothesis that people are more likely to stop if they see a choice of restaurants.

Not all fast-food restaurants are franchised; many are independently owned. Every country around the world has its own variety of single, often mobile restaurants with fast-food menus. They tend to serve products that are popular in their specific region. Canadian units will serve the standard hamburger fare, but in Quebec, tourists will want to try poutine: french fries topped with cheddar cheese curds and smothered in gravy. This dish is so popular in the region that even some McDonald's restaurants now offer it. In Ottawa, T.J. Hooker's Beavertails serves a must-try treat, popular all year round but particularly in the winter. A beavertail is a deep-fried French pastry, shaped like a flat beaver's tail, served with a variety of toppings such as maple syrup, cinnamon sugar, or strawberry jam. Many regions have developed specialty treats, although tourists are sometimes reluctant to try these new foods. After a brief description of the beavertail, the fear a tourist may have had that Canadian beavers are roving the countryside without tails soon gives way to the desire to sample this tasty treat. In 1996, T.J. Hooker's Beavertails made the move south to Disney World and can be found at the Canadian Pavilion in the EPCOT Center.

Coffee houses are popular once again, serving coffees from faraway places like Kenya, Jamaica, and Hawaii, providing a full range of specialty coffees such as cappuccinos and lattes as well as specialty teas. Second Cup and Starbucks are the leaders of this trend. They sell bagels, muffins, Danishes, and cookies as well as coffee. Independent coffee houses serve salads and sandwiches to expand their customer base.

Cafeterias are also gaining popularity in this day of the fast-food empires. A cafeteria differs from a buffet house in that, although clients choose their food from a long line of different dishes, the portions are preset and may be served by kitchen staff. Staff on the floor are only responsible for cleaning tables. In a cafeteria, real tableware may be used, and if this is the case, the staff generally pick up and sort the trays for a departing customer. Cafeterias are commonly found in contract food services—in colleges and universities, hospitals, and in some shopping centres.

in practice

Divide a piece of paper into eight columns and put one of the following food service types at the top of each: independent fast food, hotel restaurants, theme restaurants, family-style, cafeteria, coffee shop, specialty, and ethnic. Write the names of restaurants you have patronized in each of the appropriate categories (no more than five in a column). Compare and contrast the restaurants within each column and among columns on food quality, quantity, service, and price. Do you notice any significant trends in your data?

Hotel Food and Beverage Service Most hotel food-service areas are owned and operated by the hotel, although some hotels opt to rent out space to franchised companies or independent restaurant owners, with a percentage of gross food and beverage sales going to the hotel. As mentioned in the previous chapter, a hotel's

Dining rooms often reflect the personality of the restaurant owner, and many restaurants are providing small separate areas for parties.
(Photo: Paula Kerr.)

food-service component can provide up to half of the hotel's overall revenue. Hotel food and beverage service comes in many forms: fine dining, fast food, coffee shop service, room service, buffets, banquets, poolside bars, snack bars, and lounges. Room service and banquets are unique to the hotel food and beverage department. Although banquets can be hosted by other restaurants, most do not have the capacity to compete with the hotel's banquet capabilities.

S N A P S H O T

Auguste Escoffier

Escoffier! "King of Chefs and Chef to Kings." Georges Auguste Escoffier was the creator of the modern kitchen and the person most responsible for applying scientific principles to culinary arts.

To become outstanding in anything you do, you must give the subject your time, devotion, and energy. You must recognize that continual learning is part of your daily life. Escoffier did just that. His day often began at breakfast and ended only when the kitchen closed. No detail was overlooked, and at all times his staff members knew he was there to teach and support them. No fits of temper were displayed in his establishment, and he constantly worked to achieve the perfection that was his trademark in both preparation and service.

Perhaps his greatest achievement was his book, *Le Guide Culinaire*, which he wrote in collaboration with several of his fellow expert chefs. He attempted to end the period of cooking when a pinch and spoonful were the measurements and few recipes were properly recorded. In Escoffier's cookbook, exact weights and measures were indicated along with the correct method of preparation.

He brought order to the kitchen where little order had existed before. Cooks changed into uniforms while working in his kitchen and into proper attire when they left. Although the French kitchen had been departmentalized, Escoffier integrated and coordinated it. He created the triplicate order pad so that the cashier, server, and cook would each have a copy, and the guest's name was clearly written on the top, allowing Escoffier to cater to the personal preferences of his special guests. The *aboyeur* ("barker") became the *annonceur*, who called the orders out in a polite manner.

Escoffier was the originator of the modern menu. He wrote it so that the guest could easily decide which foods should be eaten first, and which foods were better suited to the palate at the end of the meal. These general principles of order are still found in today's classic French menu.

Much of the world recognition Escoffier enjoyed was due to the successful partnership he had with Cesar Ritz of the renowned Ritz Hotel chain. Madame Ritz remarked: "The collaboration of Ritz and Escoffier must be counted as one of the most fortunate events of their lives." Escoffier worked the back of the house while Ritz concentrated on the front of the house, each striving for perfection and complementing the other's work.

Escoffier died in 1935 at the age of 91. During his lifetime, he had been accorded many honours, but none so great as the Legion of Honour—France's way of recognizing his work and his genius.

Room service on a bicycle? Why not? It grabs attention and tempts other guests at the Jasper Lodge, Alberta, to be served in such a manner.
(Source: Fairmont Hotels & Resorts.)

Room Service Room service is a travel luxury. The guest is pampered by having another person deliver the meal directly to the room. Many people get this type of pampering only on vacation, so why not? All first-class hotels are expected to provide this service to their guests even if it is not a profit-making venture. Room service is expensive to operate and requires a great deal of organization to be successful. The equipment must keep hot food hot and cold food cold, and the food needs to be delivered as quickly as possible to satisfy the guest. Some hotels have special service elevators, which help staff provide fast service without disrupting other guests.

Breakfasts account for 70 percent to 90 percent of room-service orders, with continental breakfasts topping the list.[9] Some hotels provide a doorknob program, which allows guests to check off their desired menu and delivery time on a small menu hung on the outside doorknob. During the night, the menu is collected, and breakfast is served at the requested time.

To help cover additional costs, room-service meals are generally more expensive than the same meals served in the restaurant. Some hotels also add a service charge. Room service may be limited to certain hours of the day or may be offered on a 24-hour basis. The type and size of the hotel will determine the extent of room service available.

Banquets Banquet catering is the responsibility of the catering director or banquet manager. Catering is usually set up as a separate function within a hotel's food and beverage department because it requires different services and meals from a hotel restaurant. Banquets range in size from a small business meeting of perhaps 15 people to a group of more than a thousand for a convention. Weddings, conventions, bar mitzvahs, anniversary dinners, reunions, and business meetings account for the majority of banquets. All convention hotels have catering services.

Catering services can be profitable if well organized because banquets are usually priced higher than restaurant menus and the income is guaranteed. Revenue from the sale of alcohol, either through a **cash bar** or an **open bar** (where the host pays for the alcohol), makes banquets even more profitable. The group holding the banquet orders the bar service and tells the caterer the number of settings to fix. Even if some people do not show up for the meal, the group must pay for the number it guaranteed. Because of economies of scale, labour and food costs per customer are normally reduced. Servers, for example, can be hired only for the time needed.

Contract/Institutional Food Service

Contract/institutional food service differs from commercial food service in several ways. Perhaps the greatest distinguishing factor is the client. In the case of contract food service, the client is different from the customer: the customer is the person who eats the food prepared, but the client is the institution that signs the contract with the food-service operator. It is, of course, important that the customer is happy with the service, but it is even more important that the client institution is content because it renews the contract!

At first glance, it may appear that this division of the food and beverage sector has no effect on the tourism industry, but that assumption is wrong. Contract food-service operators are the only food suppliers to the airlines and rail systems. They run the food service at recreational camps, in museums and at historic sites, at sports arenas like the SkyDome, at many major special events, and at any tourist destination that chooses not to run its own food service.

Institutions often contract out their food services because they have no expertise in running a food service and no desire to be in the food business. Using professional food providers relieves them of many headaches and provides their staff and customers with a better product. The airlines recognized years ago that their business was transportation, not food service. They use Canada's largest contract food-service company—Cara Operations. Cara's in-flight kitchens provide on-board food and beverage service for airlines using Canadian airports.

Train, bus, and air terminals offer meals to their travellers either through contract services or by leasing space to franchises. It is becoming more common for terminals to use nationally known restaurants. Cara Operations and McDonald's are just a few of the big corporations that understand the valuable link between food service and transportation. Restaurants in a terminal have a valuable captive audience. The restaurant's brand name offers travellers comfort from the stress of travel. The terminal avoids worries about feeding the traveller yet still makes money from the rented space. It seems to be a win-win situation for everyone!

There is a growing market for contract food services in the recreational area of tourism. The Corel Centre in Ottawa is a good example. This facility is home to the NHL Ottawa Senators, but also hosts events ranging from concerts and special events such as Disney on Ice to trade shows for yachts, trucks, or home renovation supplies. During the "dollar dog hockey night," the Corel Centre can sell more than 15 000 hotdogs in three hours. As well as fast-food outlets, the Corel Centre has a fine-dining restaurant called the Air Canada Room, a theme restaurant called the Hard Rock Café, and a casual dining experience called Marshy's. In addition, for $45 a guest can book a seat in the Penalty Box and get not only the hockey game, but an all-you-can-eat sandwich buffet as well. The Compass Group is the world's largest contract food service and recently purchased Cara's Health Services Division. It is best known for its ability to handle food service for large events and was responsible for the Winter Olympics in Salt Lake City, 2002. In the summer of 2002, Compass took on the responsibility of feeding the participants at the World Youth Day celebrations. Compass served more than 3.5 million meals at each event, facing the challenging logistics of making, holding and serving such quantities safely and quickly at a reasonable price. In Toronto, during one of the hottest summers on record, 700 Compass managers along with 5000 volunteers managed to serve the food with minimal difficulties.

In Canada, contract food service has not yet reached the size and scope of its U.S. counterpart. However, some colleges and universities offering "board plans" have moved to professional food providers, such as ARAMARK, Sodexho, the Compass Group, and Cara. With changing demographics, such as an increase in

Schools often contract out their food service and some, like the University of Alberta, choose well-known fast-food chains like, Pizza Pizza, Tim Hortons and Taco Bell.
(Photo: Paula Kerr.)

the number of seniors looking for upscale retirement homes, many new opportunities will arise in this area of food service.

Marketing the Restaurant Business

How does a single-unit restaurant survive in the huge, highly competitive marketplace of food and beverage? Many do not, and research shows that 80 percent of owner-operated businesses go bankrupt in their first five years of operation. For many, the growth and proliferation of large chains heralds the end of the privately owned and operated restaurant. Yet the single-unit restaurant continues to exist, and new establishments quickly open in the spaces vacated by failed ventures. The challenge of the restaurant business is often underestimated by new owners, but the dream of success drives them to try to succeed where others have failed.

Success is often linked to knowledge of

- the target market's needs and demands
- food products—purchasing specifications, inventory controls, preparation, service, and storage techniques
- cost control systems for both food and labour
- sales and promotion

How do you sell the products your restaurant creates? You sell them with your most effective in-house marketing and sales tool—your **menu**. Your menu also helps define who you are and how well you will be able to satisfy a customer's needs. Descriptions need to be well written and well designed to tantalize and intrigue customers so they purchase that special soup, salad, or dessert and decide to come back again to try a different entrée. Pricing should reflect the quality and value of your selections as well as your customer's pocketbook. Menus may rely on colour, design, material, or shape to create uniqueness. The menu should be displayed so that passing pedestrians can easily read it. This helps entice tourists, and locals who have never tried your restaurant, to stop and dine with you.

Restaurants advertise and promote their business externally in a variety of ways, including local radio stations and newspapers. One common method of promotion is **couponing**, such as a limited-time two-for-the-price-of-one coupon. This strategy is similar to airline seat sales. The additional customers must be weighed against the loss in sales revenue. Research has indicated that clients who use coupons seldom make a return visit. "Early Bird Specials" are a promotion method that provides an additional revenue stream during a slow period of the day. In imitation of the airlines' frequent flier plans, restaurants are introducing frequent diner cards to reward guests for their loyalty. Although this type of promotion is unlikely to attract the casual tourist, it might encourage frequent business guests to return whenever they are in town. Creative restaurateurs can come up with some intriguing promotional activities. One small neighbourhood restaurant thanks its loyal customers several times a year with a "lottery-style" evening. On chosen Mondays or Tuesdays, instead of a bill, the customer receives a note from the owner saying *"thank you for your patronage (but please remember to tip your server)."* However, the least expensive, most effective method of promotion is still word of mouth: one customer telling friends that your restaurant is terrific. It costs nothing and says a lot—what you do, you do well. Beware, however, of the double-edged sword of word of mouth. Statistics show that customers tell an average of nine people about bad experiences and only three about the good![10]

Learning how to partner with the community and with other tourism products is becoming more important in today's competitive world. Local restaurants will sponsor sports teams and take part in community activities such as food drives and charity fundraisers. Restaurants located in the tourist area of town often partner with accommodations, tourist attractions, festivals, or events. Join your convention and visitor bureau and be sure your restaurant is listed in its local information guide. Provide "order-in" service for a hotel with limited food services to add value to the hotel product and bring more customers to your business. Link your product with tour operators to reach an additional source of revenue. Become an active participant in a festival or special event by setting up food booths for the event. This allows both the local resident and the tourist to taste your product and experience your hospitality. Understanding tourism and the needs of the tourist can provide you with opportunities other establishments miss, and that can mean your business joins the 20 percent of restaurants that learn how to thrive in this highly competitive sector.

in practice   Flip through any edition of your local newspaper and list the various promotional techniques used by restaurants. What types of restaurants are advertising? How are they drawing the value-driven customer? What restaurants are not advertising? Do you believe they are doing better, worse, or the same as those that advertise? In your experience, which restaurant in your community has best responded to current trends in dining out?

Tourism and the Food-Service Industry

Other than airline ticket costs, the average traveller spends more money on food and beverages than on any other vacation expenditure. Determining the number of restaurants dependent on tourism dollars is difficult. In some communities, 40 percent of all restaurant sales are to tourists. However, the total percentage for either Canada or the United States is unknown. Individual restaurant managers generally know how many of their customers are travellers. Restaurants can be divided into three types: tourism-sales-dependent, tourism-profit-dependent, and resident-sales-dependent.[11]

Tourism-Sales-Dependent Restaurants

Because tourism-sales-dependent restaurants earn more than half of their sales revenues from tourists, the tourist is the primary market. Obviously lodging restaurants fit into this category, but what others? In communities that prosper from tourism, nearly all restaurants will depend on tourist sales. Ski resorts are a classic example. Without Banff National Park, Banff Township in Alberta might not exist, along with all the restaurants located in Banff. Dependence is determined by location, not type of ownership. A McDonald's located across the street from a train depot may be tourism sales dependent, whereas another McDonald's just three miles east may be resident sales dependent.

The easygoing atmosphere of pubs is popular with both tourists and locals.
(Photo: Paula Kerr.)

Tourism-Profit-Dependent Restaurants

These restaurants make 20 percent to 50 percent of their sales from tourists. Most restaurants fit into this category. Even though residents make up half or more of their market, these restaurants could not maintain profitability without tourists. Location is key. The restaurant must be close enough to a major highway, an attraction, a high-traffic shopping area, or lodging establishment to attract tourists and yet be easily accessible to the community. When a restaurant starts attracting more tourists than residents, the manager must be careful not to offend local people. Especially when tourism is seasonal, local traffic must be maintained to keep the restaurant open during slow tourism periods.

Resident-Sales-Dependent Restaurants

A restaurant that derives less than 20 percent of its sales from tourists is in the resident-sales-dependent category. These restaurants may profit

OPPORTUNITIES IN FOOD & BEVERAGE

	RESTAURANT/HOTEL DINING/CATERING	KITCHEN	BEVERAGE FACILITY	INSTITUTIONS
OPERATION (FRONT LINE)	Foodservice Helper/Busperson Food & Beverage Server Bartender Wine Steward Doorkeeper/Bouncer Dishwasher/Potwasher Cook (1st, 2nd, Camp, Chef de Parti, Journeyman Cook, Garde Manger) Cook's Helper Kitchen Steward	Kitchen Helper Dishwasher/Potwasher Cook (1st, 2nd, Camp, Chef de Parti, Journeyman Cook, Garde Manger) Cook's Helper Kitchen Steward	Foodservice Helper/Busperson Food & Beverage Server Bartender Wine Steward Doorkeeper/Bouncer	Foodservice Helper/Busperson Kitchen Helper Dishwasher/Potwasher Cook (1st, 2nd, Camp, Chef de Parti, Journeyman Cook, Garde Manger) Cook's Helper
SUPERVISORY	Food & Beverage Service Supervisor Maître d'Hôtel Host/Hostess Catering Functions Supervisor Sous Chef Assistant Chief Steward Merchandising Outlet Supervisor	Baker Pastry Chef Sous Chef Banquet Chef Food Production Supervisor	Food & Beverage Service Supervisor Maître d'Hôtel Host/Hostess	Food & Beverage Service Supervisor Baker Pastry Chef Sous Chef Food Production Supervisor Merchandising Outlet Supervisor
MANAGEMENT	Comptroller Human Resources Manager Public Relations Manager Catering Functions Manager Beverage Services Manager Night Club Manager Assistant Manager Restaurant Sales Manager Dining Room Manager Room Service Manager Executive Sous Chef, Executive Chef Chief Steward Foodservice Manager/Food & Beverage Director Restaurant Manager Human Resources Director	Comptroller Chef de Cuisine Kitchen Manager Food Production Manager Head Chef Foodservice Manager/Food & Beverage Director Executive Chef/Owner	Comptroller Beverage Manager **Night Club Manager** Beverage Services Manager	Comptroller Food Production Manager Foodservice Manager/Food & Beverage Director Executive Chef
EXECUTIVE	Restaurant Chain Manager/Owner/Operator Corporate Vice President General Manager		Night Club Owner General Manager	Senior Administrator/Executive Director of Institution

SOURCE: Courtesy of Canadian Tourism Human Resource Council, *The Student's Travel Map*, 1995.

JOB DESCRIPTION FOR. . .

NIGHT CLUB MANAGER

Industry Sector	Food and Beverage or Accommodation
Division	Food and Beverage Department (hotel)
Industry Setting	Hotels, resorts, private clubs
Job Level	Middle Management
Description of Duties	Direct, plan, and control all aspects of night club operation involving efficient management and supervision, plus participation in development of sales potential including the following:

Management—set goals and objectives, prepare budgets and forecasts; study possible improvements in operation to increase profits and make necessary presentation to owner; *Service*—develop and implement policies and set standards regarding the type of service to be offered and procedures for the operation; conduct regular daily inspection of facility and inspect security; verify competition techniques; resolve customer complaints; *Staff*—collaborate with supervisory and management staff; set and monitor staff work schedules; recruit staff and oversee their training; *Inventory/Suppliers*—control inventory, monitor revenues, and modify procedures and prices when appropriate; negotiate purchasing arrangements with suppliers for the provision of supplies; *Catering*—negotiate arrangements with clients for catering or use of facilities for banquets or receptions.

Skills	Managerial (recruitment, training and evaluation, short- and long-range planning, guest relations, team development, written/oral communications, policy and procedure implementation, delegation, staff coordination, problem solving, discipline maintenance, and conflict resolution).
Knowledge	Operational (cost control, music/entertainment design and development, security, product specifications, purchasing, receiving, storage, fire regulations, facility design, portion control, sanitation requirements, food preparation, wine merchandising and service, financial planning and accounting, union relations, industry laws and regulations, and space utilization).
Education	Completion of a community college program related to restaurant/hotel management is a definite asset.
Industry Experience	5 to 10 years of supervisory-level hospitality experience is an asset.
Career Paths	Night Club Owner/Operator, Beverage Services Manager, Food and Beverage Director, General Manager
HRDC Reference	NOC 0631 Restaurant and Food Service Managers

from tourist dollars but could operate without them. In metropolitan areas, resident-sales-dependent restaurants can succeed easily, but in smaller communities with some tourist traffic they tend to be less successful.

Dining out on Vacation

According to surveys, people tend to eat differently when on vacation. They are more likely to treat themselves to a midscale or upscale restaurant. Fourteen percent of all vacationers choose full-service, fine-dining restaurants; 32 percent choose midscale restaurants, and 53 percent eat at fast-food establishments. Compare that to resident choices: 8 percent of local clientele choose fine-dining establishments, 23 percent opt for family-style/midscale restaurants, and 69 percent choose fast food. Vacationers tend to choose fast food for breakfast and lunch to get a quick start on the day's activities. At night they are ready to relax and enjoy their meal and tend to choose a full-service restaurant. Some restaurateurs have discovered the advantages of group tours. Many tours offer meal services, and tour operators are willing to schedule dinner a little earlier than normal if the price is right. Partnering with tour operators by providing quality food and service at a discounted price may mean additional revenue during the early, slower dining period. As the meal is usually a set menu and the number of guests is known in advance, profit margins should be good. As we enter the next decade, with a growing boomer market, partnering with other tourism businesses may mean the difference between success and failure for the independent restaurateur.

in practice

Identify 12 restaurants in your community and classify them as tourism sales dependent, tourism profit dependent, or resident sales dependent. If possible, talk to some of the restaurant managers to confirm your guess. Next, identify which factor discussed in the previous section has the greatest effect on the sales status of the restaurants.

summary

The food and beverage sector of the tourism industry is the largest of all eight sectors. It has two divisions: commercial and contract food service. Commercial food service is further divided into two distinct categories: full service and fast food. Restaurants can be owned by an individual, as part of a multi-unit corporate group, or as a franchise. There are many different kinds of restaurants available to the public, each serving a different need. Hotel food service features two distinct departments besides the restaurant or coffee shop: room service and banquet service. A hotel must know the needs of its clientele and structure its food-service department accordingly.

Contract food service is found in establishments whose primary reason for existence is not the service of food. Contract food services are found in museums, sports arenas, schools, hospitals and retirement homes, at festivals and special events, and within the transportation system. This division is growing fast. Canada's largest contract food server is Cara Operations. Trends and concerns in the industry are quality of service, fast food/takeout, nutrition, eating out with children, allergy awareness, and legislation affecting alcohol consumption and smoking.

Restaurant advertising and promotion entice the local crowd to eat in the restaurant. Public relations promotions tend to produce more loyal local traffic than any other type of promotion. Unless the tourist is camping or staying at the home of friends or relatives, dining out is part of the vacation experience. Breakfast and lunch are more likely to be eaten at a fast-food restaurant, whereas the evening meal, with time to relax, is spent at a midscale or upscale restaurant. Restaurants that depend on tourist dollars for their existence, such as lodging restaurants, are tourism sales dependent. Restaurants that are tourism profit dependent need both the tourist dollar and the local dollar to maintain profits. Most restaurants, however, depend on local residents, which is why many restaurateurs miss appealing to visitors who are looking for good places to eat. Tourism is a financial boost for the food-service industry that has often been overlooked.

questions

1. Restaurants, like hotels, may be owned and operated in several different ways. Briefly explain the differences and the pros and cons of owning (i) an independent restaurant unit, (ii) a multi-unit restaurant chain, and (iii) a franchise.

2. Commercial restaurants are categorized by level of service, style of the restaurant, and menu. Briefly describe eight different types of restaurants found in your area and give at least two examples of each.

3. Suppose you are running a large downtown hotel. What services will your hotel provide, what services will you decide not to offer, and what services will you contract out? Justify your decisions in terms of value to customers and profit.

4. a) List and briefly explain food service trends identified in the text. Now list them in order of importance.

   b) Justify your ranking of the top three trends and the bottom trend on your list.

   c) Which of these trends do you feel is most prominent in the industry today? Why?

5. "Contract food services will continue to play an increasing role in the tourism industry."

   a) Agree or disagree with this statement, supporting your answer with examples.

   b) If you were to choose contract food services as your career, design your career ladder and discuss the benefits you would enjoy working in this industry.

6. Differentiate between a tourism-sales-dependent or tourism-profit-dependent and a resident-sales-dependent restaurant, and provide an example of each from your area.

7. Define the following terms as they relate to the food and beverage sector: *couponing, menu, bistro, open bar, opportunity costs, cash bar, cafeteria, contract, commercial food services.*

weblinks

www.crfa.ca

The Canadian Restaurant and Foodservices Association has more than 15 000 members ranging from restaurants and hotels to foodservice suppliers.

www.restaurant.org

The (American) National Restaurant Association provides lots of information and good links to food-service and association sites.

www.cara.com

Cara Operations runs Swiss Chalet, Harvey's, and Second Cup and it provides airline food services.

notes

1. Dr. M. Mohan, G. Gislason, and B. McGowan, *Tourism Related Employment: An Update* (Ottawa, Ontario: Canadian Tourism Human Resource Council, 1998).
2. www.crfa.ca/research/research_tourismontheroadtorecovery.htm
3. Donald E. Lundberg, *The Hotel and Restaurant Business*, 4th ed. (New York: Van Nostrand Reinhold Co., 1984), pp. 17–27.
4. Harold McGee, *On Food and Cooking* (New York: Collier Macmillan, 1984), p. 131.
5. Lundberg, *The Hotel and Restaurant Business*, p. 31.
6. *New York Times*, September 11, 2002, p. 1.
7. *Ontario Restaurant News*, May 2002, p. 3.
8. www.crfa.ca/issues
9. *Ontario Restaurant News*, May 2002, p. 9.
10. SuperHost Training Manual.
11. Uel Blank, *The Community Tourism Industry Imperative* (State College, PA: Venture Publishing, 1989), p. 17.

8 The Attractions Sector

key terms

amusement park
aquarium
art museum
Canadian Heritage
casino gambling
children's museum
clustering
family entertainment
  centre (FEC)
gateway

heritage or cultural
  tourism
historic site
historical museum
living history museum
market match
megamall
museums
oceanarium
pari-mutuel gambling

partnership
scientific museum
sense of place
site specific
theme park
UNESCO World
  Heritage Site
unique selling
  proposition (USP)
virtual reality centre

learning objectives

Having read this chapter you will be able to

1. Describe the responsibilities of Canadian Heritage in the attractions sector.

2. Define the scope and variety of tourist attractions.

3. Discuss UNESCO's criteria for designated World Heritage Sites, using Canadian examples.

4. Discuss how public, private, and nonprofit attractions differ.

5. Provide examples of public attractions and compare them with private or commercial attractions.

6. Discuss six key factors that help determine a destination/attraction's success.

- -

Much of Canada's attraction lies in its natural resources (mountains, lakes, rivers, ocean shores, and forests), but tourism also depends on artificial attractions to entertain and educate visitors and residents alike. This sector of the tourism industry is growing and must continue to grow if Canada is to remain competitive, especially in international markets. What differentiates the attractions sector from the events and conferences sector is the permanence of the attraction. Canada has more than 3000 permanent sites, including amusement parks, water parks, theme parks, museums, theatres, zoos, aquariums, and heritage sites. Added to these attractions are the shopping experiences found across Canada, which include the world famous megamall, West Edmonton Mall; the harbourfront shops of Halifax; Granville Island in Vancouver with its fresh

Visitors from across Canada and around the world come to Drumheller, Alberta, to visit the Royal Tyrrell Museum, take daytrips to dig for dinosaur bones, and gaze at nature's spectacle, the hoodoos.
(Photo: Tom Hadley.)

seafood, vegetables, and crafts; and the historic Byward Market in Ottawa. It is reasonable to say that almost everyone has visited an attraction in some form or another. In many cases, attractions are the reason people travel. Attractions may be the primary destination or only one component of a larger vacation trip, but without them, vacation travel would not be what it is today. It is estimated that more than 120 000 people are employed in this sector, making up about 1 percent of the total Canadian work force.[1] This chapter looks at the variety of experiences available to the visitor in the attractions sector of tourism. It also looks carefully at six key factors that help create a successful tourism destination.

Canadian Heritage

The federal department that plays the largest role in the attractions sector is **Canadian Heritage**. This huge department manages two major divisions that affect the tourism industry: the National Parks System and the Cultural Development and Heritage division. The latter department is responsible for

- all of our national historic sites
- our seven heritage canal systems
- our national battlefields

- our national heritage river systems
- all national museums and galleries
- the national library and archives
- Canadian cultural activities, including television, radio, film, and the arts

Also reporting to Canadian Heritage is the crown corporation called the National Capital Commission (NCC), which was discussed in chapter 3.

History in Brief

Attractions are not a recent invention; many of the global attractions the tourist travels to see are historic remnants of earlier times. The Great Wall of China and the Pyramids of Egypt are two such examples. In Canada, ancient sites are beginning to interest tourists from across the country and from around the world—sites like L'Anse aux Meadows, the Viking settlement in Newfoundland, or the Tyrrell Museum in Alberta, located in one of the world's largest dinosaur gravesites. Attractions such as Disney World have provided tourists with even stronger travel motivations and made small towns like Orlando into huge destinations.

Amusement parks are centres of entertainment offering rides, shows, food, candy, and arcades. Amusement parks date to the nineteenth century, when the traditional carousel was a highlight. These parks were positioned at the end of streetcar lines to be accessible to all city dwellers. But as the automobile became popular, people ventured further in search of recreation, and the amusement park business fell on difficult times. Today, only about 150 permanent amusement parks are in operation, including Busch Gardens in Florida, Lakeside Park in Denver, and Canada's Wonderland in Ontario. Although popular attractions within the region, these parks generally do not draw national or international travellers. Modern amusement parks provide rides, entertainment, refreshments, and souvenirs.

The theme park concept is most widely attributed to Walt Disney. **Theme parks** are family entertainment centres (FECs) oriented to a particular subject or historical area. They combine costuming and architecture with entertainment and merchandise to create a fantasy-provoking atmosphere.[2] Theme parks trace their roots to the amusement park business. With the opening of Disneyland in California in 1955, Walt Disney transformed the amusement park from a run-down hangout for teenagers to a wholesome family entertainment centre with a full day's worth of thrills and fantasy. Disneyland showed that theme parks can experience great success. And they *are* great! Fantasies and dreams come true for a short time in theme parks such as Disneyland.

Walt Disney wanted to realize a perfected vision of his own childhood, right down to a small version of a Main Street like those in the midwestern towns of his youth. It was to have the virtues of an amusement park with none of the vices: dirt, carnival barkers, and general sleaziness. And it was to offer the public the Disney Studio's fantasies as a means of escape.[3]

Disneyland's success was undeniable, and 15 years later Disney announced the creation of Disney World in Florida. Disney Tokyo followed in 1984. In 1991, Disney Corporation was selected to join in the Dow Jones Industrial Average, a group of 30 large American corporations whose business health and shareholder acceptance are used as measures of the U.S.'s economic strength. Disney replaced USX (formerly U.S. Steel) and became the only representative of the tourism industry, signifying that recreation and travel have become a staple in the American economy. Disney's Dow Jones status also reflects the shift in focus from an industrial society to a leisure society.

In 1992, Euro-Disney opened in France. Although Disney has been very successful in the United States and Japan, the Euro-Disney concept has fallen on hard times. According to Michael Eisner, Disney's CEO, "We didn't have quite the affection built into our products there. We're a business story there. We're a cultural story here. I've never dealt with a business story. I like to talk about how Aladdin is doing.... All of a sudden, it's all about debt, which is not what we're used to."[4] The main problem is not the park itself, but a combination of events and rules. More than 17 million people visited the park in its first 18 months of operation, but visitors spent little and did not stay at Disney's six hotels. A recession, higher than expected interest rates, strict employee dress codes, and no wine at the restaurants have been blamed for the problems. Disney has been trying to fix the problems by adding wine to four restaurants, reducing hotel prices, and encouraging winter attendance through lower admission fees.[5] In 2000, Disney opened its "Adventure" park next to Disneyland. This theme park focuses on activities such as white-water rafting and rock climbing and is a good example of how attractions continue to bring back old customers with new facilities.[6]

Other theme parks have emulated the Disney model. Canada's Wonderland Park just outside Toronto, for example, has theme areas such as "International Street," with restaurants, stores, and boutiques in the style of Mediterranean, Alpine, and Scandinavian countries; "World Expo 1890," which features period architecture and rides; "The Medieval Faire," with live theatre, rides, restaurants, and boutiques in the style of medieval Europe; and "The Happy Land of Hanna-Barbera,"

S N A P S H O T

Walt Disney

He gave the world a bit of magic to ease the stress of modern living and added laughter and joy to a sometimes sorrowful world. He also created a new tourism product—entertainment that was family oriented, clean, safe, and well run. Walter Elias Disney was born in 1901, fourth son in a family of five. His childhood was spent following the dreams of a father who never achieved the success he had hoped for, whether it was farming in Kansas or Florida, or working in Missouri. At the age of 17, Walt went to war and served with the Red Cross in France. He was soon making extra money drawing cartoon figures and selling war relics. On his return to Chicago, he applied for jobs as a cartoonist with local papers. After several rejections, he formed a small company with a young artist named Ub Iwerks. Ub became a fast friend and would become one of the Disney Company's most respected cartoonists.

Walt Disney fell in love with the movies. He spent much of his spare time and money catching the latest films and soon felt capable of producing better, funnier cartoons than the professionals. When several business attempts failed in the Chicago area, Disney set out to make a name for himself in Hollywood.

In 1923, with his brother Roy handling the finances, Walt Disney formed his first film company, Disney Productions. However, the world of early Hollywood was full of scoundrels and crooks, and Disney Productions faced many difficulties. In 1928, Disney was forced to abandon his first cartoon figure, a rabbit called Oswald, when the studio he was working with claimed Oswald as its own. Enraged, he simply abandoned the figure.

In the same year, he developed a cartoon character based on a friendly little field mouse he had saved while living in Chicago. Mickey Mouse was born, destined to be Walt's favourite cartoon character and the second most recognized figure in the world (next to Santa Claus). Mickey's first major hit was *Steamboat Willy*, which made history as the first talking cartoon short. Between 1929 and 1934, Disney created Minnie Mouse, Goofy, Pluto, and Donald Duck, as well as a series of cartoons based on classical music pieces such as *The Skeleton Dance*. In 1937 Disney took cartoons to a new height, creating a full-length feature film in colour, called *Snow White and the Seven Dwarfs*. It was a smashing success!

With the advent of the Second World War, Disney Productions confronted new obstacles. It had released five films—*Pinocchio, Fantasia, The Reluctant Dragon, Dumbo,* and *Bambi*— all of which were flops. People were not going to films; they were at war. With financial failure facing him, Disney entered the war by producing films for the U.S. Government, films such as *Victory Through Air Power*.

By 1946 Disney had ventured into a new era of filmmaking, combining cartoon figures with live action. "Zip-a-dee-doo-dah" from *Song of the South*, a film about Uncle Remus and Bre'r Rabbit, won Disney Company its first Oscar for best song of the year.

Disney's triumphs continued, but he began to lose interest in the world of fantasy. The war effort had left him depressed, and his creative energy was at an all-time low. During a short vacation to Chicago, he came up with a new project, but it was so daring that he confided in no one until his plans were ready. When he approached Roy with his idea for a theme park, he was met with complete rejection. This time he had gone too far, Roy said, and Disney Productions would not support his efforts. Never one to back down from a dream, he approached the new medium of television to help fund Disneyland. The two big networks turned him down, but fledgling ABC offered him a contract, and Disney entered the world of TV. His *Wonderful World of Disney* was an instant success, and he proceeded with his plans for Disneyland. By now Disney Company had started to produce live action films such as *The Sword and the Rose* and had begun a new series of films called *True-Life Adventures*, which included *The Beaver Pond*, filmed in Canada.

On July 17, 1955, Disneyland opened, and brother Roy was forced to admit that it was an overwhelming success. Walt's new project soon began—the building of a larger theme park to include a view of the future, a park called EPCOT Center, Experimental Prototype Community of Tomorrow.

Although Walt's fame grew, his health failed. Years of neglect finally took their toll. In 1966 he underwent surgery to remove one lung, but life cheated him at the end. He died in December of 1966, six years before the opening of EPCOT, his final dream.

Disney left behind a legacy of firsts, a legacy of magic. He was a man of great action, who believed in his own abilities, even when others did not; he showed the world that dreams do come true. Without his creative genius and dedication to excellence, tourism would be missing a little of its magic.

with Taft cartoon characters in their well-known environs.[7] In addition to themes, live entertainment is offered throughout Canada's Wonderland.

September 11 has had a major impact on large attractions like Disneyland. One of the first travel items to be eliminated from the American way of life was pleasure travel. Added to this, the financial troubles of the high-tech industry forced the layoff of many thousand workers. American economic growth has slowed and together, these events have reduced the number of visitors to this type of attraction. For the first time in its history, Disney has also been forced to lay off workers. Past experience tells us that vacation travel bounces back quickly from economic slowdowns, as people look to escape from hard times into fantasy. If no additional terrorist attacks occur in North America over the next year, visits to this type of attraction are expected to return to normal levels.

in practice

What do you think was the dominant trend in attractions for your area in the 1990s? Do you see the popularity of water parks, miniature golf, and family entertainment centres continuing through 2005? What new attraction do you think may be trendy in the next 10 years? Defend your answers.

Theme parks, museums, zoos, casinos, and Broadway-style theatres are only a few of the different types of attractions found around the world. Attractions come in so many shapes, sizes, and types of ownership that throwing them all into a single category called attractions seems incongruous. Comparing Disney World to a Niagara Falls, or the CN Tower to the Mayan ruins in Mexico, has an element of the ridiculous about it; yet, each is classified as an attraction.

Attractions differ not only in type but in ownership; they may be privately owned and operated, nonprofit, or publicly owned. What is the difference? Table 8.1 identifies the type of ownership, sources of funding, and the different types of attractions found in each category.

TABLE 8.1   *Sources of Funding in the Attractions Sector*

	Public	Nonprofit	Private
Funding	Taxes	Admission Fees	Admission Fees
	Admission Fees	Donations	Food & Beverage
	Donations	Grants	Merchandise
	Grants	Memberships	Entertainment
			Parking
Types	Museums	Museums	Theme Parks
	Zoos/Aquariums	Zoos/Aquariums	Amusement Parks
	Historic Sites	Historic Sites	Carnivals/Circuses
	Casinos		Theatres
			Shopping Malls
			Family Entertainment Centres

Public and Nonprofit Attractions

As provincial and federal governments cut budgets, money for the upkeep and enhancement of public and nonprofit attractions has dwindled. Many Canadians fear that these funding cuts will undermine institutions that support heritage, culture, and the arts.

Public attractions are owned and operated by governments. Taxes are often the prime source of funding, although government cutbacks have forced public institutions to become more creative in raising funds. In addition, some taxpayers are less tolerant of the idea of fully supporting a public attraction. As a result, public attractions are now charging entrance fees and are bringing in exciting special events or shows to boost ticket sales and provide added revenues. Additional money is made from parking fees and the sale of souvenirs and gifts.

Many attractions raise additional revenue through their food and beverage service. After hours, space is rented for private functions. For example, the Vancouver Aquarium provides a fascinating setting for people attending a conference in the city. It provides guests with the opportunity to view the attraction at their leisure and to enjoy a meal away from the hotel setting.

Nonprofit attractions are just that—they are not in the business of making a profit, and any revenue they earn is funnelled back into the attraction. They may be created in a variety of ways. Some began as public attractions and are no longer funded by government. The Log Farm in the Ottawa region is a perfect example. One of the area's earliest farms, it was used as a living history site, showing tourists and local residents the farming methods of the early nineteenth century. When the Government of Canada ended its funding, a group of concerned citizens took over the operation. It now exists on revenue received from grants, donations, membership fees, and special events such as the Sugaring Festival. In the early spring, visitors come to watch maple syrup being made in huge cauldrons. Volunteers boil the maple sap to make fresh syrup and maple taffy, which is sold to the public.

The Diefenbunker in Carp, Ontario, is another example of how nonprofit attractions begin. Between 1959 and 1961, at the height of the Cold War, this huge four-storey bunker was built into the Carp Escarpment to protect government officials in the event of nuclear war. In 1994 the bunker was abandoned and purchased by the citizens of the town of Carp. Prior to sealing its entrance forever, final tours for interested area residents were conducted and it soon became apparent that this unique site was an important glimpse into the Cold War era in Canada. The bunker has been restored and operates as the only Cold War museum of its kind in the world. Funding comes from grants provided by the Ontario government and the Regional Municipality of Ottawa-Carleton, as well as admission fees and donations. Some nonprofit attractions are started by wealthy philanthropists who amass a collection on the subject of their passion (art, history, etc.) and who then provide funds to house and maintain the collection.

Admission fees and the sale of souvenir items often bring in revenue for nonprofit attractions. Additional revenues are generated from the sale of memberships, donation boxes at the entrance, benefit dinners, and special events. What benefits would a membership in a nonprofit organization bring? Members receive monthly newsletters, get free admissions, and have the satisfaction of knowing they are contributing to a cause in which they believe. It is sometimes hard to distinguish between a public and nonprofit attraction but, in the end, the tourist doesn't care as long as the staff are knowledgeable and the experience enjoyable.

Museums

Visiting **museums** is an important part of many itineraries and is sometimes the main focus of a trip. A museum can display just about anything, from trains and motorcycles to books and letters. Museums are either historical, scientific, or artistic. Although they are usually sponsored by government or nonprofit organizations, some are commercial for-profit enterprises.

Most museums have a permanent area on the property that displays the same exhibit at all times. Another section usually houses a succession of travelling shows. These special events keep local people coming to the museum, so changes in artists, new historical displays, or recent scientific discoveries are promoted to local residents as well as tourists.

A museum has a director, various assistants, and volunteers, depending on the size of the museum. Volunteers usually outnumber paid staff, especially in smaller communities. The director is responsible for searching for new displays, scheduling travelling shows, obtaining permanent displays for the museum, and completing paperwork such as budgeting and payroll. A board of directors is responsible for hiring and guiding the director, and is often elected from the membership of the museum. The board and the director decide on themes for the upcoming year, special events, and marketing ideas.

Art galleries and museums were once primarily cultural centres in metropolitan areas, where people of sophisticated tastes gathered to express their opinions about the works of a particular artist. Canadians have long had the opportunity to visit both nationally and provincially funded **art museums**. The National Art Gallery in Ottawa is noted for its permanent displays of Canadian art, European art, and special exhibits. For example, in 1996, art treasures belonging to Queen Elizabeth II were put on public display for the very first time. The exhibit was shown for a five-month period and proved to be a big tourist attraction.

Art museums can be found in communities throughout North America. Young artists usually get their start by displaying their work in smaller galleries,

The National Art Gallery of Canada in Ottawa, Ontario, displays the works of prominent Canadian painters such as Tom Thomson and the Group of Seven. The gallery also exhibits a special show every summer for visitors.

(Photo: John B. Kerr.)

which in turn support the local art museum. Support is garnered by displaying and advertising the work of local artists, who provide art classes to residents of all ages. By starting with the young, the art museum is able to maintain citizens' life-long support. The artist may also autograph a limited number of prints during a showing, giving tourists and locals alike an opportunity to rub elbows with the artist. Open houses, dignitary social hours, and other small events are held to reach more people and to show off what the museum has to offer. Art museums strive for variety by providing all types of artwork, including sculptures, oils, watercolours, and carvings. Operating trends are similar in small and large museums.

Historical museums are more likely than art or scientific museums to be in small communities, because all communities have a history of which they are proud. History is usually presented by showing the antiques of the time along with a written explanation of the pieces. Museums, especially the smaller ones, struggle to achieve an uncluttered display, as they receive more and more items that the donor expects to see displayed. Before long, the museum looks like an antique shop. Although museums need donations, they may also need to tell the donating party that the item may not be shown.

Trends in historical museums include **living history museums**, which re-create a period of time with people in costume portraying historical figures. These museums are popular among all age groups. Colonial Williamsburg in Virginia is the largest and best-known living history museum. It interprets eighteenth-century American history by presenting 400 buildings inhabited by people acting as bakers, apprentices, shopkeepers, and other colonial residents. On a smaller scale, Upper Canada Village, located just outside Morrisburg, Ontario, and the fortress of Louisbourg in Cape Breton, Nova Scotia, provide visitors with a similar early Canadian experience. Living history museums are successful because they are both fun and educational; they also provide jobs to local people and bring tourist dollars into the area.

A drummer at Fort Louisbourg in Cape Breton, Nova Scotia, announces the changing of the guard.
(Photo: Paula Kerr.)

Another historical museum trend is to replace the old "DO NOT TOUCH" signs with displays that can be touched. It is frustrating trying to keep young hands off a horseless carriage or an old-time rocking horse. Many museums now display the authentic piece behind an enclosure and provide a replica for children and adults to climb, touch, feel, and smell. People learn more when they have fun and can experience the past, even if only by holding the object; and when people have fun, they are more likely to return and tell their friends.

Scientific museums showcase items ranging from dinosaur bones to spaceships. They tend to show a process, whether it be the development and extinction of dinosaurs at the Royal Tyrrell Museum of Palaeontology in Drumheller, Alberta, or the history of the space age at the Kennedy Space Center in Florida. The Tyrrell Museum is located near Dinosaur Provincial Park, one of the world's most extensive dinosaur graveyards. Here tourists from all over the world visit the museum, which houses one of the world's largest collections of dinosaur bones. The most spectacular feature of the museum is Dinosaur Hall, where more than 50 skeletons are displayed, including a very rare, complete skeleton of the Tyrannosaurus Rex. Another interesting feature of the museum is the Palaeoconservatory, a room filled with plants whose origins have been traced back over 140 million years. Not to be missed is a spectacular film illustrating how scientists believe the world was created. At the other end of the timeline, the Kennedy Space Center presents the advancements of space exploration, from the first rocket ship to the shuttles being used today.

One of Canada's most respected museums, the Royal British Columbia Museum, is located in Victoria, B.C. It is typical of a large museum and blends both science and art. The museum houses the best collection of totem poles and Aboriginal art in North America. One floor is dedicated to dioramas of west coast forests and seashores, and another floor presents the human history of the province. The Royal B.C. Museum is also noted for its strong programs on ecology.

Many scientific museums are **site specific**: that is, they are located where the scientific event took place. The Tyrrell Museum is an example. Small communities that claim a scientific history can easily create a museum in honour of the person, animal, or event. The latest trend in science museums is the **children's museum**, which allows young children to experiment with various forms of scientific discoveries. These science museums, such as the Ontario Science Centre in Toronto, provide hands-on experience for visitors; it is impossible to simply stroll through without getting involved. As in a living history museum, visitors are encouraged to learn while having fun.

Overall, museums are trying to involve the younger generation on the theory that if youngsters become interested, the museum will have their support for life. Museums are becoming more family oriented and more visible in community events and tourist advertisements for the area. In the off-season, museums become classrooms. Local support is increased through school events at the museum—a smart way to be a tourist attraction.

Historic sites

Historic sites are located in every country that has taken the initiative to commemorate them, and Canada has thousands of special interest sites. Some have just a marker, explaining the historic importance of the site, but many have interpretive centres or small museums. The **United Nations Educational, Scientific and Cultural Organization (UNESCO)** has placed several national parks and historic sites on their list of **World Heritage Sites** in recognition of the outstanding universal value of the area. UNESCO Heritage Sites are carefully reviewed by an international panel before being given this title (see Table 8.2). L'Anse aux Meadows, on the northwestern tip of Newfoundland, is a UNESCO Heritage Site that commemorates the arrival of the first Europeans to the New World a thousand years ago. This site is the only authenticated Norse settlement in North America. Nearby at L'Anse-Amour, tourists visit the 7500-year-old burial mound of the first residents of Newfoundland and Labrador, the Maritime Archaic Indians.

Prince Edward Island's Province House is considered to be the "birthplace of Canada." The first meeting to discuss federal union was held here in 1864. Several rooms, including the Confederation Room, have been restored to their nineteenth-century appearance. This building also houses the provincial legislature. In New Brunswick, tourists may visit the Acadian Historical Village, which presents

TABLE 8.2   *Canadian World Heritage Sites*

Name	Province/Territory	Year Designated
Nahanni National Park	Northwest Territories	1978
L'Anse aux Meadows Archeological Site	Newfoundland and Labrador	1978

Kluane National Park
    Wrangell—St Elias/Glacier
    Bay/Tatshenshini Alsek Park
	Canada & USA	1979
		added in 1994

Dinosaur National Park	Alberta	1979
Head-Smashed-In Buffalo Jump Provincial Park Historic Site	Alberta	1982
SGaang Gwaii	British Columbia	1981
Wood Buffalo National Park	Alberta/Northwest Territories	1983

Canadian Rocky Mountains Parks
  • Banff National Park
  • Jasper National Park
  • Yoho National Park
  • Mount Robson Provincial Park
  • Mount Assiniboine Provincial Park
  • Hamber Provincial Park
	Alberta/British Columbia	1984 and 1990

The Historic District of Quebec
  • Fortifications of Quebec National Historic Site
  • Artillery Park National Historic Site
	Quebec	1985

Gros Morne National Park	Newfoundland	1987
Waterton—Glacier International Peace Park	Canada & USA	1995
The Old Town of Lunenburg	Nova Scotia	1995
Miguasha Park	Quebec	1999

SOURCE: Courtesy of Parks Canada.

*Canadian
UNESCO World
Heritage Sites
include the magnifi-
cent Nahanni River.*
(Photo courtesy Canadian
Tourism Commission.)

the tale of the Acadians' struggle for survival after expulsion from Nova Scotia in 1755. Nova Scotia has its own share of history. The town of Lunenburg, recently declared a UNESCO World Heritage Site, can trace its ancestry back to 1753, when the first settlers arrived. Lunenburg is famous for its shipbuilding and, in particular, for the *Bluenose*, the legendary sailing ship that was champion of the seas from 1921 to 1946.

Quebec City is Canada's oldest city. The original section is walled, with narrow cobblestone streets and ancient greystone houses, churches, and the old stone fort, still complete with its massive gates and cannons. Montreal, unlike Quebec City, was first established as a mission whose goal was to convert the Iroquois to Christianity. It is not surprising that the city has been known for its magnificent churches. Many tourists walk up Mont-Royal, following the path to the summit to see the modern cross placed on the spot where Maisonneuve placed a cross in1643.

One of the more interesting historic sites in Ottawa is Laurier House, the residence of two of Canada's most famous prime ministers, Sir Wilfrid Laurier and William Lyon Mackenzie King. The house has been left just as it was, and on the third floor is the crystal ball that King allegedly used to determine policy. In Manitoba, tourists visit the site of the last rebellion in Canada, led by Louis Riel and his band of Métis. In Saskatchewan, which has more museums per capita than any other province, the history of Canada's red-coated Royal Canadian Mounted Police comes alive when tourists visit training headquarters. Alberta is home to another World Heritage Site, Head-Smashed-In Buffalo Jump, where Aboriginal tribes of the northwest killed buffalo by driving them over high cliffs.

The Aboriginal people of British Columbia, working with cultural ecologists, have reconstructed much of their history. Both the Haida and Gitksan Indians are famous for their arts and crafts, especially their magnificent totem poles. The villages of Kitwanga and Kiwancool have some of the finest totem stands in North America. 'Kswan, a Gitksan village designed to teach its history to visitors, has replicas of ancient cedar log houses and a salmon smoke house. Tourists can watch Gitksan carve their dug-out canoes, or be guided around the museum by Gitksan women who vividly describe their ancient culture. The Frog House of the Ancient Past presents Gitksan life before the arrival of Europeans, and House of Grandfathers shows the impact that the Europeans had on the Gitksan way of life.

Heritage Tourism

Heritage tourism is to a culture what ecotourism is to nature. Prominent tourism specialists argue that ecology and culture are so intertwined that the term used should be "cultural ecotourism." The World Tourism Organization defines **heritage** (sometimes called **cultural) tourism** as "immersion in the natural history, human heritage, arts, philosophy, and institutions of another region or country."[8] Heritage is our past—what we have received from our ancestors and what we pass on to future generations. By showing people how and why cultures differ, heritage tourism becomes a strong link to world peace, teaching the value of art, traditions, culture, and history. Because both ecotourism and heritage tourism are part of a learning process, they require experienced, knowledgeable guides on the excursion. The number of people involved in these activities, both visitors and guides, continues to grow.

According to Statistics Canada, typical heritage tourists are between the ages of 45 and 64; they are better educated and have higher incomes than the average visitor. They are also willing to spend more money on their vacations than the average tourist. It is estimated that 40 percent of the overseas market, 37 percent of the U.S. market, and 33 percent of the domestic tourist market will include some form of heritage-related activities on a Canadian vacation.

One of the perceptions foreign tourists have of Canada as a destination is that it has great scenery and friendly people, but no history. Even Canadian tourists have little knowledge of our rich history. As the government works to preserve Canada's ancient heritage, new interest is being generated. The countryside is dotted with memories of a unique and colourful history, and all of these sites add to Canada's attractions.

Zoos and Aquariums

Large zoological parks and gardens are significant tourist attractions in themselves. People travel to San Diego to visit the San Diego Zoo, San Diego Wild Animal Park, or Sea World. These attractions all exhibit animals in enclosed areas or in a natural habitat where they can roam free, as in the Metropolitan Toronto Zoo. Zoos are no longer old, smelly places with bars and wires, but comfortable natural settings for breeding rare and endangered species. The newest animal park is located at Disney World and features a fully developed natural African setting that allows the animals a free and healthy life. The late Marlin Perkins, the famous curator and host of television's *Wild Kingdom*, insisted that zoos are a necessity; several animals have escaped extinction because of zoos, and most zoo animals are healthier than they would be in their wild state.

A zoo, like a museum, is and should be an educational experience for the visitor. But because the zoo is alive, the visitor learns without noticeable effort. The trend in zoos is to keep people involved. Aquariums and oceanariums are both "aquatic zoos." **Aquariums** are usually found inland and exhibit fresh- and salt-water fish. **Oceanariums** are located on the ocean coast and may include large fish such as sharks, as well as seals, otters, dolphins, and other aquatic life. The Monterey Aquarium in California is noted for its magical display of jellyfish, some measuring more than 1 m and some just 0.5 cm. Canada's best-known aquarium is found in Vancouver. It is renowned worldwide for its educational programs and creative displays. This facility also houses one of Canada's largest Imax theatres, allowing the aquarium to bring visitors back with special film events. Many oceanariums have special shows with trained dolphins, sea lions, or seals. These shows provide entertainment and allow the trainer to explain the habits of the animal. Zoos are doing the same thing by providing hourly shows with elephants, monkeys, or other animals. Elephant or camel rides are popular with youngsters and produce a small amount of revenue for the park. Petting farms allow the visitor to feel, smell, and hug the animals. The more people get involved in a zoo, the longer they stay, the more they learn, and hopefully, the more they spend.

Private/Commercial Attractions

Theme and amusement parks, carnivals and circuses, live entertainment, spectator sports, gaming, and shopping constitute the majority of private or commercial attractions. Private attractions rely on admission fees, food and beverage sales, merchandising, parking charges, and special event fees (see Table 8.1, p. 182). Admission fees are often higher than those of public-sponsored attractions, which can rely on grants. Private attractions, free of the bureaucratic red tape and committee structure of public enterprises, can make quick decisions and therefore adapt faster to markets. Other than great attractions like Disney World and Disneyland, most private attractions are regional tourist draws at best and are considered one component of a larger vacation trip.

The CN Tower and Skydome are two of Toronto's major attractions.
(Photo courtesy Canadian Tourism Commission.)

Theme Parks

Theme parks can focus on one theme, such as Sesame Place, or many themes, such as Magic Kingdom, Main Street, and Fantasyland in Disneyland and Disney World. The idea is to create a separate world around the chosen theme by building rides, creating characters, providing live entertainment, and serving food related to the theme. As mentioned earlier in this chapter, theme parks trace their beginnings to the late Walt Disney, who was able to develop a park for young and old alike and provide enough variety to please even the local residents time and time again.

Theme parks have developed into large-scale operations with sophisticated computer control of all rides and animated entertainment. Every detail of the park is carefully controlled and operated at a central point within the park. Obviously, these types of parks are billion-dollar operations. The development of large-scale theme parks in North America has come to a virtual standstill. For example, the controversial Disney park proposed for Virginia was to have a Civil War theme with rides and attractions similar to other Disney parks. Opposition from local residents and political pressure caused Disney to pull out. In general, the acquisition of appropriate land and the capital needed to build large theme parks are prohibitive.

Perhaps because of the huge capital outlay required for large theme parks, smaller-scale theme parks are becoming the trend. Sesame Place in Langhorne, Pennsylvania, is an excellent example. This park, without rides, has live entertainment, water attractions, computer and educational exhibits, dozens of "kid-powered" play elements, and storefronts representing Sesame Street and the surrounding Sesame neighbourhood. The Sesame theme is augmented by numerous park attractions. Sesame Studio is a two-storey indoor gallery featuring dozens of science and entertainment attractions. Paradise Playhouse is the exotic bird show on Sesame Island. Big Bird Theater is a Sesame Street musical revue. Amazing Mumford's Water Maze is a conglomeration of multicoloured tubes and nets for children to wriggle and crawl through while being gently sprayed with water. Cookie Mountain is a simple, padded-vinyl, blue "mountain" that children try to scale.[9]

Water theme parks are becoming more attractive to all ages, and small wading pools and slides are being built for the under-five crowd. Even miniature golf courses are turning "theme" by building their putting greens around a time period or scenic wonder. The success of theme parks is built on the "permission" granted to children and adults alike to forget the trials and tribulations of the real world and escape, momentarily, to a land of make-believe and fun.

Family Entertainment Centres

With both parents working, parents have less time to spend with their children than ever before. Few parents are willing to leave children behind as they look for leisure entertainment and so the industry has responded by creating interactive **family entertainment centres (FEC)**.[10] The mini-golf course is one example. Often combined with a driving range, these centres allow the family to play a game of mini-golf together or with one parent, while the second parent practises on the driving range. A **virtual reality centre** is similar to an FEC but focuses on interactive computer games and programs. Family entertainment centres may be stand-alone units with a variety of skill games available for the entire family, or they may be combined with a shopping mall or even a movie theatre. There is a growing need for attractions that can provide quick, interactive entertainment for families, and FECs are part of this growing trend.

Amusement Parks

Coney Island in New York, Six Flags in several locations, and Canada's Wonderland in Ontario are a few of the larger-scale permanent amusement parks remaining in North America. Amusement parks have had to overcome the stigma of being run-down freak shows with hotdogs and cotton candy, tattooed ride operators, and garbage-cluttered grounds. This image plagued amusement parks for many years and is the reason Walt Disney designed his special theme park. Today's amusement parks are touted as family entertainment centres with rides for the brave (stand-up roller coasters) and the not-so-brave (merry-go-rounds). The trend in amusement parks is to provide a new, exciting ride, or a new form of entertainment each year to bring back local clientele.

Amusement parks also have live entertainment throughout the day with local and regional entertainers, who usually come with a fan club of moms, dads, siblings, and friends who pay admission and increase park attendance. Special nationally known entertainers are brought in to boost attendance three or four times during the summer season. Amusement parks have become great places for company picnics and large group parties. The entire park can be leased for an afternoon or evening for the group's enjoyment. "Selling the park" during slow periods has proven to be successful; newcomers see what the park is all about without having to pay the high admission price.

Sources of revenue for private attractions include admission fees; profits from the food-service operations and sale of beverages, ice cream and sweets; sale of merchandise from the souvenir kiosks and shops; and special events. Special events can be a major draw, and a trained events manager is essential. Events and Festivals Management is one of the newer programs in our college and university systems, and it is one of tourism's fastest growing sectors (see chapter 9). The largest expenditure, once the park is open for business, is labour, with nearly 33 percent of total revenue going to the staff.[11] If a park is to stay on the leading edge of entertainment, it must invest in new rides or entertainment yearly. Clients will return if the quality of the experience meets their expectations, the attraction is clean, and the service staff is friendly, helpful, and knowledgeable about the attraction.

Live Entertainment

If the entertainment is supplied by local talent, and promotion of the event remains local, the tourist draw will be minimal. To make live entertainment a major tourist attraction, it must be promoted in tourist brochures and should be a regular, high-quality attraction throughout the tourism season. With competent marketing in place, word-of-mouth advertising will provide the extra tourist traffic.

Some communities thrive *because* of the live entertainment available to their audiences. For example, Nashville, Tennessee, with the Grand Ol' Opry, has become a town somewhat dependent on country singers and dancers. Many tourist attractions, such as the theme park Opryland USA, have been built in or near Nashville to capitalize on the traffic in the area.

Larger cities like New York, Boston, and Toronto have their Broadway-style productions, and gambling towns like Las Vegas have been traditional places to go for live entertainment. Other communities have started their own local theatres, restoring old buildings and re-creating the time when community theatre—plays, dancing, and singing—was all that was available to the public.

Summer theatres, with seasons that run from April through October, are found in every province. The most famous summer theatre in Canada is the Stratford Festival in the small town of Stratford, Ontario. Sitting on the banks of the Avon River, the picturesque town provides the visitor with a peaceful reprieve from the stress of daily living, as well as a wide choice of live theatre ranging from musicals to Shakespearean drama. The town and surrounding areas are a shopper's paradise and boast some of the finest restaurants in Canada.

Another beautiful town in Ontario is Niagara-on-the-Lake, home to the Shaw Festival—the only theatre in the world to specialize in the plays of George Bernard Shaw and his contemporaries. Nestled in wine country, 20 minutes from the spectacular Niagara Falls, Niagara-on-the-Lake is the 1996 winner of the "Prettiest Town in Canada" award.[12]

Gaming

Gaming and gambling have been around for centuries. In North America there are four types of gambling: pari-mutuel wagering, lotteries, nonprofit organization gambling (mainly bingo and raffles), and casinos. Ontario's commercial casinos, charity casinos/bingo halls, and race track slot operations generated more than $890 million between July 1 and September 30, 2001.[13] Gambling is a popular and controversial form of recreation. Because lotteries, bingos, and raffles have limited clientele, they usually do not increase the flow of tourists into a town. Casinos and pari-mutuel betting, however, are a different matter. Las Vegas is the perfect example of a gambling town that thrives on the tourist trade. In fact, casinos within the city compete with each other for the gambling business. To entice patrons, the casino operator may offer special discounts on lodging (if lodging is part of the casino); free drinks; coupons for coins; live entertainment; or inexpensive, quality food. **Casino gambling** includes slot machines, roulette, craps (dice), baccarat, blackjack (21), poker, and other games of chance. The popularity of casino gambling has stimulated such growth in Las Vegas that the city now has nine out of the ten biggest hotels in the world. Casino gambling is also offered on ships, riverboats, and ferries. The ferry that travels from Yarmouth, Nova Scotia, to Portland, Maine, has long had gambling available to passengers while in international waters.

Casino gambling has only been widely available to Canadians in the past decade. Not all communities welcome gambling. Recently the town of Rocky Mountain House in Alberta voted two to one to end all forms of gambling in the town. The Casino du Lac Leamy in Gatineau, Quebec, has raised some local concerns. Residents have not enjoyed the full benefits of a stronger local economy and there has been an unusually high rate of bankruptcy in the region, both personal and small business. Established bingo halls, whose operations have supported many local charities in the past, have seen a dramatic decline in business and have been forced to shut their doors. A new Hilton Hotel has just opened as part of the casino complex and that has raised hopes that more tourism revenues will benefit the local community. Casino Niagara and Casino Windsor, on the other hand, illustrate how communities can benefit from a casino. Both enjoy success due to their proximity to the U.S. border; Casino Niagara has the added benefit of being near the falls. According to Elizabeth Hamel, general manager of the Windsor, Essex County and Pelee Island Visitor and Convention Bureau, the Windsor Casino welcomed 9.1 million visitors in 2000–01, of which 7.9 million were Americans.[14] The Niagara region has enjoyed substantial benefits, including thousands of new jobs, which have helped reduce welfare lists, and increased tax revenues, which have helped finance urban renewal and the revitalization of Niagara's tourism industry.

In the week following September 11, 2001, border casinos saw a drop of 80 percent in their business as Americans chose to stay close to home. The long-term effects have still not been completely assessed, but revenues for the two casinos topped $19.5 million, with revenue generation for the area estimated at $2.4 billion in 2000–01.[15]

Pari-mutuel gambling is a betting pool in which those who bet on the winners of the first three places share the total amount minus a percentage for management. Pari-mutuel betting in Ontario, Quebec, and the Maritimes is on a sport called harness racing. People come to dine in the fine-food service facilities provided by the track and watch drivers race in two-wheeled carts pulled by horses. The track is circular, and competition intensifies as drivers race against each other doing several laps per event. Pari-mutuel betting also occurs across North America on greyhound dog races, quarter- and thoroughbred horse races, trotter and pacer horse races, and jai alai, a court game similar to handball. The Kentucky Derby is the best-known horse race in North America. Part of the excitement of pari-mutuel betting is the atmosphere surrounding the race track. Patrons can dine in exclusive restaurants while watching the event, or munch on nachos and hot dogs in the stands with thousands of other eager bettors. Betting has become a social event that lasts for an evening out on the town, or for a few days, and is an added attraction to visitors.

What effect will long-term legalized gambling have on communities in North America? Some feel social problems have been downplayed, as has a rise in criminal activities linked to gambling. However, casinos themselves have been proactive in dealing with these concerns. Many will, on request from a self-acknowledged problem gambler, bar the customer from the casino for a given period of time. It seems clear that the economic benefits often vastly outweigh these criticisms. It will be interesting to see whether gambling slowly loses its appeal or whether it proves to be an economic solution for some of our Canadian communities.

Shopping

Shopping as an attraction? Why not? Shopping has always been popular with the tourist. Tourists travelling to Edmonton put the West Edmonton Mall on their lists of activities. A trip to Halifax is commemorated by the purchase of a trinket or souvenir. With the building of malls, shopping has become regionalized, drawing customers from as far as 500 km away. Mall shopping becomes an annual or monthly event for the entire family. Most cities with regional shopping malls have other forms of entertainment, such as museums, theatre, amusement parks, swimming, or other outdoor recreation. Some malls are becoming the sole attraction by providing entertainment in the mall's corridors and parking lots. Special events have become so important that many malls hire special events coordinators to arrange daily and weekly entertainment, contests, and food festivals.

Increasingly popular are **megamalls**, huge shopping and entertainment centres with everything from retail and restaurants to indoor theme parks, game rooms, and small theatres. To keep people from migrating to warm climates such as Arizona, Florida, and California, cities in Canada and the northern United States are eyeing the megamall as a venue for year-round recreation opportunities. The megamall could become an enclosed city. The West Edmonton Mall is listed in *The Guinness Book of Records* as the world's largest shopping mall. It is about the size of 85 football fields and has 110 eating places, 900 shops, and 10 feature attractions, including an amusement park, skating rink, swimming pool, miniature golf course, and theme hotel. More than 60 000 people visit the mall every day during the summer, and it draws out-of-town visitors. It is just a matter of time before more communities adopt the megamall as the regional shopping and recreation centre.[16]

Historic marketplaces are another interesting concept. They are often located in the historic part of a city's waterfront, remodelled to suit small boutiques, fresh-product outlets, and food-service facilities. Tourists can buy regional crafts and combine a little history with their recreational shopping. Halifax, Saint John, Vancouver, Winnipeg, Toronto, New York City, Boston, Baltimore, and San Francisco all have well-known, historic waterfront marketplaces. Another trend in shopping is the factory outlet store. North Carolina has long been known for the bargains found in its factory outlets, which feature brand-name furniture, clothing, sheets, and towels. Many factory outlets have revitalized the small towns in which they are located.

Charter buses and tours will make it a point to stop at shopping areas such as megamalls, waterfront shops, or factory outlets. Shopping as an attraction has proven to be a financial boon for the entire region and will continue to provide travellers with an added site to visit.

in practice   Identify one public, one nonprofit, and one private attraction in your area. How do they differ in advertising, price, type of visitors, and service quality? What new attraction would be successful in your community? Why would it succeed? What are the risks?

Niagara's Six Key Factors to Success

How does a tourism destination area (TDA) use its region's sites and attractions to its best advantage? Why does one attraction become a tourist draw and another go bankrupt?

Unique towns and villages, such as Saint-Jean-Port-Joli, Quebec, provide tourists with the opportunity to purchase local crafts and to snap a few photographs.
(Photo: Paula Kerr.)

*Natural attractions
like Niagara Falls
are an important
part of Canada's
tourism product.*
(Photo courtesy Canadian
Tourism Commission.)

The Niagara Falls region has learned many lessons over the last few decades and has identified six keys to success: sense of place, the product/market match, clustering, transportation, partnerships, and environmental protection.[17]

Sense of place may arise from a natural resource or may be created by people through historical perspectives or design. A destination marketing organization (DMO) would call sense of place the destination's **unique selling proposition** (USP). For Niagara, it is their magnificent waterfalls. For Edmonton, it might be West Edmonton Mall. History handed Ottawa its USP as the capital of Canada. Destinations able to determine their USP and clearly communicate it to tourists have a greater chance of luring tourists to their TDA. Another element that impresses visitors right from the start is the effective use of a **gateway**: an access point that signals to visitors that they have arrived. An effective gateway may be just a noticeable and attractive sign, or it may include an information booth or other way to offer tourists accessible information on their arrival.

It is important that the product a destination is selling meet the target market's needs and expectations. This is referred to as a **market match**. For example, if you are targeting the family market, then your destination will feature reasonably priced accommodations, family-style restaurants, and activities that focus on family fun or education. The mature market has very different needs and if you target it, your product will probably reflect the higher income and the desire for cultural and learning experiences, and provide upscale accommodation and dining facilities. Targeting the group market might require special check-in/check-out procedures at a hotel. Since destinations usually attract more than one market, a variety of facilities is needed.

Tourism planning in most Canadian cities has been in the "coattail" category; in other words it has developed without much forethought. Planning for tourism is actually a very new concept. When one developer designs a destination, it is done with the tourist in mind. The various attractions are clustered: that is, arranged in a well-thought-out pattern, within walking distance for easy access. Washington, D.C. has used **clustering** effectively: the city's major monuments, the Capitol Building, the White House, and the many museums of the Smithsonian are all located in one area. In contrast, Ottawa has scattered tourist activities and sights throughout the region. A tourist who wishes to visit both the Museum of Civilization and the Museum of Science and Technology in one day must either have a private vehicle or take a cab or bus. Why would a city put its major tourist attractions so far apart? First, this arrangement allows different neighbourhoods to share both the benefits of tourism (jobs and revenue) and the burdens (congestion). Perhaps politics is responsible, as each city councillor fought for a piece of the tourism pie. Whatever the reason, this lack of clustering remains a problem for Ottawa to solve.

The Niagara Falls region addressed a similar problem by creating clusters around themes. There are five regions in the Niagara area:

- the Falls View area—for all tourists, accommodations focusing on the "falls theme"
- the Clifton Park area—family oriented
- Lundy's Lane—family oriented
- Niagara-on-the-Lake—theatre bound and mature tourists
- Welland—all tourists, displaying the world's largest outdoor art gallery

Clusters can often be created by zoning bylaws, as in the historic area of Niagara-on-the-Lake. The Niagara clusters are physically dispersed but linked by a good transportation system.

Transportation is the next key to tourism's success. The importance of a good transportation system cannot be overstated. How do tourists get around your town? Have you good, clear signage to your sights and attractions? Are they placed so that the tourist has time to move into the correct turning lane? Is the traffic flow simple, or are there many one-way streets, confusing signs, and poor parking facilities? Good, clear, visible road signs accomplish three things: they allow tourist traffic to flow more smoothly through the area, they reduce the risk of accidents, and they make it easier for tourists to find sites, accommodations, or destinations. Niagara has highly visible directional signs. Parking facilities are located at the edge of the city, and a special bus service moves tourists from one cluster to another. Tourists are encouraged to use this system, minimizing traffic congestion and pollution.

The fifth key to success lies in **partnerships**. In chapter 3 we discussed the successful partnership between the Canadian Tourism Commission and the tourism industry. Partnering with government is essential, as governments provide not only the infrastructure for tourism, but also many social and support services. Historically, tourist regions have vied against one another for customers. But the tourism marketplace has changed and competition comes not just from our neighbours, but from businesses around the world! Destinations need the strength that is found in alliances and partnerships. Tourism businesses want the same thing—a healthy, economically stable tourist product. Partnerships are hard to forge and can be difficult to maintain. Once created, however, they improve each product's chance of success by linking. For example, restaurants in the Niagara region support the wine region by using the fine Niagara wines on their menus. Partnering also means that the visitor can be supplied with a full, diverse package using one-stop shopping. "Elegant Traditions" is a tour created with products and services from the Shaw Festival, Inniskillin Winery, Fort George, and the Prince of Wales Hotel in Niagara-on-the-Lake.

The last key to successful tourism is the *environment*. The World Tourism Organization has stated that the protection and enhancement of the environment is

OPPORTUNITIES IN ATTRACTIONS

	ATTRACTION	MUSEUM/GALLERY/ HERITAGE SITE
OPERATION (FRONT LINE)	Attraction Facility Guide/Greeters Retail Sales Clerk Food & Beverage Wait Staff Gate/Cash Attendants Concession Attendant Ride Operators Assistant Floor Person (casino) Cultural Artist/Craftsperson/Entertainer	**Attraction Facility Guide** Retails Sales Clerk
SUPERVISORY	Ride Operations Supervisor Concession Operator Floor Person (casino) Dealers (casino) Amusement Park Supervisor Public Relations Assistant Human Resources Assistant Concession Supervisor Retail Shift Supervisor Guest Services Supervisor Maintenance/Grounds Supervisor Food & Beverage Assistant	Museum/Curatorial Assistant Interpretive Specialist (museums, etc.)
MANAGEMENT	Head of Visitor Services Public Relations Manager Human Resources Manager Games Manager (casino) Assistant Retail Manager Assistant Food & Beverage Manager Operations Supervisor Retail Shop Manager Site Operator Food & Beverage Manager Sales Manager Accounting Manager Retail Manager Maintenance Manager Assistant General Manager	Public Relations Manager Museum Manager/Curator Retail Shop Manager Site Operator Museum/Gallery/Heritage Site Admin./Director
EXECUTIVE	President and CEO General Manager	

SOURCE: Courtesy of Canadian Tourism Human Resource Council, *The Student's Travel Map*, 1995.

fundamental to balanced and harmonious tourism. Sustainable tourism development is a primary goal in tourism planning, and it means that a destination fulfills the needs of the tourist with as little damage to the environment as possible. It is unrealistic to expect tourism to bring in revenue and yet cause no added pollution or damage to the environment. The Niagara region believes tourism must take environmental protection two steps further if it is to flourish. Regions must learn how to continually maintain and restore as well as protect and conserve their natural resources. This can be

---

JOB DESCRIPTION FOR. . .

ATTRACTION FACILITY GUIDE

Industry Sector	Attractions
Division	Museum/Gallery
Industry Setting	Museums, art galleries, and other historical buildings and sites
Job Level	Operational (Front Line)
Description of Duties	Escort individuals and groups on sightseeing and educational tours through site and provide background information on interesting features or displays, answer questions, pass out literature, and ensure that visitors follow regulations on safety and conduct. By greeting visitors and explaining the site, the guides deliver an integral part of the attraction experience. May also be referred to as an On-Site Guide, Character Guide, or Animator.
Skills	Pleasing and outgoing personality, ability to communicate effectively with large groups, knowledge of geography and history, good memory, and lots of patience.
Knowledge	Knowledge of both official languages; an additional language may be a requirement for this position. Knowledge of artistic or historical matter and other background information may be required.
Education	Completion of Grade 12 may be required. No specific training requirements are necessary.
Industry Experience Career Paths	Previous experience is not a requirement for entry. Experience gained from this occupation may be required for employment in museum/gallery supervisory or management occupations in education and interpretation, including Museum/Curatorial Assistant, Assistant/Associate Curator, Assistant Librarian/Archivist, Interpretive Specialist, Museum Manager/Curator, Archivist Librarian.
HRDC Reference	NOC 6441 Tour and Travel Guides

done in many different ways. Streets, parks, and shopping areas must be maintained and kept clean. Something as simple as having plenty of garbage cans on city streets can help. We may need to set aside portions of our national parks as reserves, closed to tourism; we may need to limit the number of people using a resource. Most tourists do not mean to pollute and harm the environment, but they may harm it unwittingly if they are not given information on how to protect it. Why shouldn't tourists feed the cute little chipmunks and pick wildflowers as mementos? If tourists are told why, most will help conserve our environment. It is up to the government and the tourism industry to ensure that visitors have both the means and the information to help.

in practice

Do a quick SWOT analysis of one of your regional attractions by identifying its strengths, weaknesses, an opportunity it could take advantage of, and a threat to its continued success.

summary

An attraction adds to the quality of life in a community and to its economy through tourism revenue. Attractions are needed in the tourism industry. Without them, many people would not have a desire to travel. Attraction trends include the building of megamalls with gigantic family entertainment centres, an increase in water parks and miniature golf courses, the renovation of old museums, the building of state-of-the-art modern museums, and the preservation of historic sites. Attractions may be publicly supported, nonprofit, or private. Gaming has proven to be a success in the 1990s, as hundreds of casinos have popped up all over the United States and Canada. Each casino must compete to entice the serious or recreational gambler, and time will tell whether gaming is a trend or merely a fad. The Niagara Region has identified six key factors that contribute to the success of an attraction/destination: sense of place, product/market match, clustering, transportation, partnerships, and environmental protection.

questions

1. Create a table that identifies the following pieces of information:

    i)   four public, four nonprofit, and four private attractions in your area

    ii) a brief description of their products and activities

    iii) three ways in which each attraction helps fund their operations

    iv) a special event each attraction has used to attract new and repeat visitors

2. a) The gaming industry is growing in all regions of North America. List the gambling alternatives offered in your region and what type of gaming each one represents.

    b) Do you see the gaming industry as a positive influence on tourism? Defend your answer, using examples.

3. a) Is shopping a true tourist attraction? Defend your answer with examples.

    b) How does your city use clustering, partnerships, the local transportation system, and history of the region to promote tourist shopping areas?

4. Define the following terms as they relate to the attractions sector: *amusement park, theme park, UNESCO World Heritage Site, site-specific museum, children's museum, oceanarium.*

weblinks

www.attractionscanada.com

Attractions Canada is designed to inform Canadians and visitors about sights in Canada, ranging from outdoor attractions to museums and historic sites.

rbcml.rbcm.gov.bc.ca

The Royal BC Museum, one of the country's premier museums, in Victoria, B.C.

national.gallery.ca

Ottawa's National Gallery presents art from Canada and abroad in an impressive glass-and-stone building.

www.parkscanada.gc.ca / lhn-nhs / ns / halifax / visit / index_e.asp

The Halifax Citadel National Historic Site boasts the famous Citadel, a star-shaped fortification that overlooks downtown Halifax. (For more Parks Canada information, see their general site at **parkscanada.gc.ca /**)

disney.go.com / Disneyland /

This is the official Web site for Disneyland in California.

www.cast-a-way.com

This company hires for Disney and several cruise lines.

notes

1. Dr. M. Mohan, G. Gislason, and B. McGowan, *Tourism Related Employment: An Update* (Ottawa, Ontario: Canadian Tourism Human Resource Council, 1998).

2. Patricia MacKay, "Theme parks: USA," *Theatre Crafts*, September 1977, p. 56.

3. Bro Uttal, "The ride is getting scarier for 'Theme Park' owners," *Fortune Magazine*, December 1977, p. 168.

4. Martha T. Moore, "Euro Disney's Culture Shock," *USA Today*, Oct. 6, 1993, Sec. B., p. 2.

5. Roger Cohen, "Travel Advisory: Correspondent's Report; Euro Disney Trying to Warm Up Winter," *New York Times*, Dec. 12, 1993, Sec. 5, p. 3.

6. www.disneyworld.com.

7. James M. Cameron and Ronald Bordessa, *Wonderland through the Looking Glass* (Maple, Ontario: Belsten Publishing, 1982), p. 71.

8. www.world-tourism.com

9. John Anderson, "Sesame Place through children's eyes," *FUNWORLD*, August 1991, pp. 38–41.

10. John R. Graff, "1991 Outlook for Attractions," in *1991 Outlook for Travel and Tourism* (Washington, DC: U.S. Travel Data Center, 1990), p. 69.

11. *1990 Amusement Industry Abstract* (Alexandria, VA: International Association of Amusement Parks and Attractions, February 1991), p. 5.

12. *Maclean's* Magazine, September 1996.

13. *Tourism Canada's Monthly Magazine*, January-February 2002, p. 7.

14. Ibid.

15. Ibid.

16. David W. Howell and Robert A. Ellison, *Passport* (Toronto: Nelson Canada, 1995), p. 225.

17. Laurel Reid and Stephen Smith, *Keys to Successful Tourism Development: Lessons from Niagara* (Video: Pacific Production International), 1997.

9 The Events and Conferences Sector

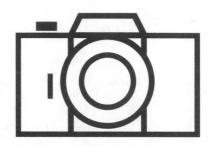

- -

key terms

breakout room	fair	seminar
civic event	festival	special event
conference	fundraising event	spectator sporting event
conference centre	hallmark event	summit
convention	Meeting Professionals	trade show
convention centre	International (MPI)	Visit Canada
exhibition	Rendez-Vous Canada	workshop

- -

learning objectives

Having read this chapter you will be able to

1. Define the terms special event, festival, fair, fundraising event, hallmark event, civic event, spectator sporting event, conference, convention, summit, and trade show.

2. Discuss the wide variety of special events that might be hosted by a community.

3. Differentiate among a conference, convention, summit meeting, and business meeting.

4. Explain the difference between a conference centre and convention centre.

5. Identify the factors that make Canada a strong competitor for the conference market.

6. Discuss the SKAs required by an events or meeting planner.

7. Explain both the good and bad effects events may have on a community.

- - - - - - - - - - - - - - - - - - - -

Events and conferences is a very important sector in the tourism industry because it makes good use of the products and services delivered by five other sectors: accommodation, food and beverage, travel trade, attractions, and adventure tourism and outdoor recreation. This sector also creates jobs for a variety of other businesses including printers, audiovisual companies, and manufacturers of exhibits. All events are similar in purpose and design but they are developed for different target markets. Special events and some trade shows target the general population while conferences, conventions, meetings, and trade shows fill the needs of the business market.

Every community, no matter how small, has frequent special events. Rural communities find that hosting a fair, festival, or sporting event brings new visitors to their town and may bring local and sometimes national recognition. Hosting an event can bring a community new full and part-time jobs, an enhanced image, strengthened community bonds, economic growth, an expanded tourism season, and an enhanced diversity of social and cultural activities. Revenues generated by events benefit not only tourism businesses, but also retail businesses and community associations. Meeting planning includes conventions, conferences, summits, and business meetings.

As business becomes more global, the need to communicate with people who do not live in the same area becomes essential. Sometimes talking on a telephone is not enough, because people tend to share knowledge and ideas best when they are face to face. Pick up any newspaper and you will read about meetings, both national and international. Recent reports estimate that more than 50 000 meetings and conventions, involving more than two million delegates, are held annually in Canada.[1] Revenue from this sector, totalling almost $4 billion dollars, will likely increase as cities expand both their convention facilities and the promotion of their special events.[2]

Canada is well suited to this business: the Canadian dollar offers a financial incentive, and Canada provides excellent convention facilities, an international appeal, a familiar lifestyle, and a wide variety of attractions. Unfortunately, some of Canada's best destinations have smaller facilities so they are unable to host large conventions or conferences. In addition, Canada is often overlooked by meeting planners who do not have enough information about our conference facilities.

People who choose to work in this field need outgoing personalities; excellent organizational techniques; good management, people, communication, and problem-solving skills; a love of detail; and a flair for public relations and working with the media. For the purpose of discussion, we will separate this sector into two divisions: special events and meeting planning.

Transportation and Events and Conferences were two of the sectors to suffer the most from the September 11 attacks. Major conferences around the world were postponed or cancelled and business travel took a serious downturn. Conscious of delegate concerns, all major events added security measures.

However, the peaceful conclusion of meetings such as the World Youth Rally, held in Toronto in July of 2002, and the Winter Olympics, held in Salt Lake City, Utah, February 2002, have helped to reassure worried organizers and delegates. Global summit meetings, such as the G-8 meetings that bring the industrial world's financial leaders together to discuss topics like international trade and globalization, have suffered not from terrorist threats but from activist demonstrations. Violence has erupted during summit meetings in Vancouver, Quebec City, and Rome. The last G-8, held in Kananaskis, Alberta, in the summer of 2002, proved to the world that Canada was able to control and contain such demonstrations, and this has helped to promote a stronger global image of Canada as a safe destination.

Special Events

Festivals and events can be half-day occurrences or year-long happenings, new ideas in a new community, or an event that occurs on a yearly basis. According to Donald Getz, a **special event** is "a onetime or infrequently occurring event outside the normal program or activities of the sponsoring or organizing body. To the customer, a special event is an opportunity for leisure, social, or cultural experience outside the normal range of choices or beyond everyday experience."[3] This is the definition used by this text.

Today special events have become big business for many Canadian municipalities. They are one of the most interesting ways of unifying and enhancing the tourist appeal of permanent structures such as museums, zoos, and arenas. A museum of art is an attraction by itself, but add a special event such as a Picasso exhibit, and the museum's appeal becomes almost irresistible to locals and tourists alike.

Special events are often designed by travel destinations to lure the tourist to the region. Some attract domestic tourists and others will appeal to the international visitor. Two examples of international events are the Olympics and the

A special event like Canada Day will bring close to 100 000 visitors to Ottawa.
(Photo courtesy Canadian Tourism Commission.)

World's Fair. In the past 30 years, Canada has hosted two World's Fairs, Expo 67 in Montreal and Expo 86 in Vancouver, and two Olympics, the 1976 Summer Olympics in Montreal and the 1988 Winter Olympics in Calgary. British Columbia has put forward a bid to host the Winter Olympics in 2010 and is one of the final three sites being considered by the Olympic committee.

Each province has its own special events, and some have gained international audiences such as the Calgary Stampede and the Nova Scotia International Tattoo. Not all special events enjoy such wide recognition, but they still remain an important part of a region's draw. Historically speaking, the turn of the millennium was one of the world's most awaited events. For the first time ever, television transported audiences to distant (and not so distant) places to record the incoming new year by time zone. Special events play a significant role in entertaining both tourists and local residents.

Festivals

Public celebrations centred around themes of local, regional, or national interest are called **festivals**. This broad category of events includes everything from jazz to the blues, from winter fun to tulips in the spring. Many rural areas of Canada use special events to lure tourists and excursionists from their region to their town. It becomes an important promotional tool for the area, as festivals will attract both local and national television coverage. Some of the bigger Canadian events include the Symphony of Fire in Victoria, B.C., Folklorama in Winnipeg, Manitoba. Small-town festivals, such as the Port Elgin Pumpkin Festival, can be equally exciting. This popular event sees the small town of Port Elgin (population 7000) swell by as many as 50 000 visitors, who spend more than $1.4 million dollars in two days. The Pumpkin festival is not only an economic boon to the region, but it also helps to raise $40 000 of much-needed revenue for the area's nonprofit groups.[4] In Toronto, Caribana, a summer celebration of Caribbean culture, generates $300 million in just three days.[5]

Quebec City's Carnival proves that even in winter, Canada has great activities.
(Photo courtesy Canadian Tourism Commission.)

Fairs

Fairs have different themes and often focus on a community's agriculture or history. Event legacies or historical fairs re-create a certain period by providing the food and entertainment of that time. Medieval and Renaissance fairs are popular examples and re-creations of historical events, such as the final battle between Wolfe and Montcalm on the Plains of Abraham in old Quebec City, are becoming more popular. Agricultural fairs feature livestock, produce, local arts and crafts, carnival rides, and food. Most farming communities have agricultural fairs, where 4-H groups (which teach young people agriculture and animal husbandry) display their goods. Ribbons are given to prize-winning animals of many breeds. Some of Canada's agricultural fairs date back to the early 1840s. They draw regional tourists by featuring nationally known singers and entertainers and are usually held in late summer to allow crops to mature for competition. These fairs are often sponsored by the local government or the community hosting the event. It is common for a carnival to join a larger event in the community and become a drawing card for nonresidents to visit. Two of Canada's biggest and best fairs are held in Toronto. The Canadian National Exhibition (CNE), held at the end of August in Toronto, combines an agricultural fair with a carnival. The CNE is the largest carnival/fair held in Canada. In November, the prestigious Royal Winter Fair brings visitors from across North America. It does not have rides or a midway but hosts a variety of competitions including horse jumping and a dog show.

Circuses

Circuses are magic for all ages; however, concern for the welfare of circus animals has caused the decline of this type of event. The only major circus left in North America is the Ringling Brothers and Barnum & Bailey Circus. Sometimes nonprofit organization such as the Shriners will sponsor a circus in order to raise money for hospitals and children's medical research. Canada's Cirque du Soleil, a circus without animals, has gained worldwide recognition for its unique creativity, using tumblers, dancers, and acrobats to enthrall its audiences.

Hallmark events

Hallmark events are major happenings such as the Olympics, the Commonwealth Games, or World Youth Day. Such events bring tourists from around the world to a destination and can have a huge economic impact on the community. Participants for World Youth Day in Toronto spent an estimated $110 million on direct tourism-related spending (souvenirs, restaurants, hotels, etc.).[6] On the other hand, the direct costs of staging the event were over budget by $3.5 million dollars, which the Roman Catholic Church, as the organizing body, has agreed to cover. If large-scale events such as this do not meet their budget, and taxes are used to cover the deficit, why do countries and communities host them? There are many reasons but perhaps the most important is the stature the event brings with it. Countries and cities bid to host the Olympics, knowing that the initial cost is great but that the media coverage will put the region on the map. The city becomes a tourist destination, not only during the Olympics, but also for many years after. When Calgary hosted the Winter Olympics in 1988, millions of people saw on television that winter can be fun and that visiting a "northern"

World-class events like the Calgary Stampede provide summer entertainment for visitors.
(Photo courtesy Canadian Tourism Commission.)

Canadian city can be an exciting vacation. This image was exactly what Calgary wanted to portray.

Fundraising events

Fundraising events have become commonplace in North America. They may be small, like a walk-a-thon to raise money for the local Humane Society, or they may be national, like the Terry Fox Run. Over the years, the Terry Fox Run has raised more than $30 000 000 for cancer research. Because of government funding cuts to hospitals and special disease research facilities, many charities now depend on these events. People have the chance to enjoy a special outdoor activity while helping to support a cause they believe in.

Civic Events

Civic events may be national, such as the celebration of Canada Day or Remembrance Day. This category includes the investiture of a new prime minister or governor general, medal presentations, or the opening of a new building. Civic events may also be global, such as a New Year's Eve celebration. Each municipality, region, and country has unique civic events, and tourists often plan their vacations to attend them.

Spectator Sporting Events

The largest **spectator sporting event** of all time is the Olympics. However, other sports such as tennis, golf, college football, and basketball also draw large crowds. Although the majority of the spectators are people who live within a two-hour drive of the event, the regional draw of tourists to sporting events has been growing rapidly. Accommodations, restaurants, and shopping areas have noticed an increase in visitors whose primary reason for coming is to watch their favourite team. Special sporting events such as the Grey Cup, the Super Bowl, the World Series, the Stanley Cup, and National Basketball Association playoffs bring in thousands of loyal fans who will spend the night and are ready to spend money on food and souvenirs.

Professional sports belong primarily to the big cities. Big-name teams like the Toronto Raptors and the National Hockey League teams bring both revenue and recognition to a region. Cities have difficulty supporting a professional team because of the influence of the U.S. marketplace. Players demand large salaries and want to be paid in U.S. dollars, making it very difficult for even a good team to be profitable. The state of Canadian hockey is a good example. Two of our National Hockey League teams have already been sold and have moved to the United States. In the United States, many teams are given tax breaks and they are not subjected to the exchange rate of the Canadian dollar. Here, we have regarded hockey as a private business and as such, seldom provide public support for the teams. The debate rages. Is hockey an integral part of Canadian culture and our lifestyle? If so, then should not some support for the game come from Canadian Heritage? Canadian Heritage provides grants to Canadian magazines, the film industry, and other embattled Canadian products. Why have they not stepped forward to aid the hockey industry? Alberta helps its teams, the Oilers and the Flames, with a hockey lottery. In Ontario, the provincial government has allowed slot machines to be placed at racetracks in support of Ontario's horse racing industry. So far, government has refused to support Ontario's hockey teams. Ottawa's is the most vulnerable NHL team, but no team is safe. Municipal tax breaks have been created for the Ottawa Senators, but unless the provincial and federal government also provide some support, it appears the team will be forced to move south. Ottawa, even though it is the country's capital city, has never enjoyed the global recognition that cities like Toronto and Vancouver have. One of the benefits of a professional team is the publicity it brings to a region. Ask a sports fan in Dallas what Ottawa is noted for and the current answer will probably be

Hockey in Canada is an integral part of Canadian culture, but a low Canadian dollar and lack of support threaten our remaining six NHL teams.
(Photo courtesy Ottawa Senators Hockey Club.)

"the Senators hockey team." The benefits of having a hockey team, especially the revenue and jobs created for the region, outweigh the disadvantages. Will we witness the demise or resurgence of Canadian professional hockey in the near future?

Most athletes never make it into the professional arena. Instead they continue to show their love for their sport by forming city leagues. These amateur leagues also bring in tourist revenue as regions host national championships for a variety of sports such as the Canadian National Skating Championship or the Brier (Canada's men's national curling championship).

Trade shows

Trade shows and expositions are a marketing and sales tool used by many industries to display and sell their products. Many trade shows are not open to the general public but are designed for specific audiences, small businesses, or entrepreneurs. They usually display the latest developments and products of an industry (such as computers, automobiles, boats, or home care products). Unlike other fairs, trade fairs are commonly held indoors and require large convention centres to display the items. Consequently, trade fairs are not generally sponsored by a public or nonprofit organization but by the pertinent industry or trade association. Revenues for the use of the facility, however, go to the community. Trade fairs are held around the world and generate a great deal of revenue for the host community. The COMDEX computer and technology trade show in Las Vegas, for example, is not open to the general public but still draws more than 100 000 participants each year. There are approximately 11 000 trade shows held annually in North America. Vendors rent space and set up booths to display their products. Demonstrations are an important part of any trade show, and special trade show prices act as a lure for those thinking of a purchase. In the hospitality industry, there are several large trade shows. The New York Restaurant Show, held every November, and the Chicago Restaurant Show, scheduled for the middle of May, are both noted for their size and for their seminars, which feature top names in both the restaurant business and the "speaker circuit." These shows are important to the entrepreneur in food service because they display the latest food products, marketing tools, and equipment for hotels and restaurants.

Many Canadian cities also hold restaurant shows. One example is the Canadian International Food and Beverage Show, held by the Canadian Restaurant and Foodservice Association (CRFA) in Toronto in February. For students, this show provides an educational opportunity that should not be missed, and special student discounts may be available. The international Travel Industry Expo is designed for travel counsellors. It displays the latest travel products, allowing participants to pick up information and make contact with a wide variety of suppliers. The Canadian Tourism Commission and the Tourism Industry Association of Canada sponsor two major trade shows for the tourism industry. **Rendez-Vous Canada**, developed by Tourism Canada in the 1980s, displays Canadian tourism products for the travel trade market—travel agencies and tour operators. The show is now sponsored by TIAC. **Visit Canada**, still operated by the CTC, focuses on the media. Canadian tourism products are made available to travel writers, photographers, and other media representatives, allowing them to do "one-stop shopping" for tourist information.

Trade shows that are open to the general public, such as auto shows, may focus on one product, or, like fall and spring home shows, may display a broad range of goods and services. The public pays an entrance fee and is free to spend the day looking and talking to experts. One example is the Wine and Food Show. Here, restaurants, wineries, distilleries, and breweries present samples of their products (for a small charge). Seminars are generally free to those who attend. Other examples of trade shows your area might enjoy would be crafts, an auto/ RV or boating/sportsman show. These shows have proven to be highly successful over the past decade. Trade shows generate more than $20 billion in North America every year. Large trade shows use spacious facilities like the Vancouver Trade and Convention Centre, the Metro Toronto Convention Centre, or the Montreal Convention Centre. All sectors of tourism benefit. For example, weeks prior to the Chicago Restaurant Show, downtown hotels are completely sold out, and during the show restaurants are booked to capacity.

Conferences, Conventions, and Meetings

An association or an organization is created by uniting a group of people with a common interest. Association meetings fall into two subdivisions: conventions and conferences. **Conventions** are large meetings where delegates come together to share ideas and to achieve some form of consensus. Perhaps the best-known convention occurs when a political party brings together delegates from across the country to elect its leader and create its party platform for the next election. Delegates to a convention usually come from varying backgrounds, so business leaders will mingle with firefighters, mechanics with consultants and those who choose to work at home. Conventions are also held by large associations such as the Kiwanis Club or Alcoholics Anonymous. There is usually a strong element of recreation in a convention program, rewarding those who have spent their time working with the organization.

Conferences are similar to conventions, except that the delegates usually come from a single industry or occupation. The Tourism Industry Association of Canada (TIAC) holds its annual conference in a different Canadian city each year, so that attendees may enjoy varied venues and attractions. Delegates come from all sectors of the tourism industry to hear about the latest research, to learn more about national certification programs, to exchange ideas, and to listen to leaders in the industry discuss current topics of interest. Many conferences take the time to recognize people who have contributed to the industry in a significant way. Conferences have a more educational tone to their programs than conventions.

Summits are similar to conferences but tend to have a political tone. The term is usually used for international meetings among high-level leaders.

Teleconferencing is the latest trend in meetings. The advances in technology allow businesses and associations to bring together a group of people via a telephone or satellite link. At more advanced sites, videoconferencing enables participants to actually see each other during the discussions. Although this type of meeting does not add to a city's tourism revenue, hotels and convention centres are beginning to provide these services in response to consumer demands.

The Association Meeting Market

Although associations may have very different reasons to exist, as a market they share characteristics:

- Their conventions and conferences usually last three to five days.
- Voluntary attendance is the norm, so delegates pay their own way.
- Destination sites must be carefully chosen to entice delegates to attend, and different cities are chosen every year.
- Accessibility is important to delegates.
- Regular meeting dates allow the delegates to plan their time well in advance.
- **Exhibitions** displaying the latest goods are important.[7]

There are about 80 000 associations in North America and many plan annual conventions or conferences. There are specific needs that must be satisfied if the convention or conference is to be a success. The choice of destination is important because delegates often bring their families along, combining business and vacation. Resorts are popular choices, and both the Banff Springs Hotel and the Jasper Park Lodge have developed good reputations as conference sites. However, both sites have a major drawback: the closest cities, Calgary and Edmonton, are some distance away. Calgary, for instance, is a 90-minute drive from Banff, forcing the delegate to either rent a car or make the last leg of the trip by bus. As members pay for their travel and accommodations, the cost of the trip is an important factor when booking the destination. Since most delegates like to try different locations every year, the organizing committee is kept busy searching out new sites. To book a site five years in advance is not uncommon.

Meeting Sites The choice of a meeting location is as varied as the products available. The first concern a meeting planner must address is the size of the facility needed. General meeting space must accommodate the entire delegation, which may be anywhere from a couple of hundred to more than 10 000 people. Smaller breakout rooms are needed to handle panel discussions, seminars, and workshops, which are an integral part of a conference. The number of rooms available at a destination and the price of accommodations are extremely important to delegates because they pay their own way. Many conferences will choose destinations that

Conference Terminology You Should Know

seminar	informal meeting in which delegates share information and ideas under the expertise of a seminar leader or presenter; seminars may also be conducted by a panel of experts who provide knowledge from differing sources
workshop	small group session that focuses on activities in which participants learn new skills or techniques
breakout room	a room in which small groups of delegates participate in seminars or workshops
Meeting Professionals International (MPI)	international, professional association of meeting planners

offer a wide choice of attractions; families can enjoy them during the day and delegates can relax together after the meetings.

Hotels today may generate 20 percent to 40 percent of their annual revenues from meetings, conventions, and conferences. Many have designed their properties to accommodate these groups, providing audiovisual support, portable food service, and a staff trained to deal with the logistics of a large meeting. Resorts also attract this market, offering recreational activities and a quiet, undisturbed setting. Older resorts such as the Algonquin in St. Andrews-by-the-Sea, New Brunswick, have done extensive renovations to accommodate this market. A multimillion dollar addition to Château Lake Louise's conference space is under way. The problem with resorts has been high room rates: many conferences are planned during peak season, when resorts are reluctant to reduce their rates.

Many large universities use their equipment and facilities during the summer months to host conferences and meetings, thus gaining revenue from rooms and services that might otherwise be idle.

Conference centres, specifically designed for meetings, provide a quiet, working environment for a conference and its delegates. Because these meetings are of an educational nature, many large universities use their equipment and facilities during the summer months to host conferences and meetings. This activity provides additional revenue for the school and makes use of rooms and services that might otherwise be idle. One of Canada's most distinctive conference centres is found in Banff, Alberta. The Banff Centre was established over 65 years ago as a retreat for musicians and artists. Arts programming is one of three distinct programming areas of The Banff Centre, which also provides conference services year-round. Here, artists come to rejuvenate their spirits and their creativity through professional development offered in a range of programs, which include Music & Sound, Theatre Arts, Media & Visual Arts, Writing & Publishing, and Aboriginal Arts. Leadership Development programming was added nearly 20 years later and is dedicated to relevant professional development for leaders and managers. It offers seminars and workshops designed to develop effective, successful leaders for all sectors, including business,

The Banff Centre provides smaller conferences and corporate meetings with unique facilities and setting.
(Source: The Banff Centre.)

government, and Aboriginal communities. Mountain Culture, the third programming area, focuses worldwide attention on mountain-related natural and cultural issues. Every year it is host to the internationally acclaimed Banff Mountain Film and Book Festivals and the Banff Mountain Photography Competition, as well as conferences and summits exploring specific mountain-related themes. The Conferences division was opened in the 1960s to provide meeting facilities for the association market. Net revenues from this area support the Centre's arts programming area. What makes this conference centre unique is the vast range of opportunities offered to guests due to the Centre's multidisciplinary environment. As well, conference delegates may hike, canoe, ski, or rock climb in the surrounding Rocky Mountains

FIGURE 9.1
The Banff Centre,
Main Auditorium
and Breakout
Rooms

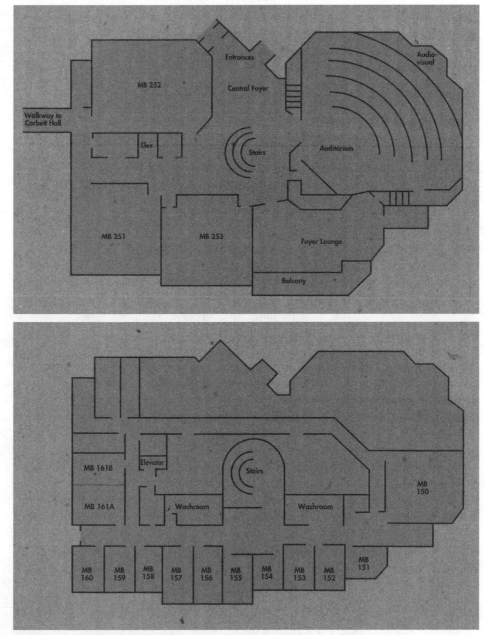

SOURCE: The Banff Centre.

using professional guiding services available in Banff; attend various arts performances and visit exhibits at the Centre; and take advantage of a full range of services, that include a travel agency and a recreation/fitness centre. Together, all these components add value to The Banff Centre's conference product (Figure 9.1).

Convention centres are specifically built to handle groups of more than 1000 people. They differ from conference centres in several ways: (a) they are larger facilities that do not have recreational opportunities on the premises; (b) they are usually located in big cities; and (c) they do not provide guest rooms. Hotels in the area will handle accommodations, and many convention centres are linked to a hotel. For example, the Vancouver Trade and Convention Centre (VTCC), located on the waterfront, is linked to the Pan Pacific Hotel.

Because building convention centres is enormously expensive, a unique partnership has developed between the tourist industry and the federal, provincial, and municipal governments, which have provided funding as well as special loans. Civic centres also play host to conventions, but their primary function is to host special events such as sporting events or cultural shows and exhibits. Some civic centres work in partnership with smaller convention facilities to help the city handle a larger number of delegates. The Saddle Dome in Calgary provides seating for an additional 16 700 participants, expanding the convention centre's capacity of 2500; the Halifax Metro Centre (capacity of 10 000) is adjacent to the World Trade and Convention Centre, with a capacity of 1300. Many cities in Canada are considering additions to their meeting spaces, and Canadians can look forward to new job opportunities as this expansion becomes a reality.

Canada's Top Convention Centres, from east to west are as follows:

- Halifax World Trade and Convention Centre
- Quebec Convention Centre
- Montreal Convention Centre
- Ottawa Congress Centre
- Metropolitan Toronto Convention Centre

Vancouver's Trade and Convention Centre has become one of Canada's most recognized buildings. It can accommodate 10 000 delegates, providing first-class service.
(Photo courtesy Canadian Tourism Commission.)

- Winnipeg Convention Centre
- Edmonton Convention Centre
- Calgary Convention Centre
- Vancouver Trade and Convention Centre
- Victoria Convention Centre

Vancouver, Toronto, and Montreal are home to Canada's top three convention centres:

The Vancouver Trade and Convention Centre: First used as the Canadian Pavilion for Expo 86, this magnificent structure with its sail-like roof has become one of the most recognized buildings in the world. The VTCC has 21 meeting rooms; 1530 m^2 of pre-function space; an 8460-m^2 exhibition hall; and a 1440-m^2 ballroom. The centre can accommodate 10 000 delegates. The Pan Pacific Hotel, which is part of the structure, does not have enough rooms for this number of delegates, so downtown hotels benefit from any large convention that comes to town. A larger convention centre has been planned for the city, funded by all three levels of government and scheduled to open in 2008.[8]

The Metropolitan Toronto Convention Centre: About 20 percent of the convention business in Canada chooses Toronto for its access to the U.S. market and its strong international corporate base. The centre has 3240 m^2 of meeting space; 18 000 m^2 of exhibition space; a 2520-m^2 ballroom; and a theatre that seats 1339 people. The Crowne Plaza hotel is situated adjacent to the centre, and an additional 10 000 hotel rooms are available within walking distance.

Montreal Convention Centre: Montreal is ranked first in Canada and third in North America as an international convention city. The ease of access from other countries, its European culture, and its reputation for fine dining and entertainment make it a popular choice, particularly for the U.S. market. It has 9220 m^2 of exhibition space; 31 meeting rooms; and a 4050-m^2 banquet hall. It is staffed by a multilingual work force and offers the latest in audiovisual services.

The Corporate Meeting Market

This segment of the meeting market has slightly different characteristics from the association market. Businesses will often hold meetings off site to avoid distractions and achieve an atmosphere in which to build a more unified team. Here are the characteristics of the corporate meeting market:

- Attendance is mandatory.
- The cost of the meeting is paid for by the business.
- The number of participants is smaller than that of a conference or convention.
- The meeting is generally shorter.
- Meetings are planned as the need arises and are booked with only a few months' or weeks' notice. As attendance is mandatory, meetings do not require visible publicity.
- The same destination may be used repeatedly, and it is often near corporate headquarters or factories.
- Exhibits are not generally part of the meeting structure.
- Emphasis is on business, so food service usually provides a "working lunch": a simple buffet of cold meats, salads or sandwiches, fresh fruit, and dessert. Beverages are supplied throughout the meeting.[9]

Corporate meetings often take place in local hotel facilities. A hotel serious about this business must provide not only quality food service, but also quiet, luxurious surroundings to fit the corporate image.

Clearly, events and festivals are an important component of the tourism industry, benefiting small and large communities alike. However, it would be naïve to think that special events have only advantages. Disadvantages do exist, but if

S N A P S H O T

Isadore Sharp

His company, Four Seasons Hotels Ltd., is one of the top hotel chains in the world. It sits at the pinnacle of the Canadian hospitality business both in quality and revenue generated. Over the past 30 years, Isadore Sharp has become one of the world's leading hoteliers. He did not start out in the hotel business but studied architecture at the Ryerson Institute of Technology in Toronto. Initially he worked for his father's construction company, but by the early 1960s he made a decision that would change the course of his life—he built his first motel in downtown Toronto.

Sharp was an innovator, a man with good instincts who focused on quality service long before it became the buzzword in the hospitality business. Having firmly established his first motel, he designed the Inn on the Park, located in what was then Toronto's northern suburbs. Around the Inn, he cultivated beautiful lawns and gardens. Using trees to provide privacy, Sharp created a refuge from the busy city. In 1970, he began to look at international locations for his third hotel. When he chose London, England, his critics felt that he had made his first mistake, for London already had many fine, luxury hotels. However, Sharp relied on his instincts, recognizing the need for a premiere property with a modern flair.

As his hotel empire flourished, Sharp never lost sight of his original tenet: quality service is worth paying for. How does he maintain such high standards? He believes that if you treat your employees as you wish to be treated, they will treat guests in a similar manner. Facilities that serve his employees are as well appointed as those he designs for his guests. Four Seasons Hotels enjoys one of the lowest staff turnover rates in the industry. For his guests he offers 24-hour room service, a complimentary shoe shine, and luxurious terry cloth bathrobes. His staff are knowledgeable, friendly, and trained to handle even the most difficult situations with dignity. Concierges in Four Seasons Hotels are among the best in the industry. They are required to have a minimum of two languages; complete knowledge of the city, its sights, restaurants, theatres, and night life; and the ability to handle any request with courtesy and professionalism under all circumstances.

By the 1980s, Four Seasons Hotels had won many awards for excellence, creating a demand for its management expertise. Sharp took his company successfully into the business of contract management, and in 1992, he moved into the luxury resort business with the purchase of Regent Hotels International of Hong Kong. Today his group owns 37 properties and generates revenues of nearly $2 billion annually.

What kind of a man is Isadore Sharp? He is man who prefers to stay quietly on the sidelines, who trusts his instincts, and is committed to exceptionally high standards of service. He understands and satisfies the needs of both his guests and his employees, and instills in his staff the belief that anything is possible. "No" and "can't be done" are not part of their vocabulary. Isadore Sharp is a Canadian who has led the way in the luxury hotel business for more than 30 years, earning respect and admiration from the hotel industry around the world.

they are addressed in the planning stages, they can be overcome or minimized. Potential disadvantages include the following: (1) volunteers may be difficult to obtain; (2) dissenting community merchants and residents may block planning; (3) inadequate planning may result in financial setbacks that jeopardize future events; (4) large numbers of visitors may tax existing accommodations, visitor services, and restaurants, posing a threat to future events if they go home dissatisfied; (5) the environment could be damaged; and (6) a community may find it difficult to attract visitors for the first until the event becomes widely known.

Managing Events

What a challenge managing a large event can be! Organizers are doomed to fail if they don't understand the complexities of planning, organizing, and staging a special event. Many colleges and universities in Canada offer excellent training programs. The CTHRC has national certification programs for events coordinator, special event manager, and meeting planner. If events management interests you, here are some of the areas of which you must develop knowledge:

- *Client needs and expectations.* It is important to start with a clear understanding of the purpose of the event, the needs of your client, and the projected outcomes. This means you must develop good communication and people skills.

- *Site selection and inspection.* For regular events such as the Calgary Stampede, the site is pre-selected. Sometimes the client chooses the site. As coordinator you must become familiar with the site on many levels to ensure you have adequate registration areas, hotel accommodations, food service capabilities, restrooms, and utilities (e.g., electrical power, power distribution, water source).

- *Designing the event environment.* Although this may be the creative side of your planning, your designs must meet your client's needs, the registrant's needs, and the budget. Some events will have a simple room set-up and others may choose to create an atmosphere and provide entertainment. As many events are held outdoors, you will need to deal with whatever Mother Nature chooses to send your way. In all cases, concern for the environment must be part of your plan.

- *Financial management.* Many events are enormously expensive to run and keeping a tight control of dollars spent is essential if they are to be a success. Besides the obvious fixed expenses, you will be dealing with a wide variety of vendors, entertainers, caterers, and paid staff. Add to these expenses marketing and promotion costs, floral and décor costs, insurance, etc. Good accounting skills are essential!

- *Training staff and volunteers.* As the event planner, you will be working with full-time/part-time staff as well as many volunteers. Volunteers willingly work for free but often lack specific skills or knowledge. You will need leadership skills to get your people working as a team.

- *Scheduling.* Much of the event is scheduled well in advance, and your client is likely to take an active part. Promotions highlight the schedule of events, and your biggest concern is ensuring that the schedule is followed.

A conference speaker who takes just 10 minutes more than scheduled can throw the rest of the day off track, affecting both food service and programmed entertainment.

• *Catering.* Food is often the highlight of any meeting or event, and knowing what your clientele wants is very important. What is a festival or fair

OPPORTUNITIES IN EVENTS & CONFERENCES

	FESTIVAL/EVENT PLANNING	CONFERENCE/MEETING PLANNING	TRADE SHOW
OPERATION (FRONT LINE)	Concession Attendant Destination Services Representative	Concession Attendant Convention/Meeting Services Guide Destination Services Representative (guide in hotel or airport) Sales Representative Registration Clerk Registration Officer Security Officer Interpreter A/V Technician	Concession Attendant Trade Show Guide Sales Representative
SUPERVISORY	Special Events Coordinator Program Specialist Catering Coordinator Banquet Supervisor Communications and Public Relations Manager Protocol Manager Registration Manager	Convention/Meeting Planner Functions Coordinator Program Specialist (AGM business meeting) Catering Coordinator (facility) Banquet Supervisor (site changes)	Trade Show Coordinator Exhibit Design Assistant Registration Manager Sales Assistant
MANAGEMENT	Concession Operator Extension Officer Fundraising Consultant/Administrator Communications and Public Relations Manager Sales Manager Human Resources Manager Special Events Manager Manager (Fair, Park, or Rec Facility) Retail Shop Manager	Fundraising Consultant/Administrator Convention/Meeting Manager (Corporate, Independent, Association) Exhibit Designer (Manager) Convention Centre Manager **Conference Service Manager**	Concession Operator Trade Show Director Exhibit Designer Sales Manager International Sales Manager Human Resources Manager Retail Shop Manager Public Relations Manager Exhibit Service Manager Facility Manager
EXECUTIVE		Executive Director/CEO	

SOURCE: Courtesy of Canadian Tourism Human Resource Council, *The Student's Travel Map*, 1995.

without the candy floss and the hotdog vendor? A conference of nutrition-
ists will be looking for freshly prepared, nutritious food while a meeting of
high-school students will want pizza or hamburgers. One of the big logis-
tical problems handled by the Compass group during World Youth Day
was ensuring the 250 000 attendees were fed within meal times. An event
planner must ensure that caterers handle special dietary needs or allergies.

- *Audiovisual equipment.* Today's meetings require a vast array of sophisticated audiovisual equipment. Planners need to know in advance who will
  supply it and what sort of technical support the company will provide.
- *Entertainment.* This varies dramatically depending on the type of event and
  the budget. Usually some sort of entertainment will be part of the package
  you create. What are your clients' interests? What is the budget? These will
  determine whether you take participants out for a night on the town or if

JOB DESCRIPTION FOR. . .

CONFERENCE SERVICE MANAGER

Industry Sector	Events & Conferences
Division	Conference/Meeting Planner
Industry Setting	Convention centres, hotels, and cruise ships
Job Level	Supervisory
Description of Duties	The Conference Service Manager works at the site of the meeting or convention with the meeting planner to ensure all needs are properly met. The Conference Service Manager understands the hotel or convention centre's functions and the responsibilities of each department. The basic responsibility is to make sure schedules are maintained and that services are rendered according to the contract. The position involves continual coordination with the various operating departments to make certain that quality service standards are maintained. It also ensures all the elements of a convention or meeting run smoothly and efficiently from the time of the attendees' arrival, through the set-up, to billing and departures. In addition to the public relations and service roles, the Conference Service Manager has a sales responsibility to the host facility for rebooking the group by providing the best service and follow-through.
Skills	Excellent communication and public relations skills; sales and record-keeping abilities; attention to detail.
Industry Experience	Most Conference Service Managers have worked in the hospitality industry where they may have gained experience in dealing with meetings and meeting planners.
HRDC Reference	NOC 1226 Conference and Event Planners

you simply set up a "dine around" night: that is, make reservations at a variety of local restaurants and allow attendees to choose one, often paying for their own meal.

- *Marketing.* Events are only successful if you have in place a smart marketing and promotion plan. Budget will determine where and how you promote the event. The better the promotions, the better the response and the higher the profit margin.

- *Finding sponsorship.* Unless you are dealing with a meeting whose costs are being covered by a specific business, sponsorship is critical to an event's success. The tourism industry can be slow to see the benefits of partnering with a special event, so finding good sponsorship is often challenging. Event organizers must learn persuasive techniques and be ready to show the benefits sponsorship brings to a company.

- *Legal, ethical, and risk management.* As with any business, legal and ethical issues will arise. You need to knowing how to read contracts and apply risk management techniques, and you must always maintain a high professional standard.

in practice

Describe 10 special events that might entice tourists to your region. Choose one event from your list and, in your own words, write an advertisement for your local newspaper that would help you promote this event.

summary

Events and conferences is an exciting sector and people who choose this field can expect long days, many challenges, and great satisfaction once the job is well done. This sector includes a wide variety of events that range from weddings to fundraising, pumpkin festivals to sporting events, corporate business meetings to world summits. Events provide a community with jobs and a stronger presence in the region. In the past, many events ended with a revenue deficit, but in today's competitive world the event must generate revenue or it faces cancellation. Planning and staging an event requires tremendous coordination skills, lots of ingenuity, and patience. To be successful in this field, knowledge, experience, and continuing professional development are essential. If you love planning and problem solving, then this may be the right sector for you!

questions

1. a)   Define the terms *special event, festival, hallmark vent, fundraising event, civic event, spectator sports event.*

    b)   Identify one example of each of the above types of event hosted by your province/region.

    c)   Describe five disadvantages for a community of hosting such events.

    d)   Explain five benefits to a community of hosting special events.

2.   a)   Create a table that compares and contrasts a convention, conference, and meeting based on the following criteria: (i) occupation of attendees, (ii) number of attendees, (iii) purpose of meeting, (iv) location of the event, (v) accessibility of the location, (vi) payment of fees and costs, (vii) duration of the event, (viii) timing of the event.

    b)   Name a recent conference and a recent convention held in your city or region.

3.   Define *trade show* and list 10 different annual trade shows in your regions. Identify each as open to the public or only to industry members.

4.   "Hockey is an important part of the tourism industry and, as such, should receive either tax considerations or financial support from a community." Agree or disagree with this statement using five different supporting factors.

5.   Define the following terms as they relate to the events and conferences sector: *conference centre, Rendez-Vous Canada, convention centre, breakout room, seminar, workshop.*

---

weblinks

www.mpiweb.org

Meeting Professionals International is the world's largest association of meeting industry professionals.

www.banffcentre.ab.ca

The Banff Centre is one of the country's most distinctive conference centres, situated on scenic Tunnel Mountain, overlooking Banff in the Alberta Rockies.

www.theex.com

Toronto's CNE, or Canadian National Exhibition ("the Ex") combines an agricultural fair with a carnival and concerts that attract thousands of visitors every summer.

---

notes

1. *The Student's Travel Map* (Ottawa: Canadian Tourism Human Resource Council, 1995), p. 11.

2. Sylvia Densmore, *Staging Successful Small Town Events*, International Festival And Events Association Presentation, February 2001.

3. Donald Getz, *Festivals, Special Events, and Tourism* (New York: Van Nostrand Reinhold, 1991), p. 44.

4. Sylvia Densmore, *Staging Successful Small Town Events*, International Festival And Events Association Presentation, February 2001.

5. *Toronto Star*, Film Festival is Economic Fuel, March 19, 2003, F1.

6. *Toronto Star*, Event's tourism boom may echo, July 30, 2002, B3.

7. David W. Howell and Robert A. Ellison, *Passport* (Toronto: Nelson Canada, 1995), p. 293.

8. *Canadian Travel Press,* December 16, 2002, p. 20.

9. David W. Howell and Robert A. Ellison, *Passport* (Toronto: Nelson Canada, 1995), p. 294.

10 The Adventure Tourism and Outdoor Recreation Sector

carrying capacity
Crown land
ecotourism
ecotourist
greenwashing

hard adventure
low-impact camping
national parks system
nonconsumptive
  tourism

outdoor recreation
recreational sports
soft adventure
sustainable tourism

Having read this chapter you will be able to

1. Describe adventure tourism, ecotourism, and outdoor recreational activities.

2. Outline the role played by Canadian Heritage/Parks Canada in this sector.

3. Discuss the key characteristics of ecotourism and the ecotourism market.

4. Define, using examples, *hard adventure, soft adventure, ecotourism, sustainable tourism, nonconsumptive tourism, and low-impact camping.*

5. Provide a brief description of 10 seasonal outdoor activities enjoyed by travellers in Canada.

6. Compare the two opposing views of tourism's impact on the environment.

7. Explain how the concept of carrying capacity is helpful to both the tourist and the environment.

8. Explain how tourism can damage vegetation, water quality, air quality, wildlife, coastlines, and mountainous terrain.

9. Explain how sustainable tourism development can be implemented by government and business.

– –

Activities found in the Adventure Tourism and Outdoor Recreation sector are major motivators for pleasure travel, and Canada has some of the world's finest outdoor experiences. Busy lifestyles and stress make vacations an important part of staying healthy. Our bodies and minds gain strength from relaxation and the chance to unwind. How do people relax? They get away from their work and their busy lives and do something they enjoy. Getting physical activity means fresh air and exercise and is a healthy choice for a vacation. This puts adventure tourism and outdoor recreation (ATOR) front and centre when vacation plans are made and explains the important role this sector plays in Canada's tourism product.

This sector includes adventure travel, activities that are part of ecotourism, and outdoor recreation. CTC statistics show an annual growth rate of 15 percent, making ATOR the fastest growing sector in Canadian tourism.[1] Our beautiful landscapes provide a wide assortment of physical activities for tourists; the challenge is to balance development with maintaining this environment.

The Canadian Tourism Human Resource Council has identified more than 80 different occupations within this sector, which employs approximately 71 000 Canadians.[2] This very broad sector encourages both entrepreneurship and small businesses and will play an increasingly important role as the baby boomers retire and make outdoor experiences an integral part of their lives. If you love the outdoors and are not interested in being stuck behind a desk, then maybe this tourism sector is the one for you. Who wouldn't like to work at play?

It is interesting to note that the events of September 11, 2001, while devastating much of the tourism industry, had little effect on adventure travel. According to IntraWest, Whistler, B.C., actually saw an increase in overnight stays. Why? First, guests felt more secure in secluded destinations than in cities. Second, allocentric tourists take risk in stride. So in the wake of 9-11, adventure tourism continues to thrive.

This chapter begins with an overview of Canada's parks and Crown lands, the site of so much ATOR activity. For purposes of study, *adventure tourism* is divided into three categories: hard adventure, soft adventure, and ecotourism, while *outdoor recreation* is divided into seasonal activities. The chapter looks briefly at risk management practices and ends with a discussion of how tourism affects the environment and how the industry is responding to these challenges.

Parks and Crown Lands

Canada's National Parks System

"National parks are a country wide system of representative natural areas of Canadian significance. By law they are protected for public understanding, appreciation and enjoyment while being maintained in an unimpaired state for future generations."[3] Parks Canada falls under the jurisdiction of the government department called Canadian Heritage. The **national parks system** was inaugurated in 1885, when 26 km² on the slopes of Sulphur Mountain in Banff were set aside to be protected for future generations. Between 1887 and 1915, five more parks were established in the western regions: Yoho, Glacier, Mount Revelstoke, Waterton Lakes, and Jasper. The St. Lawrence Islands National Park was the first in eastern Canada. Today, Canada has 41 national parks representing 24 out of 39 natural regions, and the Canadian government has set aside an additional 67 natural regions to be held under its protection, 39 land-based and 28 marine-based. The goal is to establish national parks in each region. In September of 2002, Prime Minister Jean Chrétien announced the addition of 10 new national parks.

Mandates of Parks Canada

Parks Canada does more than just manage the national parks system; it manages Canada's 131 national historic sites, historic railway stations, and more than 650 historic sites; it oversees operation of our seven historic canal systems; it coordinates the federal-provincial cooperative program for the Canadian Heritage River Systems; it directs and implements heritage tourism opportunities and programs and provides services to the more than 20 million visitors who use the national parks system every year.

Provincial Parks Systems

Each province has its own parks, natural habitats governed by ministries such as British Columbia's Ministry of Environment, Lands and Parks. The province is responsible for the management of these lands and for the safety of visitors. Park attendants patrol on land and water, to ensure that users obey the rules and regulations, issue warnings when severe weather is approaching and, in some cases, determine whether weather conditions make open fires unsafe. Provincial administrations maintain all public access such as roads, bridges, and campgrounds, and often provide rest areas and picnic tables for daytime visitors. Most parks have plans detailing future development in the region, ensuring the preservation and wise use of these protected lands.

Crown Lands

Unlike many countries around the world, much of our Canadian wilderness is not privately owned but designated **Crown land**: that is, land owned by the federal or provincial government. National and provincial parks are Crown land set aside and protected by legislation governing use and development. Not all Crown lands, however, fall under such legislation. Crown land may be leased or purchased by private organizations such as logging companies or tourism businesses. Conflict over the use of Crown land is bound to arise. For example, a clear-cut logging operation, despite reforestation programs, will blight the landscape for many years and conflict with tourism development.

Just how important is Crown land to ATOR? Most adventure tourism occurs on Crown land, and a quick look at statistics shows us why. For example, British

Columbia, our third-largest province, covers an area of 94.8 million hectares, of which 92 percent is provincial Crown land; 1 percent is federal Crown land; 5 percent is privately owned, and 2 percent is covered by fresh water. These proportions are fairly typical. Of B.C.'s Crown land, approximately two thirds (59 million hectares) is public forest and provides the basis for much of B.C.'s recreational activities. The province has begun a series of initiatives to increase the use of Crown lands for environmentally sound economic development and community uses. Almost 11 million hectares of crown land already lie within B.C.'s provincial parks system; the goal is to increase park lands by 12 percent over the next 10 years. In May of 2000, a groundbreaking treaty was signed with the Nisga'a nation, giving them complete control over 2000 km^2 of Crown land and allowing self-government. B.C. has more than 50 different First Nations, and 70 percent of these groups are currently in treaty negotiations. Settling a century-old claim of right of ownership, the Nisga'a treaty establishes a basis for future agreements. It is not yet clear how such decisions will affect tourism development.[4]

In all provinces, Crown lands form the basis of much of our outdoor recreational activities and many hunting and fishing lodges, camp sites, and resorts make good use of this land, its rivers, and its lakes. Tourism is seen as a "green industry," meaning the protection of the land it uses is paramount to the continued quality of the tourism experience. The Canadian tourism industry is active in world conferences and has learned from the experience of other tourist destinations that we must be proactive in determining proper usage of wilderness areas.

Adventure Tourism

Adventure tourism typically happens in an unusual setting, often a remote wilderness or exotic spot. It involves physical activity, sometimes quite strenuous; and often the transportation itself is part of the adventure: perhaps some type of boat or hiking or climbing. These activities are "soft" or "hard" depending on the level of risk or physical exertion. **Hard adventure**, such as mountain climbing, involves risk, challenge, often strenuous physical exertion, special equipment, and prior training. **Soft adventure**, such as hiking on a trail, is less risky, less strenuous, and requires little or no preparation. Ecotourism involves a tour of an environmentally unique area to learn about its ecology and culture. Although it may include activities that can be classified as hard or soft adventure, the focus is on ethical values and principles. **Ecotourism** is tourism that focuses on nature-related experiences that help people appreciate and understand natural resources and their conservation.[5]

Canada is world renowned for its magnificent, unspoiled scenery, so it is natural that many tourists choose to come here for adventure. Many of our rivers, such as the Nahanni, provide challenging hard adventure activities for the enthusiast. Tourists may be flown in to a rustic lodge that acts as the home base, but once they are on the river, their survival depends on how well they can handle their craft, the river, and the wilderness. No soft bed awaits them at the end of the day and meals are not catered. Accidents and injuries may be life threatening and the tourist who chooses this type of trip feels a sense of self-discovery and accomplishment once the trip has been completed.

An example of a more controlled, less risky hard adventure trip would be hiking the famous West Coast Trail (WCT) in B.C.'s Pacific Rim National Park

Hard adventure requires knowledge of the sport, prior training, and a willingness to take risks.
(Photo: Jeff Jackson.)

Reserve. The trail is easily accessible from Victoria and the two main entry points are Port Renfrew and Bamfield. Both towns have scheduled transportation services, accommodations, and stores for supplies, but neither has an ATM. This coastal area is known as "the graveyard of the Pacific" because the wild Pacific storms threw so many sailing ships and steamers up on the rocky shoals. In 1906, after the sailing ship *Valencia* sank with 133 lives lost, British Columbia built the Pachena lighthouse and the Dominion Life Saving Trail, hoping to provide survivors with a path back to civilization. As navigation techniques improved, the trail was abandoned. In 1973, when the Pacific Rim National Park Reserve was created, Parks Canada rebuilt the trail. It follows the historic route along sandstone cliffs and beaches. Here, the hiker is exposed to Canadian wilderness at its best, with breathtaking views of waterfalls, sea arches, sea stacks, and wildlife. Hikers are warned to be prepared to negotiate steep slopes; wade through rivers; use rustic ladders, bridges, and cable cars; climb steep rocks; and walk muddy trails. The entire trail lies within the territories of the Huu-ay-aht, Ditidaht, and Pacheedaht First Nations. Several sacred areas must be traversed and hikers are warned to respect Aboriginal rights. The area is patrolled by QUU'AS Guardians and park rangers ready to charge any hikers who do not obey the rules. Open to hikers from May 1 to September 30, the Trail takes five to seven days to complete, and the average temperature in July is just 14° C! Hikers must provide Parks Canada with an itinerary in case of accident, but they are warned that it may take as long as 24 hours for rescuers to arrive. The WCT Web site provides a "plan it carefully" guide including maps, a description of the area, and the type of equipment needed to successfully complete the 75-km walk. It also warns "this rugged hike is not for everyone. You and your party's fitness, knowledge, and skills must meet the challenges of the area."[6] Each province has its own form of hard adventure experiences, and demand for this product is growing. It is important for the novice adventurer to have proper equipment, a trained guide, and an understanding of the difficulties and adversities they will be expected to overcome. Being unprepared can put an entire group in death's path.

For those who crave adventure sport, Canada abounds with interesting opportunities, including mountain climbing, heli-skiing, ice climbing, spelunking (caving), sea kayaking, and white-water rafting. Along the B.C. coast is found one of our most unusual winter sports—winter surfing. Surfing along this coast can be a challenge at any time of the year, but especially when winter storms hit. Canadians first started riding the winter waves in the 1940s, and more than 4000 surfing enthusiasts brave the frigid waves and the cyclonic winds every winter. Dom Domic, president of the British Columbia Surfing Association says, "It's a misconception that surfing is only a warm weather sport."[7]

Soft adventure is similar to hard adventure with much of the risk removed. Companies who specialize in soft adventure have studiously worked to remove or control any risks to their guests. That is not to say people who participate in these types of activities will never get hurt, but with the proper equipment and trained leaders, soft adventure can be both exciting and safe. Examples of soft adventure in Canada include

- Backpacking in the Rockies: This is one of the more interesting ways for a tourist to learn about a region and its culture. The Australians were the first to use the term *backpacker*. Backpackers enjoy following self-directed itineraries and tend to use inexpensive accommodations like the hostelling system or camping. Although their daily spending is low, their stays tend to be much longer than the ordinary adventure tourist. Their tourism dollars spent on goods and services directly benefit many small communities along their journey.

- White-water rafting: Often considered a hard adventure activity, this is an exciting way to see and feel the power of a river first hand. But for most people it is a rougher ride than they would like. To capture this part of the adventure tourism market, white-water rafting companies have softened this activity by building larger rafts that are more stable in the rapids. Sometimes the rafting company will choose a quieter stretch of the river for the trip. The true adventurer would probably not be happy with this activity, but it allows a wider group of people to enjoy an experience they would have otherwise avoided.

Canadian entrepreneurs continue to expand adventure tourism to meet new market demands. The image of retirees shuffling off to sit in rocking chairs is no longer valid as the baby boomers choose to retire early. This market is looking for adventure without the physical demands of hard adventure, and it will be a good source of income for the adventure tourism and outdoor recreation sector over the next 25 years.

Ecotourism

The World Tourism Organization declared 2002 to be the International Year of Ecotourism. Ecotourism is perhaps one of the most misunderstood, overused terms in the tourism industry. Hoping to appeal to this side of the adventure tourism market, tour operators use the term loosely to mean "outdoor experiences looking at nature." As our ecosystems are a delicate balance of nature, care must be taken to ensure the area is not damaged. The Sierra Club has been an outspoken

Hiking in the Rockies provides panoramic views and can be part of a hard adventure vacation or a simple recreational outing.
(Photo courtesy Canadian Tourism Commission.)

advocate for ecotourism and has practised **low-impact camping** techniques during its tours for more than 50 years. For example, while leading rafting tours on the Colorado River, every item put to use is carried along with the guide, every item created on the trip is carried out, and participants may not pick and take out any souvenir flowers or rocks. The banks of the river are left virtually untouched and ready for the next group of adventurers. Had this style of tourism been practised by all river tours over the past half century, it is likely that the Colorado River would still be free of pollution. It is not. Sadly, too many companies engage in "**greenwashing**": that is, they use the language of ecotourism without actually protecting the environment. Oliver Hillel, tourism program coordinator for the United Nations Environment Program, cites an example of a 200-room "eco-lodge" located in the Brazilian jungle with no sewage treatment, no effort to lower environmental or cultural impacts on the local environment, and no input from the local people. Hillel argues that true ecotourism is delivered by small, locally owned and operated companies. He identifies the key characteristics of ecotourism:

1. An ecotourism venture contributes to the conservation of biodiversity. Biodiversity is defined as the variety of life on earth and the interdependence among all species.

2. Local guides and interpreters help participants to recognize the natural and cultural resources of the region and the economic benefits produced by the tour help sustain the well-being of the local community.

3. Participants become an integral part of the educational process in learning how the region's ecosystem functions and demonstrating responsible action toward the environment.

4. It requires the lowest possible consumption of nonrenewable resources. When a tourism experience takes nothing out of the ecosystem and leaves nothing behind, it is called "**nonconsumptive tourism**."[8]

Blue heron, photographed in the early morning at Lake of Two Rivers, Algonquin Park. Ecotourists leave nothing behind and take nothing with them, thereby preserving the delicate balance of nature.
(Photo: Duncan Cumming.)

The Ecotourism Market Segment

According to a recent survey by HLA and ARA consulting firms, **ecotourists** are more mature, have post–high-school education, prefer longer trips (8–14 days), and are often willing to pay a higher price for this style of tourism.[9]

Some examples of Canadian ecotourism adventures include tours flying into the heart of the Great Bear Rainforest from Klemtu, B.C., for five days with the Kitasoo and Xaixais people to learn more about this unique rainforest area and the people who live there;[10] tracing the early path of European explorers across Davis Strait to the edge of Baffin Island; travelling along the shores of Newfoundland and Labrador visiting Trinity, Battle Harbour, Gros Morne National Park, and St-Pierre-Miquelon; or travelling the coastal waters of the Arctic along the Kivilliq Coast and southern Baffin Island, visiting destinations like Rankin Inlet and Cape Dorset.[11]

Sustainable tourism occurs when tourism development and operations meet the needs of the present visitor without compromising the ability of future generations to enjoy the same experiences.[12] In simple words, the same wilderness/tourist experience you enjoy this summer should be available to your grandchildren. The best tool to ensure sustainability is environmental legislation—and enforcement. For example, the Yukon has a tough Wilderness Tourism Licensing Law that requires companies to have a permit to conduct adventure tours, which can be revoked if a company does not follow strict low-impact camping techniques.

Risk Management

In this new age of litigation, tourism companies are finding that insurance policies alone do not provide adequate financial or legal coverage if a customer is injured or killed while under their care. A risk management program identifies all the potential hazards customers may encounter and it reviews the products, services, and processes through which the product is delivered. Risk management should provide historical data on past accidents or losses and identify possible risk scenarios in the future. Each risk needs to be analyzed carefully, noting frequency, possible loss ratios, the impact of the loss to the customer, and how the incident will affect public perception of the business or activity. Then the company must ensure that all safety standards are being met. Staff must receive proper training. Environmental risks must be held to a minimum and emergency plans tested and in place. Signage identifying all risks must be clear and readily visible. It should alert users to the following:

- the obvious dangers of the activity (e.g., "not following all safety precautions may result in injury or death")

- any unusual dangers of the activity (e.g., "high water levels")

- dangers that apply to specific consumers (e.g., "this trail requires a high level of expertise, experience, and physical stamina")

If it is common knowledge that the activities your company provides have inherent risks (such as heli-skiing), why worry about risk management? A risk management policy provides an insurance company with documented proof of a high standard of care and can reduce insurance costs. Many colleges and universities are now offering risk management courses in their programs. Risk management has become a core skill for any tourism business.[13]

Outdoor Recreation

Sports and **outdoor recreation** are a big business in North America. If Canadians are to stay healthy and fit with outdoor exercise throughout the year, then the seasons dictate that they must engage in more than one sport. This benefits both the equipment suppliers and the tourism industry. A change of season means a tourist may return to enjoy your resort for an entirely different purpose: hiking, playing tennis, or golfing in the summer; skiing, snowboarding, or skating in the winter.

Canada marked the new millennium with the creation of one continuous trail that joins our country from Newfoundland and the Atlantic Ocean, to Nunavut and the Arctic, ending with the waters of the Pacific in British Columbia. It was a project designed and built by Canadian associations that represent many outdoor recreational activities such as hiking and cross-country skiing. The Trans Canada Trail (TCT), the longest trail of its kind in the world, covers 16 000 km, winds through every province and territory, and provides outdoor enthusiasts with five core activities: walking, cycling, horseback riding, cross-country skiing, and snowmobiling (in some sections). The Trans Canada Trail Foundation, a nonprofit, charitable organization, funded the building of the Trail with government grants and donations from local businesses and individuals across Canada. The trail is maintained by communities, and the shared experience of building and maintaining the Trail has strengthened the tie that binds Canadians—a love of the outdoors.[14]

Winter Sports

Some winter sports enthusiasts claim Canada has the best snow conditions in the world. Certainly British Columbia, Alberta, and Quebec provide world-class skiing on their mountains. Skiing is big business. Nearly 35 percent of the Canadian population skis during the winter. Equipment sales alone bring $2.3 billion of revenue annually to retail stores across the country.[15] The sport of skiing may be divide into groupings based on the type of trail or snow path used. *Track* skiing is done on groomed trails and *touring* skiing is done on ungroomed snow. This sport is also divided into groupings by style: cross-country/nordic, down hill/alpine, heli-skiing, and snowboarding. *Cross-country* skiing can be done anywhere, as the skier uses flat countryside or ski trails. Summer resorts looking to become four-season resorts are developing cross-country skiing as a part of their winter package. *Alpine* is downhill skiing, and most provinces have some facilities to satisfy the alpine skier. Alpine skiing has seen dramatic changes as "hot dogging" allows the skier to perform aerial manoeuvres that 40 years ago would have stunned onlookers. Heli-skiing is done in high mountainous terrain. It takes a special spirit to climb aboard a helicopter, head into the mountains, disembark at a height that few ever venture to, and then ski back down the mountain on virgin snow. It takes not only a brave spirit but a big bank balance as these trips often cost $1000 a day! Snowboarding is one of the latest winter sports in the Olympic Games. Appealing to the under-40 crowd, the single, short, ski-like board allows snowboarders greater agility and freedom of style.

For the winter athlete, Canada offers some unique experiences. In January, the Raid International Ukatak takes place. Four-person racing teams from around the globe travel across a 40-km course that tests both their endurance and skills. Over the five-day race, participants will use snowshoes, cross-country skis, mountain bikes, and ice canoes (canoes with blades on the bottom). In February, two major events take place: the Canadian Ski Marathon and the Yukon Quest International Sled Dog Race. Nearly 2000 skiers take part in the marathon, which covers a 160-km trail from Lachute in the Laurentian Mountains to Buckingham, Quebec, just outside the National Capital Region. The Yukon Quest follows the historic gold rush trail from Whitehorse to Fairbanks, Alaska. It is billed as the world's toughest dog sled race, and covers 1600 km of wild winter terrain.

Flat on your back, careening down a mountainside at 50 km per hour, all you can hear is the roar of the steel runners against compact snow. This is the wonderful world of the natural luge. Dating from the early nineteenth century, natural luge has been a fringe winter sport in Canada for fewer than 20 years. Unlike the modern luge used at the Winter Olympic games, the sled's steel edges are kept flat on the ground and riders steer with reins and flexible foot-driven wooden levers. North America's first dedicated commercial natural luge course is at Mount Washington Alpine Resort on Vancouver Island. If you live in the Toronto area, Rodle Mountain Luge Training Centre is located right in your backyard, near Bancroft.[16]

What can those of us who prefer to sit by a warm hearth do on a sunny winter day? Snowmobiling allows less active Canadians to get out and enjoy Canada's winter wonderland. People who snowmobile enjoy the camaraderie of the sport and the ease with which all members of the family can join in. It does not require any physical prowess or exceptional abilities and you don't have to be mechanically inclined. Snowmobiling is a sport even that allows even nonathletes to explore, enjoy winter, and get away from the doldrums of city life. It is, however, banned or restricted in some areas because of the noise and fumes it creates.

Other winter activities include hockey (the second most popular sport in Canada), ice skating, tobogganing, curling, and ice sailing. Ice sailing is done on the Bay of Quinte, near Belleville, Ontario. Using small sailboats equipped with

Fishing is a growing sport, and Canadian lakes and rivers have some of the finest sport fishing in the world.
(Photo courtesy Canadian Tourism Commission.)

runners, and catching the wind that blows down the bay, they speed across windswept ice at 40 km an hour. Resorts that stay open for the winter offer many of these sports, as well as a variety of indoor activities for those who are reluctant to brave the cold.

Spring, Summer, and Fall Sports

Hunting and fishing play an integral part in the lives of Aboriginal Canadians and they are major revenue generators for our tourism industry. About 5 percent of Canadians and 6 percent of Americans use their vacations enjoying these two sports. Hunters and fishers purchase equipment, lodging, food, and transportation, freshwater sport fishing alone grosses $650 million annually for the tourism industry.[17] For the best experience, hunters and fishers know that they must travel into the northern regions of a province. Fly-in fishing camps in the northern regions of all provinces appeal to the true fisher. Deep, pristine lakes, with a wide variety of fish species, are particularly attractive to the U.S. market. Accessibility of the lake or forest region often determines the quality of the sport fishing or hunting. Hunting and fishing guides with an intimate knowledge of the area may be used to further ensure a good trip. Provinces license for both hunting and fishing, placing limits on the hunting season and number of each species that may be taken. Park rangers patrol northern highways and randomly stop those leaving the area to check that limits have been respected. Although fishing continues to grow in North America, hunting is losing its appeal to younger Canadians, and decisions such as the Ontario government's cancellation of the black bear hunt in the spring of 2001 have been costly to many small businesses. Hunting plays an important role in maintaining healthy numbers of wildlife including bear, deer, and ducks. In national parks, hunting and fishing regulations are made at the federal level and Parks Canada personnel are responsible for selling the appropriate licences and enforcing regulations.

Camping   More than 14 percent of all Canadian vacations are camping trips, and 9.2 percent of U.S. travellers camp out on vacation.[18] Our parks systems encourage camping by providing a number of different services. In some parks, tourists will find interpretive centres that help them understand the region's ecosystem, small stores that provide environmentally safe soaps and other products, logs may be sold for campfires and perhaps you will find huts with shower stalls. Advance reservations are advisable if you wish to camp in a provincial park, especially at popular parks in the summer. Although camping experiences vary from major campgrounds with facilities to wilderness sites, gaining knowledge of the area and its dangers should be part of your pre-camping decision.

Golf   Golf has become one of the most popular sports in Canada. As baby boomers age, more are choosing to walk the greens of a local golf course or to fashion a winter vacation around one of the golf resorts in the southern United States. About 5 percent of Canadian travellers and 7 percent of American travellers pick up their clubs while on vacation.[19] About 2.2 million golfers take to the greens in Canada every season, spending nearly $1 billion annually in equipment, accessories, and fees. Golfers are also likely to spend their tourism dollars on other forms of entertainment, including gambling and spectator sports.[20]

Tennis   Tennis courts are also an integral part of resort life. Competent tennis instructors and knowledgeable sales clerks play a vital role in increasing the profitability of any tennis club; offering lessons and selling accessories can be very lucrative. In addition, both golf and tennis clubs must train their maintenance staff to ensure that the greens and courts are kept in excellent condition.

Marine activities   Canada has a multitude of popular marine experiences and water-based activities. Besides the sport of fishing, coastal waters provide tourists

One of the most reasonably priced vacations in Canada is camping out. Camping can be a family affair, a trip in the company of friends, or an isolated wilderness trek.

(Photo courtesy Canadian Tourism Commission.)

with opportunities to go whale watching, sea kayaking, sailing in tall ships, and deep-sea diving, to name a few. On the west coast, many companies offer marine activities. The Oak Bay Marine Group, begun 35 years ago as a small marina, is today the largest sport-fishing operation in Canada. It operates five resorts, a fleet of off-shore boats, two luxury yachts, and a 71-m steamship. In the interior, lakes and rivers provide some of the finest fishing and river rafting in the world.[21] For example, the Ottawa River near Pembroke, Ontario, offers excellent white-water rafting, and rafters come from as far away as Australia and Sweden to train on the river. Sitting on the banks of the Athabasca River in Jasper, you can watch kayakers playing on the Athabasca's challenging rapids. Swimming, water-skiing, sailing, and boating are all part of the water experience.

Walking The most popular exercise by far requires no equipment and can be done anywhere at any time. According to the National Sporting Goods Association, walking far outranks all other forms of exercise. Many cities have walking or bike paths. The large areas of green space that envelop the city of Ottawa, for example, provide safe, easily accessible paths for jogging, biking, and walking. In Vancouver, the path that follows the water's edge in Stanley Park provides residents and tourists with a scenic walk. Even large cities like New York, Boston, and Toronto offer easily accessible walking paths. If walking is part of your daily exercise, no matter where you vacation, walking provides you with the chance to meet local residents and perhaps learn more about their city and culture.

Other **recreational sports** include hiking, mountaineering, bicycling, wildlife viewing, and jogging along a beautiful beach. Outdoor activities offer tourists the chance to enjoy the climate and the scenery and to exercise at their discretion. Most accommodations whose market is the outdoor enthusiast can provide visitors with supplies and equipment, or can direct them to shops where they can rent whatever they need.

Windsurfing along the shores of Prince Edward Island.
(Photo courtesy Canadian Tourism Commission.)

Ellsworth Statler

"Life is service. The one who progresses is the one who gives his fellow human being a little more, a little better service." Ellsworth Statler was a man dedicated to details—details that made his customers happy and made the name Statler one of the best known in the industry. He began his career as a bellhop in West Virginia and ended his career as a philanthropist, donating millions to schools that taught the new generation of hospitality managers the art of hostelry.

Statler was quick to see opportunity and was always looking for ways to make work simpler and more efficient. He got his first taste of success in the concession business, selling railroad tickets and operating a billiard room in West Virginia. He diversified his interests into a bowling alley and then a small restaurant called The Pie House. By 1884, he was making the astounding sum of $10 000 a year! Leaving West Virginia, he moved to Buffalo, New York, and opened a restaurant in "the largest office building in the world." He waited for the crowds to come, but discovered that Buffalo was an "eat at home" kind of town. With creditors closing in, he gambled. Selling six dinners for the price of four and giving away prizes daily to lucky winners, he soon changed the eating habits of Buffalo. How did his business survive when he gave away 33 percent of his food? Mr. Statler was a man who believed in cost controls. First, he fired his expensive chef. Then he began to use products on his menu that were in season or reasonably priced. He developed the concept of "service side table," putting cutlery, napkins, glasses, and condiments at the side of the dining room, eliminating unnecessary trips to the kitchen for his wait staff and giving them more time to serve customers.

His first adventure into the hotel business was not exactly triumphant. He opened a 2100-room hotel for the 1901 Pan American Exposition in Buffalo, which, like the fair, was a dismal failure and nearly went bankrupt. In 1904, he tried his luck again, this time at the World's Fair in St. Louis. By the end of this event, his 2257-room hotel had a net profit of $300 000.

Statler was ready for a full-time, permanent hotel and in 1908, he opened the first Statler Hotel in Buffalo. All 300 rooms had private baths (built back-to-back using common shafts for plumbing), circulating ice water, telephones, and full-sized closets with lights. Statler also installed hooks in the bathrooms so that guests could hang up their towels and use them again instead of having to throw them on the floor. Statler was also responsible for such amenities as reading lamps attached to headboards, radios in each room, writing supplies, and the morning newspaper delivered to the door. One of his little "gem ideas" was to cut an inch off the doors so that the newspaper could be slipped under it. He hired C.B. Stoner to create a uniform auditing system to help control costs, and he put his kitchens on the same floor as his food-service outlets. Statler was the first to decorate each room with a colour scheme used throughout the hotel, allowing drapes, chairs, and bedspreads to be switched from one room to another.

What kind of man was Ellsworth Statler? Statler was not just concerned about his guests; he was one of the first hoteliers to introduce employee benefits, allowing every staff member to retire with the security of a pension. He was a man who cared deeply about his guests, his employees, and his hotels—a man who continued to invest in the development of the industry long after his death, through the Statler Foundation. This foundation provides students with scholarships and hospitality schools with funding so that learning and service will never cease.

Tourism's Impact on the Environment

The environment's role in tourism cannot be overstated. Without the scenic beauty of mountains, streams, lakes, oceans, and valleys, many people would be at a loss for what to do on a vacation. Ironically, if they do not take precautions in how they treat the environment, they may not long have the scenic beauty to visit. People may be loving their parks, mountains, and lakes to death.

Tourism is inherently a user and, in some ways, an abuser of the environment. It is an industry that makes demands on and affects the resources it uses, whether those resources are land, water, air, or any of the inhabitants thereof. Tourism around the world is, or at least should be, associated with environmental concerns. Establishing tourism management practices that limit harm to the environment is becoming a top priority for the tourism industry. There are two opposing views on the relationship between the environment and tourism.

One view holds that tourism provides an incentive for the restoration of historic sites and archeological treasures and the conservation of natural resources. The economic gain from tourism provides the means by which these areas can be restored and preserved. Tourism can also serve as an alternative to more environmentally damaging activities, such as the extraction of minerals or timber. Logging in the world's forests results in the loss of 11 million hectares a year. This deforestation increases erosion, landslides, and floods, and reduces the plant population needed to replenish oxygen in the air. Loss of forested land has also caused significant decreases in adventure tourism travel, which depends on forest-based amenities for its drawing power. The Pacific northwestern areas of Canada and the United States are scarred by clear-cutting, which decreases the scenic value and, therefore, the tourism appeal of the area. From this perspective, tourism is a friend to the environment.

The opposing view is that tourism means overcrowding, noise, litter, and disruption or extinction of animal life and vegetation. Tourism results in the dumping

To feel the power of whales playing alongside your boat is a thrill; to learn of their struggle to survive is an education.
(Photo courtesy Canadian Tourism Commission).

of waste materials into rivers and onto beaches. Individuals, groups, and experts who hold this view are adamant that tourism development should be halted or even reversed when it conflicts with the natural environment. The Great Barrier Reef near Australia is a prime example of environmental damage by tourists who knowingly or unknowingly kill the corals by stepping on them. Some may even take the corals home as souvenirs. From this perspective, tourism is a foe to the environment.

A major problem with environmental damage is that many tourists do not even realize they are the culprits. Planning and education are fundamental to understanding and preserving natural environments. In many cases, the local arm of the federal land-managing agency takes on the responsibility of educating visitors through interpretive programs, brochures, and campfire talks. The education process starts with managers appreciating the relationship between people and the natural environment. An important concept in understanding this relationship is carrying capacity.

This term was first used by researchers trying to determine how many cattle could graze on specified land without irreversibly altering the terrain. The concept has spread to human effects on natural and even some artificial environments. In this context, **carrying capacity** is the maximum number of people who can use a site with only "acceptable alteration" to the physical environment and with only "acceptable decline" in the quality of the experience for subsequent visitors. Determining carrying capacity has become a science that requires setting goals for the area, defining acceptable levels of environmental modification, and considering the kinds of use. No two areas have the same set of carrying capacity factors. Canada has been attempting to identify carrying capacity in national parks, in wilderness areas, camping areas, and front country (that is, the highly developed area consisting of road access, visitor centres, lodging, and retail outlets). There are few available studies, but a recent survey of national parks reported that two thirds of the regions suffered stress from the ecological impacts of visitors.

One successful approach is to limit privileges or access to more delicate park areas. For example, in order to preserve the Great Bear experience, Klemtu Tourism plans to limit the number of participants to 150 per year.[22]

Tourism's impact on the natural environment can be better understood by studying environmental components separately.

Vegetation Tourism may affect vegetation to the point of destroying the beauty of the area as well as the ability of plants to grow. For example, gathering twigs and branches to light a campfire has been a common practice at most campgrounds; however, stripping a campsite of live branches can permanently damage the trees. Also, fallen branches and twigs decay and become a good source of nutrients for the soil; when people remove them, the soil loses this benefit. To alleviate this problem, land-managing agencies now offer firewood to campers free or for a minimal fee. This firewood is selectively collected by rangers to minimize damage to any one area.

The collection of flowers and plants by tourists can cause changes in species distribution. Most tourists simply do not think when they pull up that pretty flower. Parks Canada is trying to educate visitors by posting signs along pathways and roads, such as "Leave only footprints. Take only pictures."

Vegetation is innocently trampled by visitors who do not understand the nature of the plant world. Most people think their footsteps cannot harm the vegetation or prevent it from growing back. The impact becomes more serious with intensive use and in delicate ecosystems and terrains. This type of problem can be minimized by building trails and walkways, allowing tourists access to controlled areas, and limiting their access in more fragile areas.

Visitors' careless use of fire has caused long-term damage to many forests and parks. In addition to educating visitors, Parks Canada restricts campfire usage during high fire-danger periods or in high-use areas. For example, some parks, such as Banff National Park and Rocky Mountain National Park, allow only small stoves in back country. Fires are simply prohibited, and the policy is strictly enforced.

Litter is also a problem. Besides being unsightly, it can damage vegetation by changing the composition of the soil, which in turn can change the ecosystem balance. Litter also kills animals who eat it.

Water Quality Tourism affects water quality in many different ways. Campers using sunscreen, soap, and dishwashing liquid in streams and lakes do not realize they leave an oily film on the water, making it unsightly and introducing chemicals. Camping has increased the level of bodily wastes in the water, and mountain lakes are particularly vulnerable to this type of damage. These waste materials carry parasites that can harm the aquatic environment as well as the next visitor who drinks from that water. Low-impact camping techniques suggest the use of non-stick pans that require no chemicals to clean or, better yet, soap-free camping. Using the proper facilities provided by the parks management services is important, and if you choose to camp in Canada's less accessible wilderness regions, you must learn the techniques for safe disposal of human wastes. Although dumping refuse is decreasing as citizens become more aware of the damage it can cause, you will still find the careless visitor throwing their drink can over the side of the boat. Other concerns relate to oil spills and overbuilding along oceans and lakes. Since 1979, more than 9000 significant oil- and tar-related spills have occurred in the wider Caribbean region, including the Gulf of Mexico, the Straits of Florida, and eastern approaches to the Caribbean Sea.[23] As a result, windward-exposed beaches have tar deposits. Water quality is also affected by activities such as recreational boating, swimming, and camping. Recreational boating on lakes and oceans leaves fuel and oils in the water, causing damage to aquatic plants and wildlife by depleting the oxygen level. The solution is to change tourists' boating habits, restricting the use of motorboats while allowing canoes, rowboats, kayaks, and other small muscle-powered craft.

Other Pollutants Tourism has been touted as the "smokeless" industry and therefore kind to the environment. However, because tourism uses automobile, buses, airplanes, and power boats, it actually increases pollutants. Noise pollution by aircraft, by power boats on a quiet lake, or from special events set in the centre of the city is also a problem.

Wildlife The impacts of tourism on wildlife are many, ranging from animals becoming too comfortable with the presence of humans to the ultimate extinction of a species. Consequences of tourism include disrupted feeding and breeding habits, reduced habitats, eliminated populations, and altered food chains. Tourism disrupts feeding and breeding habits through resort expansion, overzealous attempts to photograph wildlife, and inappropriate trail development. Elk and buffalo graze in national parks, and tourists will jump from their cars to get a close snapshot. Tourism development reduces the size of animal habitats, putting greater pressure on the remaining habitat. This condition increases the risk that animals will compete with humans for food and water or will include humans in their food source. Grizzly bears and cougars scavenge in campgrounds and garbage dumps, and some will actually stalk their human victim, looking for their next meal. Many animals have learned to tolerate the presence of tourists and, in communities like Jasper and Banff, wild animals such as elk and mountain sheep have the right of way on highways and in town. But unwary tourists may put their own lives at risk. Every year newspapers record several deaths of tourists who did not understand the dangers they faced from wildlife. Improper storage of foods while camping brings hungry bears, and a lack of respect for the ways of large animals such as elk during mating season can turn a pleasant vacation into a nightmare.

On an international scale, tourist consumption of ivory, furs, skins, heads, and tails has contributed significantly to the illegal killing of many animals. Among those savagely hunted and almost eliminated is the African elephant, hunted solely for its ivory tusks, which are made into jewellery, figurines, and piano keys. Importing and selling most ivory products is now prohibited in Canada.

Coastlines The images of sun, surf, and sand have long lured tourists to coastlines around the world. Too often, insufficient planning means that plant and animal habitats are disrupted; geological features are destroyed by excavation; water supplies are contaminated; and the natural beauty of the area is diminished. Lack of planning includes draining swamp or wetland areas for development that is incompatible with the preservation of many species and failing to properly control sewage and garbage. Littering by tourists has turned many coastline areas into dumping grounds.

Canada has three magnificent coastlines to the east, west, and north. Each is unique in its own wild and magnificent way but their beauty is easily marred by careless tourists littering and by overdevelopment. For example, on the coastlines of Nova Scotia and New Brunswick, cigarette butts carelessly tossed onto the rocks are a constant reminder that tourists seldom care for your ecosystems as you might.

Tourism planning in coastal areas needs to consider the effects of structures such as high-rise hotels and the overdevelopment of beaches. Attention must be given to issues such as unstable ground, water drainage, and eroding cliffs. Regulation of these fragile areas needs to be enforced so that visitors are able to experience coastlines in their natural form.

Mountains The human desire—or need—to leave the pressure of city life behind has put tremendous strains on mountainous ecosystems. Mountain terrains are developed as ski areas, hiking and riding trails, campgrounds, and resorts. Accessing the mountains requires roadways that disrupt wildlife habitats. Utility lines are unsightly to area inhabitants and visitors. Roads, ski trails and lifts, hiking trails, and four-wheel-drive trails all contribute to land erosion. In higher elevations where the ecosystem is extremely fragile and the slopes are often steep, the carrying capacity is small. Environmental damage may take centuries to disappear. Even "environmentally conscious" mountain climbers from around the world have abused the mountains of Nepal, leaving trails of litter and evidence of humankind everywhere.

Deserts   Once places to avoid, desert terrains are now playgrounds for tourists and local residents who travel in dune buggies and four-wheel-drive vehicles and on trail bikes. Certain desert areas have been marred by noise, dust, fuel smells, and litter. This fragile environment has lost plant species, animal life, and water holes to the overuse of off-road vehicles. Many people believe the desert is a wasteland anyway, so increasing recreation is the best way to utilize it. The only advantage desert plants and animals have over the tourist is their ability to survive on low quantities of water: without this precious resource, deserts are less likely to become popular for resorts—communities that inevitably endanger the desert ecosystem.

in practice

> In groups of three to five, design a carrying capacity plan for public land near your school. This land could be a national or provincial park or forest, or any other government-owned land used by visitors. Keep in mind how the area is used and what natural plants, animals, water, or ecosystems exist. Determine the number of people to be allowed at a given time and indicate what criteria you used to set this number. How will you enforce the carrying capacity?

Virtually all segments of the tourism industry have a detrimental effect on the environment. The degree of harm obviously differs among sectors (e.g., hotels and airlines affect the environment differently) and within the same sector (e.g., some hotel chains are more environmentally responsible than others). Environmentally conscious decision making is needed to raise the awareness of the travel industry as a whole. In the 1990s, planners and tourism promoters began to focus on environmental considerations. They pointed out that environmental concerns cannot be just an afterthought but must be integral to the planning and decision-making process. In 1990, the Canadian government presented to the public a far-reaching plan underscoring the need for a comprehensive federal action plan to create a sustainable tourism product.

Canada's Green Plan

The Green Plan is a commitment rooted in the knowledge that a concerted effort is essential if Canada is to solve its complex environmental challenges and implement sustainable economic development.[24] The Canadian government committed $3 billion in new funds to federal environmental expenditures between 1991 and 1997.

Tourism is explicitly a part of the Green Plan, which recommends that 12 percent of Canada's lands be protected space for parks, historic sites, and wildlife. Currently, only 7.1 percent of Canada's lands and waters have some degree of legal protection. Perhaps most important, however, is the effort to educate all Canadians. The underlying philosophy of the government's sustainable development policy is changing decision making. These changes will only come about if the decision-making process includes environmental considerations. However, funding promised by the government for scientific and technical research has not appeared.

The tourism industry, however, has not abandoned the sustainable tourism concept. For example, several years ago the Tourism Industry Association of Nova

Scotia (TIANS) produced a self-audit book and made it available to all tourism businesses. *A Question of Balance* explains the groundwork of a sustainable tourism program and suggests simple ways to conserve energy and water and reduce waste. For example, did you know that a leaky hot water tap, at a rate of one drop per second, wastes 800 L of hot water a month?

Environmentally sound practices will never become a reality without the support of business management and employees. The Fairmont Hotel chain has become a leader in environmental responsibility, with the support of both groups. Employee Ann Layton initiated the CP Green Partnership. Based on a professional environmental consultant's report, she developed a plan that called for

- reducing waste to landfill sites by 50 percent
- redesigning purchasing policies to ensure waste reduction at source
- collecting and recycling all recyclables—cans, glass, paper, etc.
- using environmentally friendly hotel supplies

Fairmont Hotels was one of the first chains to ask guests to use their bed linen and towels more than once. Hotels have formed Green Committees and earn "trees" for suggestions for environmentally sound practices. Once a year, the teams who have earned the most "trees" win trips to places like Jamaica or Acapulco. Competition can be fierce! The program enlists guests as well as employees in the effort to reduce, recycle, and reuse (Figure 10.1). Not only does the program benefit the environment, but the company also saves thousands of dollars yearly.[25]

Yet it is hard to break Canadians of their consumer habits. A recent survey on tourism activities identifies the following facts:

- Over the summer months, 20 000 Canadians will use a personal, motorized watercraft.
- A one-week cruise generates 7.3 tons of garbage, 3.8 million litres of waste water, 800 000 L of sewage, and 95 000 L of oil-contaminated waste.
- By recycling 275 kg of paper, Toronto's Royal York Hotel saves six trees a day.

Knowing the facts helps us to make wiser decisions. For Canadians keeping our country's environment healthy is a good goal. For the adventure tourism and outdoor recreation sector, it is not just good, it is essential.

FIGURE 10.1
Fairmont Hotels
Statistics on
Recycling

Did you know that at Fairmont Hotels
- blue recycle boxes have reached 100% compliance
- 86% of paper used is recycled or kraft paper
- 90% of all used soap is recycled to local charities in Canada and less developed countries
- Chateau Montebello uses its own compost as fertilizer
- the Royal York donates leftover food to relief agencies in the city

SOURCE: Adapted from "Shades of Green," *Lodging Magazine,* October 1999.

OPPORTUNITIES IN ADVENTURE TOURISM & OUTDOOR RECREATION

	SKI RESORT	GOLF/TENNIS FACILITY	PARKS	OUTDOOR/ADVENTURE/ ECOTOURISM	MARINE FACILITY
OPERATION (FRONT LINE)	Slope Grooming Operator Lift Operator Ski Patroller Ski Area Guest Service Representative Ski Area Retail Clerk Trail Crew Worker Snow-Making Operator Ski Rental Shop Clerk/Repair Shop Technician Sales and Marketing Representative	Retail Pro Shop Clerk Golf/Tennis Fitter Golf/Tennis Repair Person Sales Representative	Park Interpreter/Naturalist Park (Gateway) Attendant Retail Shop Clerk Visitor Service Staff Information Service Officer Interpretive Audiovisual Technician	Retail Shop Clerk Recreational Facility Attendant Adventure Guide/Tour Director Rental/Repair Technician	Marina Attendant Retail Shop Clerk Lifeguard Marine Rental/Repair Technician
SUPERVISORY	Supervisor of Lift Operations Snow Cat (Grooming) Supervisor Rental and Repair Supervisor Ski Instructor Retail Ski Shop Supervisor Snow-Making Supervisor Avalanche Control Trainee Ski Patrol & Risk Supervisor Ski Guide Guest Services Supervisor Ski School Supervisor Human Resources Housing Supervisor Sales and Marketing Supervisor Ski Area Supervisor	Golf/Tennis Instructor Golf/Tennis Pro Retail Pro Shop Supervisor Sales and Marketing Supervisor Assistant Greenskeeper	Assistant Park Warden	Outdoor Guide Outdoor Sport/Rec Instructor Fishing Guide Recreational Facility Supervisor Marketing Supervisor	Outdoor Guide Diving Instructor Swimming Instructor Canoeing/Kayaking Instructor Marketing Supervisor
MANAGEMENT	Recreation Director Human Resources Manager Public Relations Manager Rental and Repair Shop Manager Retail Ski Shop Manager Avalanche Control Manager Ski Patrol Director/Manager Ski School Director/Manager Operations Manager **Ski Area Manager**	Golf Operations Manager Human Resources Manager Public Relations Manager Greenskeeper Maintenance/Court Superintendent Retail Pro Shop Manager Sales Manager Golf Club Manager	Human Resources Manager Public Relations Manager Park Warden Curator Park Conservator Exhibit and Media Park Planner Service/Park Planner Chief of Visitor Activities Chief Park Warden	Human Resources Manager Public Relations Manager Recreational Facility Operator Trip Leader/Senior Guide Outfitter Wrangler Resort/Leisure Ops Manager Hostel/Lodge Manager Stable Manager Sports/Recreation Consultant Accommodations/Facilities Manager Outfitter/Owner/Operator	Marina Manager/Owner Human Resources Manager Public Relations Manager Boat Rental Operator Marine Tour Operator Resort/Leisure Operations Manager Hostel/Lodge Manager
EXECUTIVE	General Manager		Park Superintendent		

SOURCE: Courtesy of Canadian Tourism Human Resource Council, *The Student's Travel Map*, 1995.

JOB DESCRIPTION FOR . . .

SKI AREA MANAGER

Industry Sector	Adventure Tourism & Outdoor Recreation
Division	Ski
Industry Setting	Ski area hotel, motel, resort facility, student residence, and other accommodation establishments
Job Level	Senior Management
Description of Duties	Deal with business, financial management, and administrative aspects of the ski industry, including plan, organize, direct, and control the operations of an accommodation establishment or a department within such an establishment; develop and implement policies regarding type of accommodation service to be offered; monitor staff performance; control inventories; recruit staff; negotiate with suppliers and clients.
Working Conditions	Long hours of work, shift work, and weekend work require good health, stamina, and mental alertness.
Skills	Strong leadership and decision-making skills essential; ability to get along with all kinds of people and to adapt to unexpected situations in a calm manner. Good communication skills, both written and verbal.
Knowledge	Ski industry operations in general, accommodation facility operations in general and for particular facility and surrounding area, company policies and practices, and all applicable areas of provincial and federal legislation (e.g., Radio Act of Canada).
Education	Grade 12 completion required; graduation from a ski area management program, a hotel management program, or related course at the college or university level is usually required.
Industry Experience	3 to 5 years of experience as a Hotel Front Desk Agent is usually required and may substitute for formal educational requirements. Significant ski industry work experience is also beneficial.
Career Paths	Advancement to other senior management or executive positions is possible in other accommodation establishments and chain operations.
HRDC Reference	NOC 0632 Accommodation Service Managers

in practice
How could you affect the environment on the following types of vacations?
- Alaskan cruise
- river-rafting vacation in Idaho
- dude ranch holiday in Alberta
- backpacking trip along the Great Bear Trail
- bicycle trip around Nova Scotia

summary

The adventure tourism and outdoor recreation sector is one of great activity. People who partake of the activities in this sector fall into four categories: those who are looking for hard adventure such as mountain climbing, those who prefer a softer adventure such as hiking up a mountain path, those looking for a unique ecotourism experience, and those looking for an outdoor, recreational sport such as golfing, fishing, skiing, or boating.

The federal department that oversees the adventure tourism product is Canadian Heritage. Through the national parks service, Canadian Heritage maintains our nationally protected wildlife areas and historic sites and canals.

It is important for the student aiming for a career in tourism to remember that tourism is not without its negative effects. Development of any sort will put some form of stress on the area's vegetation, water, and animal life. Establishing goals and minimizing environmental impacts through a well-thought-out carrying capacity plan will benefit both the visitor experience and the natural environment. Some areas should not be developed based on the fragility of the terrain, but in general, if a good plan is implemented, tourists will cause minimal damage to the environment.

Sustainable tourism development encourages tourism while maintaining the natural environment. Canada's Green Plan provides us with a governmental code of ethics. For the tourism industry to be environmentally aware, education is the key. Some segments are already working toward an environmentally safe industry. Examples include limiting the number of participants; switching to recyclable or reusable materials, using biodegradable soaps, turning down thermostats and lights; and developing a resort or hotel *around* the landscape rather than destroying the landscape itself. As travellers become concerned about the environment, businesses will need to respond to consumer demands.

questions

1. The federal government department Canadian Heritage interacts with the tourism industry in two of our sectors. Identify these two sectors and show how "tourism illiteracy" on the part of this department could undermine the overall Canadian tourism product.

2. Tourists use both federal and provincial parks during outdoor vacation experiences.

    a) Explain the differences and similarities you might see in these parks.

    b) List all of the federal and four of the provincial parks found in your province.

3. a) Ecotourism is based on what four principles?

    b) Are all ecotourism experiences also considered to be nonconsumptive tourism? Explain your answer using definitions and examples.

    c) Is ecotourism an important part of your province's overall tourism product? Justify your answer by referring to the characteristics of the ecotourist and how they relate to your province's tourism product.

4. Briefly summarize a minimum of five outdoor recreational experiences available to the tourist in your region.

5. Choose four inconsistencies between the needs of the tourist and the need to protect Canadian wilderness. Explain how tourists might enjoy these regions with little or no impact on the environment.

6. Is the Canadian tourism industry doing enough to protect our environment? Defend your answer using examples.

7. Define the following terms as they relate to adventure tourism and outdoor recreation: *hard adventure, soft adventure, sustainable tourism, carrying capacity, Trans Canada Trail.*

---

weblinks

iisd.ca

The International Institute of Sustainable Development is a Canadian organization that focuses on various aspects of environmental degradation, sustainability, and policy.

www.out-there.com

Out There is a Canadian site featuring information about various adventure sports pursuits, including outdoor endurance races, caving, mountain biking, and river sports.

www.orcaspirit.com   www.knappett.com/spyhop.htm

Orca Spirit and Spyhopper are two of a number of whale-watching links in Victoria, B.C.

www.planeta.com/ecotravel   www.worldsurface.com   www.ecotourism.sk.ca

Three sites with information on ecotourism.

notes

1. ctx_news@ctc.cct.ca October 18, 2002 article.

2. Dr. M. Mohan, G. Gislason, and B. McGowan, *Tourism Related Employment: An Update* (Ottawa, Ontario: Canadian Tourism Human Resource Council, 1998).

3. www.parkscanada.ca

4. www.gov.bc.ca

5. *Heritage Tourism: Discover the Opportunity,* Industry Canada and Canadian Heritage.

6. www.parkscanada.ca

7. *Canadian Geographic,* Travel Adventure Booklet, winter 2003

8. Laszlo Buhasz, "Searching for the eco in ecotourism." *The Globe and Mail,* April 27, 2002.

9. www.ecotourism.org

10. Nathalie Southworth, "Under the Great Bear's Spell." *The Globe and Mail,* October 2, 2002.

11. *Canadian Geographic,* Summer Eco-Adventure Tours, 2002.

12. *Heritage Tourism: Discover the Opportunity,* Industry Canada and Canadian Heritage.

13. *Risk Management and Insurance Guide for the Adventure, Ecotourism and Alpine Skiing Industries.* Canadian Tourism Commission.

14. *The Trail Story,* Trans Canada Trail Web Site, http://www.tctrail.ca.

15. *Canadian Geographic,* Travel Adventure Booklet, winter 2003

16. www.tourism.gov.on.ca Outdoor Segmentation TAMS 1999.

17. Ibid

18. Ibid.

19. Ibid.

20. *The Student's Travel Map* (Ottawa: Canadian Tourism Human Resource Council, 1995), p. 62.

21. *Tourism Industry Product Overview,* prepared for Tourism British Columbia and the Council of Tourism Associations of British Columbia by Price Waterhouse and the ARA Consulting Group Inc., June 1996.

22. Nathalie Southworth, "Under the Great Bear's Spell." *The Globe and Mail,* October 2, 2002.

23. Judy Crawford "Environmental Responsibility in the Tourism Industry," in *Tourism: Building Credibility for a Credible Industry* (22nd conference of the Travel and Tourism Research Association, Long Beach Ca 1991), p. 98.

24. R.W. Slater, "Understanding the Relationship between Tourism, Environment and Sustainable Development," in *Tourism—Environment—Sustainable Development: An Agenda for Research* (proceedings of the conference of the Canadian Chapter of the Travel and Tourism Research Association, Hull, Quebec, 1991), p. 11.

25. Lou Cook, "Shades of Green," *Lodging,* October 1999, p. 67.

11

The Travel Trade Sector

learning objectives

Having read this chapter you will be able to

1. Compare and contrast the role of tour operator, tour wholesaler, and retail travel agent in the travel industry.

2. Explain the steps in creating and costing a packaged tour.

3. Define the terms *packaged tour, independent tour, group tour, fully escorted tour, hosted tour, validity dates, gateway city.*

4. Identify 10 distinct types of tours offered in today's travel market.

5. Explain the process of regulating tours and tour operators in Canada.

6. Discuss the advantages and disadvantages of taking a packaged tour.

7. Describe the travel agency by size, clientele, and ownership.

8. Summarize the changes occurring in travel agency operations and describe ways in which agencies are dealing with these changes.

9. Discuss the value and role of incentive travel in today's corporate world.

Selling travel is fun. It is a chance to put together someone's long-awaited dream vacation, to provide a tour to the hard-to-reach country, or to plan the best route at the lowest cost for a business traveller. The travel trade sector is the sales force of tourism. Travel can be sold at the wholesale level by a tour operator or wholesaler, or at the retail level by a travel counsellor. Tour operators sell packages *through* retail travel counsellors, not *to* them. They pay the retail travel counsellor a **commission** and sometimes a volume incentive, often referred to as an **override.** Tour operators, then, are restricted to selling travel arrangements that they have contracted for ahead of time. Travel counsellors can sell all types of travel anywhere, including components offered by tour wholesalers or the prepackaged tours offered by tour operators. Unlike the average tourism worker, travel agents are highly educated; 82 percent have post-secondary schooling. More than 47 000 Canadians work in this sector, and it is expected that new jobs will continue to be generated. This chapter discusses the business of wholesaling, retailing, and incentive travel.

The History of Tours

Tours are a relatively new concept in the history of tourism. Their beginnings can be traced back to the early seventeenth century, when noblemen from England arranged educational tours for their sons and heirs. "Le grand tour" was designed to educate their sons in the ways of the civilized world. The first stop might have been Paris, France. Here the student was expected to learn the ways of the court, manners and social etiquette, and the French language. Next on the itinerary were Rome and Florence where religion, art, Latin, and the antiquities (ancient history) became the course of study. In Zurich or Geneva, finance was the priority. The tour, by now entering its third or fourth year, would often end in Vienna, where all that had been learned would be polished and perfected. Upon graduation from this "school of the world," the educated and worldly young man returned to the staid life of a British nobleman. Similar tour routes can still be found in travel books, but instead of three years, today this tour may take only seven days!

The first recognized packaged tour was developed not by a travel agent (for no such thing existed at that time) but by a minister. Thomas Cook was a firm believer in the evils of liquor, so when the opportunity came to take his parish to a temperance meeting in Leicester, England, he arranged transportation by rail, a small picnic lunch, and entertainment for 570 of his followers. At the end of the day, after all bills had been paid, Mr. Cook discovered he had actually made a

A chance to see wildlife may play an important part in a Canadian tour package.
(Photo courtesy Canadian Tourism Commission.)

profit. The success of this afternoon was repeated many times over, so Mr. Cook left his ministerial calling to form the world's first travel agency.

Early tours were individually designed and were affordable only to the wealthy, a situation that changed with the new age of jet travel. What had been a costly 18-hour flight or six-day ocean crossing to Europe now became a seven-hour trip. The new Boeing 707 could carry a larger passenger load, so the cost of the trip was also substantially reduced. Tours suddenly became affordable for the middle class, and in 1958 more than 700 000 people took tours to Europe. By 1989, this figure had risen to more than 7 million! Tours are not only less expensive than booking the transportation, lodging, and attractions separately, but their cost is also a known figure right from the time of booking. Tours are prepaid, so the traveller need not worry about running out of money. Entrance to sights is guaranteed, because admission fees have been prepaid, and the sights have been chosen by a travel professional for their safety and appeal.

Wholesaling

People are often confused about the terms **tour wholesaler** and **tour operator**. Traditionally, tour wholesalers went from one travel supplier to another, booking space for their tours. They did not buy the product but acted as intermediaries between the supplier and the travel agency. No money was exchanged until an actual purchase took place. By the mid-1960s, the marketplace had changed. Most of the suppliers requested a pre-purchase of the products to guarantee the low price. Tour operators became those companies willing to invest in advance, purchasing all the components of a tour prior to packaging it. There is still a distinction between these roles, although the lines have become blurred, and the players may overlap.

For example, Sunquest acts both as a wholesaler, selling individual products to retail agencies, and as a tour operator, selling complete tour packages, including the services of a destination representative. In contrast, the Toronto-based Holiday Network sells only as a wholesaler and does not operate its own tour product. The major distinction between the wholesaler and the operator is financial risk. Tour operators assume the greatest risk, so they usually aim their sales efforts directly at the consumer (purchaser) through travel agencies.

The latest type of operator to enter the tour business is called a **consolidator**. Consolidators act as wholesalers or intermediaries between the airlines and travel agencies and pay a commission on tickets sold. Most airlines no longer pay commissions to travel agencies, so the consolidator becomes an additional source of agency revenue. Consolidators purchase a large number of airline seats at a bulk price. They then sell these seats at a net price to travel agents, who pass the savings on to their customers. The savings may be as great as 50 percent—but a word of caution if you plan to use one of these tickets. Each ticket has restrictions, which may include advance purchase dates, minimum stay requirements, and no itinerary changes. Furthermore, they are non-endorsable, meaning no other airline will accept them, and flights may not be available every day. Most consolidators are reputable, but an agency must be cautious when dealing with a newer company. One of Canada's largest consolidators is Aventours. As long as international markets are regulated by IATA and deep discounted tickets are not available to the travelling public, you can expect the role of consolidators to continue to expand.

There are four types of tour operators in Canada. The first is *an independent tour operator*, a category that includes large corporations such as American Express or individual operators such as Sunquest. The second type is a travel agency that packages tours and sells them to its clients. The third is an in-house tour operator owned and managed by a large company such as Air Canada. The last type does not sell to the public, but focuses on clubs, associations, and incentive travel groups. These tour packages must fit the special needs of the group (perhaps seniors or students) and may deal with such concerns as wheelchair accessibility or special medical equipment.

Tours are designated as either **outbound** or **inbound**. An inbound tour brings guests from a foreign country to Canada, generating jobs and revenue for Canadians. When Canadians travel to Santo Domingo using a packaged tour, they are outbound and their tourism dollars are being spent in a foreign country.[1]

Tour Development

A tour is "the services on a tourist's itinerary, usually consisting of, but not limited to, transportation, accommodation, transfers and sightseeing in one or more countries, geographical regions or cities. The services are entirely reserved or contracted for in advance by a travel agent, a tour wholesaler or a tour operator and are fully prepaid by the tourist."[2]

Tours are divided into two major categories: independent tours and packaged tours. Individuals or groups who prefer to create their own independent tour may do so using the services of a travel agent and a tour wholesaler. These customers choose between the assorted components offered by the tour wholesaler. A packaged tour, on the other hand, has a set itinerary with all of its components in place. Packaged tours may or may not have an escort and are sold to individuals as well as to groups.

There are four steps in the creation of a tour: the tour idea, negotiations, costing, and promotion (Figure 11.1).

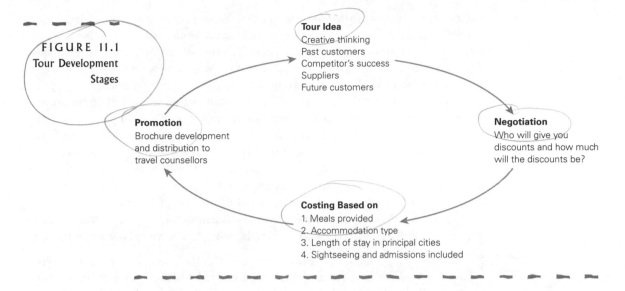

FIGURE 11.1
Tour Development
Stages

Tour Idea
Creative thinking
Past customers
Competitor's success
Suppliers
Future customers

Negotiation
Who will give you
discounts and how much
will the discounts be?

Costing Based on
1. Meals provided
2. Accommodation type
3. Length of stay in principal cities
4. Sightseeing and admissions included

Promotion
Brochure development
and distribution to
travel counsellors

The Tour Idea Every tour has to be new once. After its first venture, the tour can be offered time and time again if it was initially successful. New ideas, however, require creativity and the ability to listen to what people want. The idea may come from a supplier who provides a super deal for accommodations if the operator books a trip to the supplier's hotel. It may be an offshoot of a current trip, such as switching from a whale-watching tour to visiting Shediac, New Brunswick, to see the world's largest lobster and enjoy a lobster feast. It may be a product that tour operators already offer but that one company can provide with better service at a lower price. Market research is needed to determine whether there is a need or a desire for the tour concept. Without consumer demand, the tour, no matter how exciting, will not be a success. Most tours are developed around a central theme or destination: for example, learning more about polar bears in their natural habitat on Baffin Island. The theme or destination is the skeletal plan, which the planner must flesh out by providing other interesting or exciting reasons for people to take the tour.

Negotiation Once you have determined where you want your tour to go and what sites and experiences you wish to include, the negotiation phase of planning begins. Are there rooms available at the price you wish to pay? Is there a suitable restaurant in the area for dinner? Will the attractions you have chosen provide you with guaranteed entry at a group rate? Will you need a tour guide with specialized skills and knowledge for a part of the tour? What form(s) of transportation will you use? These questions and more need to be answered before you begin the next phase—costing and pricing.

Costing and Pricing Costing is the process of determining the total cost of providing the tour for an anticipated number of customers. **Pricing** is the process of deciding the amount each customer should pay to cover costs, including a markup, operating expenses, and profit. In the costing stage, you need to determine the direct cost of each component of the tour, such as transportation, lodging, attendance fees, and exchange rates. Then add indirect costs such as promotion, the tour planner's salary, and other overhead items. In the pricing stage, you need to calculate a markup or profit on the net cost of the tour. Once total cost is determined, you need to make an assumption about the volume, or number of tour participants, to work out the price of the tour to the traveller. Correct costing requires an accurate assessment of certain variables, especially sales—usually projected based on past experience and projected load factors. As simple as it may sound, costing is an art. It is also the most vital step in running a profitable tour operation.

Tour costing can be accomplished in a number of ways, but there are two common methods. **Base cost per participant** involves calculating the cost of transportation, meals, accommodations, and attractions for each participant and then adding a markup sufficient to cover all promotional costs, staff salaries, overhead, commissions, exchange rates, and a fair profit to establish a selling price. **Cost for use** involves negotiations with suppliers whereby tour participants only pay for what they use. For example, a hotel room is a cost only if it is occupied.

Several factors will affect the price to the consumer. In each case, the operator, and the travel agent, should try to find the balance that best suits the target market.[3]

1. *Meal costs.* The tour operator can significantly lower the cost of the tour if the traveller pays for each meal separately. Advantages include less paperwork for the operator and perhaps greater choice for the traveller. The disadvantage is that tour participants will need to budget and pay for each meal. Many people like to pay one price and not have to worry about other costs during the trip. A tour operator who permits unlimited choice from the menu (à la carte) is offering more than an operator who arranges a set menu (table d'hôte); the tour price will reflect this.

2. *Accommodation type.* The level of accommodation significantly affects the price of the tour. An economy tour books less expensive motels, usually in smaller towns or out-of-the-way locations in larger cities. Deluxe tours are booked with the finest hotels in locations convenient for side trips, shopping, restaurants, and attractions.

3. *Length of stay in principal cities.* Usually deluxe tours spend more time at a principal destination because a good tour should be relaxing. The pacing of a tour (the amount of free or leisure time within a tour's schedule) is an important sales feature. This free time allows individuals to pursue specific interests, explore the destination, shop, or simply relax. Driving long distances every day is not a hallmark of a deluxe tour.

4. *Sightseeing.* On the other hand, itineraries that indicate "the remainder of the day is open to explore…" may be tours trying to keep costs down. Built-in sightseeing increases the tour cost. Some people prefer to have every minute accounted; they want pampering and lots of supervision. Others prefer to make their own decisions and want more open time.

5. *Attractions.* Although the cost of the tour is higher when admission fees are included in the tour price, inclusion saves the traveller money in the long run because group discounts have usually been negotiated with the attraction manager. There is no general rule in costing a tour. Many people do not want to be "nickel and dimed to death," whereas others prefer a low-cost tour that requires them to pay for meals and amenities along the way. The choices are usually greater in the low-cost type of tour. Tour operators can specialize in either deluxe or economy tours, or provide packages at a variety of prices so the consumer has the choice of being pampered or merely driven from place to place.

Promotion The sale and promotion of tour packages has become very sophisticated. Bright, glossy brochures with pictures featuring the excitement of a rafting experience or the comfort of a hotel are all designed to attract a broad range of clients. Television advertisements, travelogue presentations, and a well-designed home page on the Internet also entice tourists. Without good promotional material, even the best tour product may find itself without customers.

Tour Categories

There are two main types of prearranged packaged tours. It is important for the customer as well as the travel counsellor selling the tours to understand the advantages and disadvantages of each type.

Independent Tour Both travel counsellors and tour operators can arrange independent tours for customers. As the name suggests, travellers obtain all the benefits of volume discounts and prearranged, guaranteed rates without sacrificing independence and flexibility. Customers can determine departure and return dates as well as budget. Independent tours vary in flexibility and complexity. Some tours allow the customer to choose accommodations at different hotels listed in the brochure, while others provide car rentals, increasing flexibility for the traveller. Other tours may offer fly/drive, rail/drive, rail/fly, cruise/fly, or other combinations. The key to independent tour success is the cost savings for the traveller and flexibility.

Independent tours may use more than one tour wholesaler in the creation of the package, and a distinct disadvantage of taking an independent tour is that you are on your own. There is no company representative available to help find solutions in case of a problem or difficulty encountered during the trip.

Group Tours The original group tour was based on a true group—a club or a society that wished to take a trip. In order to partake in the tour, you had to be a

Tour guides may travel with a group of tourists throughout the entire trip, or they may be hired just to show the group around a specific city or site. Tour guides must be extremely knowledgeable and must possess excellent interpersonal skills.
(Photo: Paula Kerr.)

member of the club. Today, the main difference between a group tour and an independent tour is in the costing. Group tours are usually based on a given number of participants and may be cancelled or delayed if the required number of spaces for that departure date have not been sold. There are two types of group tours: ground/land package and all-inclusive.

Ground package/land package tours include the land arrangements for the purchaser: hotel and attractions, and perhaps some meals, and perhaps a rental car. They do not include airfare in the price.

All-inclusive tours have a specific combination of features, usually include transportation, accommodations, meals, attractions, special events, service charges (such as tips, baggage handling), and may include amenities such as free travel bags and discount coupons. These tours may be fully escorted, partially escorted (hosted), or unescorted (independent).

- Fully **escorted tours** have a company representative travelling with the group. The escort is responsible for the participants' safety and enjoyment, makes sure that the tour operates smoothly, and handles any problems or difficulties. Although the escort is usually well prepared to describe the sights of an area, many companies hire **step-on guides** when visiting a city. Step-on guides have special training and a deep knowledge and love for their city, region, or site. This makes their presentation more responsive to the needs of the group and provides participants with reliable answers to their questions. This type of tour is often preferred by first-time travellers and is most useful when travelling to a country whose culture is very different.

- In a **hosted** or partially escorted tour, the group travels from destination to destination as a group, but without an escort. At each destination, a new company representative greets them and stays with them throughout their stay.

- In an **unescorted tour**, the group has their itinerary and travels without any company representative.

Types of Tours

Tours may be defined by destination and by their focus on a specific country, region, or city. A trip to the Cabot Trail in Nova Scotia is a good example of a regional tour. A two-city tour might bring visitors from Buffalo, New York, to both Montreal and Quebec City, giving them a varied experience of Canada's French culture. Tours defined by purpose are even more varied. Here are some popular examples:

- *adventure tours:* white-water rafting on the Clearwater River through Skull Canyon in Saskatchewan
- *religious tours:* visiting a religious site such as Bethlehem at Christmas
- *ethnic tours:* being immersed in a different culture, or returning to cultural roots
- *educational tours:* travelling to learn something new, whether it is visiting museums, historical sites, or art galleries, or enjoying a series of lectures on and theatrical productions of George Bernard Shaw's plays
- *soft adventure tours:* enjoying the thrill of adventure while appreciating the comforts of life, an experience provided by most safaris to Africa
- *sports and recreational tours:* golfing or skiing at a resort, or biking along the old highways of France

- *ecotourism tours:* with an expert local guides, going on expeditions to the rainforest or other ecosystem to learn about wildlife, vegetation, and ecological importance
- *special interest tours:* gambling in Windsor, visiting the wineries of British Columbia, or going to see the Calgary Stampede

Special needs tours are organized for groups of people with special medical problems. For example, a group of senior citizens with emphysema would require not only medication, but also a supply of oxygen and special handling and permits to transport it, especially if crossing borders. *Incentive tours* are created for a company as a reward for employees who have done outstanding work. They are considered gifts and are not taxable.

Tours can also be defined by the number of days, such as a seven-day tour or a two-week tour. The newest trend is the three-day weekend tour. This package fits into the changing lifestyle of North Americans who, according to statistics, are taking shorter, more frequent vacations.

The Travel Counsellor's Responsibility with Tours

Although tours can be sold directly to the consumer by the company that designs the tour (provided they hold a retail licence), most tours are sold through travel counsellors. Tour wholesalers provide a commission to the travel agency for each tour sold. Even though travel counsellors work for the wholesaler, they are responsible for helping potential travellers choose the right tour for them. The counsellor must understand tour requirements and provide accurate details, including the following:[4]

Validity Dates Tour brochures indicate when the tour is available at the stated price as well as the dates of departure from the gateway city for international or

Experiencing Canadian Aboriginal culture is an example of an ethnic or educational tour.
(Photo courtesy Canadian Tourism Commission.)

charter tours. It is important that the counsellor know these dates, as tour prices may change depending on the season.

Gateway City   The **gateway city** is the point from which the flight will leave or where the client can join the tour. It is the responsibility of the travel counsellor to get the client to the gateway city on time for departure with the group.

Itinerary and Amenities   Once again, the brochures describing the tour may or may not be explicit. Counsellors need to read all the fine print of the brochure to tell clients what to expect. The number of meals paid for in the tour price may not be obvious. Where sightseeing is "suggested" or "optional," the cost is not included in the tour. If the brochure says the tour will "see" rather than "visit" an attraction, it means travellers will view the attraction from the bus window. If the counsellor does not read the fine print critically, the client will probably be dissatisfied with the tour.

Price   Tour prices will vary depending on (a) the season, (b) modes of transportation used, (c) length of stay in principal cities, (d) type of accommodation, (e) number of meals provided, (f) sightseeing and other activities that are pre-booked, and (g) additional service charges such as tips and baggage handling that are included. Some brochures quote their low-season price, which sounds like a good deal until the client realizes the tour is to the Caribbean during hurricane season! Brochures are often confusing and contain fine print that must be explained to the customer. The travel counsellor must inform the client of items included in the price, items that are optional at an additional charge, surcharges (e.g., for currency fluctuations or fuel costs), and items that must be paid for by the customer.

Name of the Tour Operator   Both the client and the travel counsellor need to know the name of the operator or wholesaler for further reference. In some provinces, it is a legal requirement to name the tour operator. When problems occur, the travel counsellor should check into them to prevent a recurrence or stop recommending this particular operator or wholesaler to clients.

A final concern shared by travel counsellors and travellers alike is safety. Disreputable operators may use equipment that has not undergone a thorough safety check, putting the client at risk.

In summary, the travel counsellor is responsible for relaying accurate and reliable information to the prospective traveller. A counsellor who neglects to point out disadvantages as well as additional costs to the client is not providing good service, and dissatisfied customers do not return!

Regulating the Tour Industry

Canadian tour operators are regulated by many different organizations. If the tour contains an air or rail component, the tour operator must obtain approval from the National Transportation Agency prior to promoting and operating the tour. Tour operators are also licensed by the individual province, and the interests of the purchaser are protected by provincial consumer affairs departments. In recent years, a number of tour operators have gone bankrupt. Who protects the purchasers and their deposits when this happens? The tour operator is required to have a special type of insurance policy called a "performance bond," which guarantees payment to all parties (clients, travel agencies, and suppliers) in the case of financial difficulties. British Columbia, Ontario, and Quebec all require that tour operators maintain trust accounts and compensation funds and provide the province with detailed financial statements. The brochure and its information is also controlled by some provinces.

IATA plays an important role in the creation of international tours. It requires that every IATA-approved tour have the following components:

- air transportation on an IATA carrier
- accommodations for the duration of the tour
- at least one additional feature (which might be sightseeing, an activity or transfers)
- a tour brochure that meets IATA standards

If approved, the tour is given an identification number called an **IT number**. This number provides information that identifies the name of the tour operator, the year in which it was approved, the air carrier used, the area in which it can be sold, and the tour type.

Finally, the brochure must contain some very specific pieces of information:

- what is and is not included in the package
- how to place a reservation
- deposit and payment schedules
- travel documents needed (passport, visas, health card)
- cancellation and refund policies
- status of fares, rates, and itinerary (which may be subject to change)
- the tour operator's limited responsibilities and liability

S N A P S H O T

Debra Ward

Debra Ward was born and educated in Montreal. The last vocation on her mind was working in the tourism industry, and like many tourism professionals, she entered through the back door. Debra was looking for a career in public relations when the Tourism Industry Association of Canada (TIAC) hired her in 1982. She began as manager of special projects; her first major assignment was to mount a public service advertising campaign focusing on the value of tourism. She generated more than $3 million in donated radio time and magazine space. Her next project, designing an information kit to be used during TIAC's National Tourism Week campaign, won her the prestigious Best Corporate Communications award from the International Association of Business Communicators.

By 1992, her strong advocacy for the tourism industry had established Debra as one of tourism's most prominent members. As with many tourism organizations, TIAC was entering a period of restructuring, and the board of directors asked Debra to take on the role of general manager. Her knowledge of the industry and her ability to communicate and work as a team leader has allowed TIAC to realign its goals and objectives. Membership has increased significantly, providing TIAC with an even stronger voice in the field of tourism.

In 1994, TIAC's board of directors recognized Debra's outstanding contribution to the association and appointed her to the position of president, a position that had not been filled since 1983. As president of TIAC, she worked tirelessly to strengthen the tourism industry. In 1996, TIAC and the Canadian Tourism Human Resource Council held their first joint conference in Jasper, Alberta. In November of the same year, the Canadian Tourism Commission announced it would relinquish control of Rendez-Vous Canada, the industry's largest trade show, allowing TIAC to organize and promote it. These moves are examples of the partnerships that are being created within the tourism industry, illustrating the high regard both the CTHRC and the CTC have for Debra Ward and TIAC.

As president of TIAC, Debra was responsible for providing a sounding board for the industry, for taking industry concerns to the government, and for lobbying to improve not only the quality of the product as a whole, but also the quality of the individual tourist experience. She has now left TIAC to become a private consultant and continues to be is a strong advocate for upgrading work force skills and for recognizing professional standards. She also speaks out on issues that affect either the viability or profitability of Canada's tourism industry.

What kind of person is Debra Ward? Debra is full of enthusiasm for Canada's tourism industry. She exudes the warmth and vibrancy that typify the Canadian tourism professional. She has a strong belief in the tourism work force and says she owes her success to her ability to stick with a problem until it is solved. Her legacy to tourism will be the following maxim: Success is easy when your customers are treated in the same open, honest, and ethical manner in which you yourself wish to be treated.

The Advantages of Taking a Packaged Tour

Tours are becoming more popular because they offer one-stop shopping. From the colourful brochures, a customer can glimpse the facilities available at their destination. If they choose a reputable firm, purchasers can be assured that the tour's components will be of high quality. Everything is prearranged and the customer knows that tickets and accommodations have been reserved, and all the other details of the trip including transfer of baggage have been taken care of. Instead of waiting in line for tickets, prepaid tour admission gives immediate access to sites and events. Volume buying saves money, and the only money travellers need for the trip is for shopping. Most tours use direct flights, and ground transportation is waiting on arrival. In addition, tour companies recognize the need for some individualization and will build preferences into their package. Finally, one of the most important motivators of travel is companionship, and with a tour you are assured that your fellow travellers have similar interests and needs—which is why they have booked the same tour package you did. Baby boomers enjoy this style of travel, and growth in the tour industry is expected to be strong.

The Disadvantages of Taking a Packaged Tour

There are some drawbacks to taking a tour. Dissatisfaction is sure to occur if the tour operator does not provide what has been promised in the brochure—a quality product. Travel counsellors and clients are dependent on the operator's integrity and financial stability. Because a tour is a prearranged trip, it is inflexible. Your time is not your own. When the tour moves on to the next site, so must you. Do the advantages of taking a packaged tour outweigh the disadvantages? Only the consumer can answer that question.

Travel Agencies

Thomas Cook and Son, the world's first travel agency, dominated the nineteenth century. The company represented various forms of transportation and was the forerunner of the organized travel trade industry. By the turn of the century, Thomas Cook and Son had competition from upstarts such as American Express, an offshoot of the Wells Fargo Company. These early agencies provided services for the wealthy traveller and specialized in selling "grand tours" and steamship and rail tickets. As with any business, wherever there was a consumer need, an entrepreneur appeared to meet it. At the beginning of the Second World War, there were approximately 1000 agencies operating in North America. By the 1950s, with the advent of jet travel, the number of travel agencies in North America increased dramatically. Deregulation in the United States created a multitude of changes for the industry and its effect was immediately felt by Canadian agencies, too. New routes, schedules that changed quickly, and price wars among the airlines created havoc for travel agencies. Agents struggled to keep up with the latest fares and regulations. What had been a steady flow of commissions changed as agencies realized that low airfares meant a higher volume of sales was needed if they were to stay in business. Today, the complexity of airfares and their restrictions make the services of a travel counsellor more important than ever. Canada currently has more than 8000 agencies in operation, and the United States has 35 000.

The travel agency is a retail business, somewhat like a store. Customers interested in purchasing something, in this case a trip, will shop at their favourite travel agencies. The agency arranges for travel services with suppliers such as airlines, cruise ships, bus companies, railroads, car rental firms, hotels, tour wholesalers, and sightseeing operators, serving as a vital link between the traveller and the suppliers. The big difference is the amount and quality of personal service provided at a travel agency. Because of the type of business, the travel agency requires a relationship between the customer and the travel professional. Advice has become such an important part of the job, especially with leisure travel, that the more common term *travel agent* has been replaced with *travel counsellor*. Travel counsellors are knowledgeable and persuasive about the products, which makes them invaluable to travel suppliers. Travel agencies are firmly established as the principal distribution system for travel suppliers and they provide the most efficient way for the consumer to sort out the ever-increasing array of travel options.

Types of Travel Agencies

Agencies in Canada are categorized in several ways: by size, by the services they offer, and by ownership.

Small agencies have annual sales of a million dollars or less and generally employ one to three travel counsellors. Much of their business is through word of mouth, and personal service provides them with a small but loyal customer base. Medium-sized agencies employ a staff of eight to ten travel counsellors. They rely on word of mouth too but also invest in local promotions and advertising. They often focus on both business and pleasure travel. Larger agencies are usually highly diversified. Competition has been so fierce over the past decade that many smaller agencies have sold out to larger, more stable firms or have become part of a merger. These agencies have departments that specialize in travel market segments, such as the corporate market or group tours. They can often compete more effectively because they can afford top-of-the-line equipment and a larger marketing budget.[5]

Agencies may be full service (handling both vacation and business travel), corporate (dealing with business travel only), and specialty (handling specific products such as cruises or clients with special needs).

Full-Service Agency Most agencies fit into the full-service category, and are equipped to serve all categories of traveller needs, from bus tours to wilderness guide tours to business trips. The business of a **full-service agency** is typically divided 60/40: 60 percent leisure travel and 40 percent business travel, or vice versa. The combination provides a more consistent customer base: business travel may be busy when vacation travel is slow. Larger agencies usually have divisions and counsellors that specialize in categories of travel such as business, international, domestic, tours, or cruises. As a result, customers feel comfortable going to one full-service agency for all travel needs.

Corporate Agency The **corporate travel agency** specializes in business travel. Many corporate agencies do not even identify themselves as travel agencies in order to discourage walk-in vacation requests. The emphasis in service differs. The nature of the client's business dictates when and where the travel will occur. The counsellor is responsible for finding the best-priced airfare, a convenient hotel, and a car rental. Whereas a vacation counsellor may have time to plan, business travellers often call requesting a flight, accommodations, and a car rental for the next day. Most corporate agencies either charge their clients a management fee or a per ticket fee and change fee.

Some corporate agencies get so much business from a major client that they establish a branch in the workplace to deal solely with that client's needs. The agency becomes an integral part of the work place, saving the client time and money, while the agency is assured of a constant customer base. Some large corporations have developed their own travel departments, which not only plan individual business travel for employees but also arrange conventions and meetings. Travel counsellors working directly for a corporation typically get higher salaries and company benefits than agency employees.

Specialty Agency Most agencies cannot deal exclusively with one type of travel because the people needed to fill a tour do not live in one geographic area. However, in large urban centres, some **specialty travel agencies** exist.

Some agencies may be certified cruise specialists. They represent the full line of cruise products, and their agents have had additional training on various cruise ships and on how to sell a cruise package. The wide variety of vacations available from the cruise lines, the different ships and their service styles, and the niche markets that are targeted often complicate the choice of a cruise vacation. A cruise

A specialty agency deals with a single type of travel product, such as Canadian wilderness adventures.
(Photo courtesy Canadian Tourism Commission.)

specialist will know if the ship the client is looking at provides a product suitable for families with children, the seniors market, travellers with disabilities, or single passengers looking for fun and romance. These companies will often promote cruises with a theme such as Country & Western or the Big Bands.

Adventure travel is a fast-growing segment of the travel market. Agencies specialize in arranging exotic trips to places inaccessible to the everyday traveller: a river trip down the Amazon, an African safari, cross-country skiing in the Arctic, or hiking in the Himalayas. With more people looking for the unusual, adventure travel agencies can please the "hard to please." Travel can be arranged for both the hard adventurer who prefers primitive accommodations and the soft adventurer who wants the comforts of a fine hotel and restaurant each evening.

Senior travel is another specialty market. Planning seniors' trips may require knowledge of places with wheelchair accessibility, restaurants that will cater to specific dietary requirements, or motels with handrails in the bathrooms. To be successful with the mature travel market, tours should be designed to spend less time travelling and more time at attractions and destinations.

Clients with disabilities form another specialty market. In spite of the cost, the number of tours for travellers with special needs is growing.

Ethnic agencies focus on creating connections between immigrants or the children of immigrants and their countries of origin. Canada has welcomed people of all nations to its shores for centuries and Canadians of all backgrounds may decide to research and visit their ancestors' homeland. Any ethnic group that has a large representation in Canada is a prime target market for a specialized agency.

Forms of Ownership

Like hotels and restaurants, agencies may be owned privately or part of a chain, franchise, or consortium/cooperative.

Private Ownership In the early days of the travel agency, private ownership was most common, with many family-run agencies. Today, independently owned agencies must work hard to thrive in the competitive travel world. They serve local clientele and provide a high level of service to meet the needs of their clientele.

Chain Agencies Chain agencies operate under one corporate ownership, one management policy. A larger volume of business allows more vigorous promotion, more buying power, and a higher net profit than independents. Some brand names, such as American Express and Thomas Cook, have gained worldwide recognition. Employees often receive better fringe benefits and more training, and have greater opportunities to focus on special skills or to rise in the management structure. The major difficulty faced by chain operations is their impersonal approach to the client and their inability to focus on local needs.

Franchises Travel agency franchises were not introduced until the 1980s but have become popular. The benefits and the drawbacks are similar to those of any franchise system. Most customers don't know whether an agency is an individually owned and operated franchise or part of a chain. Franchises, like chains, are rigidly controlled and thus have difficulty filling the special needs of a local clientele. Employees also receive good training and have good job opportunities. Canada's largest franchised agencies are Uniglobe and Goliger's Travel. Carlson Wagonlit operates both a chain and a franchise system.

Consortiums In an attempt to survive the fierce competition of the 1980s and 1990s, smaller travel agencies have formed **consortiums** or cooperatives. In this system, similar to hotel referral systems such as Best Western, the agency keeps its independence and personal identity but joins with other independents to get large-scale advertising campaigns, better purchasing power, and a brand name. Each member pays an initial membership fee and a continuing services fee. The central office arranges advertising and promotional activities, negotiates supplier agreements, and administers the affairs of the organization. Canada's best-known cooperatives are Advantage, GIANTS, the Rider Group, GEM, and T-Comm.

Agency Operations

How do travel agencies make their money? What do they sell? Who regulates them? Travel agencies form an important distribution channel for all our tourism products. Most suppliers of tourism products pay the agency a commission on every sale. Most of an agency's income used to come from the sale of airline tickets but major airlines have dropped commission entirely. Agencies still receive commissions from consolidators, cruise lines, tour operators, car rental agencies, and railways. They now charge customers cancellation or change fees. A smaller portion of revenue is generated from the sale of insurance policies or travel accessories (e.g., guidebooks). Travel agencies may earn additional revenue from "override commissions," commissions paid at a higher rate once an agency reaches a set sales total over a given period of time. The increase provides an additional incentive to sell the supplier's products. On the other hand, some operators require that agencies reach a minimum in sales over a period of time. Tour operators must provide travel agencies with promotional and sales materials such as brochures, posters, and window displays. These are necessary but costly items and if they fail to generate sales, operators may be reluctant to continue to supply these colourful displays.

Several factors are changing the way agencies earn revenue.

- After deregulation, major airlines first reduced the amount of commission they would pay on each ticket sold, and then eliminated commissions entirely. To replace this loss of revenues, many agencies now charge customers a service fee of $35 to $100 per ticket.

- The Internet has become a competitor for travel agencies, providing interactive sales sites for hotels and attractions, allowing clients to book directly with the supplier. In addition, the latest in discounted last-minute sale prices are quickly put on the Internet, providing the surfer with last-minute travel bargains and the supplier with additional revenue on products that might have gone unsold.

- New self-ticketing devices allow travellers to book and ticket themselves on flights, including the check-in process. These kiosks provide a fast alternative to using a travel counsellor.

- Expenses that might have been absorbed by the agency 10 years ago are now being charged to the client. These include services like booking a bed-and-breakfast; long-distance calls or faxes; or passport applications.

It is becoming more difficult for travel agencies to make a profit. For decades they depended on commissions from airline ticket sales, but with most airlines giving no commission, they have been forced to charge fees for service. For example, to research a vacation package might be $50, with $40 being applied to the purchase price of the package if it is booked by the client. With more and more opportunities for individual travellers to use the Internet to research and book their own vacations, agencies must become more creative in bringing in additional revenue.

Is the travel agency business coming to an end? As with any business, technology forces changes that are sometimes difficult to adjust to, and those businesses unwilling or unable to rethink their product and its delivery are eliminated. The travel trade is facing such a challenge over the next decade. Two factors will help it survive. Businesses are discovering that travel counsellors do save them money. The latest study by Topaz International of Portland found that fares generated by a corporate travel agency saved the company an average of $116 per ticket. Malcolm Read, vice president of global sales for the Uniglobe Group, warns Internet purchasers to beware: "most web fares are non-refundable, non-changeable and have restrictions...travelers may not be aware of." As the large baby-boom market begins to retire, travel is expected to flourish. Many boomers are uncomfortable with the latest computer technologies, including the Internet. They prefer the personal touch of a travel counsellor and, although the way a travel agency earns revenue may change, the professional expertise and friendly service of the travel counsellor will remain an essential element of tourism's channel of distribution—the travel trade.

Regulating Travel Agencies

Before a travel agency can begin full operations, it must obtain an "appointment," a form of permission to conduct business. There are three major **conference appointments** required:

1. The Air Transport Association of Canada (ATAC) represents commercial aviation in Canada. The ATAC Traffic Conference handles the Canadian Travel Agency program as well as all matters dealing with interline standards, ticketing, and passenger and baggage processing. ATAC runs its programs by contract with IATA.
2. The International Air Transport Association (IATA) regulates the sale of international airline tickets.
3. VIA Rail allows agencies to sell domestic rail tickets on both VIA and Amtrak, the American rail company.

To apply for ATAC and IATA certification, a travel agency must be open and operating: it must have the cash to purchase tickets directly from the airlines or it must have an agreement with a fully accredited agency to do the ticketing on its behalf. New agencies must have at least two full-time employees—a qualified management person and a qualified ticketing agent. The location must be visible to the public and clearly identified as a travel agency. The agency must maintain a tight security system to ensure the safety of its airline tickets (called "stock"), documents, and equipment. It must have in place sufficient financial backing to ensure continued operation and must maintain its financial records according to the BSP accounting procedures. Finally, the agency must show that it is actively promoting travel through any method of advertising including brochures, flyers, direct mail, or newspaper advertisements. In addition to these regulations, British Columbia, Quebec, and Ontario all have legislation to protect the traveller, and new agencies must register with their provincial registrar. Ontario's Travel Industry Act includes a specific section to protect the consumer. Agencies must take out special insurance and bonding to protect their customers in case the tour operator files for bankruptcy prior to the completion of the trip.[6]

Two organizations in Canada work with the travel trade to ensure that professional standards are met. The Association of Canadian Travel Agents (ACTA) represents the travel trade as a whole and includes membership for travel agents, wholesale tour operators, and travel service suppliers. It deals on a national level with the government and with global organizations such as IATA. Because ACTA is concerned with professional standards, it has created a code of ethics that members agree to follow. Together with the Canadian Institute of Travel Counsellors (CITC), ACTA has established ACCESS, a body set up to standardize education through national examinations, awarding professional credentials to successful applicants. The CITC has developed a code of ethics members agree to follow, and it has been active in the pursuit of professional development and certification of Canadian travel agents since 1960. Prior to 1990 when the ACCESS examination process was instituted, the CITC administered the national examination for agents, offering the designations of **CTC (certified travel counsellor)** and certified travel manager (CTM). Certification was based on knowledge and experience. The role of the CITC has changed; it now focuses on training and instructional materials. Under the auspices of the CITC and ACTA, the Canadian Tourism Human Resource Council has developed a new program for national certification based on skills, knowledge, and attitudes.

Marketing the Travel Trade Products

Travel agencies promote the tourism *products* of other suppliers and are not considered to be a product themselves. However, they are the channel of distribution, that is, the *place* where tourism products are sold. *Pricing* the products is not usually the agency's concern, as many products are already packaged and priced. Retail stores build in their profit margin by setting the difference between their buying and selling price. Since travel agencies cannot set the price of the products they sell, they are trying to restore profits by adding service charges. *Promotion* is an important part of any business' survival strategy. Tour companies help to promote their products by supplying tour operators with colourful brochures and displays. They also have sales representatives drop by to discuss the products and provide sales help to the agents. To remain competitive, travel agencies must promote both the products they represent and their own services. Larger chains and franchises may use television, but as the majority of clients are local residents, most agencies use the travel section of local newspapers or local radio stations.

Marketing efforts should reflect the philosophy of the travel agency. What type of people does it serve? What are their needs and how are they fulfilled? To sharpen their focus, travel agencies sometimes undertake formal or informal research on their customers' needs, which may include preparing **customer profiles**. Personal sales are also important. Sales agents must know the product well to describe its advantages and disadvantages to their clients. Finally, a good sales agent must know how to close the sale.

Image is what brings a client through the door—colourful displays and a professional looking staff. The final success or failure of the travel agency, however, depends on the competence of its travel counsellors and the effectiveness of their personal selling techniques. More than any in other sector in tourism, lifelong learning is an essential part of a travel counsellor's job.

in practice

Many people use a travel agency only for airline ticketing. As a travel counsellor, what techniques would you use to convince the traveller that you can and should arrange the car rental, hotel, or rail ticket? What carefully chosen words would you use to sell more to your client?

Incentive Travel

Another area of selling travel is the growing field of **incentive travel**: trips used as a prize to for employee performance. Incentive travel is on the upswing because it creates a winning situation for all parties involved: the corporation wins with more sales, increased employee productivity, less absenteeism, and better safety records; the employees win by being treated to an exclusive trip; and the incentive travel company wins by increasing sales and profits.

Incentive travel will grow because it is said to be the ultimate motivator. A trip increases an employee's status among peers and family members and provides the opportunity to go to places and experience things never dreamed possible. Not only does the potential trip motivate extra effort, but the winning employee returns feeling good and continues to work hard. By using incentive travel, companies show they believe in their people.

A good travel counsellor must have strong knowledge of many different tourism products, be detail-oriented, and enjoy working with people.
(Photo: Paula Kerr.)

The other side of incentive travel is the destination. Resorts, hotels, and tourism bureaus are starting to see the benefit of bringing in hundreds of people through incentive travel programs. They are actively involved in persuading incentive planners that they have the perfect destination, and offering inspection tours to make their point.

How Incentive Companies Operate

Although simple on paper, developing an incentive travel program is quite complex. Initially, the manager in an incentive house or a specialty incentive travel agency approaches the marketing manager of a company and suggests how incentive travel could help solve the corporation's problem, which could be anything from the need to sell more product to reducing absenteeism.

For example, the incentive travel manager would work out the savings for the company if absenteeism could be reduced by 50 percent. A portion of these savings would be put toward travel costs. The incentive company would be responsible for setting rules, promotion, program administration, and awards. Accurate records of absenteeism and tardiness over the specified time period would be kept, and letters of encouragement would be sent to participants. To motivate those who have already missed too many days, the incentive company could provide opportunities for employees to buy in (i.e., people who do not meet the quota or criteria are allowed to pay the difference, enabling them to go with their peers and fill the empty slots of the trip).

The Society of Incentive Travel Executives (SITE) conducts training programs and seminars on how to succeed in incentive travel and publishes a newsletter. Most important, SITE is the sounding board for problems and opportunities in incentive travel.

OPPORTUNITIES IN THE TRAVEL TRADE

	RETAIL	WHOLESALE
OPERATION (FRONT LINE)	Reservation (Ticket) Agent Retail Sales Clerk Travel Counsellor Tour Guide/On-Road Guide International Counsellor Sales Representative Outside Sales Agent Customer Services Representative	**Local Tour Guide** Bus Greeter Sales Representative
SUPERVISORY	Tour Planner Group Sales Representative Commercial Account Specialist Incentive Travel Specialist Destination Development Specialist Tour Leader/Director/Manager/Tour Escort/Specialty Tour Guide/Long-Distance Guide Sales and Marketing Supervisor	Tour Planner Group Sales Representative Sales and Marketing Supervisor
MANAGEMENT	Senior Travel Counsellor Public Relations Manager Human Resources Manager Tour Manager Tour Promotions Manager Operations Manager Reservation/Ticketing Manager Sales Manager Travel Agency Manager/Owner Tour Operator/Wholesaler	Package Tour Coordinator Sales and Marketing Manager Tour Operator/Wholesaler Tour Broker
EXECUTIVE	Managing Director General Manager Corporate Vice-President	Managing Director General Manager Corporate Vice-President

SOURCE: Courtesy of Canadian Tourism Human Resource Council, *The Student's Travel Map*, 1995.

JOB DESCRIPTION FOR. . .

LOCAL TOUR GUIDE

Industry Sector	Travel Trade
Division	Retail, Wholesale
Industry Setting	Travel agencies, tour/travel-related companies
Job Level	Operational (Front Line)

Description of Duties

Escort and/or transport individuals or groups on local tours; ensure prepared itineraries, transportation, and accommodations are met; describe points of interest; plan and carry out recreational activities, including:

Escort on local tours—ensure adequacy of transportation and accommodation; organize baggage and look after special needs; may also be responsible for special events and entertainment, paying bills, recording cheques issued, organization and promotion of tours including selling tickets, handling bookings, and accompanying tours; *Sightseeing tour guides*—conduct local city tours, operate transportation vehicles and provide commentary about local site; *Establishment tour guides*—escort on sightseeing and educational tours through particular sites and buildings of interest, describing features of interest, answering questions, and passing out literature.

May also include On-Site Guide, Step-On Guide, Character Guides, or Animators.

Skills

Pleasing and outgoing personality, ability to communicate effectively with large groups, knowledge of geography and history, good memory and lots of patience, ability to create a friendly, enthusiastic atmosphere on tours, must have appropriate motor vehicle licence if required to transport tourists on job. Tour escorts should be at least 21 years of age to accompany groups on night club tours.

Knowledge

Knowledge of both official languages or an additional language may be a requirement for this position. Knowledge of artistic or historic matter and other background information may be required.

Education

Completion of Grade 12 may be required. No specific training requirements are necessary.

Industry Experience Career Paths

Previous experience is not a requirement for entry.

With experience, may progress to supervisory, middle, and senior management occupations including Tour Planner, Tour Leader/Director/Tour Escort, VIP Guide, Tour Manager/Long-Distance Guide/Freelance Guide, Tour Operator/Wholesaler.

HRDC Reference

NOC 6441 Tour and Travel Guides

in practice

> Make a list of companies in your community that could benefit from an incentive travel program. What problem would you try to solve for those companies? Write down a convincing statement you would use to persuade the company.

summary

The selling of travel takes three basic forms: wholesaling, retailing, and incentive travel, which is a combination of the other two. A wholesaler/operator plans and organizes a tour package but gives the retailer (travel counsellor) the challenge of selling it to the customer. The travel counsellor is the retailer for every type of travel. The incentive travel planner organizes a trip for the employees of a company, but only those employees who meet the criteria set up by the planner will win the trip.

Most wholesale travel is in the form of packaged tours. The tour operator decides on an attractive trip, negotiates prices with the suppliers, and sets the consumer price. There are three types of tours: the independent tour allows clients to travel on their own without supervision; the hosted tour is similar to the independent tour but has a host in each city to arrange excursions and to order tickets to attractions; the escorted tour provides a tour guide to accompany the group and to make sure all scheduled activities go as planned.

A travel agency survives on the service and management fees it charges its clients and on commissions from selling various travel products to the general public. Travel counsellors can no longer collect commissions on most airline tickets but do get commissions from cruise, hotel, and car rental bookings. Three types of agencies exist: the full-service agency provides both vacation and business travel arrangements; a corporate agency works with business travellers; and specialty travel agencies work with a single type of product (e.g., cruises, adventure travel) or a single target market (e.g., seniors, travellers with disabilities).

Incentive travel is a growing field because travel is an excellent motivator, encouraging employees to work harder, sell more, or stay with the company longer. The company gains increased productivity or sales, and the employee wins a trip. The destination chosen for the award also wins by hosting a group of people who ordinarily would not be visiting.

questions

1. Using the steps outlined in developing a tour, create a packaged tour of your region.

   i. Identify the type of tour and its target market.

   ii. Determine whether it will be a fully escorted tour or hosted tour. Justify your choice.

   iii. Explain the four individual steps you will follow as you create your tour. Use examples and list the items included in the tour.

   iv. Set validity dates, a gateway city, and a suggested price.

      v.   Describe four advantages for a traveller taking your tour.

     vi.   Describe two disadvantages and explain how you will attempt to minimize them.

   vii.   Identify the regulating agencies you will need to get approval from and how they will affect your final product.

2.   Describe the different ownership/management styles found in the travel agency business.

3.   Summarize three different changes in the travel agency business and how agencies are dealing with the challenges they pose.

4.   What is incentive travel and why is it a growing part of the travel trade industry?

5.   Define the following terms as they relate to the travel trade sector: *conference appointment, override, specialty agency, tour operator, tour wholesaler, consolidator, consortium, full-service agency, IT number, inbound tour.*

weblinks

www.citcontario.com

The Ontario branch of the Canadian Institute of Travel Counsellors offers industry surveys and a "Scam Watch" feature, along with a section on employment in tourism.

www.citc.ca

The Web site for the Canadian Institute of Travel Counsellors, a membership organization for individual Canadian travel professionals.

www.clearwaterrafting.com www.riversearch.com

Riversearch.com offers an international directory of what they consider to be the world's finest rivers and best companies for white-water rafting, including a number in British Columbia, Ontario, Quebec, and Yukon.

www.thomascook.com

Thomas Cook offers a wide range of travel services, including tours categorized as "Sun," "Lakes and Mountains," "Ski," "Over 50's," "Club 18-30," and "Villas and Pools."

notes

1. Dr. Marilyn Mohan, G. Gislason, and B. McGowan, *Tourism Related Employment: 1998 Update* (Ottawa, ON: Canadian Tourism Human Resource Council, 1998), p. 230.

2. David Wright, CTC, *Professional Travel Counselling*, 4th ed. (Toronto, ON: Canadian Institute of Travel Counsellors, 1998), p. 294.

3. Patricia J. Gagnon and Karen Silva, *Travel Career Development*, 5th ed. (Homewood, IL: Irwin, 1990), p. 169.

4. Aryear Gregory, *The Travel Agent*, 2nd ed. (Rapid City, SD: National Publishers of the Black Hills, Inc., 1985), p. 136.

5. David Wright, CTC, op. cit., p. 33.

6. David W. Howell and Robert A. Ellison, *Passport* (Toronto: Nelson Canada, 1995), p. 323.

12 The Tourism Services Sector

key terms

chamber of commerce
convention and visitor
   bureau (CVB)

destination marketing
   Organization (DMO)
familiarization (fam) tour

front-line training
site inspection

learning objectives

Having read this chapter you will be able to

1. Describe the five industry components of tourism services.

2. Explain the role that the Department of Foreign Affairs and International Trade, Citizenship and Immigration Canada, and Canada Customs and Revenue Agency play in the tourism industry.

3. Summarize the activities of the provincial and municipal governments as they relate to tourism.

4. Explain the functions of destination marketing organizations such as convention and visitor bureaus and the role of a chamber of commerce.

5. Discuss the membership, mandate, and goals of the Tourism Industry Association of Canada.

6. List the miscellaneous services that ensure the tourism industry in Canada remains competitive, modern, and in a positive state of growth.

The tourism industry is somewhat akin to a stage production: the setting consists of landscape and buildings; the cast of actors is represented by the entire community, with everyone playing the part of tourism host. Behind the scenes are those who really make the production work. This support group of backstage workers is called tourism services. People in tourism services specialize in serving the needs of the industry rather than the needs of the visitor. A wide variety of organizations, associations, government agencies, and businesses supply these services. Because many tourism businesses are small and privately owned, they rely on this sector for help in dealing with marketing and promotions, taxation, government regulations, safety, education, and staff training. Tourism services is their link to the world of tourists.

This sector also includes retail sales and media coverage and the services of construction companies, financial institutions, and telecommunications and computer industries. Together, the businesses that compose tourism services ensure that the product offered is modern and competitive and that the tourism industry as a whole runs smoothly.

This chapter provides information on the inner workings of the tourism industry—a whole new set of job opportunities! The tourism services sector can be divided into five components, each handling a different tourism need:

- government agencies
- tourism associations and organizations
- marketing services
- research and consulting
- miscellaneous services[1]

Governments and Tourism

The government of any country plays an extremely important role in tourism. If the tourism industry does not have the support of the government, it cannot flourish. For instance, when the Shah of Iran was overthrown in 1979, the new government closed the borders of Iran to foreigners. The streets of Tehran, once bustling with tourists eager to spend their money in the city known as the "Paris of the East," suddenly had no visitors. Shops, hotels, and restaurants had difficulty surviving. Tourism, once a profitable business for Iran, became virtually nonexistent. Japan provides another example of the impact of government regulations. Until the 1960s, travel to and from Japan was tightly controlled. The Japanese were seldom allowed to vacation outside the country, and foreigners were not encouraged to visit Japan. When the ban on travel was lifted, tourism began to flourish, opening Japan to the world and providing new revenues for the Japanese government and its people.

The Federal Government and Tourism

Throughout the text, we have been examining the roles played by the federal government in the tourism industry. In chapter 3 we looked at Industry Canada and two Crown corporations: the Canadian Tourism Commission, responsible for creating a viable tourism industry through strong promotions and marketing plans, and the National Capital Commission, responsible for maintaining the "capital experience" for all Canadians. In chapter 5, we examined the role of

Transport Canada in ensuring safe travel within our borders. In chapters 8 and 10, we looked at the important role played by Canadian Heritage in preserving our natural resources and our cultural heritage. Now let's look at three more departments:

The Department of Foreign Affairs and International Trade (DFAIT) is responsible for issuing Canadian passports and Canadian entrance visas.

Passports are official documents that allow holders to travel from and return to their own countries. The United States and Canada have one of the least restrictive border-crossing policies in the world; however, September 11 forced both countries to revisit the way they regulate border crossings. The federal government has redesigned Canadian passports to make forgery more difficult, by digitally printing the bearer's picture on a secure page and adding a hologram. Children used to travel on their parents' passports but must now carry their own. Background checks on new applicants are more vigorous, and tighter security measures at all border crossings are now in place. Of course, with these changes came an increase in the cost and turnaround time of processing a passport. For business travellers who frequently cross the border, Canada and the United States are considering a special identification card that will allow expedited access to both countries. To qualify for these cards, the businessperson must first submit to a rigorous background investigation. Iris identification scanners and visual scanners that can quickly identify travellers as "safe" or "safety risks" are also being considered.

Visas are official documents that give travellers permission to enter a country for a specified period of time. For example, a Hungarian who wishes to visit Canada must now go to the Canadian embassy in Budapest to obtain a visitor's visa. DFAIT has imposed new, tighter restrictions on all visas issued and has added eight countries to the "visa required" list. The easiest visas to get are those granted to students enrolling in a school or university. Most of the terrorists involved in the World Trade Center/Pentagon attack entered the United States on student visas. Travel agents are able to provide their customers with correct visa information.

Because of growing tensions throughout much of the world, the government has created a Web site covering recent developments in 220 foreign countries (www.voyage.gc.ca). The information includes any internal developments that might put the Canadian traveller in jeopardy and ranges from current conflicts to weather problems or health concerns.

The first Canadians a foreign tourist meets are employees of the department of *Citizenship and Immigration Canada*. They are responsible for checking the travel documents for every person arriving in Canada, including Canadians. Prior to September 11, Immigration's computer system was not linked to any other law enforcement agency. In recent years, several terrorists have entered Canada first, then crossed the border into the United States. To try to stop this traffic, immigration officials will now be linked to the RCMP system, which will in turn link to U.S. law enforcement agencies.

Every country requires arriving travellers to pass through customs control, where everything recently purchased and being brought into the country must be declared. The *Canada Customs and Revenue Agency* not only collects personal income taxes but is also responsible for customs services. Airline passengers who reside in a foreign country must complete declaration forms and immigration forms. For returning Canadians, proof of citizenship and the declaration form serve as both entry and customs declaration documents. Canadians must list all items purchased abroad. If entry is via private vehicle, declaration may be verbal. However, drivers may be asked for proof of ownership or for the rental agreement for the vehicle. Customs inspectors, constantly on the lookout for missing children, often query children accompanying adults.

What *cannot* be brought into the country? Most countries do not allow animal or agricultural items across the border. It is believed that a piece of uncooked sausage brought into Canada in the 1950s caused an outbreak of foot-and-mouth disease in Saskatchewan that cost taxpayers $800 million to eradicate. Dutch elm disease, introduced from Europe in the early 1960s, destroyed native elm trees. Two major problems Canadian environmentalists are dealing with today have "stolen" across the border: zebra mussels clog waterways, and purple loosestrife is choking native wildflowers. What a cost to the environment and to the taxpayers! When tourism becomes a destructive force rather than a beneficial one, it is important to discover the causes quickly and to rectify the problem. Tourists must be responsible and leave plant and animal life for the next tourist to enjoy.

Returning Canadians may bring back up to $50 worth of goods duty-free after a minimum absence of 24 hours; after 48 hours the maximum amount is $200, and after a week it rises to $750. It is wise to keep receipts and make goods easily accessible for inspection. Customs inspectors have the legal right to examine luggage as part of their responsibility to protect Canada's safety, economy, and environment. As a tourist visiting a foreign country, travellers must be sure to follow not only immigration and customs policies, but also all laws, legal or cultural. Many regions are not as tolerant as North America when a law is broken.

in practice   All levels of government become involved in the eight sectors of tourism to ensure the safety, health, and welfare of the visitor. What laws, rules, or regulations would protect tourists as well as residents in your region?

Provincial Governments and Tourism

Provincial governments also have ministries or departments responsible for provincial tourism matters. All have similar mandates, which include the following:

1. **Promote travel opportunities and increase the number of visitors to the province.** Provinces advertise their tourism products in many ways. Many set up booths at trade fairs across Canada and the United States to promote their resorts, adventure activities, attractions and historical sites, accommodations, food services, and transportation services. Once potential visitors request information from a provincial tourism board, they are amazed at the response. A simple request for information on fishing lodges will result in a deluge of brochures on a wide variety of fishing vacations, equipment rentals, and maps.

2. **Encourage the development of the tourism industry through market research and planning.** All provinces use strategic planning to ensure that they are developing sustainable tourism products with a significant market base. Many programs focus on existing resources: cultural heritage, recreational activities, natural attractions, and historical sites.

3. <u>**Work with the tourism industry in the province to continually improve the product.**</u> Recognizing the need for skilled workers, provincial governments have helped fund tourism education councils (TECs; see chapter 3), which provide training and certification programs for a wide variety of tourism occupations. Workers dealing directly with tourists may take a short customer service course offered in all provinces under a variety of names, including "SuperHost," "Alberta Best," and "FirstHost." These courses cover quality service and good hospitality practices—in other words, how to handle customers in a friendly, professional, and informed manner. Provinces may also create "info-mercials" to educate residents on the value of tourism as a revenue generator.

4. <u>**Produce literature that promotes the seven front-line sectors of the industry.**</u> Provinces fund television commercials, travel videos, and CD-ROMs that market their regions. They all have Web pages on the Internet and are investing in state-of-the-art tourist information centres. Most provinces also have a 1-800 number that provides advice for planning everything from weekend getaways to extended trips.

5. <u>**Liaise with federal and municipal ministries.**</u> Many tourism events require participation from all levels of government. For example, as Toronto pushed its bid for the 2008 Summer Olympic Games, municipal, provincial, and federal input was required not only to raise funds for the submission, but also to ensure the Olympic selection committee of government commitment.

Outside the tourist information centre in Cape Breton, Nova Scotia, beside a newly erected totem pole, a piper ushers in the annual Highland Games.

(Photo: Judy McArthur.)

Municipal Governments and Tourism Associations

Municipal governments have similar needs and perform similar activities to their provincial counterparts. To promote their tourism products (attractions, hotels, restaurants, etc.) some cities have a tourism marketing department. Others turn to private, nonprofit associations like convention and visitor bureaus (CVBs) or local chambers of commerce.

Chambers and CVBs These groups work with the city to promote local events and attract visitors. They advertise in newspapers and magazines and on radio, television, and the Internet, and produce booklets, most notably a visitor's guide. These guides, placed in hotel rooms, offer information on attractions, festivals and events, shops, restaurants and bars, and transportation systems. Some are hard-cover, and guests are requested to leave them in the room on departure. Others resemble magazines, which guests can take home as souvenirs and hopefully pass along to friends.

Chambers of commerce and CVBs have similar operational styles and functions. Chambers of commerce are nonprofit, private organizations; convention and visitor bureaus may be either nonprofit organizations or municipal governmental departments. In some areas, a chamber or CVB may serve an entire county or region.

A **chamber of commerce** is an association of voluntary business and professional people who work together to solve community problems and to promote and develop the community. The first known chamber of commerce was established by the city council of Marseilles, France, toward the close of the seventeenth century. The oldest chamber of commerce in North America was in New York State, chartered by King George III in 1770 for the protection of commerce following passage of the Stamp Act by Parliament in 1765. The early North American chambers, like their European prototypes, were associations of tradespeople organized for the protection and promotion of commerce.[2] It was not until much later that chambers became community organizations, as business owners realized that their own prosperity depended on the prosperity of the community.

Recognizing the financial impact tourism has for its members, chambers of commerce become involved in all aspects of tourism. For example, the Ontario Chamber of Commerce (OCC) actively participates in Ontario's certification process. Their representatives, in conjunction with the Ontario Tourism Education Corporation (OTEC), promote and set up training courses for Ontario's tourism work force.

The fundamental mission of a **convention and visitor bureau** is to enhance the economic stability of a community by soliciting and servicing conventions and other types of events that generate overnight stays. In addition, a CVB promotes vacation travel to the area. The CVB is the community's liaison between potential visitors and the businesses that will host them. It is a city's information clearinghouse, convention management consultant, and promotional agency, and is often the catalyst for urban development and renewal. CVBs have a sensitive and important role in leading the community's tourism industry. A dynamic and professional CVB creates a favourable image of the community for tour and meeting planners, which can increase tourism volume and profits.

Chambers of Commerce and CVBs run on membership fees. Both organizations offer members cooperative advertising programs and trade shows. The CVB usually coordinates these programs and sometimes charges a commission on each convention booking. Destination publications include visitor's guides, maps, meeting planner's guides, and brochures on attractions, hotels and restaurants, activities, and city tours. These may be sent out by direct mail, given to walk-ins, mailed to people inquiring about the destination, and given to meeting planners.

Another way to promote sales is to arrange a **familiarization tour (fam tour)** for a group of prospects to show off the city's charms and suitability for conventions. A fam tour, free to the prospective client, is sponsored by city businesses. A **site inspection**, in contrast, is held for a single prospective client (usually an association) at the client's expense and is tailored to its needs and desires. While a fam tour solicits business from associations that have not yet considered the site, a site inspection provides final details to associations that have narrowed the choice to two or three locations.

After all the marketing techniques have been employed and the association or client wants to do business, the CVB puts together a bid presentation. The presentation may be given to a single person, a select group, a board of directors, or to the entire association. The bid should answer all the client's questions, so the CVB needs to understand all the client's needs and desires. Many CVBs contact the client's previous convention sites before the bidding to gather information.

Convention Services In most cases, CVBs are not designed to perform the actual convention setup, although they can provide a wide array of assistance. Some services are performed for all associations, whereas others are written in as part of the host city's responsibilities. The CVB convention division may provide city and site information to generate interest among association members or it may host an event at the association's current convention as a welcome to the following year's meeting. The CVB arranges pre-convention tours to assist the client in planning the convention and may organize programs to encourage spouses to come along. The CVB may also set up a speaker's bureau to book local speakers for the upcoming convention or conference. Finally, if more than one hotel is needed, the CVB may set up a housing bureau to help with hotel reservations and confirmations.

During the convention, services range from simple items such as a welcome banner strategically placed at the airport and convention centre to registration and shuttle services. CVBs have a list of trained personnel who can perform many of the tedious convention duties, from typing name badges to collecting registration fees. The CVB may also be asked to provide the speaker for the opening ceremony. When given enough advance notice, it can arrange for the premier, mayor, or other prominent person to welcome the convention delegates. Often the CVB will provide an information desk to give tourist information. Finally, the convention services department helps the meeting planner with last-minute details: that extra roll of tape or slide projector, or an adjustment in room temperature. This kind of help takes the stress off the meeting planner, which in turn makes for a successful convention and a happy client.

Tourist Information Centres

Tourist information centres act as gateways and provide visitors with their first impression of a province, region, or town. All levels of government fund information centres to tell tourists about the region: its accommodations, attractions, special events, food service choices, historical sites, and unique environmental experiences. In the Ottawa region, the National Capital Commission has a large information centre on Parliament Hill, open from June to September. Bilingual guides offer visitors tours of the grounds and buildings. Brochures on historical sites are also available. Provinces usually locate tourism information centres along major highways and at border crossings. These centres offer general information on the province as a whole. Information centres all across Canada are easily identified by their question mark symbol **(?)**. Because information centres are usually open in the summer, the jobs are often filled by students, who can practise their customer relations skills and apply their knowledge of the region.

in practice List 15 attractions in your region. How would you promote them to tourists at a visitor centre? If you were a CVB, which ones would you emphasize to an association considering a convention? How would you promote them?

Tourist information centres may be operated by federal, provincial, or municipal organizations.
(Photo: Paula Kerr.)

S N A P S H O T

Ray Kroc

"Find out where your talents lie and then do whatever you are doing better than anybody else. But be willing to pay the price." With that philosophy in mind, Ray Kroc, at age 52, set out to build the McDonald's empire. What makes Kroc's story even more interesting is that he did nothing new, came up with no great innovation, and yet rose higher in the hospitality business than any other pioneer. Ray Kroc had what it takes to make it in the business: skill in organization, great perseverance, and a talent for marketing his product. Kroc purchased the rights to McDonald's and its golden arches from two brothers who ran the original burger restaurant. His first major task was to simplify and standardize the menu. The KISS principle (keep it simple, stupid) was developed by Kroc, as was the acronym QSC&V— quality, service, cleanliness, and value. How important these concepts are, even in today's market, 50 years later! In fact, the great success of McDonald's is due to a simplified system of operation, cleanliness, friendly service, and a menu that appeals to both children and adults in taste and price.

Ray Kroc focused on making hamburgers and fries better than any other restaurant in town. He accomplished this feat by instituting an operating manual that clearly spelled out every little detail of the business. McDonald's, like most restaurants today, uses standardized recipes. Over the past 50 years, the corporation has developed tools that ensure that the amount of sauce is exact, that the egg in the Egg McMuffin is the perfect size, and that the hamburger bun is precisely 9 cm in diameter. This precision reassures McDonald's customers that wherever they travel, they will get exactly what they expect in a hamburger.

McDonald's has been careful in maintaining the quality of its menu. Tremendous research goes into each new menu item offered. For example, Ray knew that a closed restaurant did not produce revenue and that there was a demand for a quick breakfast, but it took several years of research before he was satisfied with his menu. Breakfast at McDonald's was launched in the 1960s with excellent results. Little of the McDonald's menu has changed over the years, proof that his care in creating and maintaining the quality of his products has paid off.

Kroc was a genius at marketing. He chose his staff carefully, looking for men and women with specific talents (finance, training, management) who shared his vision and his enthusiasm. One of the features of a McDonald's restaurant is its visibility to passers-by. The golden arches are recognizable, no matter the province, state, or country. Over the past decade, McDonald's has chosen to design specific restaurants to blend in with the local neighbourhood, especially when that neighbourhood has a historic past. For example, nestled quietly in a narrow, cobblestone street in the city of Salzburg, Austria, is a McDonald's, recognizable only by its interior decor and menu—a familiar place to eat in a town full of history.

Ray Kroc was not only a genius at marketing and at choosing the right personnel to help develop and run McDonald's, but he also believed in community spirit. Ronald McDonald Houses are found in many major cities across North America, providing living quarters for out-of-town family members of hospitalized children.

What kind of man was Ray Kroc? He was an entrepreneur who believed that anything was possible if a person had drive, dedication, persistence, and a dream. He encouraged training, promotion from within, and excellent customer service. He was a man who maintained that McDonald's has a duty to give back to the community the support it receives.

Tourism Associations and Organizations

Because of the complex nature of the tourism industry, a variety of industry associations have developed in the past century. They can be divided into two categories: organizations that focus on marketing and those that focus on advocacy or lobbying. CVBs are marketing-oriented organizations; another example is the Canada West Ski Marketing Council. These organizations strive to attract visitors to a destination or to encourage people to participate in a specific pursuit. They develop and execute marketing plans, design special promotions, coordinate publicity, and work with advertising agencies. Tourism advocates and lobbying organizations are more concerned with the welfare of the tourism industry as a whole or with the success of a specific sector such as travel trade or food and beverage. Many of these associations have already been discussed in previous chapters. Nationally recognized advocacy groups in Canada include

- Tourism Industry Association of Canada (TIAC)
- Association of Canadian Travel Agents (ACTA)
- Canadian Restaurant and Foodservices Association (CRFA)
- Canadian Federation of Chefs and Cooks (CFCC)
- Canadian Food Service Executive Association (CFSEA)
- Aboriginal Tourism Team Canada (ATTC)

- Hotel Association of Canada (HAC)
- Meeting Professionals International (MPI)
- Association of Tourism Professionals (ATP)

All of the groups listed above are private, except ATTC, which is quasi-public; that is, it receives some funding from the federal government.

These associations represent their members to governing bodies and the public in general. They put on seminars, sponsor events, conduct research, and keep their members informed about all the activities within their sectors. They prepare briefing papers for governments on issues such as taxation and regulations that affect their sectors. They have also been instrumental in writing national occupational standards and in providing training and certification (see chapter 3).

The Tourism Industry Association of Canada (TIAC) is a good example of a lobbying organization. TIAC is a private organization, founded in 1931 and funded by membership dues. It serves the industry as its national voice. Members come from all areas of the tourism industry: businesses, institutions, associations, and individuals. TIAC's mandate is to strengthen tourism by lobbying the federal government on tax issues, federal tourism initiatives, training programs for tourism workers, and legislation that promotes a proactive tourism industry. Here are some of TIAC's goals:

- Provide a forum for discussion and action in order to offer valid feedback regarding pending legislation.
- Improve the quality of the industry through seminars, workshops, and conferences.
- Provide networking opportunities and current information to all eight sectors of tourism.

Associations will remain vital to the future of tourism. The collective weight of their membership influences government policies and legislation, creating a healthy environment for workers and visitors alike. Becoming active in tourism organizations gives members the chance to network with professionals in their field and to have a say in the future of their industry.

Marketing Services

For the most part, travel is not an activity essential to our survival. Consequently, advertising and promotion need to entice the traveller. Canadian destinations compete not only in the global tourism marketplace, but also province against province, city against city. The tourism industry as a whole is also competing against other discretionary purchases, such as home renovation and consumer goods. A strong marketing program often includes the services of an advertising agency (artists, creative directors, copy writers, and musicians) as well as a public relations company. The contract for Fairmont Hotels, Disney World, or Air Canada can be worth millions of dollars to an advertising agency. The CTC and its industry partners spent $100 million in 2001 to promote tourism in Canada.

Destination marketing organizations promote their cities, regions, provinces, or country. Our national DMO is the CTC and we have already dis-

Marketing services use a variety of tools to sell a destination: commercials, posters, perhaps a safari hat.
(Photo: Paula Kerr.)

cussed its marketing approaches for Canada. Most DMOs are run by some level of government, but the trend is for government to stand back, allowing the industry to take a larger role in its promotion and costs. Every province has some form of DMO: in British Columbia this role is filled by Tourism B.C. CVBs are another example of a DMO and usually perform the tourism marketing activities for a city or region.

A strong destination marketing organization can significantly increase tourist volume and in turn revenue. Working for a DMO is challenging and can be exciting. You must have good knowledge of your region and strong marketing and communication skills. No two days or groups are alike, and your ability to meet these challenges with ease will ensure your success in this field.

Research and Consulting

Not all products appeal to all people. How do you decide who will use your products? Will your product suit their needs? Those questions are answered through market research and analysis. Research can be done informally, simply by asking clients about their satisfaction. Many tourist operations leave comment cards in hotel rooms or in restaurants, or train staff to ask "Was everything to your liking?" However, such casual questions do not always identify problem areas. Many customers are uncomfortable criticizing, and will often answer "fine." Do staff really want to know what was wrong with the service? No server is looking for a critique during the dinner rush! To get a better image of how well a product meets customers' needs, a business can hire independent research professionals.

Tourism research firms usually focus either on tourism products in general or specific products, providing important information to help guide decision making. Here are some of the questions that research on your product should answer:

- Is your product unique?
- How does the quality of your product measure up against similar products?
- Does your product have enough capacity to handle demand?
- What are the benefits of purchasing your product?
- What drawbacks have been identified with your product?
- Is your product sustainable? easily accessible?
- What do clients expect when they purchase your product?
- What needs does your product fulfill for the client?
- What needs are left unfulfilled?

Research also provides the industry with a track record of its performance, and it measures the impact of tourism on the economy. Some companies, such as Air Canada, have their own research divisions. Others hire consulting firms. Many large multinational consulting firms work with the industry, such as PricewaterhouseCoopers and KPMG Consulting. The nonprofit Conference Board of Canada is the lead agency responsible for research in Canada. The Canadian Tourism Research Institute (CTRI) is the division that concerns itself with tourism issues. Its members' mandate is to "assist their customers in the Canadian tourism industry to anticipate and respond to emerging trends in a manner that will enhance their competitiveness."[3]

Consultants may work for a large firm but they are often entrepreneurs with specific expertise. For example, if you have worked extensively in the food and beverage industry, you may be able to use your knowledge of foods to help a restaurateur create an exciting menu using colours, shapes, and good descriptive copy. Perhaps you are an accountant with a specialty in food and beverage labour cost control. Whatever your field of knowledge, being a consultant means you sell your expertise to those willing to pay for your services. When you work for yourself, you can have greater flexibility with your work hours but you must also have a strong skill set and the willingness to take a risk, because unemployment is just one contract away! Many consultants find that the satisfaction of being their own boss outweighs all of the risks.

Miscellaneous Services

Miscellaneous services is the final component of the tourism services sector. Below is a short list of some of these businesses and occupations:

- Education and training services for tourism are provided by a variety of institutions and businesses: high schools, colleges, and universities; private trainers; and organizations such as tourism education councils (TECs) and the Canadian Tourism Human Resource Council (CTHRC). TECs focus on **front-line training**, that is, training staff who deal directly with the tourist. Because tourism businesses are also interested in creating and maintaining a professional work force, they will often provide in-house training for staff.
- Travel writers and photographers for the tourism industry combine their love of travel with their creative or artistic abilities. A travel writer or photographer may work for one magazine (such as *Canadian Geographic*) or may work freelance.

- Construction engineers and architects design and build facilities for the tourism industry. Often a firm will specialize in the construction of restaurants, cruise ships, or hotels.
- Duty-free shops and retail merchants provide opportunities for travellers who love to shop. Many department stores are offering SuperHost training to their floor staff to provide good customer service.
- Web page and site designers are quickly establishing themselves as indispensable to the small business. Good Web designers must have not only strong computer skills, but also a good knowledge of the tourism product or business they are creating the Web site for.

OPPORTUNITIES IN TOURISM SERVICES

	ASSOCIATIONS/ GOVERNMENT	MISCELLANEOUS TOURISM SERVICES
OPERATION (FRONT LINE)	Tourism/Visitor Information Counsellor (Info Centre, Auto Club, etc.) Information Centre Clerk/Guide	Retail Sales Clerk in a Tourism Operation Sales Representative
SUPERVISORY	Tourism/Visitor Information Centre Supervisor	Business Travel Specialist Destination Development Specialist Tourism Research Assistant Tourism Market Researcher
MANAGEMENT	Auto Club Travel Manager Tourism Association Administrator Key Tourism Positions in Government Director, Policy, Research & Planning Director, Domestic Marketing Director, Tourism Services Director, Tourism Development Director, Human Resources Tourism Information Centre Manager Manager, Media Relations Manager, Meetings & Incentive Travel Manager, Travel Trade Sales Manager, International Marketing	Travel Writer/Photographer **Tourism Consultant/Researcher** Tourism Educator Public Relations Manager Media/Trade Press Specialist Tourism Research/Statistical Specialist Reservation Services Manager Retail Merchandiser (Tourism Operations)
EXECUTIVE	Deputy Minister of Tourism Minister Responsible for Tourism	

SOURCE: Courtesy of Canadian Tourism Human Resource Council, *The Student's Travel Map*, 1995.

JOB DESCRIPTION FOR . . .

TOURISM CONSULTANT/RESEARCHER

Industry Sector	Tourism Services
Division	Research/Consulting/Miscellaneous
Industry Setting	Tourism and research departments of government (federal, provincial, regional, municipal), private consulting and research firms, information centres, professional associations, marketing associations
Job Level	Middle Management
Description of Duties	Duties include providing research, analysis, and planning services to tourism-related public and/or private sector clients on the tourism industry, markets and marketing channels, industry organizations, and government programs. May also include identification of marketing opportunities and preparation of marketing and development strategies for specific projects; coordination of agenda and speakers for tourism-related conferences.
Education	Bachelor's degree and preferably a master's degree in tourism, business, or social science.
Career Paths	Ministry of Tourism senior management and executive-level occupations; private sector tourism-related business opportunities in senior management and executive-level positions.
HRDC Reference	NOC 4163 Economic Development Officers and Marketing Researchers and Consultants

- Specialty farms and cheese factories (Balderson), vineyards (Inniskillen), food manufacturers (Heinz), and food distributors (Summit Foods) all help to make Canadian foods a culinary adventure. Food photographers working with culinary or tourism magazines preserve for all time outstanding dining experiences found in Canada.

- Auto clubs around the world are important to any vacationer who uses a private vehicle. Auto club counsellors design travel routes for CAA (Canadian Automobile Association) customers to avoid construction areas and bypass large cities. Counsellors must have knowledge of the region, updated highway information, and the skill to explain a route.

- Manufacturers produce items used by different sectors in the industry, such as commercial ovens, machines, furniture, and amusement park rides.

The list goes on. So many people work in and with the tourism industry that it is easy to see why it is known as a labour-intensive industry. The work can be fun, and the rewards, even just a warm hello or a hearty thanks, make a tourism job a special event every day.

summary

The tourism services sector has a wide range of occupations that are instrumental in creating a quality Canadian tourism product. The sector can be broken down into five components: government agencies, tourism associations and organizations, marketing and promotional firms, research and consulting firms, and miscellaneous services. All levels of government become involved in the tourism industry through research, development, promotion, education, funding, and legislative and regulatory initiatives.

Tourism associations are either promoters of or advocates for the industry. They provide information to members and help set the direction of tourism. Marketing and promotional firms know how to sell the industry's products. Understanding the unique characteristics of the tourism product is essential. Research and consulting firms provide the industry with a wealth of information, including an analysis of current market trends and projections for the future. The remaining occupations that keep the industry progressing and running smoothly fall into the miscellaneous category and include educators, architects, construction engineers, and companies that supply the industry with products such as fresh produce, cleansers, and landscaping services. Although this sector remains behind the scenes, it plays a vital role in the tourism industry.

questions

1. a) The government of any country plays a crucial role in the planning, development, maintenance, and promotion of a country or region. Summarize briefly the various roles played by (i) the federal government, (ii) your provincial government, and (iii) your municipal government.

    b) List two pieces of legislation or regulations, created by each level of government, that help or hurt the tourism industry as a whole, or the tourist as an individual. Explain why you believe this legislation is helpful or harmful.

2. Research your city's convention and visitor bureau and describe four different services it performs for the tourism industry in your region.

3. Tourism services provides the industry with many different support services.

    a) Choose any five services that appeal to you from this sector and explain why you might be interested in this line of work.

    b) Would you require further education to work in each of these businesses? If so, what courses would you be looking for?

4. Define the following terms as they relate to the tourism industry: *familiarization tour, site inspection, DMO.*

weblinks

www.cthrc.ca

The Canadian Tourism Human Resources Council promotes professionalism in the industry by means of training, setting industry standards, and professional certification.

www.conferenceboard.ca / ctri /

The Canadian Tourism Research Institute (CTRI) specializes in travel analysis and forecasting.

www.tourisme-montreal.org

Montreal's official tourist information Web site includes accommodation links, a planner's guide, and much more.

notes

1. *The Student's Travel Map* (Ottawa: Canadian Tourism Human Resource Council, 1995), pp. 102–103.

2. *Chamber Executive Handbook* (Helena, MT: Montana Association of Chamber Executives, 1989), p. 2.

3. Harry French, 1996 National Conference on Tourism, Jasper, Alberta, conference proceedings, p. 41.

13 Challenges and the Future

key terms

code of ethics   time poverty

learning objectives

Having read this chapter you will be able to

1. Explain how the eight concerns/challenges identified by the CTC for the tourism industry may slow or expand the industry's growth rate.

2. Identify and explain the impact of current trends in lifestyles, travel, and technology on the tourism industry.

3. Explain the importance of ethical behaviour in the tourism industry.

4. Discuss trends in each tourism sector identified by the Canadian government.

5. Outline briefly the challenges that face tourism in the new millennium.

Tourism is like a snowfall. During blizzard periods, the sheer number of tourists makes life for a community difficult. Tourism produces overcrowded streets, hour-long waits for restaurant tables, overbooked flights and hotels. The Olympic Games is a good example of an event where all the planning in the world cannot lessen the strain on the entire community. As with a massive snowfall, the aftermath of such an event requires a tremendous amount of cleanup. At other times, Canadian snowfalls are beautiful, soft and steady; this is the equivalent to tourism's peak periods, when the number of tourists is constant but workable. Attractions are busy, hotels and restaurants are full, and the crowds are friendly. At times, the snow falls sporadically, enough to tell us that it is snowing, but not enough to bother us—the equivalent of tourism's shoulder or off-peak period. The tourists are still coming, but there is no inconvenience to residents. Hotels and restaurants experience a slow cycle, and often the airlines cut back on their flights. Finally, there comes a time when no snow falls at all. Not all destinations experience a total lack of tourists, but some inaccessible resorts must close for the winter.

Snowfalls are similar to tourism in other ways: just as no two snowflakes are alike, no two tourists are alike. The impact of a snowfall is affected by external factors (winds, time of day, day of the week, amount of snow already on the ground); tourism, too, is affected by factors beyond the industry's control (weather, political unrest, recession). Finally, no matter how annoying snow may be, there is always a positive side: skiing, snowshoeing, making snowmen in the yard. In tourism, the benefits are revenues generated and additional work for local residents.

Canadians have no choice about how much snow they get—but they do have a choice about tourism. The future of the tourism industry in Canada promises to be very bright if governments and industry act wisely. Tourism revenues—currently $54.6 billion—will grow, and occupational opportunities will expand. This chapter examines the future of tourism. Why does Canada believe tourism will continue to grow? Where is the industry going and how will it get there?

Issues Raising Concern in the Industry

In a 1996 paper, the CTC addressed eight key issues that the industry felt the federal government needed to deal with.[1] All these issues still exist; in fact, some have been exacerbated. If these issues are not resolved, they will likely weaken the Canadian tourism product in the next decade. This section will explore those key issues.

Transportation Easy, reasonably priced access to and around a country is critical if tourism is to flourish. Canada's transportation system is slowly deteriorating. The quality of highways, roads, and roadside facilities has diminished, and with recent government cuts, upgrading is slow. Deregulation appears to have helped create a near-monopolistic air system, with Air Canada our only remaining national carrier. Lack of governmental structuring has allowed it to begin low-cost services with subsidiaries like Tango and Jazz competing directly with smaller low-cost carriers like WestJet. Air travel has become increasingly expensive as governments and the airlines tack on additional taxes and surcharges. Although the industry feels that a less expensive ticket price will encourage Canadians to travel within their own country, reasonably priced air transportation is becoming a rare event.

The Role of Parks and Historic Sites National parks and historic sites are important to the tourism industry because many product offerings have some natural or historic significance. However, conflicts arise when Parks Canada, for example, attempts to balance the need for better tourist accessibility with the need to preserve land, flora, and fauna for future generations. The industry has raised concerns because demand for our national parks' experience is growing (Banff and Jasper are perhaps the most pressured), while deteriorating facilities threaten the overall quality of the tourist experience. Wilderness areas such as Nahanni and Tateshini/Alsek national parks are already showing signs of pollution.

The Evolving Role of Canada Customs and Immigration More than two million border crossings take place daily between the United States and Canada. While Europe reduces the formalities at border crossings, making travel on the continent easier, borders in North America will have stricter controls and be more time consuming to cross as customs and immigration officials try to ensure only citizens, residents, and bona fide tourists enter their country. Officials are being given broader powers to ensure those crossing have proper papers and legitimate business. Terrorism is a constant concern and freedom of access between our two countries is disappearing. Is the Canadian government willing to invest the hard dollars required to upgrade technology at our borders? Will our border guards get the promised computer links between the RCMP and U.S. and British security agencies? Will these changes ensure a smoother, safer border crossing for tourists while eliminating potential terrorist threats?

The Tax Issue Taxes have always been a thorn in the side of tourism, and with the introduction of the goods and services tax (GST) in 1991, they became a major concern for tourism. Since the GST is not levied on Canadian exports, and tourism is one of Canada's biggest exports, why is the GST charged on tourism products? Even if a foreign tourist purchases a Canadian tour package outside Canada, the GST must still be paid. Tourism advocates feel strongly that this discriminates against tourism products that are already costly. In 1998, after lobbying by the TIAC, the government agreed to remove the GST paid by international conferences choosing a Canadian destination. Of course, delegates must still pay GST on any purchases while in Canada. TIAC also lobbied for remuneration rights for tourists on GST paid while in Canada. If they keep their receipts and fill out the correct paperwork, a cheque in Canadian funds for GST paid will be mailed to their home address. At the 1999 Hotel Association of Canada Conference, a panel of tourism professionals discussed this issue. Ken Hine, CEO of the International Hotel and Restaurant Association, described the tax situation as it had existed in New York City. Taxes there reached a high of 21.25 percent, and the industry was able to prove to both municipal and state governments that these taxes were driving more business away than they were generating in tax revenues. Consider the case of a tourist visiting Ontario who must add 15 percent (PST and GST) to all their purchases, plus a liquor tax and a hotel tax! Add to that an entertainment tax levied on some forms of entertainment, Airport Improvement Fees, and numerous municipal taxes and you may agree with the panel, who pointed out: "It's called killing the golden goose. Political bodies find it easier to tax their non-constituents (tourists) because no one in the community... thinks it is a bad idea." Our dollar may be low against other currencies, but high taxes chip away at the advantage.

Training of Tourism Workers Service is one of the most important problems faced by the tourism industry today. Because many workers have direct contact with the tourist, proper training is essential. If Canada is to compete in a global market, our tourism professionals must have the skills, knowledge, and attitudes (SKAs) to deliver the product effectively. Training programs developed by the tourism education councils and the industry are an important advance. Certification provides the employee and the work place with a visible sign (certification pins and certificates) that the establishment has invested in training to ensure a pleasurable guest experience.

Grading of Facilities The industry has asked for a national assessment program that would grade tourism facilities, making choice easier for tourists, especially when they must choose at a distance. The quality of the tourism product is strengthened if high standards are set and consistently met by tourism facilities. Programs such as Atlantic Canada's Canada Select Program are a big step in the right direction.

Financing the Future of Tourism The financial community has not perceived tourism to be a sound financial investment. There are several reasons for this perception: tourism consists of a series of small businesses, many of which have a track record of financial difficulties or bankruptcy; it is hard to define the tourism business and its potential revenues in a financial statement; and financial institutions have never possessed a clear vision of the tourism industry (a problem that exists within the industry itself). As tourism moves front and centre in the world of financial investment, Canadian lending institutions should reconsider their position.

Aboriginal Tourism Both the federal and provincial governments, along with the industry, recognize the growing demand for experiences centred on the cultural heritage of Aboriginal Canadians. All too aware of the harm tourism can bring, the industry strongly supports the development of Aboriginal tourism as long as it meets the government's requirement for sustainability. This development must enhance Aboriginal culture, respect Aboriginal lands and lifestyle, and produce viable employment for the community. In the end, Aboriginal tourism should improve the quality of life, both financially and culturally, for Aboriginal Canadians.

Heritage and cultural tourists have become an important market for Aboriginal tourism.
(Photo: Kate Sarbutt.)

Terrorist Threats

In the past decade, there have been many threats against nations around the world. Terrorist acts have plagued U.S. facilities on foreign soil but the destruction of the World Trade Center brought the fear of terrorism home to Americans. In the 1970s, hijackings were more commonplace than they are today but passengers were used as bargaining tools, allowing the terrorists to achieve certain demands. September 11 showed the world that aircraft can become effective bombs, bringing about massive destruction. Passengers are now just the unlucky participants. Israel's tourism industry has suffered more than most from terrorist actions. In Malaysia, tourists were captured and held for more than three months while their captors' demands were being considered. In Bali, three Canadian tourists died when a nightclub was bombed. Travel in less-developed countries is less safe than it was. Canada has actually benefited loosely from the chain of events. We are still viewed by the world as a safe place for travel and our tourism industry has rebounded much faster than has tourism in the United States. There is no doubt, however, that if terrorists continue to make headlines around the world, tourism will continue to suffer.

Ethics and Tourism

What are ethics and why are they so important to the tourism industry? According to *Webster's Dictionary*, ethics are a system or code of morals, or the ability of a particular person, group, association, or profession to distinguish right from wrong.[2] One of the problems people encounter when discussing or applying ethical principles is the vast differences among cultures, nations, and religions.

In North America consumers are protected by laws against false commercial claims. Yet how easy it is with new computer technology to create a brochure that shows mountains in the backyard of a cute little chalet, when in truth they are 30 km away! Another shady marketing ploy is the bait and switch: a company advertises a deeply discounted price for, say, a cruise, but sets aside only a few tickets at this price. Once potential customers are on the line, a clever sales agent can easily sell a space at a higher price. As tourism workers, we have a very close relationship with our guests and they entrust us with their personal belongings and their lives. Few businesses are given this type of trust and it is important to tourism products and services everywhere that this trust is not misplaced. The Canadian tourism industry—hotels, attractions, restaurants, and transportation systems—must develop a **code of ethics** based on the values of right and wrong that helped found this nation. If you are working in the industry, does your business have a code of ethics? Is it posted? Does the staff believe in it and follow it?

As you enter the tourism industry, remember that trust between a tourist and a supplier is essential. The tourism product is intangible and cannot operate without trust. You are the only link between your product and the tourist. Tourists entrust you with their lives, their security, and their possessions. You accepted this responsibility when you entered the tourism industry. Serve it with honesty and concern for your customers and you will be rewarded with happy customers, a profitable business, a sense of pride, and the satisfaction of having done your job well.

Technology and Its Impact on Tourism's Future

The impact of new technology on the industry will continue to be as great a changing force as were the technological changes in the last half of the twentieth century. Those changes, in transportation, the media, and the financial world, to mention only a few, have created this huge global business called tourism. About half the population in North America is comfortable with computers and use them daily. That number is growing steadily. How does that affect the market-place? Consumers are logging on to the Internet for information on destinations, hotels, attractions, and adventure opportunities. A recent survey showed that 59 percent of Web users retrieve travel information. Air Canada's online travel agency, Destina.ca, attracted more than a million surfers in its first 60 days of operation. The study projected that by 2003, 50 percent of Canadians who travel would book on the Internet.[3] Travellers can search the Web to find interesting vacation opportunities. User-friendly Web sites are the wave of the future and if you aren't on the Web, you are missing marketing and sales opportunities. The Internet is be-coming a clearing house for unsold or "distressed" tourism products. As an exam-ple, airlines sell off deeply discounted seats to last-minute travellers via the Web. This method of sales helps counter the extreme perishability of our tourism prod-ucts. Another new trend is the online auction. Similar to the seat sale, this allows the consumer to determine what they are willing to pay for the product. However, although most customers are willing to search the Internet for vacations and bar-gains, many prefer to do the actual purchase through a travel agent. Security of a purchase over the Internet still remains a concern to many would-be purchasers. The success of any tourism business will depend on the owners understanding their customers' ever-changing needs and tailoring their product to meet them.

Trends in the Tourism Industry

How have people, their motivations, their needs, and their wants changed in the past decade? Peter Yesawich, a leading expert in the field of marketing research has identified some of the newer trends in lifestyle, travel, and technology.[4] After the

Experiencing our wildlife is often an important part of a Canadian vacation; however, tourists often disregard their own safety and the safety of others by attempting to get too close.
(Photo: Paula Kerr.)

tough years of recession in the early 1990s, North Americans emerged with a renewed sense of possibility. Employment increased and with it, discretionary income. The increase in sales of homes and cars coupled with lower interest rates has helped to create a stronger demand for tourism. Customers are demanding and expecting more from suppliers and look for value for their dollar. They have become smarter shoppers and search out the best price for the product they are purchasing.

As business becomes more competitive, as companies try to produce more product for less, we are burdened by **time poverty**. Many people find they have less time for everything, including vacations. The average North American lunch "hour" is just 28 minutes long! How will restaurants handle the need for quicker service or the "work while you eat" lunch? The number of hours that we work is increasing. However, the time we allot for vacation and business trips is getting shorter and the need for efficient service is greater. Today's consumers are willing to pay more for convenience. With the work week lengthening, time spent at home is focused on family and family activities. Research has shown that our priorities have changed. We want more control over our lives and what we do. We want the ability to take time off when needed, and our health, successful relationships, and family life have become more important than personal wealth. This gives rise to a growing demand for safe, fun family attractions. The number-one symbol of success is no longer money, but satisfaction with life.

Consumers are also becoming "street smart." There has been an erosion of trust in the marketplace, which hits tourism hard. Remember, we sell a product that is both expensive and intangible, and if a business is to succeed and thrive, it must deliver a product that surpasses customer expectations.

Businesses that survived the last recession are now struggling with the current economic downturn caused by the collapse of technology stocks and recent stock scandals among big, respected businesses Although business travel has largely rebounded from the sharp drop after the attacks on the World Trade Center, studies conflict about the overall trend in business travel, with some projecting a continued decline. Trips are often shorter, less frequent. The Internet and teleconferencing have the potential to replace face-to-face business practices. This reduction applies mostly to individual trips and small meetings rather than conferences and conventions. Having successfully hosted the G-8 Conference at Kananaskis in August 2002 with no major disruptions or outbreak of hostilities, Canada is being recognized as a safe alternative to U.S. destinations. Growth is forecast in this area of the business meeting market.

Branding has become an important ally to sales, and small businesses are having more difficulty staying profitable. The growing demand for high-profile brand names is expressed by the forming of alliances and associations, and the buyout of smaller businesses by larger ones. Using a brand name provides customers with a familiar product, one that they have confidence in. Fifty-one to seventy-one percent of consumers choose a brand name over an unknown one, especially when dollar values are similar.

Consumers are looking for products that are easy to purchase and use. This need can be filled by creating partnerships among tourism businesses. Package deals—for example, putting accommodations together with a rental car and some entertainment and dining options—are growing in popularity. This "one-stop shopping" method of purchase may be seen not only in the tourism industry, but also in many areas of the North American lifestyle. Consider the new megastores that supplies customers with groceries, clothes, furniture, appliances, and drugs under one roof. This trend reflects the longer work week and the erosion of personal, discretionary time. Packages that provide the traveller with short, relaxing holidays are expected to gain a greater share of the market. For example, hotels should be looking at strategic pricing: a Sunday-through-Thursday stay coupled with a Thursday-through-Sunday package. This fills the need for business travellers looking to reduce the cost of their travel, and the vacation traveller who wants to take a four-day weekend.

Over the years, North Americans have become increasingly jaded in their views of government, authority, and the media. Advertising has even less credibility. Consumers are more willing to complain if the product or service does not meet expectations, and everyone "wants it their way." This increased demand for personalized service will require a better trained staff and a more flexible way of doing business.

Transportation trends include ticketless air travel, with do-it-yourself, computerized check-in, and discount airlines that offer little or no service. Aircraft manufacturers are designing larger, much faster planes. Expect to see continued alliances and code sharing between the major airline companies. Trains are becoming an attractive alternative to air travel because they seem less likely to attract terrorist activity. With the added surcharges on an airline ticket in Canada, at least on short-haul runs like Montreal to Toronto, the train is more affordable. VIA Rail has recognized the tourist demand for luxury train travel and has added newly refurbished cars and more service. North American short-haul markets are considering replacing conventional trains with high-speed service using the technologies like the Maglev. Cruise lines seem convinced that bigger is better and are making cruises even more luxurious and elaborate, including facilities such as wedding chapels, bowling lanes, ice rinks, and jogging paths! Smaller ships are beginning to focus on specific target markets such as the convention or ecotourism market.

Trends in the accommodation sector include the move to smaller, boutique-style hotels, providing customers with a high level of personal services through enhanced training programs. One of the newer product services offered by many hotels is high-speed Internet connection. The larger hotel chains are expected to continue their partnerships with smaller properties, including buyouts. Finally, hotel commissions to travel agents will likely drop or be phased out entirely.

Food and beverage will remain a growing and entrepreneurial industry. As baby boomers age, they become increasingly concerned about nutritious food. Fresh, local products will score high with this knowledgeable market. A good wine list will be a selling point for upscale restaurants. Smaller establishments will continue to struggle against the larger, well-known chains and must be able to reach a target market that believes that "smaller is better." Alliances and buyouts will continue to be commercially successful. Technology will play an ever-increasing role in this industry and businesses must keep tighter controls of their food costs using modern computer and cash systems.[5] Finally, the demand for contract food services and for food service aligned with upscale retirement homes will provide hospitality and culinary students with interesting career options.

The experiential sectors of tourism will flourish as more baby boomers enjoy their retirement years. Attractions and special events that focus on culture and historical themes will be popular. More attractions are getting the visitor involved

Where is McDonald's? This view of a busy street in Salzburg, Austria, shows how hotels and restaurants are becoming more sensitive to cultural values and are making an effort to blend in with the local landscape. (McDonald's is at the third sign on the right.)
(Photo: John B. Kerr.)

with hands-on workshops or seminars. Communities looking to expand their economic base are hosting a variety of special events to help extend their tourist season and increase revenue generation. Special events are not only important for the tourism industry, but are also a main source of revenue for charities and bring needed recognition to local enterprise. According to a September 2002 CTC report, business travel will increase by 8 percent over the next year.[6] The low Canadian dollar and the sense of security Canadian destinations create will lead to new growth in the conference and convention business.

Adventure tourism and outdoor recreation has strong growth potential. A high level of safety will be an essential component for much of this market. Ecotourism in the true sense of the word, will continue to intrigue the adult market. Resorts that boast of a unique natural setting will be held to a higher standard of sustainable development and their design must ensure minimum harm to the environment. Boomers looking for a healthy retirement will lead increasingly active lifestyles that will include daily exercise. Golf courses and walking trails within suburban sites will become an integral part of the tourism experience.

The travel trade will remain an important piece of the tourism industry but methods of doing business will change. Customers' use of travel agencies depend on the agencies' expertise and accountability. Tour companies will need to align many of their products with an older audience, providing well-paced, intellectually stimulating tours.

Tourism services will expand with the other sectors. As higher service levels are demanded by consumers, employees will need better customer service skills. Good trainers and quality training programs will be increasingly popular with all service sectors. There is a need for good consumer research and statistics. For smaller businesses, niche marketing will become important as they work against the tidal wave of branding and big business. If brands are to remain competitive, they will have to produce more cost-effective advertising campaigns that clearly identify with their target markets' needs.

John Gow

With a love of skiing and the mountains, it is no wonder that John Gow set his sights high early in life. He began his career in 1964 at Sunshine Village in Banff, Alberta, as a ski instructor and mountain guide. It was soon recognized that his instinctive skill and knowledge base were too great to leave him on the mountain. With his first promotion, he became director of ski school operations. From there he moved to the position of director of marketing for Sunshine Village. Then he became its general manager and, finally, chief executive officer. John Gow was an integral part of the development strategies that led to Sunshine Village's great expansion (including one of the world's largest gondola systems) and its ability to operate at virtual capacity.

By 1981, John reached the pinnacle of success at Sunshine Village. His next move, along with several associates, was to purchase Silver Star Mountain Resort in British Columbia. As president of his own company, John discovered that his responsibilities included not only the day-to-day operations of the resort, but also the challenges of working alongside government agencies, planning for future expansion, and determining how to finance his ideas. How Silver Star Mountain resort has changed under his guidance! What had once been a local ski hill has now become a major resort area for the Okanagan region and all of British Columbia. He added a themed village centre, hotels, restaurants and bars, shops, and special recreation facilities that satisfy the needs of both day visitors and tourists. Recently he expanded the resort,

tripling its skiable acreage, installing two express quad chairlifts, and increasing the vertical drop by 40 percent. Plans for the future include an 18-hole golf course, making Silver Star Mountain Resort a year-round property.

John Gow is not a man to sit around. In Banff, he became an active member of the chamber of commerce, serving on the hospitality board and the municipal council. During his 17 years in Banff, he was a major catalyst in the construction of two housing developments, improving the quality of life for residents who lived and worked in the mountain resort area. Working with the local transportation companies, he formed a partnership with the ski schools, creating a joint marketing program along with ticketing and transportation facilities, which allowed them to penetrate markets in Eastern Canada, Japan, and the United States.

When he made the move to British Columbia, he became even more active. Among the positions he currently fills are chair of the Pacific Rim Institute of Technology and Rendez-Vous Canada, board member with Tourism British Columbia, and past chair of TIAC.

Who is John Gow? He is a man of energy, with a passionate commitment to the ski industry, to the development of the western ski product, and to tourism as a whole. His ability to work with all levels of government and industry and his vision for a sustainable and profitable future have made him one of the most respected voices in Canadian tourism. There are few who can balance life and its challenges as well as John Gow.

Tourism Challenges

Challenges provide opportunities for people to grow and expand their vision. Challenges frequently lead to greater achievement and new inventions. Some challenges are life changing. Where would the world be if physicians did not challenge disease, searching for cures? Some challenges simply make life interesting. As tourism enters the new millennium, many challenges need to be faced. Today's biggest challenge is the continued threat of terrorism. Keeping tourists safe has always been important but now it has become a priority. September 11 has forced Canada to deal with the ongoing problem of fake Canadian passports and has forced the government and the airlines to take additional security precautions.

All eight tourism sectors face a challenging future. Transport Canada must find ways to deal with declining road conditions and the rising costs of travel. At last, the Trans Canada Highway will have two new lanes added between Fredericton and Quebec City. Our airlines must deal with increased congestion at major airports. Many of the smaller and discount carriers are choosing to use airports such as Hamilton as hubs to help curb costs. Rising fuel costs and the aging of Air Canada's fleet will not help our national airline in its battle for cost control. Many question the security surcharge the federal government has added to each airline ticket. Why is the GST, already collected on every airline ticket, not being redirected for this purpose? Are we getting value for our dollar? Security, while tightened at the boarding gate, still remains lax at other airport entry points. The car rental business will need to deal with the declining business market by increasing use of rental cars by the vacation traveller. This means providing a wider assortment of cars and pricing options for the traveller or seeking niche markets such as the demand for specialty vehicles like vans and SUVs. Canadian trains have seen a recent upsurge in traffic and VIA Rail is focusing on providing a higher level of service by training staff and renovating its cars. Many short-haul markets are looking at faster trains in order to better challenge the air system. Cruise lines face a variety of problems: overcrowd-

Expanding Canadian airports and improving Canada's immigration and customs services are important if the country is to remain globally competitive.

(Photo: Paula Kerr.)

ing at popular ports, particularly in the Caribbean; concerns for the environment as ships get bigger and the cruise lines add to their fleet; and passenger safety. In August of 2002, a major cruise line had to deal with a food poisoning outbreak, causing the ship to return to the port of Vancouver. Other problems include dealing with onboard robberies and rape as well as the terrorist threat. Halifax and Vancouver have seen strong growth in this market and will need to expand port services in the near future. Finally, how do the cruise lines reach that 90 percent of North Americans who have never taken a cruise?

Service has been identified as the weakest link in the tourism business and with growing global competition, the industry must focus on service training and education. Using the occupational standards developed by provincial tourism education councils makes training reasonable and easily accessible for even small business operators. The accommodation sector must provide customers with knowledgeable staff; faster, more personal check-in and check-out procedures; and a new awareness of customers with special needs. Hotels must provide an aging boomer market with well-lit facilities, bathrooms ergonomically designed for less agile people, and information in larger print. Analysts predict that over the next 20 years, baby boomers will begin to sell their homes, moving into retirement communities. Already some small hotels have been converted to retirement condominiums, using existing facilities such as commercial kitchens, dining rooms, a pool or exercise area, and meeting spaces. Resorts will need to think in terms of all four seasons. By adding spas, winter activities and special events, they can extend revenue seasons and appeal to a broader clientele.

The food and beverage sector faces a broad spectrum of challenges. Service and training will continue to be priorities. More competition means restaurants will need to use service as a discriminating factor in choice. Legal issues such as alcohol consumption and no smoking bylaws will need creative solutions from restaurateurs. Perhaps the most important challenge is an age-old one—food safety. Scandals continue to plague the industry, including *E. coli* outbreaks and other food poisoning incidents. One of the best ways to ensure safe food handling is to put into place the Hazard Analysis Critical Control Point (HACCP) system. Devised by the U.S. space program to ensure food safety during space missions, this method of ensuring food safety is highly recommended by the Canadian Restaurant and Foodservice Association.

Growth in the attractions and events and conferences sectors must provide tourists with a greater array of sites and events than ever before. Tourists are beginning to look for unique educational experiences with hands-on activities[7] such as learning how to weave, to make wine, or to work a ranch. There is a shortage of trained, experienced event coordinators and meeting planners. The event business gets bigger every year as companies from all industrial sectors recognize the financial returns of a well-planned festivity. The convention market has suffered from September 11, but as planners begin to look for safe sites, Canada has a great opportunity to become a major destination. Can we meet the challenge with newer conference facilities and well-trained staff?

Adventure tourism and outdoor recreation has also seen tremendous growth. As boomers retire, exercise and fresh air becomes an important health issue. They will be looking for destinations that provide a wide variety of physical activities. Young, single travellers are searching for excitement while on vacation and finding it backpacking around the country, hiking in the mountains, and boating on our beautiful lakes and challenging rivers. Even the cruise lines are hopping on the activity wagon, creating on-board golf courses and "rock climbing" experiences. Canada is well positioned to take full advantage of this trend, but will we have the trained personnel to ensure the experience is not only exciting but safe? Canadian colleges and universities now offer a wide variety of adventure tourism courses.

The travel trade faces a quickly changing industry. Use of the Internet by potential customers is slowly eroding business. With many commissions lowered or dropped completely, new streams of revenue must be generated. That great hotelier Cesar Ritz was doing it at the turn of the twentieth century. Now travel agencies must use his techniques, learning as much as they can about customer needs and meeting them in a professional and friendly manner. Keeping customer profiles will be more important than ever. Customers are more likely to return if they feel comfortable and well looked after. Travel agents have more education than any other sectors' work force but now they are expected to know more and work faster than ever before.[8]

Tourism services, an often ignored sector of the industry, will also experience a boom. Why? As the other sectors struggle to keep up with new demands, these support groups become even more important. Architects and designers will need to be more ecologically driven, ensuring new products cause minimum harm to the environment. Research, consulting, and marketing firms, retail outlets, government services, educators, and trainers—these are the unseen backbone of the industry. To fulfill the needs of the industry, these services must find ways for tourism sectors to link together to create a strong, sustainable product. These companies must supply reliable, easily understood information. On the other hand, industry professionals need to learn how to apply the information they receive from tourism services. The tourism services sector is creating a new vision of the Canadian tourism product for an era of change.

summary

The tourism industry has experienced phenomenal growth over the past 50 years. With the retirement of the baby boomers, dramatic growth will continue for the next 20 years. Much of this expansion is due to changes in lifestyle brought about by technological advancements. Although the industry is looking at growth potential, it has also identified challenges. If the industry is to succeed, it must be aware of global trends and must clearly identify the motivations of its markets and be ready to meet their needs and expectations. The industry is gearing up to start a new era and the snapshot of Canada's tourism future looks both bright and exciting!

questions

1. a) Look at the challenges identified by the Canadian Tourism Commission. Rearrange them in order of importance as you see it.

   b) Provide a brief description of the issues.

   c) How do you feel each issue/challenge might best be overcome?

   d) Justify your placement of your first three and last-place challenge.

2. Are the following scenarios examples of unethical behaviour? Explain why or why not.

    a) A customer is given a poolside room instead of the beachside room requested.

    b) Two customers arrive 10 minutes prior to their aircraft's scheduled departure and the agent refuses to board them.

    c) Just as the kitchen is plating the entrée for a 125-person gala banquet, the cook trips and drops 25 tenderloin steaks onto the kitchen floor. The kitchen staff pick them up and continue to serve them, reasoning that what the customers don't know can't hurt them.

    d) The bartender at a local pub gives frequent customers free drinks once a week.

3. List, in order of importance, three lifestyle trends that you believe will affect your chosen sector of the industry. Explain how your business is fulfilling, or might fulfill, these new customer needs.

---

weblinks

www.mcb.co.uk / htgf / analysis

The Hospitality and Tourism Global Forum includes a wealth of information about current issues in tourism; it includes papers, analysis, industry news, and more.

www.tourism.govt.nz

The New Zealand Tourism Policy Group provides a number of its publications online, covering topics such as sustainability and tourism policy.

www.projectplanetcorp.com

Project Planet focuses on sustainable tourism and environmental measures for tourism-industry operators.

There are a number of job-search sites that include tourism-related careers, among them

www.hcareers.com (Hospitality Careers Online)
www.workopolis.com (operated by *The Globe and Mail*)
www.monster.ca

---

notes

1. *Tourism: A Canadian Growth Industry* (Ottawa: Canadian Tourism Commission, 1996).

2. *Webster's II New Riverside University Dictionary* (Boston: Riverside Publishing Co., 1984).

3. www.realontario.ca

4. Peter Yesawich, Trends in the Tourism Industry, address to the TIAC Conference, Jasper, Alberta, November 1996.

5. *The ADitus White Paper.*

6. ctx_news@ctc.cct.ca, September 25, 2002.

7. *The ADitus White Paper.*

8. *Future Skill Requirements in the Retail Travel Industry* (Ottawa: Canadian Tourism Human Resource Council, 1997).

Appendix: Tourism Education Councils

Hospitality Industry Education Advisory Committee (HIEAC)
15225–104th Avenue, Suite 306
Surrey, British Columbia V3R 6Y8
Tel: (604) 930-9770   Fax: (604) 930-9971
e-mail: info@hieac.com
Web site: **www.hieac.com**

ATEC (Alberta's Training for Excellence Corporation)
1600 College Plaza Office Tower
8215– 112th Street NW
Edmonton, Alberta T6G 2C8
Tel: (780) 423-9225   Fax: (780) 437-6655
Toll-free: 1-800-265-1283
e-mail: info@atec.ca
Web site: **www.atec.ca**

Saskatchewan Tourism Education Council (STEC)
Division of Tourism Saskatchewan
101–230 22nd Street East
Saskatoon, Saskatchewan S7K 0E9
Tel: (306) 933-5900   Fax (306) 933-6250
Toll-free: 1-800-331-1529
e-mail: stec@sasktourism.com
Web site: **www.stec.com**

Manitoba Tourism Education Council (MTEC)
Airport Place
Unit 115, 1821 Wellington Avenue
Winnipeg, Manitoba R3H 0G4
Tel: (204) 957-7473   Fax: (204) 956-1700
Toll-free: 1-800-820-6838 (MTEC)
e-mail: general@mtac.ca
Web site: **www.mtec.mb.ca**

Ontario Tourism Education Corporation (OTEC)
21 Four Season's Place, Suite 300
Toronto Ontario M9B 6J8
Tel: (416) 622-1975   Fax: (416) 622-7476
Toll-free: 1-800-557-6832 (Ontario only)
e-mail: info@otec.org
Web site: **www.otec.org**

Conseil Québécois des Ressources Humaines en Tourisme (CQRHT)
boulevard Jacques-Cartier est, bureau 200
Longueuil, Québec J4N 1L7
Tel: (450) 651-1099   Fax: (450) 651-1567
e-mail: info@cqrht.ca
Web site: **www.cqrht.qc.ca**

Tourism Industry Association of New Brunswick (TIANB)
500 Beavercourt Court, PO Box 23001
Fredericton, New Brunswick E3B 7B3
Tel: (506) 458-5646   Fax (506) 459-3634
Toll-free: 1-800-668-5313
e-mail: tianb@nbnet.nb.ca
Web site: **www.tianb.com**

Tourism Industry Association of Nova Scotia Human Resource Council (TIANSHRC)
1099 Marginal Road, Suite 201
Halifax, Nova Scotia B3H 4P7
Tel: (902) 423-4480   Fax: (902) 422-0184
e-mail: information_central/TIANS@tourism.ca
Web site: **www.tians.org**

Tourism Industry Association Of Prince Edward Island (TIAPEI)
25 Queen Street, PO Box 2050
Charlottetown, Prince Edward Island
Tel: (902) 566-5008   Fax (902) 368-3605
e-mail: tiapei@tiapei.pe.ca
Web site: **www.tiapei.pe.ca/**

Hospitality Newfoundland and Labrador (HNL)
107 LeMarchant Road
St. John's, Newfoundland A1C 2H1
Tel: (709) 722-2000   Fax: (709) 722-8104
Toll-free: 1-800-563-0700
e-mail: hospitality@hnl.nf.ca
Web site: **www.hospitality.nf.ca**

Yukon Tourism Education Council (YTEC)
202 Strickland Street, Suite C
Whitehorse, Yukon Y1A 2J8
Tel: (867) 667-4733   Fax (867) 667-2668
e-mail: yukontec@internorth.com
Web site: **ytec.yukon.net**

Northwest Territories Arctic Tourism
P.O. Box 610
Gogacho Building, 47th Street, #4916, 3rd Floor
Yellowknife, Northwest Territories X1A 2N5
Tel: (867) 873-7200   Fax: (867) 873-4059
Toll-free: 1-800-661-0788
e-mail: nwtat@travel.nt.ca
Web site: **www.nwttravel.nt.ca**

Nunavut Tourism
PO Box 1450
Nortex Building
Iqaluit, Nunavut Territory X0A 0H0
e-mail: nunatour@nunanet.com
Web site: **www.nunatour.nt.ca**

Glossary

activation—Guest's level of excitement, alertness, or energy, which is either high or low.

agricultural tourism—A tourism experience that teaches travellers about the agricultural industry in Canada through hands-on farm life experiences.

all-inclusive tour—A tour package that provides the guest with transportation, food and beverage service, entertainment, and lodging for one price. Service charges may also be included.

allergy awareness—Consumer demand to know the ingredients used to create food products, to avoid allergic reactions.

allocentric—A traveller willing to take risks, willing to go without the normal conveniences of life in order to gain a fuller travel experience. These travellers prefer to go where few people have before and are often referred to by marketers as *innovators*, first to try a new travel destination in its development stage.

American plan (AP)—A hotel room rate that includes the room plus three full meals.

amusement park—A centre of entertainment that offers rides, shows, food, candy, and arcades.

aquarium—An aquatic zoo that features a wide variety of fish and sea creatures in tanks for viewing. It may include marine mammals such as porpoises.

art museum—An institution that provides a variety of artwork including sculptures, oils, watercolours, and carvings.

back of the house—Operative employees who do not come into direct contact with guests.

balanced development—A component of the integrated development theory, in which one portion of the development can operate at a loss that is compensated for by a lucrative operation elsewhere in the resort.

base cost per participant—A method for setting the selling price for a tour by taking the cost of transportation, meals, accommodations, and attractions (base cost), then adding a markup to cover promotion cost, salaries, and overhead.

bed-and-breakfast (B&B)—An accommodation that is generally family owned and managed, accommodates three to ten groups per night, and includes a family-style breakfast.

Bermuda plan (BP)—Room rate that includes a full American breakfast: juice, coffee, eggs, sausage/bacon, and toast.

bilateral agreement—In transportation, an agreement between two countries that often deals with the number of flights permitted from each country into a specific airport, the size and capacity of the airplanes, and special fares.

bistro—A small, casual restaurant that serves fresh, eclectic food.

breakout room—Smaller rooms made available for seminars or workshops at a conference.

BritRail pass—A train pass allowing unlimited travel in the British Isles.

buffet house—An "all you can eat" restaurant that offers a wide assortment of hot and cold food, which customers can help themselves to.

bullet train—A high-speed Japanese train.

business guest—An individual travelling for work purposes, who usually has few choices in deciding where, when, how, and how long to travel.

cafeteria—A type of restaurant at which customers can choose their food from a serving line of different dishes, with the portions preset and served by kitchen staff.

campground—The place where campers can set up their tents or park their recreational vehicles.

cannibalization—A situation in which a franchiser allows two independent units to locate too near each other, causing loss of revenue.

Canadian Heritage—The federal department responsible for managing two major divisions affecting Canada's tourism industry: Parks Canada (our National Park system) and the Cultural Development and Heritage division, which oversees all of Canada's national historic sites, heritage canal and river systems, national battlefields, museums, galleries, libraries and archives, and cultural activities. The National Capital Commission (NCC) also reports to this department.

Canrailpass—A train pass that allows unlimited travel on VIA trains over specific travel periods; can be purchased by both domestic and foreign tourists.

carrying capacity—The maximum number of people who can use a site with only acceptable alteration to the physical environment and with only acceptable decline in the quality of experience gained by subsequent visitors.

cash bar—Alcohol service at a banquet at which guests pay for the alcohol consumed.

casino gambling—Gambling including slot machines, roulette, craps, blackjack, poker, and other games of chance.

catalytic development—Development of a destination in which a single developer encourages complementary businesses in and around the property.

centralized development—A component of catalytic development; refers to the major developer who provides the basic facilities, major accommodation units, and promotion for the destination.

certification—Industry recognition of individuals who have demonstrated their competencies for a particular occupation as they relate to occupational standards.

certified travel counsellor (CTC)—A person who has satisfactorily completed a certification process provided by the Canadian Institute of Travel Counsellors.

chain ownership—A single corporate identity that operates more than one property, with all properties reporting to corporate headquarters.

chamber of commerce—A city organization that promotes industry and retail development and markets tourism to the city.

channel of distribution—Where a product is sold; "place" in the four P's of marketing.

charter—A bus, plane, or ship rented for the purpose of transporting people from one location to another, usually at lower rates than regularly scheduled rates.

children's museum—A museum that involves young children in activities to educate and entertain them. May be one component of a larger museum.

circle trip—A type of round trip in which the route taken to the destination differs from the route taken from the destination.

civic event—Event sponsored by a government organization (e.g., swearing in a new prime minister, Remembrance Day).

clustering—Locating a variety of tourism sites and products in one area to create easy access for visitors.

coattail development—Development of a destination that occurs naturally, without community planning. A lack of common theme often means duplication of services and general lack of direction for the destination.

code of ethics—A system of beliefs based on the values of right and wrong in a specific culture.

coffee house—A type of restaurant that serves a variety of specialty coffees from around the world but little food.

commercial food service—A division of the food-service industry that serves the public and is available to anyone wishing to eat out.

commission—The percentage of a selling price paid to a retailer by a supplier (e.g., an airline paying to a travel agency).

common currency—The use of credit cards, traveller's cheques, automated banking, and currency exchange machines to allow travellers easy access to money and credit while on vacation.

condominium—An individually owned apartment-style unit located in an area filled with recreational amenities; can be rented out to other travellers when not occupied by the owner.

conference—A large meeting where delegates from the same industry or occupation come together to exchange ideas, learn, and network.

conference appointment—Permission to conduct business in a travel agency.

conference centre—A location specifically designed for meetings that provides a quiet, working environment for a conference and its delegates. Conference centres have accommodations within the complex.

conference hotel—A hotel with conference facilities that caters to large groups, usually in the downtown area of major cities.

confirmed reservation—An oral or written confirmation by a hotel that a room has been reserved usually with an agreed upon time of arrival (e.g. 6 p.m.); also called *tentative reservation.*

consolidator—An operator that purchases a large number of airline seats every year from individual airlines at a low price, which it then sells to tour operators and travel agents at discounted prices.

consortium—A group of independent businesses who work together for a common purpose (e.g., independently owned travel agencies who promote their products through the brand name of GIANTS).

continental plan (CP)—A hotel room rate that includes the room and a continental breakfast.

contract food service—A division of the food-service industry that serves a specific clientele, not the general public; found in establishments whose main purpose is not to serve food, such as museums, stadiums, airlines.

convention—A large meeting where delegates from different occupations come together to share ideas and achieve some form of consensus.

convention and visitor bureau (CVB)—A municipal or private organization that promotes tourism and provides convention facilities and informational services for visitors to the city.

convention centre—A location specifically built to handle groups of more than 1000 people but that provides no accommodations.

corporate rates—Reduced rates given to companies to encourage sales.

corporate travel agency—An agency that deals almost exclusively with business travel arrangements as opposed to leisure travel.

cost for use—A type of tour pricing in which each separate component of the tour is priced with a markup, and tour participants only pay for what is used.

costing—The process of determining the total cost of a package, such as a tour, for a specific number of customers.

couponing—Promotion of a restaurant, etc., through coupons offering discounts.

Crown land—Land that is not privately owned. Crown land may be owned by the province or by the federal government but unlike protected park lands, it often does not fall under specific protective legislation. Much of Canada's wilderness is designated Crown land.

cuisine tourism—Tourism that focuses on culinary products, such as a tour of wineries, a short course at a cooking school, or a series of lectures on foods of a region, combined with a local food festival.

cultural motivators—A desire to know and learn more about the music, architecture, food, art, folklore, or religion of other people.

cultural tourism—See *heritage tourism.*

customer profile—Information about customers used by service providers to identify client needs and expectations.

day rate—A hotel room rate charged between 9 a.m. and 8 p.m. (no overnight stay).

day tour—A bus tour that lasts less than 24 hours and has no accommodation arrangements, usually in one specific region.

demand—The need or desire for goods and services; the number of people who wish to purchase a product.

demographics—Statistics that include age, marital status, occupation, sex, income, and place of residence, used for understanding who the travellers are to a particular site.

destination life cycle—The stages through which a destination moves: conception, growth, maturity, and decline.

destination marketing organization (DMO)—An organization that is responsible for creating a marketing plan for a destination and promoting it. The CTC is Canada's federal DMO, with CVBs usually representing a city or region.

direct flight—A flight that carries a traveller from one destination to another, making at least one stop along the route.

discretionary income—The money that one may spend as one pleases.

discretionary time—Time away from work and other obligations.

domestic tourist—A person travelling in the country in which he or she resides who stays for a period of 24 hours and travels at least 80 km from home.

double double—A hotel room with two double beds.

dude or guest ranch—An accommodation that is either a working ranch where guests help in the everyday work, or a luxury ranch resort for horseback riding, swimming, hiking, or tennis.

ecotourism—Responsible travel aimed at learning about the interrelationships and physiology of organisms and their environment; focuses on nature-related experiences that help people appreciate and understand our natural resources and their conservation.

ecotourist—A person who believes in responsible travel to natural areas and who aids in conserving the environment and improving the welfare of local people.

elastic demand—Demand that changes significantly when price changes (e.g., demand drops when price rises).

empty nest—The life stage of married couples whose children have grown and left home.

escorted tour—An organized tour led by a professional tour guide.

ethnic restaurant—A restaurant that serves food from a specific culture, country, or region.

Eurailpass—A ticket to travel by rail in 16 European countries over a specified time period; sold only to non-Europeans.

European plan (EP)—A hotel rate that includes the room, with no meals.

excursionist—Any person who travels at least 40 km from the place of residence, stays less than 24 hours, and is not commuting to work or school or operating as part of a crew on a train, airplane, truck, bus, or ship.

exhibition—At a convention or congress, a display of goods and services used by the delegates in their work place.

external locus of control—A personality dimension of believing that events are determined by other powerful individuals, fate, or chance.

extrovert—An individual who is outgoing and uninhibited in interpersonal situations.

fair—A special event with a theme, such as an agricultural fair, historical fair, trade fair, or World's Fair.

familiarization tour (fam tour)—A free or discounted trip for travel professionals, designed to acquaint them with the area in order to help them choose a convention site.

family entertainment centre—Indoor facilities (usually built in malls) that offer video games, carnival games, miniature golf, electric go-karts, miniature merry-go-rounds, and other amusements.

family life stage—A person's position in his or her lifetime.

family plan—A plan in which there is no extra charge for children under a given age staying with their parents at a hotel.

family-style restaurant—Restaurant, often located in the suburbs, that offers full, fast, and friendly service, "comfort" food, and a welcoming environment for children.

fast-food restaurant—Restaurant where customers order and pick up their own food and clear their tables when finished. Prices are low and menu is limited.

festival—A public celebration centred on a theme of local, regional, or national interest or importance.

fine dining—Restaurants that provide elegant décor, high-quality food prepared from scratch, and professional, attentive service.

fly/coach tour—a tour that combines airfare with an escorted bus tour.

forecasting—The process of attempting to determine future demand in an area.

foreign tourist—A person visiting a country other than the one in which he or she usually resides and staying for a period of at least 24 hours.

franchise—A business purchased as a turn-key operation, with everything in place.

franchise advisory councils (FACs)—Bodies that represent franchisees, providing them with a forum through which to address concerns with the franchise contract or the franchiser.

franchisee—The purchaser of a franchise operation.

franchiser—The company that owns the franchise rights to a product and sells it to other operator/investors.

Freedoms of the Air—Global rules regulating aircraft/airline activity dealing with rights of passage for an airplane, traffic rights, and the granting of special rights to certain airlines under specific circumstances; also known as *rights of the air*.

front of the house—Employees who deal actively with customers, usually in a hotel or a restaurant setting.

front-line training—Training provided for staff members who deal directly with the public.

full-service travel agency—A travel agency staffed and equipped to answer and serve all categories of traveller needs.

functional form—Within integrated development, adherence to a common theme.

fundraising event—Public event that encourages people to participate in order to raise money for a specific cause or organization.

gateway—The welcoming sign to a destination informing tourists they have arrived; an information centre near the edge of town that provides tourists with brochures and help in arranging their stay.

gateway airport—Airport from which major international flights arrive and depart.

gateway city—The city where a tour begins.

greenwashing—Using the "eco-label" to lure unsuspecting tourists into believing your company uses sound environmental practices.

ground/land package—A tour that includes the land arrangements of a tour but no air transportation.

guaranteed reservation—A room reserved with payment by the guest (by credit card) regardless of whether the guest arrives.

guests—Another term for tourists.

hallmark event—Major happening that brings tourists from around the world to a destination and has a huge economic impact on the community (e.g., the Olympics).

hard adventure—Tourism activity that takes place in an unusual, exotic, remote, or wilderness setting and involves some form of unconventional means of transportation, high or low levels of physical activity, and some risk or challenge.

haute cuisine—An elegant and expensive style of restaurant noted for its outstanding food, opulent atmosphere, and highly trained staff.

heritage tourism—Immersion in the natural history, human heritage, arts, philosophy, and institutions of another region or country. A trip that educates the visitor on the architecture, food, folklore, or religion of another culture. Also called *cultural tourism*.

high-speed transportation (HST) system—A train that can travel at 250 km an hour.

higher-value tourist—A tourist looking for upscale destinations and experiences and willing to pay more.

historic site—A place of special historical interest.

historical museum—A museum depicting some historical event or place.

hospitality of host—An intangible concept referring to the genuine warmth extended to visitors by the host destination.

hospitality suite—A hotel room with a parlour that has a bar and sitting area for guests.

hosted tour—A tour on which participants travel between destinations without a guide but are met at each destination by a host guide from that community.

hostel—A lodge with communal washrooms and bedrooms designed for four to twenty people.

hosts—People, communities, or regions that entertain visiting guests.

hotel—Accommodation that provides access to guest rooms from a central lobby.

HST—See *high-speed transportation system*.

hub and spoke—A pattern of transportation in which an airline uses one airport as the collecting point for incoming and outgoing flights. This system is also used in the motor coach industry.

inbound tour—A tour that brings guests from a foreign country to Canada, generating jobs and revenue for Canadians.

inbound tourist—See *foreign tourist*.

incentive travel—The practice of using a trip as an award for performing to a certain set of standards.

independent restaurateur—An individual owner of a restaurant.

industrial tourism—Tourism that includes visits to industrial sites, such as the oil fields of Alberta or the salmon fisheries of British Columbia.

inelastic demand—Demand that does not change, or changes very little, with a price increase or decrease (e.g., gas).

infrastructure—A basic system that includes facilities such as roads, sewage systems, electricity, and water supply.

integrated development—The development of a large parcel of land by a single individual or company to the exclusion of all other developers.

interdependency—A component of catalytic development; entrepreneurial activities of other businesses within the development succeed because the initial developer succeeds, and the initial developer succeeds because of the entrepreneurs. Each is dependent on the other.

interline connection—Air travel between two destinations during which the traveller is forced to change airline companies in order to complete the journey.

internal locus of control—The belief that people are in charge of what happens in their lives.

International Air Transport Association (IATA)—A privately run international organization whose principal function is to facilitate the movement of persons and goods from and to any point on the world air network by any combination of routes.

International Civil Aviation Organization (ICAO)—An agency of the United Nations that ensures that the development of the airline system is both safe and orderly.

interpersonal motivator—A reason for travel based on family and friends and the seeking of comradeship

introvert—A person who is more concerned with personal thoughts and feelings than those of others.

isolation—A component of integrated development; a development is located away from existing settlements.

IT number—An identification number for an approved tour that identifies the operator, air carrier, type of tour, and year approved.

jetway—A hallway that joins a plane to the airport terminal.

joint venture—An arrangement between two partners in which one partner supplies the expertise in a business and the other partner provides the financial investment.

kilometre cap—Limitation used by rental car agencies that allows a certain number of kilometres for a flat fee each day.

landing fee—Fee charged by an airport to an airline for the right to land and use airport services.

land package—See *ground/land package.*

"le grand tour"—An educational tour of Europe taken by young English noblemen in the seventeenth and eighteenth centuries.

leakage—A community's need to import workers and/or goods in order to sustain its tourism industry.

living history museum—A museum in which people act the parts of historical characters.

load factor—The percentage of seats filled on an airplane by paying or revenue-producing passengers.

loading apron—The cement parking area for the aircraft, located at the terminal gate, in which planes are serviced and fuelled, and bags are loaded and unloaded.

low-impact camping—A type of camping in which every item carried in is carried out; every item created on the trip is carried out; enclosed fires and biodegradable products are used; no souvenirs are taken from the area; and the area is left virtually untouched and ready for the next group of adventurers.

LRC (light, rapid, comfortable)—VIA Rail service between Quebec and Windsor, which is provided by new trains. Passengers are offered a choice of service level and price.

management contract—A method of hotel management and operation in which one company owns the property and another company operates it.

marketing—A continual, sequential process through which management plans, researches, implements, controls, and evaluates activities designed to satisfy both customers' needs and wants and the organization's objectives.

marketing mix—Controllable factors that may be selected to help satisfy customer needs or wants (product, price, place, promotion).

marketing plan—A written plan used to guide an organization's marketing activities for a period of one year or less.

market match—The satisfactory situation in which the product on offer meets the needs of the target market.

market performance—Global product trends, growth rates, and past and current demand for the product.

market segmentation—The division of the overall market into groups of people who share common characteristics or have similar needs.

Meeting Professionals International (MPI)—A professional association of North American meeting planners.

megamall—A large shopping and entertainment centre offering everything from retail stores and restaurants to indoor theme parks, game rooms, and small theatres for live performances.

menu—A listing of all the products a restaurant sells.

midcentric—The halfway point in a tourist personality classification system between allocentrics and psychocentrics. Most people fit into this category.

MNEs—The motivation, needs, and expectations of travellers.

modified American plan (MAP)—A hotel room rate that includes the room plus breakfast and lunch or dinner.

motel—Tourist accommodation that provides free parking and access to a guest's room directly from the parking lot.

motivator—A "promoter of action" whose purpose is to fulfill a need or want.

motor coach package—A bus tour that lasts from 3 to 30 days and includes one or more of these four components: accommodations, meals, attractions, sightseeing.

multiplier effect—Ripple effect; the mechanism whereby the benefits of tourism dollars spread through a community, profiting businesses and residents not directly involved in tourism.

multi-unit corporate restaurant—A chain of restaurants in which one person or company controls all the units; typically, all restaurants have similar décor, menu, and management style.

museum—A building that displays a wide assortment of memorabilia ranging from artworks, historical, or scientific items to agricultural tools or cartoons.

national parks system—A country-wide system of representative natural areas of Canadian significance. By law they are protected for public understanding, appreciation, and enjoyment while being maintained in an unimpaired state for future generations. Under the jurisdiction of the federal government department called Canadian Heritage/Parks Canada, the system includes 41 national parks.

national tourism office (NTO)—An office established by the federal government in one of a number of international locations to promote tourism in Canada.

natural resources—The physical means of supporting and attracting tourists, such as land and agriculture, a habitable climate, a water supply, and natural beauty.

niche (target) marketing—Creating products to fulfill the needs of a specific segment of the total market; also known as *target marketing.*

nonconsumptive tourism—A type of tourism in which the tourist takes nothing away from the destination and leaves nothing behind.

nonstop flight—A flight that does not stop between point of departure and destination.

occupancy rate—The average percentage of rooms rented.

occupational standards—Documents that outline the skills, knowledge, and attitudes that an individual must demonstrate and practise to be deemed competent in a given job.

oceanarium—An aquatic zoo located on the shores of an ocean that features saltwater fish and animals such as dolphins, seals, whales, and shore birds.

online connection—Air travel between two destinations during which the traveller is forced to change aircraft but not airline in order to complete the journey.

open bar—Alcohol service at a banquet at which the host pays for the alcohol consumed.

open-jaw trip—A type of air travel in which travellers can fly to one city but return from a different city.

Open Skies—Bilateral agreement between the United States and Canada for North American airlines, which provides tourists with greater choice of carrier and types of flights.

Orient Express—Operating from 1833 to 1977, the famous train that travelled from Paris to Istanbul, carrying royalty, political leaders, the very rich, and the very powerful.

outbound tour—A tour in which Canadians travel to a foreign country.

outbound tourist—A Canadian who travels to a foreign country as a tourist.

outdoor recreation—Activities that occur outdoors, such as hiking, backpacking, canoeing, sailing, kayaking, bicycling, horseback riding, wildlife viewing, and heli-hiking.

overbooking—The practice of selling more hotel rooms, airplane seats, etc., than exist, on the assumption that not all reservations will be picked up. This practice can leave guests without a room at the hotel or a seat on the airline.

overnight/short tour—A bus tour that is two days long.

override—A bonus or extra commission earned for doing volume business.

pari-mutuel gambling—A betting pool in which those who bet on the winners of the first three places share the total amount minus a percentage for management.

partially escorted tour—

partnerships—Alliances formed among various sectors of the tourism industry. By working together they ensure a better quality product for the consumer and shared business opportunities for the industry.

people resources—The talents and abilities of people in the community.

physical motivator—A reason for travelling to an area related to health, including relaxation, sports participation, recreation, medical exams, or health treatments.

place—One of the marketing P's, referring to the location in which a product is sold; also known as *channel of distribution*.

pleasure guest—Someone travelling for pleasure on discretionary time and money.

price—One of the marketing P's: the amount charged for a product, which includes all costs and profit.

pricing—The process of deciding the amount each customer should pay to cover costs, including a markup, operating expenses, and profit.

product—One of the marketing P's—the good or service being sold.

product capacity—The number of facilities, the accommodations/rooms available, and the transportation system capacity.

product/market match—See *market match*.

promotion—One of the marketing P's, referring to advertising and other means of generating customer interest in the product.

psychocentric—A traveller who enjoys travel only when it is just like home and is often anxious; the "armchair" traveller.

psychographics—Marketing information based on people's activities, opinions, motives, behaviours, and interests.

pub—Small casual restaurant that emulates an English, Irish, or Scottish bar, including the ambiance, the menu, and the types of beer and whiskey available.

pull factors—Tangible reasons for travel choices, such as friends, mountains, and beaches.

push factors—Intangible reasons for travel choices, such as the need to escape, the need for culture, or a need for physical fitness.

qualitative forecasting—The use of experts and their accumulated experience and knowledge to predict the likely outcome of events.

quantitative forecasting—The analysis of numerical data (current and historical) to help predict the future.

rack rate—A standard day rate for a hotel room.

rapid development—A component of integrated development; refers to the speed at which development can occur because a single developer can make decisions quickly.

recreational sports—Major sports that affect the tourism industry, including skiing, golf, tennis, and water sports.

referral system—A marketing strategy whereby hotels band together, receiving instant brand-name recognition and access to a worldwide reservation system and national and global advertising campaigns (e.g., Best Western).

REIT (Real Estate Investment Trusts)—A company that buys hotel/resort properties then sell shares of the property on the stock market.

Rendez-Vous Canada—A trade show that brings together Canadian tourism suppliers and international tour operators.

resort—A destination hotel that is usually located in the countryside, near water or the mountains. Resorts provide their guests with a wide variety of outdoor recreational activities, indoor services such as spas, pools, and workout rooms, and a variety of in-house dining experiences.

resort hotel—A hotel, usually located in a natural or wilderness setting, that provides high-quality rooms, food service options, and a wide variety of entertainment and outdoor activities.

revenue performance—Past and projected growth levels and estimated future revenues.

round trip—An airline routing that originates in a city, goes to a destination, and returns to the original city.

run-of-the-house rate—A discount rate for block bookings.

same-day visitor—See *excursionist*.

scheduled air carriers—Airplanes that operate on defined routes, whether domestic or international, for which licences have been granted by the government or governments concerned.

scientific museum—A museum centred on some study of science ranging from dinosaur bones to space ships.

secondary developers—Developers who build complementary facilities near a primary development, such as a major resort.

seminar—An informal meeting in which participants share ideas, knowledge, and expertise under the supervision of a leader or presenter.

sense of place—The special feeling of a destination, created by its unique feature(s), and used in marketing it.

Shinkansen—A Japanese bullet train that connects major Japanese cities and operates at speeds of 200 km per hour.

sightseeing tour—See *day tour*.

single—A hotel room occupied by one person.

site inspection—First-hand view of a potential conference site by the organizers to determine whether it meets the group's needs.

site specific—a museum located where the event took place.

soft adventure—outdoor activities, such as hiking and snorkeling, with a sense of adventure but little risk. They are usually less strenuous than hard adventure and no pretraining is required. If equipment is needed, it is supplied by the organizing company.

spa—A hotel or resort that encourages healthy, rejuvenating activities such as massage therapy, body wraps, steam baths, aerobic exercise classes, etc. As part of the vacation package, guests often are provided with low-calorie gourmet meals.

special event—A one-time or infrequently occurring event outside the normal program or activities of the sponsoring or organizing body.

special interest cruise—A cruise that focuses on a specific topic of interest, usually from an educational standpoint, such as ecotourism, history, opera.

specialty restaurant—A type of restaurant that serves one kind of food, such as chicken or ribs.

specialty travel agency—An agency that specializes in a particular type of travel, such as adventure travel or cruises.

spectator sporting event—A sporting event that has audience audience appeal, such as professional hockey, baseball, or basketball.

status and prestige motivators—Reasons to travel related to a need for recognition, attention, appreciation, and good reputation; same as social and ego factors.

step-on guide—A sightseeing guide who has particular knowledge about the history, people, and events that have shaped the region and who is specifically trained to show the sights of the city.

suite—A hotel room with one or more bedrooms and a sitting room or parlour.

summit—an international meeting of high-level government leaders.

supply—The amount of product available.

suprastructure—All of the buildings located at the destination; that is, structures that are "built up" from the ground such as lodging facilities, restaurants, terminals, and stores.

sustainable tourism—When tourism development and operations meet the needs of current tourists and host regions while protecting and enhancing opportunities for the future.

target marketing—Selecting a market segment for marketing attention. Also known as *niche marketing*.

taxiway—The lane used by an aircraft to travel between the air terminal and runway.

tentative reservation—See *confirmed reservation*.

theme cruise—A cruise that focuses on a particular event or topic (e.g., Super Bowl Cruise, Rock and Roll Cruise); also called *special-interest cruise*.

theme park—A family entertainment centre oriented to a particular subject or historical area that combines the continuity of costuming and architecture with entertainment and merchandise to create a fantasy-provoking atmosphere.

theme restaurant—Restaurant that "transports" customers to a different time or place through ambiance, server costumes, menu, and entertainment reflecting the theme (e.g., Medieval Times).

time poverty—Having too much to do and too little time.

time-sharing—Buying a vacation segment, usually of two weeks, in a condominium unit.

tour operator—A company that contracts with and pays in advance for services provided by hotels, transportation companies, and other suppliers in order to create a tour package.

tour wholesaler—A company that contracts for space with hotels, transportation companies, and other suppliers to create a tour package. Historically it differs from a tour operator because no money changes hands until the space is purchased by a client. Today, there is no noticeable difference between the two types of operation.

tourism—The activities of persons travelling to and staying in places outside their usual environment for not more than one consecutive year for leisure, business, and other purposes.

tourism education council (TEC)—Organizations with provincial mandates to stimulate and coordinate the development of tourism education in their provinces.

tourism illiteracy—The condition of not knowing or understanding the benefits of the tourism industry.

tourist court—Tourist accommodation that provides customers with a small cabin and a parking space.

tourist dollars—Revenue produced by the tourism industry.

trade show—A marketing and sales tool used by many industries to display and sell their products.

transfer—Any change in transportation, between modes or within the same mode, during a journey.

transportation systems—The vehicles that use the infrastructure of a destination.

travel deficit—The difference that occurs when the dollars spent by tourists choosing to vacation outside their country (outbound tourists) exceeds the revenue generated by foreign tourists (inbound tourists) who visit the country.

trend—Current style or preference; in tourism, a popular destination or activity.

trend analysis—The use of historical data to predict future trends.

trinketization—The process of producing and selling cheap, mass-produced, imported goods as if they were genuine artifacts of local culture.

trip—Any travel that takes a person 80 km away from his or her place of residence for any reason other than a commute to work or school, travel in an ambulance, to a hospital or clinic, or a trip that is longer than one year.

turn down service—Service provided by luxury hotels, bedspread is folded down and a chocolate placed on the pillow.

twin—A hotel room with two single beds.

unescorted tour—A tour in which the group travels without a company representative.

UNESCO World Heritage Site—A place designated by the United Nations Educational, Scientific, and Cultural Organization in recognition of its outstanding universal value.

unique selling proposition—The one identifier for a destination that makes it unique; the destination's sense of place.

unlimited kilometres—A car rental package that charges travellers a flat fee regardless of distance driven.

value—The customer's mental estimate of the worth of a product.

variety—Change or novelty, which the guest either seeks or avoids.

VIA Rail Canada—A Crown corporation, created by the merger of Canadian National Railways and Canadian Pacific Railway, responsible for all long-distance passenger rail traffic in Canada.

virtual reality centre—An entertainment centre similar to an FEC but that focuses on interactive computer games and programs.

Visit Canada—A trade show that introduces travel writers from around the world to the Canadian tourism product.

visitor—A generic term used for both domestic and foreign tourists in Canada.

visitor use—The total number of tourists or excursionists to visit a destination or attraction or to attend an event over a specified period of time.

walking—The practice of sending guests who have reservations that cannot be honoured to other available hotels.

weekend rate—Special discounted rates used by hotels that rely upon corporate business during the week. These discounted rates encourage business people to bring their families in for a weekend vacation or encourage locals to use the hotel and its services as a quick "weekend getaway".

workshop—A small group session in which participants learn new skills or techniques.

World Heritage Site—see *UNESCO World Heritage Site*.

Index

A3XX, 94
Aboriginal tourism, 290
Aboriginal Tourism Team Canada
    (ATTC), 279
Acadian Railway company, 103
ACCESS (ACTA/CITC Canadian
    Educational Standards System),
    20
accessibility, as travel barrier, 35
accommodations sector
    see also lodging industry
    Canada select accommodations pro-
        gram rating categories, 146
    career opportunities, 148–149
    classifications within, 137–144
    described, 4
    marketing, 144–148
    trends, 294
activation, 30
adventure tourism
    backpacking, 227
    ecotourism, 225, 228–230
    greenwashing, 228
    hard adventure, 225, 227
    low-impact camping, 228
    nonconsumptive tourism, 228
    risk management, 230
    soft adventure, 225, 227
    sports, 227
    sustainable tourism, 229
    travel agencies, 261
    West Coast Trail (WCT), 226–227
    white-water rafting, 227
adventure tourism and outdoor recre-
        ation sector
    adventure tourism, 225–230
    career opportunities, 241–242
    described, 5
    outdoor recreation, 230–234
    September 11, impact of, 26, 223
    trends, 295
adventure tours, 254
advertising, 148, 170
age, as travel barrier, 36
agricultural tourism, 5
Air Canada, 85, 86, 87
air carrier airports, 89
Air France, 94
Air Transport Association of Canada
    (ATAC), 264
Airbus Consortium, 94
airfares, 91
airline associations, 92–94
airline terminology, 90–91

airlines
    airfares, 91
    airports, 89–90
    alliances, 86
    Canada's air system, 88–89
    charter air services, 89
    code sharing, 86
    commuter airlines, 86
    deregulation, 86–87, 263
    discount airlines, 86
    "feeder" airlines, 86
    future of passenger flight, 94–95
    history of air travel in Canada,
        84–87
    hub and spoke system, 87
    international air transport system,
        92
    load factor, 91
    "no frills" airlines, 86
    reservations, 92
    scheduled air carriers, 89
    September 11, impact of, 87
    supersonic air travel, 94
    terminology, 90–91
    transfer, 87
airport hotels, 138
airports, 89–90, 119
Alberta Tourism Education Council
    (ATEC), 54
all-inclusive tours, 254
allergy awareness, 158
allocentric, 29
the *Allouette*, 102
alternative action plans, 71–72
amenities, 256
American Automobile Association
    (AAA), 131
American plan, 147
American Youth Hostel, Inc., 144
amusement parks, 179, 191–192
aquariums, 189–190
ARA Consulting Group Inc., 78
area beautification, 43
Armstrong, Peter, 103
art museums, 184–185
association meeting market
    characteristics, 210–211
    conference centres, 212–214
    convention centres, 214–215
    meeting sites, 212
Association of Canadian Travel Agents
    (ACTA), 20, 54, 264, 279
Association of Tourism Professionals
    (ATP), 280

Associations touristiques regionales
    associées du Québec, 54
attraction facility guide, 200
attractions sector
    Canadian Heritage, 178–179
    career opportunities, 200
    described, 5
    history of, 179–182
    key factors to success, 195–200
    private/commercial attractions,
        190–195
    public and nonprofit attractions,
        183–190
    September 11, impact of, 182
    trends, 295
automobile travel
    car rental industry, 98–100
    popularity of, 97
    reasons for, 97
    trends, 97–98
Avis, 98
Avis, Warren E., 98

back of the house staff, 135
backpacking, 227
balanced development, 74
Banff (Alberta), 75
banquets, 167
barriers to tourism acceptance
    congestion, 42
    crime and unwanted behaviour, 41
    diversion of government funds, 42
    increases in costs of services, 42
    inflation, 42
    leakage, 42
    local resentment, 42
    pollution, 42
    seasonality, 42
barriers to travel
    accessibility, 35
    age, 36
    cost, 34
    distance, 35
    fear, 37
    health, 36
    lack of time, 35
    travel tastes and experiences, 35–36
base cost per participant, 252
Baumgarten, Jean-Claude, 26
Bay of Pigs, 93
B.C. tourism
    constraints on growth, 80
    financial benefits, 79
    higher value tourists, 79

Japanese tourists, 78
market performance, 78
methodology for assessment of product areas, 78
product capacity, 78
revenue performance, 78
seasonality, 79
sustainability, 78
Tourism Industry Product Overview, 78
tourist types, 79
vision, criteria for defining, 78–79
visitor experience, quality of, 79
visitor use, 78
Bearskin Airlines, 86
bed-and-breakfast (B&B), 142–143
Bell 609, 95
benefits of tourism
area beautification, 43
better choices in services, 42
cultural preservation, 42
cultural support, 43–44
economic diversification, 42
educational facilities, 43
enhanced travel, 43
favourable world image, 43
financial benefits, 79
foreign capital, 43
infrastructure improvements, 43
modernization, 43
recreational facilities, 43
societies, effects on, 43–44
tax revenues, 43
Bermuda plan, 147
bilateral agreements, 92
bistros, 162
the *Blue Train*, 106
Boom, Bust and Echo, 8
breakout room, 211
British Airways, 94
BritRail pass, 106
Buchanan Report on tourism, 20–21, 56
Budget Car Rental, 98
budget hotels, 140
buffet house, 164
bullet train, 106
bus transit system, 119
buses. *See* motor coach travel
business guests, 26–27
business hotels, 140
Business Improvement District (BID) approval, 77
business market, 26–27

cabotage, 93
Cabrita, Judith, 51–52
cafeterias, 165

Calm Air, 86
campgrounds, 144
camping, 233
Canada Customs and Revenue Agency, 47, 274
Canada select accommodations program rating categories, 146
Canada's Wonderland Park, 182
the *Canadian*, 102
Canadian Air Transport Security Authority (CATSA), 87
Canadian Airlines International (CAI), 86
Canadian Automobile Association (CAA), 131
Canadian Federation of Chefs de Cuisine (CFCC), 54, 279
Canadian Food Service Executive Association (CFSEA), 279
Canadian Government Travel Bureau, 45
Canadian Heritage, 47, 178–179
Canadian Institute of Travel Counsellors (CITC), 54, 264
Canadian National Railways, 85, 102
Canadian organizations/associations, 19–20
Canadian Pacific Airlines (CP Air), 85, 86
Canadian Pacific Railway, 40, 102
Canadian Restaurant and Foodservices Association (CRFA), 54, 159, 279
Canadian tourism
Canada-U.S. border, after September 11, 46
Canadian Government Office of Tourism (CGOT), 45
Canadian Government Travel Bureau, 45
Department of Regional Industrial Expansion (DRIE), 45
federal government and, 47–50
history of, 44–46
industry numbers, 48
national tourism office (NTO), 45
Tourism Canada, 45
Canadian Tourism Commission (CTC), 11, 19, 47–48
Canadian Tourism Human Resource Council (CTHRC), 19, 20, 55, 223
Canadian tourism product. *See* tourism product
Canadian Tourism Research Institute (CTRI), 20
Canadian World Heritage Sites, 187

Canadians travelling abroad, distribution of, 12
CanJet, 86
cannibalization, 133
Canrailpass, 105
car rental industry
corporate rates, 100
dynamics of business, 98–99
fly-and-drive vacation package, 100
kilometre cap, 100
locations, 98, 100
marketing strategies, 100
origins of, 98
price factor, 100
top four rental agencies, 98
unlimited kilometres, 100
careers
see also job descriptions
in accommodations sector, 148–149
in adventure tourism and outdoor recreation sector, 241–242
in attractions sector, 200
in events and conferences sector, 218
food and beverage sector, 172–174
steps to success, 18
tourism as good career choice, 17–18
in tourism services sector, 284
in transportation, 120–121
in travel trade sector, 266
carrying capacity, 237
cash bar, 167
casino gambling, 193
casual dining, 157
catalytic development, 74, 75
centralized development, 75
certification, 55, 56
certified travel counsellor (CTC), 264
certified travel manager (CTM), 264
chain agencies, 262
chain ownership, 132
chambers of commerce, 20, 276
channel of distribution, 60
charter, 89, 108
charter air services, 89
charter yachts, sailboats and houseboats, 115
children, dining out with, 157
children's museum, 186
circle trip, 90
circuses, 206
Citizenship and Immigration Canada, 47, 273
civic events, 207
clients with disabilities, 261
clustering, 197

Coach USA, 107
coastlines, 239
coattail development, 74, 75–77
code of ethics, 291
code sharing, 86
coffee houses, 165
commercial attractions. *See* private/
commercial attractions
commercial food service
banquets, 167
bistros, 162
buffet house, 164
cafeterias, 165
coffee houses, 165
described, 161
dining, 162
ethnic restaurants, 163
family-style restaurant, 163
fast-food restaurants, 164
fine dining, 162
haute cuisine, 162
hotel food and beverage service,
166–167
pubs, 162
specialty restaurant, 163
theme restaurants, 164
commission, 248
Committee of Statistics Experts of the
League of Nations, 10
common currency, 9
common theme, lack of, 75
commuter airlines, 86
competition
car rental industry, 98–99
in coattail development, 77
increase in, 53
Competition Act, 86
computers, and growth in tourism, 7
conception, 67
condominiums, 141
Conference Board of Canada, 20
conference centres, 212–214
conference hotels, 140
conference service manager, 218
conference terminology, 211
conferences, 210–217
confirmed reservation, 148
congestion, as tourism acceptance barrier, 42
consolidator, 250
consortiums, 262
consulting services, 282
Continental plan, 147
contract/institutional food service,
161, 167–169
convention and meeting market, 139
convention and visitor bureau (CVB),
20, 276, 277

convention centres, 214–215
conventions, 210–217
corporate meeting market, 215–217
corporate rates, 100, 138
corporate travel agency, 260
cost for use, 252
costing, 252
costs
increases in, as tourism acceptance
barrier, 42
integrated development, 75
of travel. *See* travel costs
Council of Tourism Associations of
British Columbia (COTA), 78
couponing, 170
crime against tourists, 41
Crown corporations
Canadian Tourism Commission
(CTC), 47–48
National Capital Commission
(NCC), 49–50
VIA Rail Canada, 102
Crown lands, 224
Cruise Lines International Association
(CLIA), 60, 112
cruise specialists, 261
cruise travel
"booze cruise," 111
Canadian cruise ships, 112
charter yachts, sailboats and houseboats, 115
ferries, 114
freight cruises, 115
history of cruising, 110–112
lake cruises, 114
marketing strategies, 115–118
repositioning cruise, 113
river cruises, 114
sea cruises, 112–113
special interest cruises, 113
theme cruises, 113
types of cruises, 112–115
during war, 111
CTC (certified travel counsellor), 264
CTM (certified travel manager), 264
Cuba, 93
cuisine tourism, 5
cultural motivators, 32
cultural preservation, 42
cultural support, 43–44
cultural tourism, 189
customer-oriented marketing, 61
customer profiles, 265
customer service director/purser, 121
customs services, 274

day rate, 138
day tours, 108

Delphi technique, 70
Delta Hotel chain, 134
the *Delta Queen*, 114
Delta Queen Steamboat Co., 114
demand, 59
demographics, of guests, 26, 29
Department of Foreign Affairs and
International Trade, 47, 273
Department of Regional Industrial
Expansion (DRIE), 45
Deregulation Act, 85
deserts, 240
destination life cycle, 67
Destination Marketing Organizations
(DMO), 56, 196, 281
dining, 162
dining out on vacation, 174
direct flight, 91
discount airlines, 86
discretionary income, 27
discretionary time, 27
Disney, Walt, 179, 180–181
Disney Corporation, 180
the *Disney Magic*, 116
Disney theme parks, 67, 74,
179–180
disposable income, 8
distance, as travel barrier, 35
domestic tourists, 10
the *Dorchester*, 101
double, 138
double-decker buses, 118
double double, 138
dude ranches, 142
duplication, 77

economic diversification, 42
economic environment, 69
economy/budget hotels, 139
ecotourism, 225, 228–230
ecotourism tours, 255
ecotourists, 229
educational facilities, 43
educational systems, 8
educational tours, 254
ego/self-esteem, 32
eight tourism trade sectors, 3
Eisner, Michael, 180
elastic demand, 59
Employment and Immigration
Canada, 54
empty-nest stage, 27
the environment
carrying capacity, 237
coastlines, 239
deserts, 240
Green Plan, 240
mountains, 239

pollutants, 238
    tourism's impact on, 236–241
    vegetation, 237–238
    water quality, 238
    wildlife, 238–239
Escoffier, Georges Auguste, 166
escorted tours, 254
ethics, and tourism, 291
ethnic agencies, 261
ethnic restaurants, 163
ethnic tours, 254
Eurailpass, 106
Euro-Disney, 180
European plan, 147
event management, 217–220
events and conferences sector
    association meeting market,
        210–215
    career opportunities, 218
    conferences, 210–217
    conventions, 210–217
    corporate meeting market,
        215–217
    described, 5
    meetings, 210–217
    special events, 203, 204–210
    trends, 295
excursionists, 11
exhibitions, 211
external locus of control, 30
extrovert, 30

facilities, grading of, 290
Fairmont Hotels, 134, 241
fairs, 206
fall sports, 232–234
familiarization tour (fam tour),
    276
family entertainment centres (FEC),
    191
family life stage, 27–28
family plan, 138
family-style restaurant, 163
farming out, 148
fast-food restaurants, 164
favourable world image, 43
fear, as travel barrier, 37
federal government
    Canada Customs and Revenue
        Agency, 47
    Canadian Tourism Commission
        (CTC), 47–48
    Citizenship and Immigration
        Canada, 47
    Department of Foreign Affairs and
        International Trade, 47
    Heritage Canada, 47
    Industry Canada, 47

National Capital Commission
        (NCC), 49–50
    Transport Canada, 47
federal government, and tourism,
    273–274
"feeder" airlines, 86
female business traveller, 26
ferries, 114
festivals, 205
financial benefits, 79
fine dining, 162
fly-and-drive vacation package, 100
fly/coach tours, 109
food and beverage sector
    allergy awareness, 158
    career opportunities, 172–174
    casual dining, 157
    children, dining out with, 157
    commercial food service, 161, 167
    contract/institutional food ser-
        vice, 161, 167–169
    described, 4
    dining out on vacation, 174
    history of food-service industry,
        154–156
    legal issues, 159
    major divisions, 161–169
    marketing, 169–170
    menu, 170
    nutrition, 158
    resident sales-dependent restau-
        rants, 171–174
    restaurant ownership, 159–161
    service, 157–158
    size of, 154
    takeout and delivery, 157
    tourism-profit-dependent restau-
        rants, 171
    tourism-sales-dependent restau-
        rants, 171
    trends, 156–159, 294
food-service industry. *See* food and
    beverage sector
Foot, David, 8
forecast trends, 70
forecasting, 70
foreign capital, 43
foreign railways, 105–106
foreign tourists, 10
Four Seasons Hotel Ltd., 216
Franchise Advisory Councils
    (FACs), 133
franchisee, 132
franchiser, 132
franchises
    hotels, 132–133
    restaurants, 161
    travel agencies, 262

Freedom to Move, 85, 102
Freedoms of the Air, 93
freight cruises, 114–115
frequent business traveller, 26
front-line training, 282
front of the house staff, 134
full-service agency, 260
fully escorted tours, 254
functional form, 74
fundraising events, 207

gambling, 193–194
gaming, 193–194
gateway, 196
gateway airport, 90
gateway city, 256
general aviation airports, 89
Global Passenger Systems, 107
global trends, 78
goals, 70–71
golf, 233
goods and services tax (GST),
    289
government funds diversion, as
    tourism acceptance barrier, 42
governments
    federal government, 273–274
    municipal governments,
        275–277
    provincial governments,
        274–275
    and tourism, 272–277
    tourist information centres,
        277
Gow, John, 296
the *Grand American Queen*, 114
"le grand tour," 15
Green Plan, 240
greenwashing, 228
Greyhound US, 107
ground package tours, 254
group tours, 254
guaranteed reservation, 148
guest ranch, 142
guest services attendant, 149
guests
    business guests, 26–27
    classification of, 26–30
    defined, 25
    demographics, 26, 28–29
    motivation, 26, 31–34
    motivation, needs, and expecta-
        tions (MNEs), 33–34
    personality dimensions,
        29–30
    pleasure guests, 27–28
    psychographics, 26, 29–30
    reasons for travel, 31–34

terrorism, impact of, 25–26
top activities participated in, in
     Canada, 33
transient guests, 141
Le Guide Culinaire, 166

hallmark events, 206–207
hard adventure, 225, 227
haute cuisine, 162
health, as travel barrier, 36
heritage tourism, 189
Hertz, 98
hierarchy of needs, 31–32
high-speed transportation (HST)
     system, 103
high turnover, 53
higher value tourists, 79
Hillel, Oliver, 228
Hilton, Conrad, 16
Hilton International, 16
Hine, Ken, 289
historic marketplaces, 195
historic sites, 186–189, 289
historical museums, 185
historical perspective
     air travel in Canada, 84–87
     attractions sector, 179–182
     Canadian tourism, 44–46
     cruise travel, 110–112
     food-service industry, 154–156
     lodging industry, 127–130
     railways, 101–103
     tourism, 13–17
     tours, 248–249
Hospitality Newfoundland and
     Labrador (HNL), 54
hospitality of the hosts, 66
hospitality suite, 138
hosted tours, 254
hostels, 143
hosts
     defined, 25
     hospitality of the hosts, 66
     tourism illiteracy, 41–44
     training, 52–56
Hotel Association of Canada (HAC),
     54, 131, 280, 289
hotel industry. *See* lodging industry
hotel REITS (real estate investment
     trusts), 134
hotel terminology, 138
hotels
     see also lodging industry
     airport hotels, 138
     budget hotels, 140
     business hotels, 139
     conference hotels, 139
     confirmed reservation, 148

convention and meeting market,
     139
downtown location, 137
economy/budget hotels, 139
farming out, 148
food and beverage service,
     166–167
guaranteed reservation, 148
length of stay, classification by, 141
location, classification by, 138
luxury hotels, 139
luxury properties, 140
midscale hotels, 139, 140
moderate hotels, 139
vs. motel, 137
motivation or purpose, classifica-
     tion by, 139
overbooking, 148
pleasure/vacation guest, 140
residential hotels, 141
resort hotels, 139
resorts, 139
room rate, classification by, 139
room service, 167–300
service level, classification by, 140
small towns, 139
suburban location, 137
tentative reservation, 148
top five hotel companies in
     Canada, 137
transient guests, 141
upscale hotels, 139, 140
walking, 148
houseboats, 115
HSCT, 94
hub and spoke system, 86
human resource challenges, issues and
     concerns, 52–53

in-house tour operator, 250
inbound tourists, 10
inbound tours, 250
incentive tours, 255
incentive travel, 265–266
income
     discretionary income, 27
     disposable income, 8
Independent Motel Association
     (IMA), 131
independent restaurateurs, 160
independent tour operator, 250
independent tours, 253
industrial tourism, 5
Industry Canada, 47
industry image, 52
inelastic demand, 59
inflation, as tourism acceptance
     barrier, 42

infrastructure
     described, 65
     improvements, 43
     inventory of, 69
institutional training, lack of recogni-
     tion for, 53
integrated development, 74, 75
interdependency, 75
interline connection, 91
internal locus of control, 30
International Air Transport Association
     (IATA), 19, 92, 93, 257, 264
international air transport system, 92
international business traveller, 27
International Civil Aviation
     Organization (ICAO), 18, 92,
     94
international organizations, 18–19
international tourists to Canada, distri-
     bution of, 12
Internet
     and growth in tourism, 7
     impact of, 292
     travel agencies, competition for, 263
interpersonal motivators, 32
introvert, 30
inventory, 68–70
isolation, 75
IT number, 257
itinerary, 256

Japan
     bullet train in, 106
     white glove pushers, 119
Jazz, 86
JetsGo, 86
Jetway, 90
job descriptions
     see also careers
     attraction facility guide, 200
     conference service manager, 218
     customer service director/purser,
          121
     guest services attendant, 149
     night club manager, 173
     ski area manager, 242
     tour guide, 267
     tourism/consultant researcher, 283
joint ventures, 131

Kennedy Airport, 119
kilometre cap, 100
Korean Airlines flight 007, 92
Kroc, Ray, 278–279

lack of time, as travel barrier, 35
Laidlaw, 107
lake cruises, 114

land package tours, 254
landing fee, 90
language barrier, 53
late community involvement, 77
leakage
    defined, 13
    as tourism acceptance barrier, 42
legal issues, and restaurants, 159
light rail transit (LRT) systems, 119
live entertainment, 192–193
living history museums, 185–186
load factor, 91
loading apron, 90
local resentment, as tourism acceptance barrier, 42
lodging industry
    see also hotels
    chain ownership, 132
    franchises, 132–133
    functions, 134–137
    history and trends, 127–130
    individual ownership, 131–132
    joint ventures, 131
    management contract, 133–134
    marketing strategies, 132
    meal plans, 147
    occupancy rates, 129
    organization, 134–137
    referral systems, 132
    REITS (real estate investment trusts), 134
    September 11, impact of, 130
    technological changes, 129
    tourist courts, 129
lodging industry staff
    accounting staff, 135
    administrative staff, 135
    back of the house staff, 135
    engineering staff, 136
    food and beverage staff, 136
    front of the house staff, 134
    front office staff, 135
    guest services staff, 135
    housekeeping staff, 136
    sales and marketing staff, 135
    security staff, 137
lodging options
    bed-and-breakfast (B&B), 143
    campgrounds, 144
    condominiums, 141
    dude ranches, 142
    hostels, 144
    hotels. *See* hotels
    motels, 137, 141
    spas, 143
    time-sharing, 142
low-impact camping, 228
LRC (light, rapid, comfortable), 103

the *Lusitania*, 111
luxury business traveller, 26
luxury hotels, 139
luxury properties, 140

Maglev, 103
management contract, 133–134
the *Maple Leaf*, 102
marine activities, 233
market match, 196
market performance, 78
market segmentation, 61
marketing
    accommodations, 144–148
    better methods, and tourism growth, 9
    bus tours, 109–110
    car rental industry, 100
    cruise travel, 115–118
    customer-oriented marketing, 61
    defined, 56
    elasticity of demand of tourism, 59
    events, 220
    food and beverage sector, 169–170
    foreign railways, 106
    lodging industry, 132
    niche marketing, 61
    rail travel, 104–105
    referral systems, 132
    target marketing, 61
    tourism products, 56–61
    tourism services, 280–281
    travel trade products, 264–265
    uniqueness of tourism product, 57–58
marketing mix
    defined, 59
    place, 60
    price, 59
    product, 59
    promotion, 60–61
marketing plan, 61
Marriott, J. Willard, 35–36
Marriott 3 W.T.C., 130
Marriott Company, 35–36
Marriott Corporations, 140
Maslow, Abraham, 31
Maslow's hierarchy of needs, 31–32
the *Mauritania*, 111
McDonald's, 278–279
meal plans, 147
media coverage advancements, 7
Meeting Professionals International (MPI), 211, 280
meetings, 210–217
megamalls, 195
menu, 170

Metropolitan Toronto Convention Centre, 215
midcentrics, 29
midscale hotels, 139, 140
mission statement, 70–71
the *Mississippi Queen*, 114
mode of transportation, 120
moderate hotels, 139
modernization, 43
modified American plan (MAP), 147
Mont Tremblant (Quebec), 75
Montreal Convention Centre, 215
motels, 137, 141
motivation, needs, and expectations (MNEs), 33–34
motivation of guests, 26, 31–34
motivators
    cultural motivators, 32
    defined, 31
    interpersonal motivators, 32
    Maslow's hierarchy of needs, 31–32
    physical motivators, 32
    purpose of, 31
    push and pull factors, 32
    status and prestige motivators, 32
    visiting friends and relatives (VFR), 31
motor coach packages, 109
motor coach travel
    advantages of, 108
    charter, 108
    decline, 107
    fly/coach tours, 109
    grading tour packages, 109
    marketing strategies, 109–110
    motor coach packages, 109
    overnight/short tours, 108
    qualified tour director or escort, 110
    regulation of, 107
    scheduled, inter-city services, 107, 108
    seniors market, 110
    sightseeing/day tours, 108
    specialty markets, 110
    tour categories, 108–109
    tours, 108
mountains, 239
multi-unit corporate restaurant, 160
multiplier effect, 12
municipal governments, and tourism, 275–277
municipal organizations, 20
museums, 184–186

National Capital Commission (NCC), 49–50, 277
National Car Rental, 98

national parks system, 223–224
national tourism office (NTO), 45
National Transportation Act, 85, 102
National Transportation Agency
    (NTA), 85, 257
natural luge, 231
natural resources, 65
NAV CANADA (NAVCAN), 88
Needham, Douglas, 159
Newfoundland and Labrador, 67
Niagara Falls (Ontario), 75, 195–200
Niagara Region, 77
niche marketing, 61
night club manager, 173
"no frills" airlines, 86
nonconsumptive tourism, 228
nonprofit attractions. *See* public and
    nonprofit attractions
nonstop flight, 91
the *Norweta*, 114
nutrition, 158

occupancy rates, 129
occupational standards, 55–56
oceanariums, 190
the *Olympic*, 111
online connection, 91
Ontario Motor Coach Association
    (OMCA), 108, 109
Ontario Tourism Education
    Corporation (OTEC), 54
open bar, 167
open jaw trip, 90
Open Skies agreement, 92
Organisation for Economic Co-opera-
    tion and Development, 86
Orient Express, 107
Ottawa International Hostel, 144
outbound tourists, 10
outbound tours, 250
outdoor recreation
    see also adventure tourism and out-
        door recreation sector
    fall sports, 232–234
    spring sports, 232–234
    summer sports, 232–234
    Trans Canada Trail (TCT), 230
    winter sports, 230–232
overbook, 148
overnight/short tours, 108
override, 248

Pacific Asia Travel Association (PATA),
    19
the *Pacific Express*, 102
Pacific Rim Institute of Tourism
    (PRIT), 54
Pacific Western Airlines, 85, 86

the *Paddlewheel Queen*, 114
Pan American, 76–77
Pan American World Airways, 111
pari-mutuel gambling, 194
Paris, France, 43
parks
    issues concerning role of, 289
    national parks system, 223–224
    Parks Canada mandate, 224
    provincial parks systems, 224
Parks Canada mandate, 224
partially escorted tours, 254
partnerships, 197
passports, 273
Pearce, Douglas, 74
PEI Air, 86
people resources, 52
performance bond, 257
personality, as psychographic data, 29
physical environment, 69
physical motivators, 32
physiological needs, 31
place
    accommodations sector, 147
    cruise travel, 118
    marketing mix component, 60
plan implementation, 73
planning. *See* tourism planning
pleasure guests, 27–28
Plog, Stanley, 29
political atmosphere, 68
political stability, 10
pollutants, 238
pollution, as tourism acceptance
    barrier, 42
poor attitudes/self-image, 53
poor training practices, 53
poorly trained managers, 53
prestige motivators, 32
price
    accommodations sector, 147
    cruise travel, 117
    marketing mix component, 59
    tours, 252, 256
Price Waterhouse, 78
pricing, 252
private/commercial attractions
    amusement parks, 179, 191–192
    family entertainment centres
        (FEC), 191
    gambling, 193–194
    gaming, 193–194
    live entertainment, 192–193
    shopping, 194–195
    theme parks, 179, 190–191
    virtual reality centre, 191
product
    accommodations sector, 146

cruise travel, 116–117
    marketing mix component, 59
product capacity, 78
profits, decline in, 53
promotion
    see also marketing
    accommodations sector, 148
    advertising, 148
    couponing, 170
    cruise travel, 118
    marketing mix component, 60–61
    public relations, 148
    tours, 253
provincial governments, and tourism,
    274–275
provincial parks systems, 224
psychocentric, 29
psychocentric-allocentric continuum,
    30
psychographics, of guests, 26, 29–30
public and nonprofit attractions
    aquariums, 189–190
    described, 183
    heritage tourism, 189
    historic sites, 186–189
    museums, 184–186
    zoos, 189–190
public relations, 148
public transportation, 118–119
pubs, 162
pull factors, 32
push factors, 32

the *Quaker City*, 111
qualitative forecasting, 70
quantitative forecasting, 70
A Question of Balance (TIANS), 241

rack rate, 138
rail travel
    auto/train option, 105
    bullet train, 106
    challenges, 105
    decline in, 102
    foreign railways, 105–106
    high-speed transportation (HST)
        system, 103
    history of the train, 101–103
    LRC (light, rapid, comfortable),
        103
    marketing strategies, 104–105
    Orient Express, 107
    Shinkansen, 106
    trains of the world, 106–107
rapid development, 74
reasons for travel, 31–34
recreational facilities, 43
recreational sports, 234

recreational vehicle (RV) travel
    advantages of, 97
    new industry, emergence of, 100
    tour and rally companies, 100–101
    trends, 97–98
redundancy, 77
referral systems, 132
REITS (real estate investment trusts),
    134
religious tours, 254
Rendez-Vous Canada, 46, 209
repositioning cruise, 113
research services, 281–282
reservations, 92
resident sales-dependent restaurants,
    171–174
residential hotels, 141
resort hotels, 139
resorts, 139
restaurant ownership, 159–161
restaurants. *See* commercial food ser-
    vice; food and beverage sector
revenue performance, 78
risk management, 230
Ritz, Cesar, 145, 166
river cruises, 113–114
Rocky Mountaineer Railtours, 103
room service, 167–300
round trip, 90
the *Royal Hudson*, 103
the *Royal Scotsman*, 106
run-of-the-home rate, 138

safety needs, 31
sailboats, 115
same-day visitors, 11
scheduled air carriers, 89
scientific museums, 186
sea cruises, 112–113
seasonality
    in B.C. tourism, 79
    as tourism acceptance barrier, 42
    tourism product, 58
secondary developers, 75
self-actualization needs, 32
self-ticketing devices, 263
seminar, 211
seniors market, 110, 261
sense of place, 196
September 11 terrorist attack
    adventure tourism and outdoor
        recreation, impact on, 26,
        223
    airlines, impact on, 87
    attractions, impact on, 182
    Canada-U.S. border, impact on, 46
    casino gambling, impact of, 194
    described, 15–17

effect on tourism, 10
    lodging industry, impact on, 130
service, 157–158
Sharp, Isadore, 216
Shinkansen, 106
shopping, 194–195
shrinking labour pool, 53
the *Siberian Express*, 106
Sierra Club, 228
sightseeing/day tours, 108
single, 138
site inspection, 276
site specific, 186
ski area manager, 242
skiing, 231
snowmobiling, 231
social atmosphere, 69
social needs, 31
Society of Incentive Travel Executives
    (SITE), 266
soft adventure, 225, 227
soft adventure tours, 254
spas, 143
special events
    circuses, 206
    civic events, 207
    defined, 204
    fairs, 206
    festivals, 205
    frequency of, 203
    fundraising events, 207
    hallmark events, 206–207
    purpose of, 205
    spectator sporting event, 207–209
    trade shows, 209–210
    trends, 295
special interest cruises, 113
special interest tours, 255
special needs tours, 255
specialty restaurant, 163
specialty travel agencies, 260–261
spectator sporting event, 207–209
sports and recreational tours, 254
spring sports, 232–234
SST Concorde, 94
Statler, Ellsworth, 235
Statler Foundation, 235
status and prestige motivators, 32
step-on guides, 254
strategy development, 73
stressful lifestyles, 8
suite, 138
summer sports, 232–234
summits, 210
Super 8 Motel franchise, 133
the *Super Continental*, 102
supersonic air travel, 94
supply, 59

suprastructure
    described, 66
    inventory of, 69
sustainability, 78
sustainable tourism, 229

takeout and delivery, 157
Tango, 86
target marketing, 61
tastes and experiences, as travel
        barrier, 35–36
tax issues, 289
tax revenues, 43
taxiway, 90
technology
    computers, 7
    and growth of tourism, 6–8
    and hotel industry, 129
    impact on tourism industry, 292
    Internet, 7
    media coverage advancements, 7
    transportation system advances, 7
teleconferencing, 210
tennis, 233
tentative reservation, 148
terminology
    airline terminology, 90–91
    conference terminology, 211
    hotel terminology, 138
    tourism terminology, 10–13
terrorism
    customs and immigration, evolv-
        ing role of, 289
    fear, as travel barrier, 37
    guests, impact on, 25–26
    impact of, 290–291
    September 11. *See* September 11
        terrorist attack
    tourism as target for, 17
theme cruises, 113
theme parks, 179, 190–191
theme restaurants, 164
Thomas Cook and Son, 259
Tilden, 98
Time Air, 85
time poverty, 293
time-sharing, 142
the *Titanic*, 111
tour guide, 267
tour operators, 250
tour wholesaler, 250
tourism
    benefits of, 42–44
    as career. *See* careers
    elasticity of demand, 59
    environmental impact of,
        236–241
    and governments, 272–277

growth of, 6–10
societies, effects on, 43–44
tourism acceptance, barriers to. *See*
    barriers to tourism acceptance
tourism associations and organiza-
    tions, 279–280
Tourism British Columbia, 78 *see also*
    B.C. tourism
Tourism Canada, 45, 54
tourism/consultant researcher, 283
tourism development
    balanced development, 74
    catalytic development, 74, 75
    centralized development, 75
    classification of, 74
    coattail development, 74, 75–77
    described, 74
    functional form, 74
    integrated development, 74, 75
    isolation, 75
    rapid development, 74
tourism education councils (TECs),
    53–55
tourism illiteracy
    barriers to tourism acceptance,
        41–42
    benefits of tourism, 42–44
    challenges of, 41
    described, 41
tourism industry
    challenges, 297–299
    ethics, 291
    financing, 290
    issues, 288–290
    technology, impact of, 292
    terrorist threats, 290–291
    trade sectors, 3
    trends, 292–295
Tourism Industry Association of
    Canada (TIAC), 20, 46, 54,
    210, 257–258, 279, 280
Tourism Industry Association of
    Manitoba (MTEC), 54
Tourism Industry Association of New
    Brunswick, 54
Tourism Industry Association of Nova
    Scotia (TIANS), 51, 54, 241
Tourism Industry Association of
    Prince Edward Island (TIAPEI),
    54
Tourism Industry Association of
    Saskatchewan (STEC), 54
Tourism Industry Association of the
    Northwest Territories, 54
tourism industry associations and
    organizations
    Canadian organizations/associa-
        tions, 19–20

international organizations, 18–19
    municipal organizations, 20
Tourism Industry Product Overview, 78
Tourism Industry Standards and
    Certification Committee
    (TISCC), 51, 54
tourism planning
    alternative action plans, 71–72
    cyclical nature of, 68
    described, 67–68
    forecast trends, 70
    goals, 71
    inventory, 68–70
    mission statement, 70–71
    plan implementation, 73
    planning model, 68
    preferred alternative, selection of,
        72
    provincial approach. *See* B.C.
        tourism
    review, evaluation, revision and
        continuation, 73
    strategy development, 73
tourism product
    accommodations sector, 4
    adventure tourism and outdoor
        recreation sector, 5
    attractions sector, 5
    British Columbia. *See* B.C. tourism
    costs of, 57
    described, 52
    eight tourism trade sectors, 3
    elastic demand, 59
    events and conferences sector, 5
    fixed supply, 58
    food and beverage sector, 4
    global trends, 78
    inability to store, 58
    intangibility of, 57
    marketing. *See* marketing
    overview, 2–6
    perishable nature of, 57–58
    quality of, 58
    seasonality, 58
    time constraints, 58
    tourism services sector, 6
    transportation sector, 3
    travel trade sector, 5–6
    uniqueness of, 57–58
tourism-profit-dependent restaurants,
    171
tourism-sales-dependent restaurants,
    171
tourism services sector
    career opportunities, 284
    chambers of commerce, 276
    convention and visitor bureau
        (CVB), 276, 277

described, 6
Destination Marketing
    Organizations (DMO),
    280–281
governments and tourism. *See* gov-
    ernments
marketing, 280–281
miscellaneous services, 282–284
research and consulting, 281–282
tourism associations and organiza-
    tions, 279–280
trends, 295
tourist courts, 129
tourist destination areas (TDAs), 65
    components of, 65–67
    development of, 65
    hospitality of the hosts, 66
    infrastructure, 65
    life cycle of destination, 67
    natural resources, 65
    suprastructure, 66
    transportation systems, 66
tourist dollars, 12
tourist information, 154
tourist information centres, 277
tourist types, 79
tours
    advantages of, 258
    base cost per participant, 252
    categories, 253–254
    cost for use, 252
    costing, 252
    development, 250–253
    disadvantages of, 258–259
    history of, 248–249
    idea, 251
    inbound, 250
    industry regulation, 256–257
    IT number, 257
    negotiation phase of planning, 251
    outbound, 250
    pricing, 252
    promotion, 253
    travel counsellor's responsibility,
        255–256
    types of, 254–255
    wholesaling, 250
trade shows, 209–210
Trailways, 107
training
    certification, 55, 56
    education and training services,
        282
    front-line training, 282
    human resource challenges, issues
        and concerns, 52–53
    issues, 290
    occupational standards, 55–56

people resources, 52
tourism education councils
(TECs), 53–55
trains. *See* rail travel
Trans Canada Airlines (TCA), 85
Trans Canada Trail (TCT), 230
transfer, 87
transient guests, 141
Transport Canada, 47, 88
transportation sector
airlines, 84–96
automobile and recreational vehicle
travel, 97–101
buses, 107–110
careers, 120–121
cruise industry, 110–118
described, 3
issues, 288
motor coach industry, 107–110
public transportation, 118–119
rail, 101–107
selecting mode of transportation,
120
trends, 294
transportation systems, 7, 66, 197
travel agencies
chain agencies, 262
conference appointments, 263–264
consortiums, 262
corporate travel agency, 260
early agencies, 259
franchises, 262
full-service agency, 260
operation of, 262–263
private ownership, 261
regulation of, 263–264
retail business, 259
specialty travel agencies, 260–261
as tour operator, 250
types of, 259–261
travel agent. *See* travel counsellors
travel barrier. *See* barriers to travel
travel costs
as barrier to travel, 34
decline in, 9
travel counsellors, 255–256, 259

travel deficit, 11
travel trade sector
career opportunities, 266
commission, 248
described, 5–6
incentive travel, 265–266
marketing, 264–265
override, 248
tours. *See* tours
travel agencies, 259–264
trends, 295
trend analysis, 70
trends
accommodation, 294
adventure tourism and outdoor
recreation sector, 295
attractions sector, 295
branding, 293
defined, 70
economic downturn, 293
food and beverage sector, 294
package deals, 294
personalized service, demand for,
294
special events, 295
street smart consumers, 293
time poverty, 293
tourism services sector, 295
transportation, 294
travel trade sector, 295
trinketization, 44
trip, 10
Trippe, Juan, 76–77
twin, 138

UNESCO World Heritage Sites, 187
unescorted tours, 254
Unique Selling Proposition (USP), 196
uniqueness of tourism product, 57–58
United Airlines, 86
United Nations, 10–11, 17
United Nations Educational, Scientific
and Cultural Organization
(UNESCO), 187
unlimited kilometres, 100
unskilled labour, 52

upscale hotels, 139, 140
validity dates, 255
value, 61
Vancouver Trade and Convention
Centre, 215
variety, 30
vegetation, 237–238
VIA Rail Canada, 102, 103, 104–105,
264
virtual reality centre, 191
visas, 273
Visit Canada, 45, 209
visiting friends and relatives (VFR), 31
visitor experience, quality of, 79
visitor use, 78
visitors, 25

walking, 148, 234
Ward, Debra, 257–258
Ward, Max, 95–96
Wardair, 86, 95–96
water quality, 238
weekend rate, 138
the *Wendebee II*, 114
West Edmonton Mall, 194, 195
WestJet, 86
Whistler (B.C.), 75
white glove pushers, 119
white-water rafting, 227
wildlife, 238
Windows on the World, 156
winter sports, 230–232
Woodall's World of Travel, 101
workshop, 211
The World, 112
World Tourism Organization (WTO),
17, 18, 189, 200, 228
World Travel and Tourism Council
(WTTC), 19

yachtaminium, 115
yachts, 115

Zip, 86
zoos, 189–190